Computers

Brief Edition

Computers

SIXTH EDITION

Larry Long
Nancy Long

Prentice Hall   Upper Saddle River, New Jersey   07458

Acquisitions Editor: DAVID ALEXANDER
Editor-in-Chief: PJ BOARDMAN
Executive Marketing Manager: NANCY EVANS
Sales Specialists: AUDRA SILVERIE, KRIS KING,
                        GREG CHRISTOPHERSON
Production Coordinator: CAROL SAMET
Managing Editor: BRUCE KAPLAN
Copy Editor: ANNE GRAYDON
Senior Manufacturing Supervisor: PAUL SMOLENSKI
Manufacturing Manager: VINCENT SCELTA
Design Director: PATRICIA SMYTHE
Cover Designer: OH! JACKIE, INC.
Illustrator (Interior):   BATELMAN ILLUSTRATION
Senior Manager of Production & Technology: LORRAINE PATSCO
Print/Media Project Supervisor: DAVID SALIERNO
Supervising Electronic Art Specialist: WARREN FISCHBACH
Electronic Artist: STEVEN FRIM
Interior Design/Formatting Supervisor: CHRISTY MAHON
Formatters: ERIC HULSIZER, CHRISTY MAHON, JOHN NESTOR,
                 ERIK R. TRINIDAD, PATRICE VAN ACKER
Cover Art: MICK WIGGINS

 ©1999, 1998, 1996, 1993, 1990, 1986 by Prentice-Hall, Inc.
A Simon & Schuster Company
Upper Saddle River, New Jersey 07458

Library of Congress Cataloging in Publication Data

Long, Larry E.
   Computers / Larry Long, Nancy Long.—6th ed., Brief
     304 p. cm.
     Includes index.
     ISBN 0-13-096254-6
     1. Computers. 2. Electronic data processing. I. Long, Nancy. II. Title.
  QA76.L576 1999   98–19193
  004—dc21   CIP

Prentice Hall International (UK) Limited, London
Prentice Hall of Australia Pty. Limited, Sydney
Prentice Hall of Canada Inc., Toronto
Prentice Hall Hispanoamericano, S.A., Mexico
Prentice Hall of India Private Limited, New Delhi
Prentice Hall of Japan, Inc., Tokyo
Simon & Schuster Asia Pte. Ltd., Singapore
Editora Prentice Hall do Brasil, Ltda., Rio de Janeiro

Printed in the United States of America
10   9   8   7   6   5   4   3   2

To Our Children
Troy and Brady,
The motivation for all that we do.

CONTENTS OVERVIEW

CONTENTS

SPECIAL INTEREST SIDEBARS

PREFACE TO THE STUDENT

Welcome to the computer revolution. You've taken the first step toward computer competency, the bridge to an amazing realm of adventure and discovery. Once you have read and understood the material in this text and have acquired some hands-on experience with computers, you will be poised to play an active role in this revolution.

- You'll be an intelligent consumer of PCs and related products.
- You'll be better prepared to travel the rapidly expanding information superhighway and you'll know where to exit to get the information or services you need.
- You'll become a participant when conversations at work and school turn to computers and technology.
- You'll be better able to relate your computing and information processing needs to those who can help you.
- You'll know about a wide variety of software and services that can improve your productivity at work and at home, give you much needed information, expand your intellectual and cultural horizons, amaze you, your family, and your friends, and give you endless hours of enjoyment.

Achieving computer competency is the first step in a lifelong journey toward greater knowledge of and interaction with more and better applications of information technology (IT). Computer competency is your ticket to ride. Where you go, how fast you get there, and what you do when you arrive is up to you.

Learning Aids

Computers is supported by a comprehensive learning assistance package that includes these helpful learning aids:

The Long and Long INTERNET BRIDGE

The Long and Long INTERNET BRIDGE http://www.prenhall.com/long is a site on the Internet that is accessible from any PC with Internet access. The site, which is designed to help you make the transition between textbook learning and real-world understanding, has three main components:

- *Internet Exercises.* The INTERNET BRIDGE invites you to go online and explore the wonders of the Internet through a comprehensive set of Internet exercises. These entertaining exercises challenge you to learn more about the topics in this book and to do some "serendipitous surfing."
- *Online Interactive Study Guide (ISG).* The INTERNET BRIDGE's comprehensive online Interactive Study Guide gives you an opportunity to sharpen your problem-solving skills and to gauge your understanding of the material in the chapter. For each chapter, the ISG has multiple choice, true/false, and essay quizzes. The built-in grading feature gives you immediate feedback in the form of a report. The report also includes a question-by-question summary with an explanation or hint, your response, and the correct response (if needed).
- *Monthly Technology Update.* The printed book alone is no longer sufficient to keep you abreast of a rapidly advancing technology. The INTERNET BRIDGE's

Monthly Technology Update section helps you bridge this technology gap. Each month the authors post a chapter-by-chapter update to the INTERNET BRIDGE. The monthly update includes summaries of important technological events that occurred during the previous month.

The INTERNET BRIDGE icons in the margins throughout the book relate material in the book to applicable Internet exercises and online *Interactive Study Guide* chapters.

Edu.cis: Distance Learning with Computers

Edu.cis http://www.prenhall.com/edu.cis is the online course Internet site for this information technology concepts book and the software skills books by Robert Grauer and Maryann Barber. The site lets you take computer competency courses via distance learning or allows you to enhance your classroom experience. That is, you log on to the *edu.cis page* on the Internet to interact with instructors and classmates, go over chapter summaries, evaluate your understanding of course material, participate in on-line discussion groups, take quizzes and tests, gain access to class information (schedule, homework, and so on), make inquiries about your grades, and much more.

IT Works CD-ROM: Courseware for Information Technology

IT Works is a CD-ROM–based multimedia learning tool that interactively demonstrates many important computer concepts and applications. The IT Works icons in the margins throughout the book relate material in the book to applicable modules in *IT Works* (ISBN: 0-13-366766-9).

You, Computers, and the Future

Whether you are pursuing a career as an economist, a social worker, a politician, an attorney, a dancer, an accountant, a computer specialist, a sales manager, or virtually any other career, the knowledge you gain from this course ultimately will prove beneficial. Keep your course notes and this book; they will prove to be valuable references in other courses and in your career.

Even though computers are all around us, we are seeing only the tip of the computer-applications iceberg. You are entering the computer era in its infancy. Each class you attend and each page you turn will present a learning experience to help you advance one step closer to an understanding of how computers are making the world a better place in which to live and work.

PREFACE TO THE INSTRUCTOR

The Paradigm Shift

The rules are changing. The criteria by which we make decisions, the way we do things, and even what we do is changing, dramatically. The explosion of the Internet, a rapidly expanding worldwide network of computers, coupled with increased interest in personal computing has resulted in an acceleration in the pace of change. We are now members of an interconnected society where we can shop at online Wal-Mart Supercenters, research our family tree, take virtual tours of thousands of sites from the White House to the pyramids, take courses for college credit, and much, much more, all from a linked PC.

This paradigm shift is causing radical changes in all facets of society, including the way we teach and learn. We are entering a new era of education in which technology plays an increasingly significant role. This is especially true of introductory computer courses in which the integration of the technology is a natural extension of the learning process. After all, the best place to learn about computers is at the computer.

Computers, 6th Edition: A Technology Update

This sixth edition of *Computers* is a *technology update* intended to bring *Computers* abreast with a rampaging technology. About six Internet years pass in one real-time year—the elapsed time between the fifth and sixth editions. For the past 15 years, your peers have told us that we consistently publish the most up-to-date computer concept textbooks. We take great pride in your confidence in us and are committed to offering you and your students a timely IT concepts textbook.

The sixth edition retains the same familiar look and feel as the fifth edition (and also that of *Introduction to Computers and Information Systems*, 5th ed., by Long and Long). The sixth edition reflects hundreds of changes in information technology over the past year, but its organization is the same as that of the fifth edition. This consistency in organization should enable a smooth, seamless transition for those colleges moving from the fifth to the sixth edition. The sixth edition includes:

- Over 100 new or updated images to reflect the latest releases and innovations in software.
- Many new photos showing new hardware and applications (for example, an in-dash automobile PC).
- Scores of updated Internet and America Online examples.
- A new Windows appendix, reflecting both Windows 95 and 98 concepts.
- 1999–2000 capacities and speeds for modems, disks, RAM, processors, printers, and so on.
- Major changes in PC architecture, such as the Pentium II, AGP video technology, and SDRAM.
- Coverage of new issues, such as *spamming*.

A Mixed-Media Learning Tool

This textbook is one component of a *mixed-media learning tool*. Although it can be used as a stand-alone resource, it's effectiveness is enhanced when used in conjunction with the Long and Long INTERNET BRIDGE and edu.cis, its companion Internet sites, IT Works, its multimedia CD-ROM-based courseware, and other media-based ancillaries. The mixed-media orientation of this edition of *Computers* gives students a power boost up the learning curve and instructors an innovative vehicle for delivery of course content. The margin icons throughout the book direct students to applicable INTERNET BRIDGE and IT Works activities.

We've designed the *Computers*, 6th ed., mixed-media resource to give you maximum flexibility in course design and instruction. Use this resource to offer computer competency education in whatever formats meet your student and curriculum needs, from traditional classroom/lab instruction to courses offered completely online via distance learning.

Throughout all aspects of this mixed-media approach to learning, we play to the student's sense of exhilaration by projecting the excitement of the age of information. We have attempted to include something on every printed page, every Internet page, and every CD-ROM–based exploration that will tickle their senses and inspire them to learn more. Eventually anxieties and fears fade away as students recognize the dawning of a new era in their life, an era bursting with opportunity.

The Intro Course

The introductory computer course poses tremendous teaching challenges. To be effective, we must continually change our lecture style and even the vehicle by which we convey content and interact with students. Throughout the term we are continually changing hats. Sometimes we are historians. Much of the time we are scientists presenting technical material. On occasion we are sociologists commenting on social issues. In the same course we now toggle between lecture and lab. Moreover, we are teaching an ever-increasing amount of material to students with a wide range of career objectives and technical abilities. Prentice Hall and we have done everything we can to help you meet this challenge.

Opportunity, challenge, and competition are forcing all of us to become computer competent and to prepare ourselves for a more interconnected world. *Computers,* 6th ed., its mixed-media components, and its ancillary materials provide a launch pad toward these objectives. The target course for this text and its teaching/learning system:

- *Provides overview coverage of computing concepts and applications for a wide variety of introductory courses.* The Right PHit custom-binding solution allows you to select only those modules required to meet your course's educational objectives.

- *Accommodates students from a broad spectrum of disciplines and interests.*

- *May or may not include a laboratory component.* The Right PHit offers an extensive array of optional hands–on laboratory materials.

The Right PHit: Prentice Hall's Custom Binding Solution

Prentice Hall's custom binding program offers the Right PHit for everyone. The Right PHit program allows you to create the book that is right for your course, curriculum, and college. *Computers* is organized into four modules. The Core Module, the foundation of the Right PHit program, can be combined and bound with any or all of the other three conceptual modules.

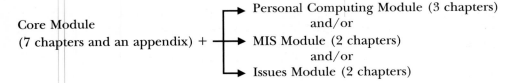

Core Module
(7 chapters and an appendix) +
→ Personal Computing Module (3 chapters)
   and/or
→ MIS Module (2 chapters)
   and/or
→ Issues Module (2 chapters)

Core The seven core chapters introduce students to the world of computing, concepts relating to interaction with computers, and fundamental hardware, software, communications concepts, and going online (the Internet, online information services). This module includes Focus on ITs (photo essays) on the making of integrated circuits and on computer history, plus an appendix on the Windows environment.

Personal Computing The three personal computing chapters introduce students to the most popular personal computing applications (word processing, desktop publishing, presentation, spreadsheet, database, browser, graphics, and multimedia). This module includes a buyer's guide Focus on IT.

MIS This two-chapter module introduces students to the various types of information systems (MIS, DSS, expert systems, software agents, and so on) and includes an overview of the latest approaches to systems development.

Issues The two issue-oriented chapters discuss computing in context with society, addressing the many issues raised by the coming of the Information Age. Also, in these chapters students travel the information superhighway, making frequent stops to discuss current and future applications.

The Right PHit program offers a complete solution for introductory computer courses, from concepts to applications. Any component of the Grauer/Barber *Exploring Windows 95* or *Exploring Windows 98* series can be bound with *Computers,* 6th ed., via Prentice Hall's Right PHit program. A complete array of Office 95 and Office 97 titles is available in this custom binding program, as are modules on Visual Basic, Netscape, and Internet Explorer. The *Exploring Windows* series is part of the most extensive array of hands-on laboratory materials offered by any textbook publisher. These hands-on manuals can be bound together with *Computers,* 6th ed., or, if you prefer, bound separately and shrinkwrapped as a package so students can carry them to the lab one at a time. Your Prentice Hall representative will be happy to work with you to identify that combination of student support materials and packaging that best meets the needs of your lab environment.

Popular Features Retained in the 6th Edition

- *Applications-oriented.* The continuing theme throughout the text is applications. Hundreds of applications are presented from on-line universities to telemedicine to robotics.
- *Readability.* All elements (photos, figures, sidebars, and so on) are integrated with the textual material to complement and reinforce learning.
- *Presentation style.* The text and all supplements are written in a style that remains pedagogically sound while communicating the energy and excitement of computers and computing to the student.
- *Currency-plus.* The material actually anticipates the emergence and implementation of computer technology. Included is coverage of digital convergence, Win-

dows 98, ADSL, DVD (digital videodisk), webcasting, hypermedia, audio mail, NCs, online documents (HTML and PDF formats), e-money, data warehousing, intelligent agents, SDRAM, rapid application development using CASE, the Pentium II, AGP video boards, compact disk-rewritable (CD-RW), Zip and SuperDisk drives, morphing, firewalls, flaming, Internet-based videophone links, hot plugging, IrDA ports, workplace ergonomics, and applets.

- *Flexibility.* The text and its mixed-media teaching/learning system are organized to permit maximum flexibility in course design and in the selection, assignment, and presentation of material.

- *Extensive coverage of Internet applications and concepts.* Students are given an opportunity to take an extended trip on the information superhighway. Internet and general online capabilities and concepts are covered in detail.

- *Analogies.* Analogies are used throughout the book to relate information technology concepts they are learning to concepts they already understand, such as airplanes (computer systems), audio CDs (random processing), and cars/parking lots (files/disks).

- *Colorful new Focus on ITs.* Focus on ITs combine dynamic photos with in-depth discussions of topics that are of interest to students: how chips are made, the history of computers, and how to buy a PC.

- *Walkthrough illustrations.* Every attempt has been made to minimize conceptual navigation between the running text and figures. This was done by including relevant information within the figures in easy-to-follow numbered walkthroughs.

- *Mixed-media margin icons.* The INTERNET BRIDGE and IT Works icons in the margin point students to interactive multimedia learning resources on the Internet and the IT Works CD-ROM. The INTERNET BRIDGE icons invite students to check out the Monthly Technology Update, do applicable Internet exercises, and use the Interactive Study Guide to assess their grasp of the material. The IT Works icons identify applicable explorations and challenges. These resources are designed by the authors to complement this book.

- *Chapter pedagogy.* Chapter organization and pedagogy are consistent throughout the text. Each chapter is prefaced by "Let's Talk" (an introduction to terms in the chapter) and Learning Objectives. In the body of the chapter, all major headings are numbered (1-1, 1-2, and so on) to facilitate selective assignment and to provide an easy cross-reference to all related material in the supplements. Important terms and phrases are highlighted in **boldface** type. Words and phrases to be emphasized appear in *italics*. Informative boxed features, photos, and "Memory Bits" (outlines of key points) are positioned strategically to complement the running text. Each chapter concludes with a Summary Outline and Important Terms, Review Exercises (Concepts; Discussion and Problem Solving), and a Self-test. Margin icons direct students to applicable INTERNET BRIDGE and IT Works activities.

The *Computers* Teaching/Learning System

Computers, 6th ed., continues the Long and Long tradition of having the most comprehensive, innovative, and effective support package on the market. The teaching/learning system includes the following components.

Long and Long INTERNET BRIDGE
<http://www.prenhall.com/long>

The Long and Long INTERNET BRIDGE is designed to help students studying Long and Long resources make the transition between textbook learning and real-world understanding. To use this resource, the student connects to the Internet, navigates to the INTERNET BRIDGE, and clicks on the *Computers,* 6th ed., image. The site offers a variety of activities and services, including these main components:

INTERNET EXERCISES

The Internet exercises encourage students to more fully explore computer competency topics while familiarizing themselves with the Internet. The student selects a specific chapter to begin an online adventure that will take him or her around and into the exciting world of computing. The student's journey will include many stops that can increase his or her understanding and appreciation of the technologies that change and embellish our lives.

Each chapter has from one to seven topics (for example, Printers, Telecommuting, Multimedia, and/or Artificial Intelligence), at least one of which is Serendipitous Surfing (for example, movies, sports, or popular culture). Each topic has from three to seven Internet Exercises. For each exercise, the student: 1) reads the exercise; 2) navigates to the applicable Internet site(s); 3) notes the source(s) title(s) and URL(s); 4) finds the requested information; and 5) returns to the topic page and enters the requested information in the response box. When all Internet exercises are completed for a given topic, the student clicks the "Submit Answers" button to e-mail the responses to his or her instructor/grader.

ONLINE INTERACTIVE STUDY GUIDE

The Internet-based Interactive Study Guide (ISG) helps the student learn and retain concepts presented in the text. A drop-down box on the ISG page lets the student navigate directly to the desired chapter. The student can view the chapter learning objectives, then choose from three skills quizzes: multiple choice, true/false, or essay. These quizzes are designed to give students the opportunity to sharpen their problem-solving skills and assess their grasp of concepts.

- *Multiple Choice.* When taking the multiple-choice quiz the student simply clicks the radio button for the correct response for each question. After answering all of the questions, the student submits the answers for automatic grading. A summary report is returned to the student within seconds. The summary report includes the percentage cor-

Cross the Internet Bridge and close the gap between textbook learning and real-world understanding. The focus of all Long and Long books and resources is computer education.

Welcome to the Long and Long **I N T E R N E T   B R I D G E**

 Computers **5th Edition**

 Computers and Information Systems **5th Edition**

 Computers **4th Edition**

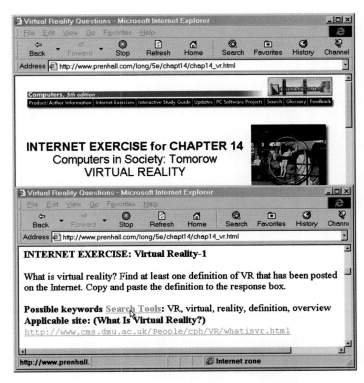

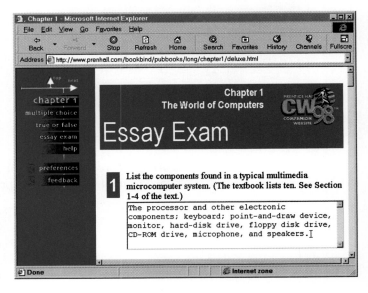

rect, the number of incorrect answers, and the number of unanswered questions. The report also includes a question-by-question summary with an explanation, the student's response, and the correct response (if needed).

- *True/False.* The true/false interface and summary report is like that of a multiple-choice quiz.
- *Essay Exam.* The essay exam includes a text response box for each question into which the student inserts the answer.

Most questions have hints or they provide a reference to the applicable section in the text. After completing a quiz, students have the option of routing the answers to their e-mail addresses and/or to that of their instructor. The summary report is sent for multiple-choice and true/false quizzes, and the questions and answers are sent for the essay exams.

MONTHLY TECHNOLOGY UPDATE
Each month we compile a summary of important changes and happenings in the world of computing. These summaries, which are keyed to chapters, are intended to help keep the student's learning experience current with a rampaging technology.

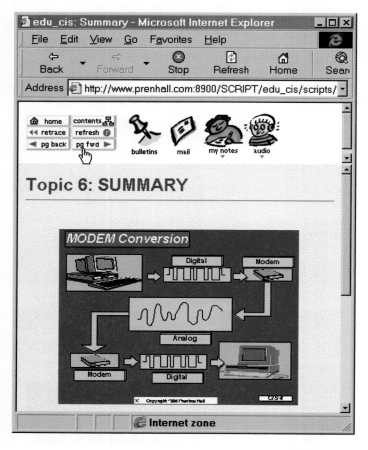

Edu.cis: The Online Course Page

Edu.cis http://www.prenhall.com/edu.cis is Prentice Hall's Internet site supporting online computer competency courses. The site supports this book and its companion lab book, *Office Professional 97* by Grauer and Barber. Edu.cis offers you and your colleagues all the advantages of a custom-built program, but without the hassle. If you are considering offering all or part of your course via distance learning, then edu.cis can help you create and implement a high-quality course with relative ease. If you already offer an online course, then edu.cis can assist you in formalizing your course. Edu.cis gives you the flexibility to integrate your custom material with the continuously updated Long and Long content. The edu.cis is packaged within the WebCT course authoring tool so that you can customize the content to meet the most demanding curriculum requirements. Whether you are off and running or this is your first online course, edu.cis can save you countless hours of preparation and course administration time.

Edu.cis includes these and many other features in each of its 28 learning modules: an introduction, objectives, summaries of key concepts, online activities that use the Internet and Office 97, offline activities that integrate the texts with Web content, self-check exercises, online quizzes (auto-scored and recorded), test item database and test preparation tools (auto-scored and recorded), e-mail accounts for students and instructors, and a bulletin board primed with interesting discussion topics. A wizard program guides you through the initial stages of course development, including the creation of a password-protected course home page. The *Course Management* feature automatically grades online tests and records scores in your electronic grade book. The *Progress Tracking* feature lets you monitor individual and overall student progress. The *Content Tracking* feature tells you how often and for how long each and every student visits an *edu.cis* page. The WebCT shell also lets you integrate files without using HTML.

IT Works CD-ROM: Courseware for Information Technology

- *IT Works CD-ROM: Courseware for Information Technology.* Accompanying *Computers,* 6th ed., is the most comprehensive and exciting multimedia courseware ever produced for introductory computing education (0-13-366766-9).

Prentice Hall has made a significant commitment and contribution to introductory computer education with the release of the IT Works CD-ROM. The IT (Information Technology) Works CD-ROM represents a new generation in college-level courseware. IT Works is an innovative multimedia educational tool that can work one-on-one with students to demonstrate interactively many important computer concepts and applications. This extremely visual and interactive courseware employs sound, motion video, colorful high-resolution graphics, and animation. Plan on students spending many informative and fun-filled hours with IT Works.

The initial version sports three modules, each of which contains the following main menu options: *Exploration* (teaches important concepts and applications); *Challenge* (tests the student's knowledge of the subject); *Review* (multiple-choice and true/false questions); *Video* (video vignettes); and *Glossary*. Cross-references to the multimedia Explorations and Challenges are included in the margins throughout the book.

Computer Explorer. This explorer exams the system unit, inside and out (front and rear). The student simply clicks on a component to learn more about it.

Peripherals Explorer. This Peripherals Explorer activity introduces you to common input/output devices, storage devices, and storage media you might configure with a PC.

Online Explorer. This explorer simulates going on-line. The student can "log on" and learn to navigate the Internet, America Online, and a BBS.

Applications Explorer. The Applications Explorer gives the student a better view of what software is available. They can explore various applications in four software categories: productivity, multiuser applications, home/personal, and system software.

IT Works, like the technology, is dynamic—ever changing and growing. As your needs change, so will *IT Works.*

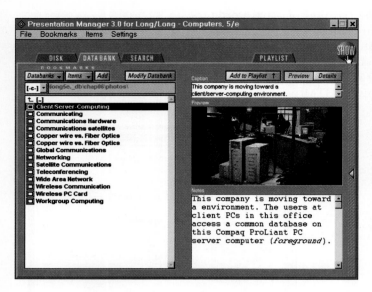

Computers Presentation Manager CD-ROM

The Presentation Manager is a truly user-friendly PC-compatible presentation program that enables you to integrate Prentice Hall-supplied resources with your own for vibrant multimedia lectures. The *Computers* Presentation Manager CD-ROM contains hundreds of images and many videos that can be organized to meet your presentation needs. The CD-ROM contains all of the figures in the text and over one hundred photo images from the book and elsewhere, plus a variety of video vignettes. All of these resources are organized by chapter for your convenience. When putting together the resources for a particular lecture, simply use the key word search and preview feature to find exactly what you need. You can also integrate images of your own; and the software enables you to include (or modify) notes for each image or video (0-13-081910-7).

PH Custom Test

PH Custom Test is an integrated PC-compatible test-generation and classroom-management software package. The package permits instructors to design and create tests, to maintain student records, and to provide on-line practice testing for students (0-13-081918-2).

Test Item File

The *Test Item File* contains thousands of multiple-choice, true/false, essay, and matching questions. The questions are listed by numbered section head. The *Test Item File* diskettes are distributed for use with PH Custom Test software (0-13-081914-X).

Instructor's Resource Manual (IRM)

The *IRM* contains teaching hints, references to other resources, PowerPoint and acetate images, lecture notes, key terms with definitions, solutions to review exercises, and much more (0-13-081913-1). Also available on the Long and Long INTERNET BRIDGE.

Color Transparency Acetates

Approximately one-hundred color transparency acetates, which support material in the text, are provided to facilitate in-class explanation (0-13-081915-8). Also available on the Long and Long INTERNET BRIDGE.

PowerPoint Slides

Several hundred colorful and illustrative PowerPoint slides are available for use with Microsoft PowerPoint. The PowerPoint slides are distributed as individual files so they can be integrated into your multimedia presentations. Available on the Presentation Manager CD-ROM and on the Long and Long INTERNET BRIDGE.

Computer Chronicles Video Library

Prentice Hall and Computer Chronicles have joined forces to provide you with a video library that offers a variety of documentary and feature-style stories on computers and applications of information technology (0-13-848060-5).

Author Link

If you have questions about the text, its package, or course planning, call us (see the *IRM* for number) or contact us via the INTERNET BRIDGE authors' page (click on the "Feedback" option).

Acknowledgments

A major mixed-media learning tool like *Computers*, 6th ed., and all its ancillaries is not simply written by its authors. That's the easy part. Literally hundreds of people and almost one hundred companies participated in the creation of *Computers* and its many supporting elements.

We would like to single out a few of the many people at Prentice Hall who made major contributions to this project. Acquisitions Editor David Alexander spearheaded the effort with zeal and vision. Production Manager Bruce Kaplan and copy editor Anne Graydon added just the right mix of patience and creativity. The end-product is proof that these and the following Prentice Hall professionals are committed to excellence: Lori Cardillo, P. J. Boardman, Carolyn Henderson, and Keith Kryszczun in Editorial; Nancy Evans, Kris King, Audra Silverie, and Greg Christofferson in Marketing; Joanne Jay, Paul Smolenski, Lorraine Patsco, Dave Salierno, Veronica Schwartz, Christy Mahon, and Richard Bretan in Production and Manufacturing; Ted Tolles, David Nusspickel, Phyllis Bregman, and Heidi Lobecker in New Media. Our good friend Henry Rowe provided valuable feedback and co-authored several of the supplements.

We would like to extend our appreciation to the following professors and to scores more who reviewed for previous editions. Their valuable insight is evident throughout the book.

6TH EDITION:
Wendell Dillard, Arkansas State University; Ken Giffin, University of Central Arkansas; Doug K. Lauffer, Community College of Beaver County; Dori McPherson, Schoolcraft College; Tom Gorecki, Charles County Community College; Dan Everett, University of Georgia; Carol Mull, Asheville-Buncombe Technical Community College; Marian Schwartz, North Central Technical College; Cindy Hanchey, Oklahoma Baptist University; Dr. Emmanuel Opara, Prairie View A&M University; Rajiv Malkan, Montgomery College; Focus Group for *Computers*, 6th ed.; Jeanann Boyce, University of Maryland; Nancy Cosgrove, University of Central Florida; Barbara Ellestad, Montana State University; Shirley Fedorovich, Embry-Riddle Aeronautical University; Wayne Headrick, New Mexico State University; Suzanne Konieczny, Marshall University; Gary Mattison, Strayer College; Rick Parker, College of Southern Idaho; Judy Scholl, Austin Community College.

For previous editions, reviewers include:

5TH EDITION:
Amir Afzal, Strayer College; Gary R. Armstrong, Shippensburg University; Shira L. Broschat, Washington State University; James Frost, Idaho State University; Jorge Gaytan, University of Texas, El Paso; Helene Kershner, SUNY, Buffalo; Ruth Malmstrom, Raritan Valley Community College; Michael A. McNeece, Strayer College; John F. Sharlow, Eastern Connecticut State University; John Stocksen, Kansas City Kansas Community College.

4TH EDITION:
Suzanne Baker, Lakeland Community College; Amanda Bounds, Florida Community College at Jacksonville; Don Cartlidge, New Mexico State University (emeritus);

Stephanie Chenault, The College of Charleston; Eli Cohen, Wichita State University; William Cornette, Southwest Missouri State University; Timothy Gottlebeir, North Lake College; Vernon Griffin, Austin Community College; Sandra Brown, Finger Lakes Community College; Mike Michaelson, Palomar College; Domingo Molina, Texas Southmost College; Joseph Morrell, Metropolitan State College of Denver; Patricia Nettnin, Finger Lakes Community College; Anthony Nowakowski, State University of New York College at Buffalo; Michael Padbury, Arapahoe Community College; Carl Ubelacker, Cincinnatti State Technical and Community College.

3RD EDITION:

Ray Fanselau, American River College; Fred Homeyer, Angelo State University; Robert Keim, Arizona State University; Carl Clavadetscher, California Polytechnic State University, Pomona; Barry Floyd, California Polytechnic State University, San Luis Obispo; Dr. Diane Visor, University of Central Oklahoma; Dr. Diane Fischer, Dowling College; Dr. Adolph Katz, Fairfield University; Constance Knapp, Pace University; Dr. John Sanford, Philadelphia College of Textiles and Science; Peter Irwin, Richland College; Al Schroeder, Richland College; Amir Afzal, Strayer College; James Johnson, Valencia Community College.

2ND EDITION:

Michael J. Belgard, Bryant and Stratton College; Roy Bunch, Chemeketa Community College; Marvin Daugherty, Indiana Vocational Technical College; Joyce Derocher, Bay de Noc Community College; Kirk L. Gibson, City College of San Francisco; Randy Goldberg, Marist College; Don Hall, Manatee Community College; Seth Hock, Columbus State Community College; Dr. M. B. Kahn, California State University at Long Beach; Michael A. Kelly, City College of San Francisco; Constance K. Knapp, CSP, Pace University; Sandra Lehmann, Moraine Park Technical College; William McTammany, Florida Community College at Jacksonville; Margaret J. Moore, Coastal Carolina Community College; Thomas H. Miller, University of Idaho; Anne L. Olsen, Wingate College; Verale Phillips, Cincinnati Technical College; Mark Seagroves, Wingate College; Bari Siddique, Texas Southmost College; Dr. Joseph Williams, University of Texas at Austin; Larry B. Wintermeyer, Chemeketa Community College; Floyd Jay Winters, Manatee Community College.

1ST EDITION:

Sally Anthony, San Diego State University; Harvey Blessing, Essex Community College; Wayne Bowen, Black Hawk Community College; Michael Brown, DeVry Institute of Technology, Chicago; J. Patrick Fenton, West Valley College; Ken Griffin, University of Central Arkansas; Nancy Harrington, Trident Technical College; Grace C. Hertlein, California State University; Shirley Hill, California State University; Cynthia Kachik, Santa Fe Community College; Sandra Lehmann, Morraine Park Technical Institute; Michael Lichtenstein, DeVry Institute of Technology, Chicago; Dennis Martin, Kennebec Valley Vocational Technical Institute; William McDaniel, Jr., Northern Virginia Community College at Alexandria; Edward Nock, DeVry Institute of Technology, Columbus; Lewis Noe, Ivy Technical Institute; Frank O'Brien, Milwaukee Technical College; Alvin Ollenburger, University of Minnesota; Beverly Oswalt, University of Central Arkansas; James Phillips, Lexington Community College; Nancy Roberts, Lesley College; Richardson Siebert, Morton College; Bob Spear, Prince George's Community College; Thomas Voight, Franklin University.

We also appreciate the efforts of the many companies that have contributed resources (information, photos, software, images) to this book and its supplements. We would like to thank those who created key ancillaries for *Computers*: Henry Rowe (content for *Interactive Study Guide, Test Item File,* and *Instructor's Resource Manual,* and C. Norman Hollingsworth (PowerPoint slides).

Finally, we wish to extend our gratitude to the hundreds of instructors, administrators, and students who have provided feedback on previous editions of *Computers*. Their input, also, has been invaluable to the evolution of this sixth edition.

LARRY LONG, Ph.D.   NANCY LONG, Ph.D.

ABOUT THE AUTHORS

Dr. Larry Long and **Dr. Nancy Long** have written more than 30 books, which have been used in over 600 colleges throughout the world. Larry is a lecturer, author, consultant, and educator in the computer and information services fields. He has served as a consultant to all levels of management in virtually every major type of industry. He has over 25 years of classroom experience at IBM, the University of Oklahoma, Lehigh University, and the University of Arkansas. Nancy has teaching and administrative experience at all levels of education: elementary, secondary, college, and continuing education.

Computers

The World of Computers

LEARNING OBJECTIVES

- Become aware of the scope of computer understanding needed by someone living in an information society.
- Describe the implications of computer networks on organizations and on society.
- Demonstrate awareness of the relative size, scope, uses, and variety of available computer systems.
- Describe the fundamental components and the operational capabilities of a computer system.
- Identify and describe uses of the computer.

Courtesy NASA

LET'S TALK

Can you follow this conversation? It includes computing concepts presented in this chapter. Read it now, then reread it once you've had an opportunity to study the chapter.

The Scene The car pool arrives at Frank's house, the last stop on a 40-minute commute into the city.

FRANK: Good morning, all. I need some help—and quick!

JILL: What's up, Frank?

FRANK: Got an e-mail last night from my boss. He wants me to put together some demographic information for our regional sales manager in Portland. And, he wants it yesterday! Any ideas?

MARIA: You know, while I was cruising the Internet this weekend I found an online version of *The World Fact Book*. It might have what you need.

SPIKE: I think we can help, Frank. Here, Jill, let's plug my new notebook PC into your cellular phone. Where did you find that information, Maria?

MARIA: On the CIA's Internet site. Just search on "CIA."

SPIKE (after about a minute): OK, we're online to the CIA site and here's the data.

FRANK (looking at Spike's PC): Fantastic, Spike! That's exactly what the boss wants. Can you download the data for Washington, Oregon, and Idaho? Say, your new PC's monitor has great resolution.

SPIKE: Thanks, it's got a top-of-the-line processor with loads of RAM. And, when I need hard copy, I've got this one-pound printer. Do you want to e-mail your boss while I've got this communications link?

FRANK: Sure. Send this to j_rossi@amicorp.com. Subject: Demographic data. Message: Jim, I'll have the data you requested on your desk by nine.

SPIKE (handing him a diskette): Frank, here's a diskette containing the file.

FRANK: Thanks, I owe you guys.

JILL: Hey, what are friends for? But next time, how about greeting us with coffee and donuts instead!

1–1 The Information Society

We live in an **information society** where **knowledge workers** channel their energies to provide a cornucopia of computer-based information services. The knowledge worker's job function revolves around the use, manipulation, and dissemination of information. This book will help you cope with and understand today's technology so you can take your place in the information society.

R_x for Cyberphobia: Computer Competency

Not too long ago, people who pursued careers in almost any facet of business, education, or government were content to leave computers to computer professionals. Today these people are knowledge workers. In less than a generation, **computer competency** has emerged in virtually any career from a *nice-to-have skill* to a *job-critical skill*.

By the time you complete this course, you will achieve computer competency. If you've got **cyberphobia,** the fear of computers, computer competency is a sure cure. Computer competency will allow you to be an active and effective participant in the emerging information society. You and other computer-competent people will:

1. *Feel comfortable using and operating a computer system.*
2. *Be able to make the computer work for you.* The computer-competent person can use the computer to solve an endless stream of life's problems, from how to pass away a couple of idle hours to how to increase company revenues.

**Monthly Technology Update
Chapter 1**

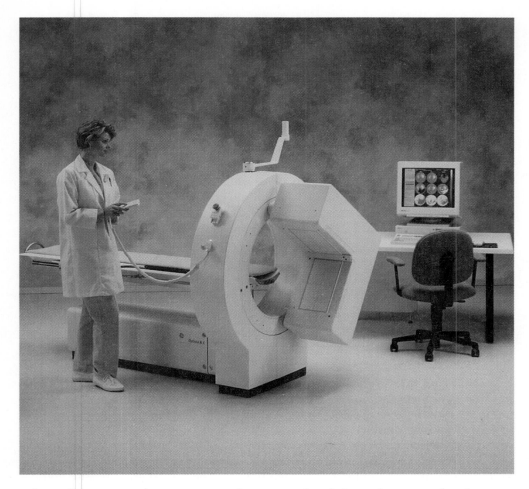

Today we belong to an information society where we are "knowledge workers," as well as doctors, engineers, and accountants. This nuclear imaging technologist uses sophisticated hardware and software to help with medical imaging and image management. Nuclear imaging looks at physiological processes rather than at anatomical structures. Nuclear medicine has a wide variety of uses, including the diagnosis of cancer and studying heart disease. Courtesy of GE Medical Systems

3. *Be able to interact with the computer—that is, generate input to the computer and interpret output from it.* **Input** is data entered to a computer system for processing. **Output** is the presentation of the results of processing (for example, a printed résumé or a tax return).

4. *Understand the impact of computers on society, now and in the future.*

5. *Be an intelligent consumer of computers and computer equipment, collectively called **hardware**.* Smart computer shoppers usually get what they need, not what they think they need. And, they can save a lot of money.

6. *Be an intelligent consumer of software and other nonhardware-related computer products and services.* **Software** refers to a collective set of instructions, called **programs,** that can be interpreted by a computer. The programs cause the computer to perform desired functions, such as flight simulation (a computer game), the generation of business graphics, or word processing.

7. *Be conversant in **computerese**, the language of computers and information technology.* In this book, you will learn those terms and phrases that not only are the foundation of computer terminology but also are very much a part of everyday conversation at school, home, and work.

This surreal scene is all the more remarkable for the way the computer artist has used graphics techniques to model light, shadow, and reflections, mimicking a photograph's realism.
Courtesy of Pixar, Inc.

The Computer Revolution

In an information society, the focus of commerce becomes the generation and distribution of information. A technological revolution is changing our way of life: the way we live, work, and play. The cornerstone of this revolution, the *computer*, is transforming the way we communicate, do business, and learn, and an explosion of computing advances is speeding this change.

- **Personal computers,** or **PCs,** offer a vast array of *enabling technologies*. Enabling technologies help us do things. For example, PCs have maps that help traveling business people navigate the streets of the world, and they have presentation tools that help them make their point when they get there. Already, you need go no farther than your home computer to get the best deal on a new car, send your congressperson a message, order tickets to the theater, play chess with a grand master in Russia, or listen to a radio station in New Zealand.

- Millions of people can be "at work" wherever they are as long as they have their portable personal computers—at a client's office, in an airplane, or at home. The *mobile worker*'s personal computer provides electronic links to a vast array of information and to clients and corporate colleagues.

- Increasingly, the computer is the vehicle by which we communicate, whether with our colleagues at work through **electronic mail (e-mail)** or with our friends through **bulletin-board systems (BBSs).** Both electronic mail and BBSs allow us to send/receive information via computer-to-computer hookups.

That's just *today. Tomorrow,* the next wave of enabling technologies will continue to cause radical changes in our lives. For example, if you're in the market for a new home, you will be able to "visit" any home for sale in the country from the comfort of your own home or office via computer. All you will need to do is tell the computer what city to look in and then enter your search criteria. The electronic realtor will then list those houses that meet your criteria, provide you with detailed information on the house and surrounding area, then offer to take you on a tour of the house— inside and out. After the electronic tour, you will be able to "drive" through the neighborhood, looking left and right as you would in your automobile. Such systems may seem a bit futuristic, but virtually all of California's real estate listings can be viewed on your computer. Systems that permit neighborhood drive-throughs are under active development!

Each day new applications, such as a national multilist for real estate, as well as thousands of companies, schools, and individuals are being added to the **National Information Infrastructure (NII).** The NII, which is also called the **information superhighway,** refers to a network of electronic links that eventually will connect virtually every facet of our society, both public (perhaps the local supermarket) and private (perhaps to Aunt Minnie's daily schedule).

Looking Back a Few Years

To put the emerging information society into perspective, let's flash back a half century and look at the evolution of computing.

- *Fifty years ago,* our parents and grandparents built ships, kept financial records, and performed surgery, all without the aid of computers. Indeed, everything they did was without computers. There *were* no computers!

- *In the 1960s,* mammoth multimillion-dollar computers processed data for those large companies that could afford them. These computers, the domain of highly specialized technical gurus, remained behind locked doors. In "the old days," business computer systems were designed so a computer professional served as

The industrial society evolved in a world without computers. The advent of computers and automation has changed and will continue to change the way we do our jobs. In the automobile industry, those assembly line workers who used to perform repetitive and hazardous jobs now program and maintain industrial robots to do these jobs.   GM Assembly Division, Warren, Michigan/Courtesy of Ford Motor Company

an intermediary between the **user**—someone who uses a computer—and the computer system.

- *In the mid-1970s,* computers became smaller and more accessible. This trend resulted in the introduction of personal computers. During the 1980s, millions of people from all walks of life purchased these miniature miracles. Suddenly, computers were for everyone!

- *Today,* one in four Americans has a home computer more powerful than those that processed data for large companies during the 1960s. The widespread availability of computers has prompted an explosion of applications. At the individual level, we can use our PCs to go on an electronic fantasy adventure or hold an electronic reunion with our scattered family. At the corporate level, virtually every business has embraced **information technology (IT),** the integration of computing technology and information processing. Companies in every area of business are using IT to offer better services and gain a competitive advantage.

Data: Foundation for the Information Society

Data (the plural of *datum*) are just raw facts. Data are all around us. Every day, we generate an enormous amount of data. **Information** is data that have been collected and processed into a meaningful form. Simply, information is the meaning we give to accumulated facts (data). Information as we now know it, though, is a relatively new concept. Just 50 short years ago, *information* was the telephone operator who provided directory assistance. Around 1950, people began to view information as something that could be collected, sorted, summarized, exchanged, and processed. But only during the last decade have computers allowed us to begin tapping the potential of information.

Computers are very good at digesting data and producing information. For example, when you call a mail-order merchandiser, the data you give the sales representative (name, address, product number) are entered directly into the merchandiser's computer. When you run short of cash and stop at an automatic teller machine, all data you enter, including that on the magnetic stripe of your bank card, are processed immediately by the bank's computer system. A computer system eventually manipulates your *data* to produce *information*. The information could be an invoice from a mail-order house or a bank statement.

Traditionally, we have thought of data in terms of numbers (account balance) and letters (customer name), but recent advances in information technology have opened the door to data in other formats, such as visual images. For example, dermatologists (physicians who specialize in skin disorders) use digital cameras to take close-up pictures of patients' skin conditions. Each patient's **record** (information about the patient) on the computer-based **master file** (all patient records) is then updated to include the digital image. During each visit, the dermatologist recalls the patient record, which includes color images of the skin during previous visits. Data can also be found in the form of sound. For example, data collected during noise-level testing of automobiles include digitized versions of the actual sounds heard within the car.

The relationship of data to a computer system is much like the relationship of gasoline to an automobile. Data provide the fuel for a computer system. Your car won't get you anywhere without gas, and your computer won't produce any information without data.

Have you ever wondered where you are or how to get to where you are going? The Rockwell PathMaster route guidance and information system tells you exactly where you are (anywhere in the world) and provides turn-by-turn visual and voice-prompted directions to get you to your destination. The system relies on a global positioning system (GPS) and map-matching to ensure accurate vehicle positioning at all times. The Path-Master is being installed in rental cars, service fleets, emergency vehicles, real estate vehicles, and many other destination-oriented markets. In a few years it may be standard equipment on your car. Rockwell/David Perry

This Course: Your Ticket to the Computer Adventure

You are about to embark on a journey that will stimulate your imagination, challenge your every resource, from physical dexterity to intellect, and alter your sense of perspective on technology. Learning about computers is more than just education. It's an adventure!

Gaining computer competency is just the beginning—your computer adventure lasts a lifetime. Information technology is changing every minute of the day. Every year, hundreds of new IT-related buzz words, concepts, applications, and hardware devices will confront you. Fortunately, you will have established a base of IT knowledge (computer competency) upon which you can build and continue your learning adventure.

1–2 Networking: Bringing People Together

So far we know that computers are extremely good at bringing together data to produce information. Computers also bring together people, from all over the world, to enable better communication and cooperation.

The Global Village

The Global Village

Three decades ago, Marshall McLuhan said, "The new electronic interdependence recreates the world in the image of a global village." His insightful declaration is now clearly a matter of fact. At present, we live in a *global village* in which computers and people are linked within companies and between countries (see Figure 1–1). The global village is an outgrowth of the **computer network**. Most existing computers are linked electronically to a network of one or more computers to share resources and information. When we tap into networked computers, we can hold electronic meetings with widely dispersed colleagues, retrieve information from the corporate database, make hotel reservations, and much, much more.

On a more global scale, computer networks enable worldwide airline reservation data to be entered in the Bahamas and American insurance claims to be processed in Ireland. Securities can be traded simultaneously on the New York Stock Exchange and other exchanges around the world by people in Hong Kong, Los Angeles, and

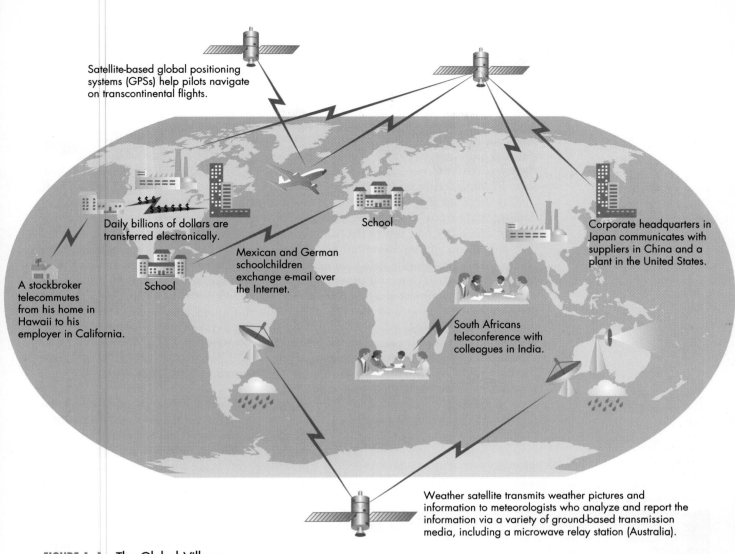

Satellite-based global positioning systems (GPSs) help pilots navigate on transcontinental flights.

Daily billions of dollars are transferred electronically.

School

Mexican and German schoolchildren exchange e-mail over the Internet.

School

A stockbroker telecommutes from his home in Hawaii to his employer in California.

Corporate headquarters in Japan communicates with suppliers in China and a plant in the United States.

South Africans teleconference with colleagues in India.

Weather satellite transmits weather pictures and information to meteorologists who analyze and report the information via a variety of ground-based transmission media, including a microwave relay station (Australia).

FIGURE 1-1   The Global Village
Computer-based communication is turning the world into a global village. We can communicate electronically with people on the other side of the world as easily as we might have a conversation with a neighbor.

Berlin. Computer networks can coordinate the purchases of Korean electronics, American steel, and Indonesian glass to make cars in Japan, and can then be used to track sales of those cars worldwide.

Thanks to computer networks, we are all part of a global economy, in which businesses find partners, customers, suppliers, and competitors around the world. The advent of this global economy is changing society across the board, often in subtle ways. For example, customer service may continue to improve as companies realize how quickly an irate customer can broadcast messages vilifying a company or a particular product to thousands of potential customers over regional, national, and international bulletin boards. Computers, related hardware, and software products are especially vulnerable to such customer attacks. If a product does not stand up to advertised capabilities, the computing community will quickly expose its shortcomings to literally millions of potential buyers. This same level of scrutiny will ultimately be applied to other products and services. For example, there are hundreds of bulletin boards devoted exclusively to discussions of restaurants in various cities and countries.

In these cities and counties, you can be sure that frequent diners know which restaurants offer good food and value and which ones do not. These and thousands of other special-topic bulletin boards can be found on the Internet.

The Internet and Information Services: Going Online

The Internet (the Net) is a worldwide network of computers that has emerged as *the* enabling technology in our migration to a global village. It connects tens of thousands of networks, millions of computers, and many more millions of users in every country. The Internet can be accessed by people in organizations with established links to the Internet and by individuals with PCs. Most colleges are on the Net; that is, they have an Internet account. A growing number of corporations are also becoming authorized Internet users. If you have access to a computer at work or at a college computer lab, you're probably "on the Net" (see Figure 1–2). If not, you can link your PC to a computer at an organization with an Internet account. As an alternative, you can subscribe to a commercial **information service,** such as America Online (Figure 1–3). These and other commercial information services have one or several large computer systems that offer a wide range of information services, including up-to-the-minute news and weather, electronic shopping, e-mail, and much, much more. The services and information provided by the Net and information services are **online;** that is, once the user has established a communications link via his or her PC, the user becomes part of the network. When online, the user interacts directly with the computers in the information network to obtain desired services. When the user terminates the link, the user goes **offline.**

The Internet emerged from a government-sponsored project to promote the interchange of scientific information. This spirit of sharing continues as the overriding theme over the Internet. For example, aspiring writers having difficulty getting read or published can make their writing available to thousands of readers, including agents and publishers, in a matter of minutes. Unknown musicians also use the Internet to gain recognition. *Surfers* on the Internet (Internet users) desiring to read a story or listen to a song, **download** the text or a digitized version of a song (like those on an audio CD) to their personal computer, then read it or play it through their personal computer. Downloading is simply transmitting information from a remote computer (in this case, an Internet-based computer) to a local computer (in most cases a PC). Information (perhaps a story or a song) going the other way, from a local computer to a remote computer, is said to be **uploaded.** Some have not only won the acclaim of fellow surfers, but have gone on to commercial success as well.

This spirit of sharing has prompted individuals and organizations all over the world to make available information and databases on a wide variety of topics. This wonderful distribution and information sharing vehicle is, of course, a boon for businesses. Thousands of publishers, corporations, government agencies, colleges, and database services give In-

FIGURE 1–2   Shopping on the Internet
You can shop the electronic malls and stores of the Internet to get bargains on everything from pasta makers to motorcycles. After you purchase a Honda Golden Wind Wing motorcycle, you use the Internet to join a touring association, chat with fellow enthusiasts, and keep in touch with happenings in the motorcycle-touring world.

ternet users access to their information—some provide information gratis and some charge a fee. Over the next few years look for more and more businesses to use the Internet to generate revenue.

Services and capabilities of the Internet and commercial information services are growing daily. For example, a hungry traveler on the Internet can now order a pizza via PizzaNet. The customer sends the order over the Internet to a Pizza Hut computer in Wichita, Kansas, where it is interpreted and rerouted to the customer's nearest Pizza Hut. Of course, you can't download a pizza—it has to be delivered in the traditional manner. Already you can order almost any consumer item from tulips to trucks through the electronic malls (see Figure 1–3).

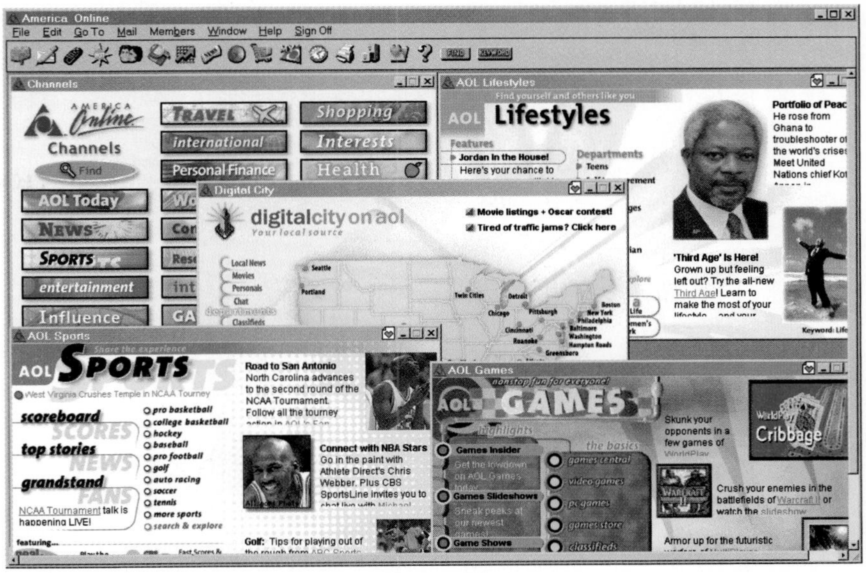

Services available from the publicly available Internet and the subscription-based information services play a major role in shaping our information society. We'll discuss both in considerable detail throughout the book.

FIGURE 1–3   America Online Channels
America Online has 21 Channels, or interest areas (upper left corner), from which to choose. Shown here are the main choice screens for the *Sports, Games, Digital City,* and *Lifestyles* channels.

1–3 Computers: The Essentials

Almost everyone in our information society has a basic understanding of what a computer is and what it can do. This book is designed to add depth to this basic understanding.

Conversational Computerese: Basic Terms and Definitions

The **computer,** also called a **processor,** is *an electronic device that can interpret and execute programmed commands for input, output, computation, and logic operations.* Computers aren't as complicated as you might have been led to believe. A **computer system** has four fundamental components: *input, processing, output,* and *storage* (see Figure 1–4). Note that the processor, or computer, is just one component in a computer system. It provides the intelligence for the computer system, performing all computation and logic operations. In everyday conversation people simply say "computer" when they talk about a computer system. We'll follow this conversational standard throughout this book. We'll refer specifically to the processor when discussing that part of the computer system that does the processing.

Each of the components in a computer system can take on a variety of forms. For example, *output* (the results of processing) can be routed to a televisionlike **monitor,** audio speakers (like those on your stereo system), or a **printer** (see Figure 1–4). The output on a monitor is temporary and is called **soft copy.** Printers produce **hard copy,** or printed output. Data can be entered to a computer system for processing (input) via a **keyboard** (for keyed input), a microphone (for voice and sound input), or a point-and-draw device, such as a **mouse** (see Figure 1–4).

Storage of data and software in a computer system is either *temporary* or *permanent.* **Random-access memory** (**RAM,** rhymes with *ham*) provides temporary storage of data and programs during processing within solid-state **integrated circuits.** Inte-

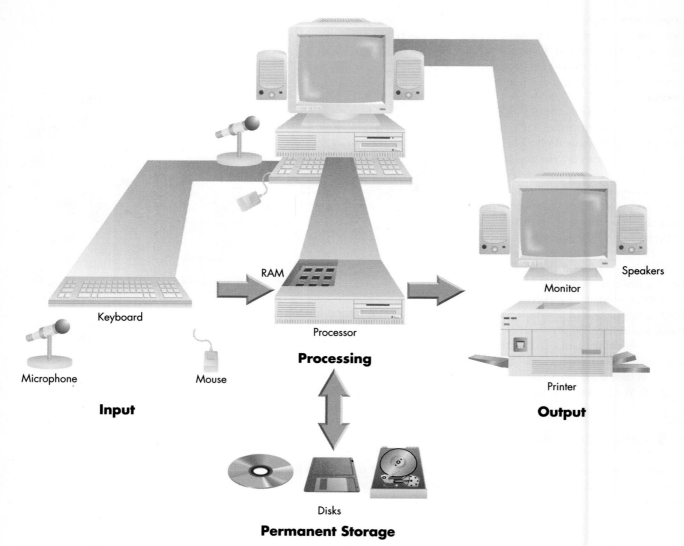

Input

Microphone

Keyboard

Mouse

RAM

Processing

Processor

Permanent Storage

Disks

Output

Monitor

Speakers

Printer

FIGURE 1–4 The Four Fundamental Components of a Personal Computer System
In a personal computer system, the storage and processing components are often contained in the same physical unit. In the illustration, the disk-storage medium is inserted into the unit that contains the processor.

grated circuits, or **chips,** are tiny (about .5 inch square) silicon chips into which thousands of electronic components are etched. The processor is also a chip. Permanently installed and interchangeable **disks** provide permanent storage for data and programs (see Figure 1–4). A computer system's **configuration** describes its internal components (for example, size of RAM and special features) and its **peripheral devices** (printer, various disk-storage devices, monitor, and so on).

Computer Systems: Commuters to Wide-Bodies

Computers can be found in a variety of shapes, from cube-shaped to U-shaped to cylindrical to notebook-shaped. However, the most distinguishing characteristic of any computer system is its *size*—not its physical size, but its *computing capacity*. Loosely speaking, size, or computing capacity, is the amount of processing that can be accomplished by a computer system per unit of time. **Mainframe computers** have greater computing capacities than do personal computers, which are also called **microcom-**

puters (or **micros**). Mainframe computers vary greatly in size from midsized mainframes serving small companies to large mainframes serving thousands of people. And **supercomputers,** packing the most power, have greater computing capacities than do mainframe computers. Depending on its sophistication, a **workstation**'s computing capacity falls somewhere between that of a PC and a midsized mainframe. Some vendors are not content with pigeonholing their products into one of these four major categories, so they have created new niches, such as *desktop mainframes*. In this book, we will limit our discussion to these four major categories (see Figure 1–5). We should emphasize that these categories are relative. What people call a personal computer system today may be called a workstation at some time in the future.

PCs, workstations, mainframes, and supercomputers are computer systems. Each offers many **input/output, or I/O,** alternatives—ways to enter data to the system and to present information generated by the system. All computer systems, no matter how small or large, have the same fundamental capabilities—*input, processing, output,* and *storage*. Keep this in mind as you encounter the computer systems shown in Figure 1–5 in this book, at school, and at work. In keeping with conversational computerese, we will drop the word *system* when discussing the categories of computer systems. Keep in mind, however, that a reference to any of these categories (for example, supercomputer) implies a reference to the entire computer system.

The differences in the various categories of computers are very much a matter of scale. Try thinking of a *supercomputer* as a *wide-body jet*, and a *personal computer* as a *commuter plane*. Both types of airplanes have the same fundamental capability: to carry passengers from one location to another. Wide-bodies, which fly at close to the speed of sound, can carry hundreds of passengers. In contrast, commuter planes travel much slower and carry fewer than 50 passengers. Wide-bodies travel between large international airports, across countries, and between continents. Commuter planes travel short distances between regional airports. The commuter plane, with its small crew, can land, unload, load, and be on its way to another destination in 15 to 20 minutes. The wide-body may take 30 minutes just to unload. A PC is much like the commuter plane in that one person can get it up and running in just a few minutes. All aspects of the PC are controlled by one person. The supercomputer is like the wide-body in that a number of specialists are needed to keep it operational. No matter what their size, airplanes carry passengers and computers process data and produce information. Besides obvious differences in size, the various types of computers differ mostly in the manner in which they are used. Discussions in the following section should give you insight into when and where a particular system might be used.

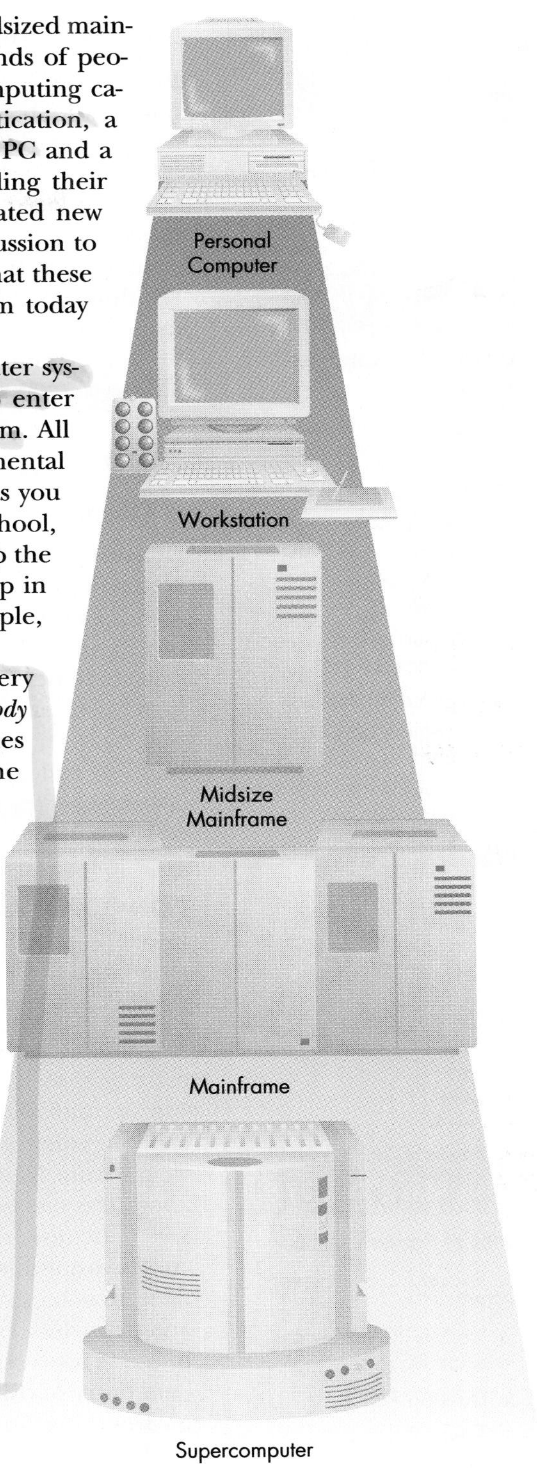

Personal Computer

Workstation

Midsize Mainframe

Mainframe

Supercomputer

FIGURE 1–5 Categories of Computers

1–4 Personal Computers to Supercomputers: Capabilities and Uses

Every 10 hours, more computers are sold than existed in the entire world 25 years ago. Back then, computers came in one size—big. Today, computers come in a variety of sizes. In this section we discuss the capabilities and uses of the four basic categories of computers: personal computers, workstations, mainframes, and supercomputers.

INTERNET BRIDGE

Personal Computers

Personal Computers

In 1981, IBM introduced its **IBM PC** and it legitimized the personal computer as a business tool. Shortly thereafter, other manufacturers began making PCs that were compatible with the IBM PC. Most of the today's personal computers (over 80%) have evolved from these original PC-compatibles. Long removed from the IBM PC, they are also called **Wintel PCs** because they use the Microsoft **Windows 9x/NT** (a collective reference to Microsoft **Windows 95**, **Windows 98**, or **Windows NT**) control software and an In*tel* Corporation or Intel-compatible processor. Each of the Microsoft Windows 9x/NT family of **operating systems** controls all hardware and software activities on Wintel PCs.

The Wintel PC represents the dominant PC platform. A **platform** defines a standard for which software is developed. Specifically, a platform is defined by two key elements:

- The processor (for example, Intel Pentium II or Motorola PowerPC)
- The operating system (for example, Windows NT or Mac OS)

Generally, software created to run on one platform is not compatible with any other platform. Most of the remaining personal computers are part of the Apple **Macintosh** line of computers, which use the **Mac OS** operating system and the Motorola **PowerPC processor**.

One person at a time uses a PC. The user turns on the PC, selects the software to be run, enters the data, and requests the information. The PC, like other computers, is very versatile and has been used for everything from communicating with business colleagues to controlling household appliances. Note that the terms *personal computer, PC, microcomputer*, and *micro* are used interchangeably in practice. The personal computer is actually a family of computers, some conventional and some unconventional.

CONVENTIONAL PCS: POCKETS, LAPTOPS, DESKTOPS, AND TOWERS Conventional personal computers have a full keyboard, a monitor, and can function as stand-alone systems. These PCs can be categorized as *pocket PCs, laptop PCs, desktop PCs*, and *tower PCs* (see adjacent photos).

Pocket and Laptop PCs **Pocket PCs** and **laptop PCs** are light (a few ounces to about eight pounds), compact, and are called "portable" because they have batteries and can operate with or without an external power source. The pocket PC, sometimes called a **palmtop PC**, literally can fit in a coat pocket or a handbag. Laptops, which weigh from four to eight pounds, are often called **notebook PCs** because they are about the size of a one-inch-thick notebook.

The power of a PC is not necessarily related to its size. A few laptop PCs can run circles around some desktop PCs. Some user conveniences, however, must be sacrificed to achieve portability. For instance, input devices, such as keyboards and point-and-draw devices, are given less space in portable PCs and may be more cumbersome to use. This is particularly true of pocket PCs, in which miniaturized keyboards make data entry and interaction with the computer difficult and slow. The display screen on some pocket PCs is monochrome (as opposed to color) and may be difficult to read under certain lighting situations. Portable computers take up less space and, therefore, have a smaller capacity for permanent storage of data and programs. Laptop battery life can be as little as a couple of hours for older models to 20 hours for state-of-the-art rechargeable lithium batteries.

The 2-in-1 PC can be used as both a notebook and a desktop PC. It has two parts: a fully functional *notebook PC* and a **docking station**. Two-in-one PCs have a configuration that allows users to enjoy the best of both worlds—portability and the expanded features of a desktop. The notebook, which supplies the processor, is simply inserted into or removed from the docking station, depending on the needs of the user. The

MEMORY BITS

Categories of Computer Systems

- Personal Computers (PCs)
- Workstations
- Mainframe computer systems
  —Enterprise-wide systems
  —Input/output-bound applications
- Supercomputer systems
  —Engineering and scientific computing
  —Processor-bound applications

MEMORY BITS

Types of Personal Computers

- Pocket PC or palmtop PC
- Laptop PC and note-book PC
- Desktop PC
- Tower PC
- 2-in-1 PC (notebook with docking station)
- Port replicator
- Slate or pen-based PC
- Personal digital assistant (PDA)
- Network computer (NC)

THE PC FAMILY

◄When searching for a personal computer, this executive identified portability and flexibility as her primary criteria. She chose a docking station for the office that she uses in conjunction with her IBM Thinkpad notebook PC. Courtesy of International Business Machines Corporation. Unauthorized use not permitted.

▲ This real estate appraiser uses an Apple Powerbook notebook PC in conjunction with a digital camera (foreground) to prepare appraisals. She inserts digital photographs of the property directly into an electronic document, which is then printed and given to her client. Courtesy of Apple Computer, Inc.

▲ This executive's day-timer is just one of many applications on his slate PC. Photo provided by GRiD Systems Corporation

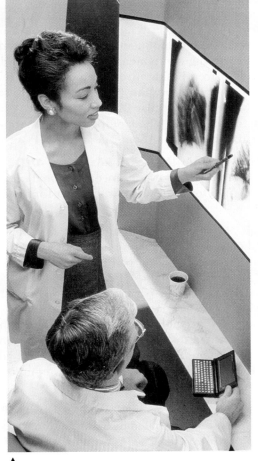

▲ Students use an Apple Newton, a PDA, to take notes for a presentation. Courtesy of Apple Computer, Inc.

▲ This Compaq Prosignia, a tower PC, can sit under, beside, or on top of a desk. The printer connected to it is shared by other PCs in this office. Reprinted with permission of Compaq Computer Corporation. All Rights Reserved.

▲ The high-performance palmtop computer being used by these doctors can run the same applications as its desktop cousin. Photo courtesy of Hewlett-Packard Company

Each year millions of people purchase desktop PCs, like this Compaq Presario, for their homes. Reprinted with permission of Compaq Computer Corporation. All Rights Reserved.
▼

◄Workers at McKesson Corporation wear their PCs. The wearable PCs weigh 13 ounces, fit over the hand and forearm, contain a small screen and key pad, and can scan bar codes. This receiving clerk can read bar codes and enter data while keeping both hands free to lift and move shipping containers. Photo courtesy of McKesson Corporation

A-30

docking station can be *configured* to give the docked notebook PC the look and feel of a desktop PC. That is, the docking station can expand the notebook's capabilities and might include: more disk storage, a CD-ROM drive, several interchangeable disk options, a magnetic tape backup unit, a large monitor, and expansion slots into which still other features can be added to the system (for example, circuitry that would enable television programming to be viewed on the PC's monitor).

Another notebook option, called the **port replicator**, works like the docking station in that the notebook PC is inserted into it and removed as needed. Once inserted the notebook can use the port replicator **ports** and whatever is connected to them. Ports are electronic interfaces through which devices like the keyboard, monitor, mouse, and printer are connected. Port replicators also provide bigger speakers and an AC power source, and some include a network connector.

Desktop and Tower PCs   **Desktop PCs** and **tower PCs** are not considered portable because they rely on an outside power source and are not designed for frequent movement. Typically, the desktop PC's monitor is positioned on top of the processing component. The processing component of the tower PC is designed to sit upright, like a desktop PC's processing component standing on its end. The taller towers (over two feet) are usually placed beside or under a desk, and the smaller mini-tower may be placed in any convenient location (on a nearby shelf, on the desk, or on the floor).

Currently, the most popular PC is the tower PC, primarily because it gives us the biggest "bang for the buck." The laptop, which cost about twice that of a comparable tower PC, is gaining ground. About one in three PCs sold are laptops.

THE EXTENDED PC FAMILY: SLATE PCs, PDAs, AND NCs   The conventional members of the PC family have several unconventional cousins. These personal computers may be designed for special applications or for use in a particular computing environment.

Slate Computers   Mobile workers in increasing numbers are using portable **slate PCs**. Slate PCs, sometimes called pen-based PCs, use electronic pens in conjunction with a combination monitor/drawing pad instead of keyboards. Users select options, enter data, and draw with the pen. United Parcel Service (UPS) couriers use slate PCs when they ask you to sign for packages on a pressure-sensitive display screen with an electronic stylus.

Slate computers are poised to make an entry into the world of many mobile professionals. Hand-written text is interpreted by handwriting-recognition software, then entered into the system. Insurance agents and claims adjusters who need to work at accident or disaster scenes have found slate computers more suitable to their input needs (which may include both text and drawings).

Peripherals Explorer

Personal Digital Assistants   **Personal digital assistants (PDAs)** or **handheld PCs** may take on many forms and are called by many names, from *personal communicators* to *mobile business centers* to *Web phones*. PDAs are smaller than slate PCs, usually weighing less than a pound. They can include a built-in cellular phone that enables the wireless sending/receiving of faxes and access to the Internet (including e-mail). Their built-in wireless communications capabilities give their users immediate access to the Internet, colleagues and clients, and needed information, virtually anytime, anywhere. PDA interaction can be via the pen (like a slate PC) or by touching the keys on an on-screen keyboard or a reduced-key keyboard.

Generally, PDAs support a variety of personal information systems, such as appointment scheduling, phone-number administration, to-do lists, tickler files, diaries, and so on. Of course, they can also support a variety of PC-type applications, such as spreadsheets and personal financial management. Also, PDAs are designed to be easily connected to other computers and printers for data transfer, network access, and printing. Coca-Cola and Pepsi-Cola distributors equip their salespeople with PDAs, which enable them to better manage their territories.

Network Computers In contrast to the conventional PC, the **network computer**, or **NC**, is designed to function only when it is linked to a server computer (normally an organization's internal local area network). The NC looks similar to a PC but with several major configuration differences. First, it has a relatively small processor and considerably less RAM than modern personal computers. Second, it does not have a permanently installed disk. And, of course, it is less expensive than a stand-alone PC.

The NC depends on a central network server computer to do much of the processing and for permanent storage of data and information. Here is the way an NC works: The network computer user has access to a wide range of applications; however, the software applications and data are downloaded as they are needed to the NC from a network's central computer. Whether or not to buy into the NC concept is one of the major debates in the information technology community. Exchanging PCs for NCs will eliminate the expensive and time-consuming task of installing and maintaining PC-based software, but it will make all NCs dependent on the server computer. If the server goes down, all NCs depending on it go down.

Many industry observers are predicting that network computers, such as this HDS@workStation Network Computer will replace PCs in the workplace. NCs eliminate the hassle associated with configuring and maintaining software on PCs. NC software is retrieved from a central network computer as it is needed.   Courtesy of HDS Network Systems, Inc.

CONFIGURING A PC: PUTTING THE PIECES TOGETHER PC users often select, configure, and install their own system. The configuration of a microcomputer or what you put into and attach to your computer can vary enormously. Common configuration options are shown in Figure 2–6.

Nowadays, the typical off-the-shelf PC is configured to run multimedia applications. **Multimedia applications** integrate text, sound, graphics, motion video, and/or animation. Computer-based encyclopedias, such as Microsoft's Encarta, provide a good example of multimedia applications. They can take you back to July 20, 1969, and let you see motion video of the Apollo 11 lunar module *Eagle* landing on the moon at the Sea of Tranquility. If you wish, you can listen to Commander Neil Armstrong proclaim, "That's one small step for [a] man, one giant leap for mankind" as he steps on the moon. Of course, the electronic encyclopedia contains supporting text that explains that he intended to say "a man." The typical multimedia-configured PC (see Figure 1–4) includes the following components.

1. A microcomputer (the processor and other electronic components)
2. A keyboard for input
3. A point-and-draw device for input (usually a mouse)
4. A monitor for *soft copy* (temporary) output
5. A printer for *hard-copy* (printed) output
6. A permanently installed high-capacity **hard-disk drive** for permanent storage of data and programs
7. A **floppy disk drive** into which an interchangeable **diskette**, or **floppy disk**, is inserted
8. A **CD-ROM drive** into which an interchangeable **CD-ROM**, which looks like an audio CD, is inserted
9. A microphone (audio input)
10. A set of speakers (audio output)

Virtually all PCs give users the flexibility to configure the system with a variety of peripheral devices (input/output and storage). A PC system is configured by linking any of a wide variety of peripheral devices to the processor component. Figure 1–6 shows the more common peripheral devices that can be configured with a PC. Many other peripherals can be linked to a PC, including video cameras, telephones, image scanners (to enter images to the system), other computers, security devices, and even a device that will enable you to watch your favorite television show on the PC's monitor.

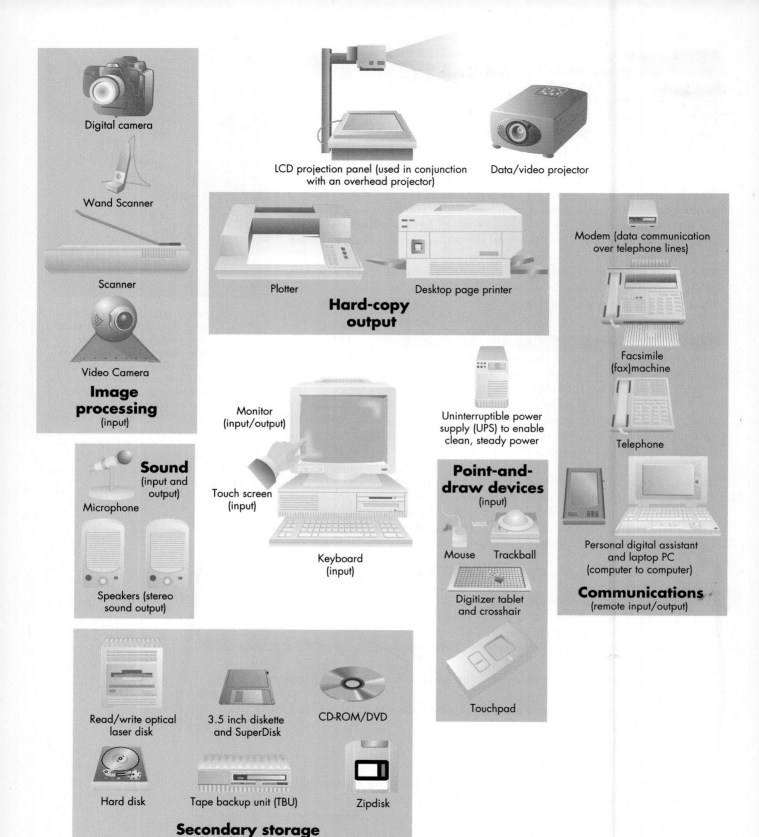

Image processing (input)
- Digital camera
- Wand Scanner
- Scanner
- Video Camera

LCD projection panel (used in conjunction with an overhead projector)

Data/video projector

Hard-copy output
- Plotter
- Desktop page printer

Sound (input and output)
- Microphone
- Speakers (stereo sound output)

Monitor (input/output)

Touch screen (input)

Keyboard (input)

Uninterruptible power supply (UPS) to enable clean, steady power

Point-and-draw devices (input)
- Mouse
- Trackball
- Digitizer tablet and crosshair
- Touchpad

Modem (data communication over telephone lines)

Facsimile (fax) machine

Telephone

Personal digital assistant and laptop PC (computer to computer)

Communications (remote input/output)

Secondary storage
- Read/write optical laser disk
- 3.5 inch diskette and SuperDisk
- CD-ROM/DVD
- Hard disk
- Tape backup unit (TBU)
- Zipdisk

FIGURE 1–6 The Personal Computer and Common Peripheral Devices
A wide range of peripheral devices can be connected to a PC. Those shown here and others are discussed in detail in later chapters.

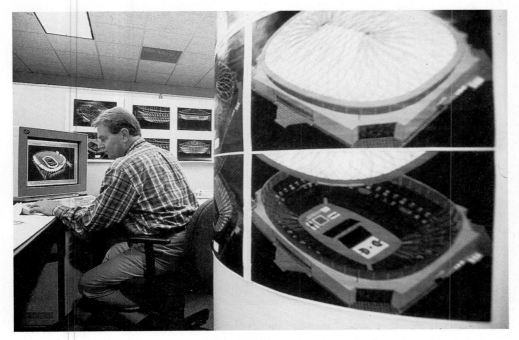

Engineers used IBM workstations to create CAD models of the venues for the 1996 Atlanta Olympics. Because his workstation is on a network with other similar workstations, all project team members can follow the progress of each design effort.   Courtesy of International Business Machines Corporation. Unauthorized use not permitted.

Workstations: The Hot Rods of Computing

What looks like a PC but isn't? It's a *workstation* and it's very fast. Speed is one of the characteristics that distinguishes workstations from PCs. In fact, some people talk of workstations as "souped-up" PCs. The PC was fine for word processing, spreadsheets, and games, but for real "power users"—engineers doing **computer-aided design,** or **CAD** (using the computer in the design process), scientists, and other "number crunchers"—the PC sometimes fell short.

The workstation's input/output devices also set it apart from a PC. A typical workstation will sport a large-screen color monitor capable of displaying high-resolution graphics. **Resolution** refers to the clarity of the image on the monitor's display. For pointing and drawing, the workstation user can call on a variety of specialized point-and-draw devices that combine the precision of a gun sight with the convenience of a mouse. Add-on key pads can expand the number of specialized function keys available to the user.

The capabilities of today's high-end PCs are very similar to those of low-end workstations. In a few years, the average PC will have workstation capabilities. Eventually the distinctions between the two will disappear, and we will be left with a computer category that is a cross between a PC and a workstation. Time will tell whether we call it a PC, a workstation, or something else.

Workstations

Mainframe Computers: Corporate Workhorses

Mainframe computers, with their expanded processing capabilities, provide a computing resource that can be shared by many people. Mainframes are usually associated with **enterprise-wide systems**—that is, computer-based systems that service enti-

Mainframe Computers

The clean lines of this mainframe computer system (in the background) hide the thousands of integrated circuits, miles of wire, and even gold that make up its inner workings. This data center provides information processing support for hundreds of end users. Photo courtesy of Hewlett-Packard Company

ties throughout an organization. For example, human resource management, accounting, and inventory management tasks are usually enterprise-wide systems handled by mainframe-based networks. Typically, users communicate with a centralized mainframe, called a **host computer,** through a PC or a **terminal,** which has a keyboard for input and a monitor for output. Depending on the size of the organization, a dozen people or 10,000 people can share system resources by interacting with their PCs, terminals, workstations, NCs, PDAs, and other communications devices.

Until the late 1960s, all computers were mainframe computers, and they were expensive—too expensive for all but the larger companies. Large companies shelled out $1.5 million and more for mainframe computers with less power than today's $1000 PCs. In the late 1960s, computer vendors introduced smaller, slightly "watered down" computers that were more affordable for smaller companies. The industry dubbed these small computers **minicomputers,** or simply **minis.** The term was used until recently, when the distinction between minis and mainframes began to blur. Today the term is seldom used. Smaller mainframes are called midsized computers.

Mainframe computers are *designed specifically* for the multiuser environment, in contrast to PCs and workstations, which are frequently used as stand-alone computers. Mainframes are oriented to **input/output-bound** applications; that is, the amount of work that can be performed by the computer system is limited primarily by the speeds of the I/O and storage devices. Administrative data processing jobs, such as generating monthly statements for checking accounts at a bank, require relatively little calculation and a great deal of input and output. In I/O-bound applications, the computer is often waiting for data to be entered or for an output device to complete its current task.

It is unlikely that you would find two mainframe computers configured in exactly the same way. For example, a large municipal government generates a tremendous amount of *external output* (output that is directed to persons not affiliated with city government, such as utility bills and tax notices) and would require several high-speed page printers. In contrast, a software development company might enter and process all data from terminals with relatively little hard-copy output.

Supercomputers: Processing Giants

During the early 1970s, administrative data processing dominated computer applications. Bankers, college administrators, and advertising executives were amazed by the blinding speed at which million-dollar mainframes processed their data. Engineers and scientists were grateful for this tremendous technological achievement, but they were far from satisfied. When business executives talked about unlimited capability, engineers and scientists knew they would have to wait for future enhancements before they could use computers to address truly complex problems. Automotive engineers were still not able to create three-dimensional prototypes of automobiles inside a computer. Physicists could not explore the activities of an atom during a nuclear explosion. A typical scientific job involves the manipulation of a complex mathematical model, often requiring trillions of operations to resolve. During the early 1970s, some complex processor-bound scientific jobs would tie up large mainframe computers at major universities for days at a time. This, of course, was unacceptable. The engineering and scientific communities had a desperate need for more powerful computers. In response to that need, computer designers began work on what are now known as supercomputers.

Supercomputers primarily address **processor-bound** applications, which require little in the way of input or output. In processor-bound applications, the amount of work that can be done by the computer system is limited primarily by the speed of the computer. Such applications involve highly complex or vastly numerous calculations, all of which require processor, not I/O, work.

Supercomputers are known as much for their applications as they are for their speed or computing capacity, which may be 10 times that of a large mainframe computer. These are representative supercomputer applications:

- Supercomputers enable the simulation of airflow around an airplane at different speeds and altitudes.
- Auto manufacturers use supercomputers to simulate auto accidents on video screens. (It is less expensive, more revealing, and safer than crashing the real thing.)
- Meteorologists employ supercomputers to study the formation of tornadoes.
- Hollywood production studios use supercomputers to create the advanced graphics used to create special effects for movies such as *Independence Day* and for TV commercials.
- Supercomputers sort through and analyze mountains of seismic data gathered during oil-seeking explorations.
- Medical researchers use supercomputers to simulate the delivery of babies.

All of these applications are impractical, if not impossible, on mainframes.

This CRAY T3E-900 supercomputer is the first commercially available computer that is capable of performing a trillion operations per second. Courtesy: Cray Research (now part of Silicon Graphics, Inc.)

INTERNET BRIDGE

Supercomputers

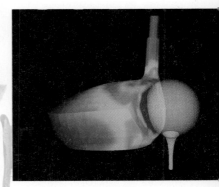

MacGregor Golf Company turned to a Cray Research supercomputer to design its titanium-head club. A supercomputer model "hits" the ball, collects and analyzes data, and makes design recommendations. The result was a club with added airfoils that yields the average duffer an extra seven to ten yards per drive. Courtesy of Cray Research, Inc.

Ethical Issues and Concerns

Monitoring of E-mail

MANY ORGANIZATIONS MONITOR BOTH E-MAIL AND TELE-phone conversations of their employees. These organizations cite productivity and quality control as justification. People who used to chat at the water cooler or snack counter do so now over office e-mail. Monitored e-mail is just as likely to surface as "meet you at the gym after work" as "meet you in the conference room."

Realistically, e-mail is monitored to discourage nonbusiness messages and to keep employees focused on job-related activities. We now know that e-mail, when used responsibly, can boost productivity. We also know that, if abused, e-mail can be counterproductive.

Once an organization decides to monitor e-mail, it can do so in several ways. Individuals can scan e-mail archives for inappropriate transmissions, often a time-consuming process. In large organizations, computers scan e-mail archives for key words (baseball, party, boss, and so on) and kick out messages with questionable content. Already many employees have been fired or disciplined for abusing e-mail.

Employees feel that monitoring of e-mail is an invasion of personal privacy. Many workers view e-mail as just another tool, such as a telephone, and that they should be allowed some reasonable personal use. The issue is being argued in the courts.

Discussion: Does an employer's right to know outweigh the employee's right to privacy?

1–5 A Computer System at Work

Now that we know what different kinds of computer systems exist, let's examine exactly what a computer can and cannot do. To get a better idea of how a computer system actually works, we will look at how it might do the processing of a payroll system.

Processing Payroll: Payday

One computer-based system makes us happy each and every payday. It's called a *payroll system.* Just about every organization that has employees and a computer maintains a computer-based payroll system. The payroll system enables input and processing of pertinent payroll-related data to produce payroll checks and a variety of reports. The payroll system walkthrough in Figure 1–7 illustrates how data are entered into a network of personal computer systems and how the four system components (input, processing, output, and storage) interact to produce payroll checks and information (in our example, a year-to-date overtime report).

In the walkthrough of Figure 1–7, the payroll system and other company systems are supported on a **local area network (LAN).** A LAN connects PCs or workstations in close proximity, such as in a suite of offices or a building. In most LANs, one central computer, called a **server computer,** performs a variety of functions for the other computers on the LAN, called **client computers.** One such function is the storage of data and applications software. In Figure 1–7, client PCs throughout the company are linked to a server computer. In the example, the server computer is a tower PC, but the server computer can be any type of computer, from a notebook PC to a super-computer.

What Can a Computer Do?

Computers perform two operations: input/output operations and processing operations.

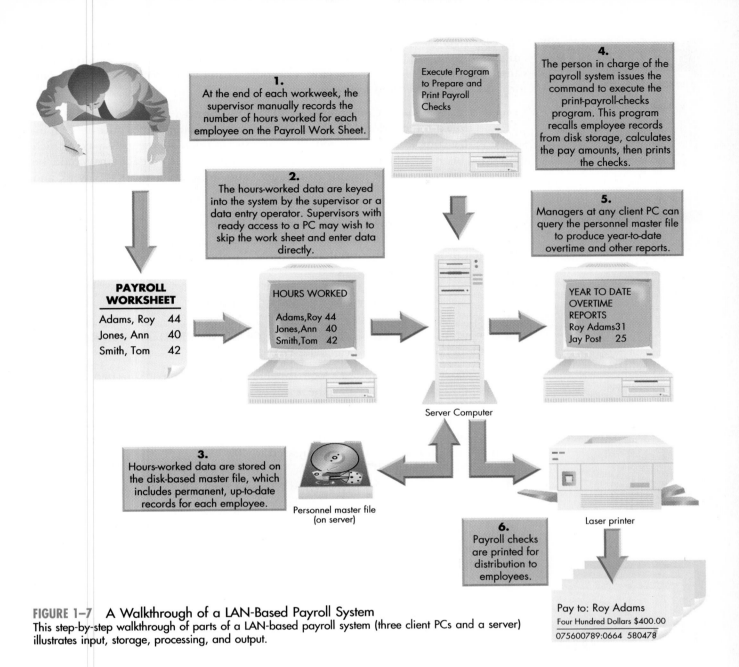

FIGURE 1–7 A Walkthrough of a LAN-Based Payroll System
This step-by-step walkthrough of parts of a LAN-based payroll system (three client PCs and a server) illustrates input, storage, processing, and output.

INPUT/OUTPUT OPERATIONS: READIN' AND 'RITIN' In performing input/output (I/O) operations, the computer *reads* from input and storage devices and then *writes* to output and storage devices. Before data can be processed, they must be "read" from an input device or data storage device. Input data can be entered directly by end users or by professional data entry operators. Typically, data are entered on a terminal or a PC keyboard or they are retrieved from data storage, such as a magnetic disk. Once data have been processed, they are "written" to a magnetic disk or to an output device, such as a printer.

Input/output (I/O) operations are illustrated in the payroll-system walkthrough example shown in Figure 1–7. Hours-worked data are entered, or "read," into the computer system (Activity 2). These data are "written" to magnetic disk storage for recall later (Activity 3). Data are "read" from the personnel master file on magnetic disk, processed (Activity 4), and "written" to the printer to produce the payroll checks (Activity 6).

MEMORY BITS

Computer Operations

- Input/output
  —Read
  —Write
- Processing
  —Computation
  —Logic

PROCESSING OPERATIONS: DOING MATH AND MAKING DECISIONS Any two computers instructed to perform the same operation will arrive at the same result because the computer is totally objective. Computers can't have opinions. They can perform only *computation* and *logic operations*.

Computation operations. Computers can add (+), subtract (−), multiply (*), divide (/), and do exponentiation (^). In the payroll-system example of Figure 1–7, an instruction in a computer program tells the computer to calculate the gross pay for each employee in a computation operation. For example, these calculations would be needed to compute gross pay for Ann Jones, who worked 40 hours this week and makes $15 per hour:

Pay = 40 hours worked * $15/hour = $600

The actual program instruction that performs the above calculation might look like this:

PAY = HOURS_WORKED * PAY_RATE

The computer would then recall values for HOURS_WORKED and PAY_RATE from the personnel master file and calculate PAY.

Logic operations. The computer's logic capability enables comparisons between numbers and between words. Based on the result of a comparison, the computer performs appropriate functions. In the example of Figure 1–7, Tom Smith and Roy Adams had overtime hours because they worked more than 40 hours (the normal workweek). The computer must use its *logic capability* to decide if an employee is due overtime pay. To do this, hours worked are compared to 40.

Are hours worked > (greater than) 40?

For Roy Adams, who worked 44 hours, the comparison is true (44 is greater than 40). A comparison that is true causes the difference (4 hours) to be credited as overtime and paid at time and a half. The actual instruction that would perform the logical operation might look like this:

IF HOURS_WORKED > 40 THEN PAY_OVERTIME

The Computer's Strengths

In a nutshell, computers are fast, accurate, consistent, and reliable. They don't forget anything, and they don't complain.

SPEED: 186 MILES/MILLISECOND Computers perform various activities by executing instructions, such as those discussed in the previous section. These operations are measured in **milliseconds, microseconds, nanoseconds,** and **picoseconds** (one thousandth, one millionth, one billionth, and one trillionth of a second, respectively). To place computer speeds in perspective, consider that a beam of light travels down the length of this page in about one nanosecond. During that time a mainframe computer can perform the computations needed to complete a complex tax return.

ACCURACY: ZERO ERRORS Computers are amazingly accurate, and their accuracy reflects great *precision*. Computations are accurate within a penny, a micron, a picosecond, or whatever level of precision is required. Errors do occur in computer-based information systems, but precious few can be directly attributed to the computer sys-

MEMORY BITS

Fractions of a Second

- Millisecond = 0.001 second (one thousandth of a second)
- Microsecond = 0.000001 second (one millionth of a second)
- Nanosecond = 0.000000001 second (one billionth of a second)
- Picosecond = 0.000000000001 second (one trillionth of a second)

tem itself. The vast majority can be traced to a program logic error, a procedural error, or erroneous data. These are *human errors*.

CONSISTENCY: ALL STRIKES Human baseball pitchers try to throw strikes, but often end up throwing balls. Computers always do what they are programmed to do—nothing more, nothing less. If we ask them to throw strikes, they throw nothing but strikes. This ability to produce consistent results gives us the confidence we need to allow computers to process mission-critical information (information that is necessary for continued operation of the organization).

RELIABILITY: NO DOWNTIME Computer systems are the most reliable workers in any company, especially when it comes to repetitive tasks. They don't take sick days and coffee breaks, and they seldom complain. Anything below 99.9% **uptime,** the time when the computer system is in operation, is usually unacceptable. For some companies, any **downtime** is unacceptable. These companies provide **backup** computers that take over automatically should the main computers fail.

MEMORY CAPABILITY: VIRTUALLY UNLIMITED Computer systems have total and instant recall of data and an almost unlimited capacity to store these data. A typical mainframe computer system will have trillions of characters and millions of images stored and available for instant recall. High-end PCs have immediate access to 2 or 3 billion characters of data and thousands of images. To give you a benchmark for comparison, this book contains about 1.25 million characters and about 300 images.

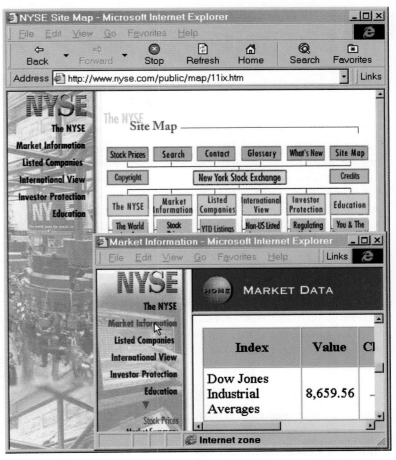

At the New York Stock Exchange, literally billions of dollars' worth of securities are routinely bought and sold with nary a penny lost, a testament to the accuracy of computers. This scene is one of many that can be found at the NYSE's Visitors Center tour on their Internet site < http://www.nyse.com/public/visit/vis-tour.html > .   Courtesy of the New York Stock Exchange.

1–6 How Do We Use Computers?

The uses of computers are like the number of melodies available to a songwriter—limitless. If you can imagine it, there is a good chance that computers can help you do it. This section provides an overview of potential computer applications, which should give you a feel for how computers are affecting your life. These applications, however, are but a few of the many applications presented throughout the book.

Serendipitous Surfing: The Movies

Information Systems

The bulk of existing computer power is dedicated to **information systems.** This includes all uses of computers that support the administrative aspects of an organization, such as airline reservation systems, student registration systems, hospital patient-billing systems, and countless others. We combine *hardware, software, people, procedures,* and *data* to create an information system. A computer-based information system pro-

EMERGING TECHNOLOGY

Going Grocery Shopping: Let Your Fingers Do the Walking

HOW WOULD YOU LIKE TO DO A WEEK'S WORTH OF GROCERY shopping in 10 minutes? Rather than loading the kids into the minivan on shopping day, you can send them out to play and do your shopping from the comfort of your home. Thousands of busy people have traded their shopping carts for keyboards. Rather than fight the crowds in the Chicago and San Francisco areas, they log on to the Peapod, an online shopping and delivery service.

Peapod is giving us a glimpse into the future of retailing—the *virtual store*. Peapod is a pioneer in a rapidly expanding industry that is dedicated to enabling us to buy almost anything from a PC. Peapod subscribers go shopping at the virtual grocery store by logging on to a system that lets them interactively shop for grocery items,

including fresh produce, deli, bakery, meat, and frozen products. Rather than running from aisle to aisle, you simply point and click around the screen for the items you want. Once online you can

- Choose from over 20,000 items
- Compare prices instantly to find the best deal
- Check your subtotal at any time to stay within your budget
- Create personal shopping lists to save time
- View images of products
- Check out store specials
- View nutritional labels for products
- Sort like products instantly by nutritional content
- Choose a delivery time that fits your schedule

Peapod's online shopping system is linked directly to its partner stores' computer systems (Safeway in San Francisco and Jewel in Chicago). When you send your shopping list to Peapod, an order is transmitted to the nearest partner store. A professionally trained shopper takes your order, grabs a shopping cart, and does your shopping for you. The professional shopper takes a fraction of the time you would take because the list is ordered by aisle and the shopper knows exactly what to get. You can redeem your coupons when the shopper/delivery person arrives with your food. Food is delivered in temperature-controlled containers.

The virtual supermarket is sure to change the way we shop. This interactive online approach helps take the hassle and the mystery out of grocery shopping. We can

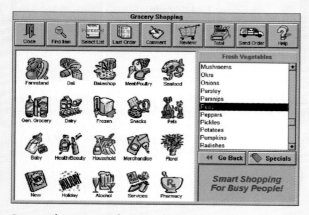

Grocery shoppers now have another option—going online. The Peapod system lets subscribers point and click their way around a virtual supermarket.

---

vides an organization with *data processing* capabilities and the knowledge workers in the organization with the *information* they need to make better, more informed decisions.

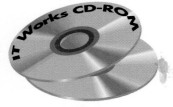

Applications Explorer

Personal Computing

The growth of **personal computing,** an environment in which one person controls the PC, has surpassed even the most adventurous forecasts of a decade ago. It's not uncommon for companies to have more personal computers than they do telephones.

A variety of domestic and business applications from the foundation of personal computing. Domestic applications include everything from personal finance to edu-

enced an 8% increase in sales. Already, online shopping accounts for over 15% of the sales volume at the partner stores. Such success has not gone unnoticed by other entrepreneurs. Shoppers Express has teamed up with grocery and pharmacy stores throughout the United States to offer an online shopping service over the information service America Online. Wal-Mart, the world's largest retailer, now offers online shopping services. Apparently a growing number of people are willing to give up the smell of fresh bread to avoid the long lines at the checkout counter.

The Peapod system has made life easier for a great many people. It has also saved them time and money. Working parents gladly trade shopping time for more time with the kids. Some people enjoy saving big on coupons and baby-sitting costs. Just about everyone saves money because the system encourages you to buy the product with the best per unit price. People who haven't set foot in a grocery store for months say their families are eating better than ever.

Shopping online means never having to leave your home.

view items by category (snack foods), by item (cookies), or by brand (Keebler). We can even peruse the items on sale. We can request that items be arranged alphabetically by brand, by price per unit, by package size, or, we can even request a listing by nutritional value.

In the minds of the busy people who shop online, the cost of the service (approximately $11 on a $100 order) is easily offset by other savings (better prices, less spent on travel, and so on). These savings do not consider the extra personal time shoppers recover by shopping online.

Online shopping is here to stay. Since linking up with Peapod, the grocery store partners have experi-

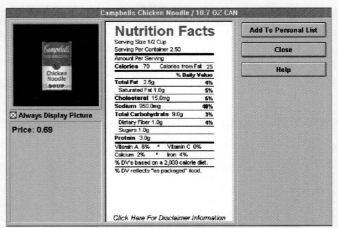

Online grocery shoppers can request nutritional facts on grocery items. They can also compare nutritional value between like products.

cation to entertainment. Microcomputer software is available to support thousands of common and not-so-common business applications.

A growing family of software for personal or business productivity is the foundation of personal computing in the home and in the business world. These are some of the most popular productivity tools.

- *Word processing.* **Word processing software** enables users to enter and edit text in documents in preparation for output (printing, faxing, or sending via e-mail). Word processing documents can include graphic images.

- *Desktop publishing.* **Desktop publishing software** allows users to produce *camera-ready documents* (ready to be printed professionally) from the confines of a desk-

Retailers have worked hard to create information systems and automate the checkout process. Now they are poised for the next step in automation—self-checkout. Already most of us are comfortable with the convenience of the automatic teller machine (ATM). Perhaps we will embrace the automated checkout machine (ACM) as well. Shoppers scan their own groceries and receive visual and verbal confirmation of each purchase from the monitor. With ACMs, checkout is faster and less expensive. Monetary transactions are handled electronically. The coming of the ACM in grocery and eventually other retail businesses moves us one step closer to the cashless society. CheckRobot Automated Checkout Machines/Courtesy of International Business Machines Corporation. Unauthorized use not permitted.

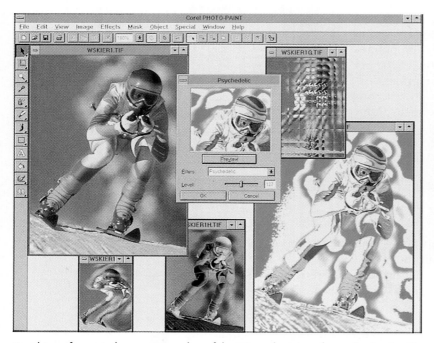

Graphics software is the newest member of the PC productivity software family. A wide range of graphics software enables you to create and work with computer-based images. Corel's Photo-Paint, shown here, allows you to edit (change) photographs. Here, the original photo (upper left) is given a psychedelic effect (lower right), warped (lower left), and recolored (bottom center). Courtesy of Corel Corporation

As we witnessed firsthand in the O. J. Simpson "trial of the century," multimedia presentations are beginning to revolutionize courtroom litigation techniques. This law firm uses a multimedia system to capture video, audio, and text information. Once these are captured, the system assists lawyers in mixing video depositions, animated simulations, graphs, and other physical evidence into a multimedia package for courtroom presentations. Courtesy of Dynatech Corporation

top. People routinely use desktop publishing to create newsletters, advertisements, procedures manuals, and for many other printing needs.

- *Spreadsheet.* **Spreadsheet software** permits users to work with rows and columns of data.

- *Database.* **Database software** permits users to create and maintain a database and to extract information from the database. In a database, data are organized for ease of manipulation and retrieval.

- *Graphics.* **Graphics software** encompasses a variety of graphics-oriented software applications that facilitate the creation and management of computer-based images, such as pie graphs, line drawings, company logos, maps, clip art, blueprints, presentation graphics (including animation and multimedia), and just about anything else that can be drawn in the traditional manner.

- *Communications.* **Communications software** is a family of software applications that enable users to send e-mail and faxes, tap the Internet, log on to an information service, and link their PC with a remote computer.

These research scientists are accessing the Merck Gene Index, a catalog of human gene sequences. The database is available to all investigators seeking insight into molecular modeling in the design of new compounds. Courtesy of Merck & Co., Inc.

Communication

Computers are communications tools that give us the flexibility to communicate electronically with one another and with other computers. For example, we can set up our computers to send e-mail birthday greetings to our friends and relatives automatically. We can log on to a commercial information service (like America Online or CompuServe) to chat online (via keyed-in text) with one person or a group of people. Recent software innovations allow us to talk to people in remote locations, using only our PCs and a link to the Internet. Communications applications and concepts are discussed and illustrated in detail throughout the book.

Science, Research, and Engineering

Engineers and scientists routinely use the computer as a tool in *experimentation, design,* and *development.* There are at least as many science and research applications for the computer as there are scientists and engineers. One of these applications is computer-aided design (CAD), which involves using the computer in the design process. CAD systems enable the creation and manipulation of an on-screen graphic image. CAD systems provide a sophisticated array of tools, enabling designers to create three-dimensional objects that can be flipped, rotated, resized, viewed in detail, examined internally or externally, and much more. Photographs in this chapter and throughout the book illustrate a variety of CAD applications.

Education and Reference

Computers can interact with students to enhance the learning process. Relatively inexpensive hardware capable of multidimensional communication (sound, print, graphics, and animation) has resulted in the phenomenal growth of the computer as an educational tool in the home, in the classroom, and in business. Computer-based education will not replace teachers, but educators agree that **computer-based training (CBT)** is having a profound impact on traditional modes of education. Available CBT programs can help you learn keyboarding skills, increase your vocabulary, study

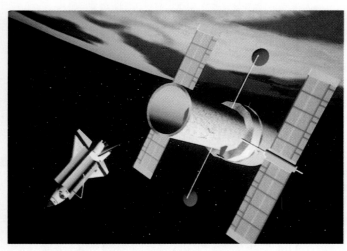

NASA used an Evans & Sutherland computer image generator to train astronauts on procedures used to repair the damaged Hubble Telescope. Shown here are the space shuttle and the Hubble Telescope. NASA was one of the early users of graphics-based simulations to train workers. Computer simulations are routinely used to train workers in many professions, including automobile mechanics and neurosurgeons.   Evans & Sutherland Computer Corporation

It's never a rainy day on the PC. Electronic miniature golfers can play some very interesting and spirited miniature golf courses without paying the course fee. Virtual golfers are confronted with challenges that rival the most imaginative real-life miniature golf courses. However, miniature golfers in the virtual world swing with the finger tips rather than with arms and a metal club. Shown here is Sierra's Ultra Mini Golf.

algebra, learn about the makeup of the atom, practice your Russian, and learn about computers. These are just the tip of the CBT iceberg.

Entertainment and Edutainment

More applications are being created that tickle our fancy and entertain us. You can play electronic golf. You can buy a computer chess opponent in the form of a board, chess pieces, and a miniature robotic arm that moves the pieces (you have to move your own pieces). You can "pilot" an airplane to Paris and battle Zorbitrons in cyberspace. Carmen Sandiego, the debonair thief of computer games and television fame, thrills children with the chase to find her and her accomplices, while teaching them history and geography. Software that combines *educ*ation and enter*tainment,* such as "Carmen Sandiego," has been dubbed **edutainment software.**

The amount of computing capacity in the world is doubling every two years. The number and sophistication of applications are growing rapidly with the increase in the number of computers and their capabilities. Tomorrow, there will be applications that are unheard of today.

Interactive Study Guide
Chapter 1

IMPORTANT TERMS AND SUMMARY OUTLINE

1–1 THE INFORMATION SOCIETY   In an **information society, knowledge workers** focus their energies on providing a myriad of information services. The knowledge worker's job function revolves around the use, manipulation, and dissemination of information.

Computer competency is emerging as a universal goal in the information society. Computer-competent people know how to purchase, use, and operate a computer system, and how to make it work for them. The computer-competent person is also aware of the computer's impact on society and is conversant in **computerese.** Computer competency is a cure for **cyberphobia.**

Software refers collectively to a set of machine-readable instructions, called **programs,** that cause the computer to perform desired functions. Computers and computer equipment, which accept **input** and provide **output,** are called **hardware.**

The computer revolution is transforming the way we communicate, do business, and learn. This technological revolution is having a profound impact on the business community and on our private and professional lives. For example, increasingly, we communicate with our colleagues at work through **electronic mail (e-mail)** or with our friends through **bulletin-board systems (BBSs).**

After the turn of the century we can anticipate traveling the **information superhighway,** a network of high-speed data communications links that eventually will connect virtually every facet of our society (also called the **National Information Infrastructure,** or **NII**). Today, millions of people have a **personal computer (PC).** This widespread availability has resulted in an explosion of applications for computers.

Through the 1970s, **users** related their information needs to computer professionals who would then work with the computer system to generate the necessary information. Today, users work directly with their PCs to obtain the information they need.

Data, which all of us create and use every day, are the raw facts from which information is derived. **Information** consists of data collected and processed into a meaningful form. The data in a computer-based system are stored on the **master file,** which is made up of **records.**

Learning about computers is an adventure that will last a lifetime because **information technology (IT),** the integration of computing technology and information processing, is changing daily.

1–2 NETWORKING: BRINGING   PEOPLE   TOGETHER   We now live in a global village in which computers and people are linked within companies and between countries. Most existing computers are part of a **computer network** that shares resources and information.

The Internet links millions of users in a global network. **The Net** can be accessed by people in organizations with established links to the Internet and by individuals with PCs. Commercial **information services** offer a wide range of information services, including up-to-the-minute news and weather, electronic shopping, e-mail, and much more. The information and services provided by the Internet and information services are **online.** When the user terminates the link, the user goes **offline.** Internet users can **download** text or a digitized version of a song directly to their PC, then read it or play it through their PC. Information is **uploaded** from a local computer to a remote computer.

1–3 COMPUTERS: THE ESSENTIALS   The **computer,** or **processor,** is an electronic device capable of interpreting and executing programmed commands for input, output, computation, and logic operations.

Output on a computer can be routed to a **monitor** or a **printer.** The output on a monitor is temporary and is called **soft copy.** Printers produce **hard-copy** output. Data can be entered via a **keyboard** or a **mouse,** a point-and-draw device.

Random-access memory (RAM) provides temporary storage of data and programs during processing within solid-state **integrated circuits,** or **chips.** Permanently installed and interchangeable **disks** provide permanent storage for data and programs. The computer system's **configuration** can include a variety of **peripheral devices.**

The differences in the various categories of computers are very much a matter of scale. **Mainframe computers** have greater computing capacities than do PCs, or **microcomputers (micros).** And **supercomputers** have greater computing capacities than mainframe computers. Depending on its sophistication, a **workstation's** computing capacity falls somewhere between that of a PC and a midsized mainframe. All **computer systems,** no matter how small or large, have the same fundamental capabilities—*processing, storage, input,* and *output.* Each offers many **input/output,** or **I/O,** alternatives.

1–4 PERSONAL COMPUTERS TO SUPERCOMPUTERS: CAPABILITIES AND USES   In 1981, IBM introduced its **IBM PC,** defining the original PC-compatible machine, now also called a **Wintel PC** because of its use of **Windows 9x/NT** operating system and the Intel processors. The Apple **Macintosh** line of computers, with its **Mac OS** and **Motorola PowerPC processor** is the other major **platform.** Personal computers come in four different physical sizes: **pocket PCs (palmtops), laptop PCs** (also called **notebook PCs), desktop PCs,** and **tower PCs.** Pocket and laptop PCs are considered portable. A 2-in-1 PC that can be used as both a notebook and a desktop has two parts: a fully functional *notebook PC* and a **docking station.** Two-in-one PCs allow users to enjoy the best

of both worlds: portability and the expanded features of a desktop. The **port replicator** works like the docking station in that the notebook PC is inserted into it and removed as needed to enable access to the port replicator **ports** and whatever is connected to them. **Slate PCs**, sometimes called **pen-based PCs** use electronic pens instead of keyboards. **Personal digital assistants (PDAs)**, or **handheld PCs**, are handheld personal computers that support a variety of personal information systems. The **network computer,** or **NC,** is designed to work only when linked to a network. The diskless NC has a relatively small processor and less RAM than modern personal computers.

Multimedia applications combine text, sound, graphics, motion video, and/or animation. The typical multimedia-configured PC includes a microcomputer; a keyboard and a point-and-draw device for input; a monitor and a printer for output; a **hard-disk drive** and a **floppy-disk drive** into which an interchangeable **diskette,** or **floppy disk,** is inserted; a **CD-ROM drive** into which an interchangeable **CD-ROM** is inserted; and a microphone and a set of speakers for audio I/O.

The workstation's speed and input/output devices set it apart from a PC. A typical workstation will have a high-**resolution** monitor and a variety of specialized point-and-draw devices. A common use of workstations is for **computer-aided design (CAD).**

Mainframe computers are usually associated with **enterprise-wide systems;** that is, computer-based systems that service entities throughout the company. Users communicate with a centralized mainframe, called **a host computer,** through their **terminals** and other communications devices. The term **minicomputer,** or simply **mini,** was used until recently, when the distinction between minis and mainframes began to blur. Mainframes are oriented to **input/output-bound** applications. Supercomputers primarily address **processor-bound** applications.

1–5 A COMPUTER SYSTEM AT WORK   A **local area network (LAN)** connects PCs or workstations in close proximity. The LAN's **server computer** performs a variety of functions for other computers on the LAN, called **client computers.**

Computers perform input/output (I/O) operations by reading from input and storage devices and writing to output devices.

Computer system capabilities are either input/output or processing. Processing capabilities are subdivided into computation and logic operations.

The computer is fast, accurate, consistent, and reliable, and has an enormous memory capacity. Computer operations are measured in **milliseconds, microseconds, nanoseconds,** and **picoseconds.** For some companies, any **downtime** (versus **uptime**) is unacceptable. These companies provide **backup** computers that take over automatically should the main computers fail.

1–6 HOW DO WE USE COMPUTERS? There are many applications of computers, including the following:

- *Information systems.* The computer is used to process data and produce business information. Hardware, software, people, procedures, and data are combined to create an **information system.**
- *Personal computing.* The PC is used for **personal computing** by individuals for a variety of business and domestic applications, including such productivity tools as **word processing software, desktop publishing software, spreadsheet software, database software, graphics software,** and **communications software.**

- *Communication.* Computers are communications tools that give us the flexibility to communicate electronically with one another and with other computers.
- *Science, research, and engineering.* The computer is used as a tool in experimentation, design, and development.
- *Education and reference.* The computer interacts with students to enhance the learning process. **Computer-based training (CBT)** is having a profound impact on traditional modes of education.
- *Entertainment and edutainment.* Every day, computer applications are being designed and created just to entertain us. Software that combines *edu*cation and enter*tainment* has been dubbed **edutainment software.**

REVIEW EXERCISES

Concepts

1. What are the four fundamental components of a computer system?
2. Which component of a computer system executes the program?
3. Associate the following with one of the application areas for computers discussed in Section 1–6: experimentation, home use, CBT, architectural design, the Internet, and business information systems.
4. What global network links millions of computers throughout the world?
5. Compare the information processing capabilities of human beings to those of computers with respect to speed, accuracy, reliability, consistency, and memory capability.
6. In terms of physical size, how are conventional PCs categorized?
7. Describe the relationship between data and information.
8. Within the context of a computer system, what is meant by *read* and *write*?
9. Name five PC productivity tools.
10. Name a PC productivity tool that would be helpful in writing a term paper. Explain.
11. List at least three services provided by a commercial information service.

12. The operational capabilities of a computer system include what two types of processing operations? Give an example of each.
13. What term is used to describe the integration of computing technology and information processing?
14. What do we call mail that is sent electronically?

Discussion and Problem Solving

15. The computer has had far-reaching effects on our lives. How has the computer affected your life?
16. What is your concept of computer competency? In what ways do you think achieving computer competency will affect your domestic life? Your business life?
17. At what age should computer-competency education begin?
18. Discuss how the complexion of jobs will change as we evolve from an industrial society into an information society. Give several examples.
19. The use of computers tends to stifle creativity. Argue for or against this statement.
20. Comment on how computers are changing our traditional patterns of personal communication.
21. Comment on how computers are changing our traditional patterns of recreation.

SELF-TEST (BY SECTION)

1–1 a. To be computer-competent, you must be able to write computer programs. (T/F)

b. A person whose job revolves around the use, manipulation, and dissemination of information is called: (a) a computerphobe, (b) a knowledge worker, or (c) a data expert?

c. _____ are the raw facts from which _____ is derived.

d. _____ is data entered to a computer system for processing, and _____ is the presentation of the results of processing.

1–2 a. A _____ _____ integrates computer systems, terminals, and communication links.

b. When the user terminates the link with a commercial information service, the user goes: (a) offline, (b) on-log, or (c) online?

c. Uploading on the Internet is transmitting information from an Internet-based host computer to a local computer PC. (T/F).

1–3 a. A printer is an example of which of the four computer system components?

b. Output on a monitor is soft copy and output on a printer is hard copy. (T/F)

c. Integrated circuits are also called: (a) slivers, (b) chips, or (c) flakes?

1–4 a. The power of a PC is directly proportional to its physical size. (T/F)

b. The four size categories of conventional personal computers are miniature, portable, notebook, and business. (T/F)

c. A 2-in-1 PC is in two parts: a fully functional _____ PC and a _____ station.

d. What is the name given those applications that combine text, sound, graphics, motion video, and/or animation: (a) videoscapes, (b) motionware, or (c) multimedia?

e. The workstation capabilities are similar to those of a low-end PC.

f. The _____, which offers input and output capabilities, is designed to be linked to a host computer.

g. Supercomputers are oriented to _____-bound applications.

1–5 a. The two types of processing operations performed by computers are _____ and _____.

b. A microsecond is 1000 times longer than a nanosecond. (T/F)

1–6 a. _____ _____ refers to the capability of producing camera-ready documents from the confines of a desktop.

b. More computing capacity is dedicated to information systems than to CBT. (T/F)

c. The microcomputer productivity tool that manipulates data organized in a tabular structure of rows and columns is called a _____.

d. _____ software combines education and entertainment.

Self-test Answers. **1–1 (a)** F; **(b)** b; **(c)** Data, information; **(d)** Input, output. **1–2 (a)** computer network; **(b)** a; **(c)** F. **1–3 (a)** output; **(b)** T; **(c)** b. **1–4 (a)** F; **(b)** F; **(c)** notebook, docking; **(d)** c; **(e)** F; **(f)** terminal; **(g)** processor. **1–5 (a)** computation, logic; **(b)** T. **1–6 (a)** Desktop publishing; **(b)** T; **(c)** spreadsheet; **(d)** Edutainment.

Focus on IT

The History of Computing: An Overview

The history of computers and computing is of special significance to us, because many of its most important events have occurred within our lifetime. Historians divide the history of the modern computer into generations, beginning with the introduction of the UNIVAC I, the first commercially viable computer, in 1951. But the quest for a mechanical servant—one that could free people from the more boring aspects of thinking—is centuries old. Why did it take so long to develop the computer? Some of the "credit" goes to human foibles. Too often brilliant insights were not recognized or given adequate support during an inventor's lifetime. Instead, these insights would lay dormant for as long as 100 years until someone else rediscovered—or reinvented—them. Some of the "credit" has to go to workers, too, who sabotaged labor-saving devices that threatened to put them out of work. The rest of the "credit" goes to technology; some insights were simply ahead of their time's technology. Here, then, is an abbreviated history of the stops and starts that have given us this marvel of the modern age, the computer.

INTERNET BRIDGE

Computer History

1623–1662: Blaise Pascal Although inventor, painter, and sculptor Leonardo da Vinci (1425–1519) sketched ideas for a mechanical adding machine, it was another 150 years before French mathematician and philosopher Blaise Pascal finally invented and built the "Pascaline" in 1642 to help his father, a tax collector. Although Pascal was praised throughout Europe, his invention was a financial failure. The hand-built machines were expensive and delicate; moreover, Pascal was the only person who could repair them. Because human labor was actually cheaper, the Pascaline was abandoned as impractical. Courtesy of International Business Machines Corporation. Unauthorized use not permitted.

3000 B.C.: The Abacus The abacus is probably considered the original mechanical counting device (it has been traced back 5000 years). It is still used in education to demonstrate the principles of counting and arithmetic and in business for speedy calculations. The Computer Museum, Boston, MA

1642: The Pascaline
The Pascaline used a counting-wheel design: Numbers for each digit were arranged on wheels so that a single revolution of one wheel would engage gears that turned the wheel one tenth of a revolution to its immediate left. Although the Pascaline was abandoned as impractical, its counting-wheel design was used by all mechanical calculators until the mid-1960s, when they were made obsolete by electronic calculators. Courtesy of International Business Machines Corporation. Unauthorized use not permitted.

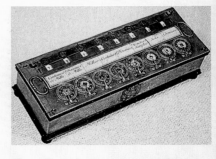

1793–1871: Charles Babbage Everyone from bankers to navigators depended on mathematical tables during the bustling Industrial Revolution. However, these hand-calculated tables were usually full of errors. After discovering that his own tables were riddled with mistakes, Charles Babbage envisioned a steam-powered "differential engine" and then an "analytical engine" that would perform tedious calculations accurately. Although Babbage never perfected his devices, they introduced many of the concepts used in today's general-purpose computer. Courtesy of International Business Machines Corporation. Unauthorized use not permitted.

1801: Jacquard's Loom A practicing weaver, Frenchman Joseph-Marie Jacquard (1752–1834) spent what little spare time he had trying to improve the lot of his fellow weavers. (They worked 16-hour days, with no days off!) His solution, the Jacquard loom, was created in 1801. Holes strategically punched in a card directed the movement of needles, thread, and fabric, creating the elaborate patterns still known as Jacquard weaves. Jacquard's weaving loom is considered the first significant use of binary automation. The loom was an immediate success with mill owners because they could hire cheaper and less skilled workers. But weavers, fearing unemployment, rioted and called Jacquard a traitor.   Courtesy of International Business Machines Corporation. Unauthorized use not permitted.

1842: Babbage's Difference Engine and the Analytical Engine Convinced his machine would benefit England, Babbage applied for—and received—one of the first government grants to build the difference engine. Hampered by nineteenth-century machine technology, cost overruns, and the possibility his chief engineer was padding the bills, Babbage completed only a portion of the difference engine (shown here) before the government withdrew its support in 1842, deeming the project "worthless to science." Meanwhile,

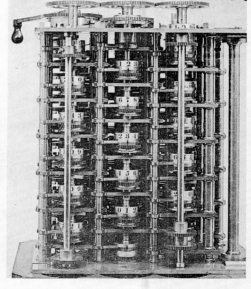

Babbage had conceived of the idea of a more advanced "analytical engine." In essence, this was a general-purpose computer that could add, subtract, multiply, and divide in automatic sequence at a rate of 60 additions per second. His 1833 design, which called for thousands of gears and drives, would cover the area of a football field and be powered by a locomotive engine. Babbage worked on this project until his death. In 1991 London's Science Museum spent $600,000 to build a working model of the difference engine, using Babbage's original plans. The result stands 6 feet high, 10 feet long, contains 4000 parts, and weighs 3 tons.
New York Public Library Picture Collection

1816–1852: Lady Ada Augusta Lovelace

The daughter of poet Lord Byron, Lady Ada Augusta Lovelace became a mentor to Babbage and translated his works, adding her own extensive footnotes. Her suggestion that punched cards could be prepared to instruct Babbage's engine to repeat certain operations has led some people to call her the first programmer. Ada, the programming language adopted by the Department of Defense as a standard, is named for Lady Ada Lovelace. The Bettmann Archive/BBC Hulton

1890: Hollerith's Tabulating Machine

Hollerith's punched-card tabulating machine had three parts. Clerks at the U.S. Bureau of the Census used a hand punch to enter data into cards a little larger than a dollar bill. Cards were then read and sorted by a 24-bin sorter box (right) and summarized on numbered tabulating dials (left), which were connected electrically to the sorter box. Ironically, Hollerith's idea for the punched card came not from Jacquard or Babbage but from "punch photography." Railroads of the day issued tickets with physical descriptions of a passenger's hair and eye color. Conductors punched holes in the ticket to indicate that a passenger's hair and eye color matched those of the ticket owner. From this, Hollerith got the idea of making a punched "photograph" of every person to be tabulated. Courtesy of International Business Machines Corporation. Unauthorized use not permitted.

1860–1929: Herman Hollerith

With the help of a professor, Herman Hollerith got a job as a special agent helping the U.S. Bureau of the Census tabulate the head count for the 1880 census—a process that took almost eight years. To speed up the 1890 census, Hollerith devised a punched-card tabulating machine. When his machine outperformed two other systems, Hollerith won a contract to tabulate the 1890 census. Hollerith earned a handsome income leasing his machinery to the governments of the United States, Canada, Austria, Russia, and others; he charged 65 cents for every 1000 people counted. (During the 1890 U.S. census alone, he earned more than $40,000—a fortune in those days.) Hollerith may have earned even more selling the single-use punched cards. But the price was worth it. The bureau completed the census in just 2½ years and saved more than $5 million. Courtesy of International Business Machines Corporation. Unauthorized use not permitted.

1924: IBM'S First Headquarters Building

In 1896 Herman Hollerith founded the Tabulating Machine Company which, in 1911, merged with several other companies to form the Computing-Tabulating-Recording Company. In 1924 the company's general manager, Thomas J. Watson, changed its name to International Business Machines Corporation and moved into this building. Watson ran IBM until a few months before his death at age 82 in 1956. His son, Thomas J. Watson, Jr., lead IBM into the age of computers. Courtesy of International Business Machines Corporation. Unauthorized use not permitted.

1920s–1950s: The EAM Era   From the 1920s throughout the mid-1950s, punched-card technology improved with the addition of more punched-card devices and more sophisticated capabilities. The *electromechanical accounting machine (EAM)* family of punched-card devices includes the card punch, verifier, reproducer, summary punch, interpreter, sorter, collator, and accounting machine. Most of the devices in the 1940s machine room were "programmed" to perform a particular operation by the insertion of a prewired control panel. A machine-room operator in a punched-card installation had the physically challenging job of moving heavy boxes of punched cards and printed output from one device to the next on hand trucks.   Courtesy of International Business Machines Corporation. Unauthorized use not permitted.

1904–1995:
Dr. John V. Atanasoff
In 1939 Dr. John V. Atanasoff, a professor at Iowa State University, and graduate student Clifford E. Berry assembled a prototype of the ABC (for *Atanasoff Berry Computer*) to cut the time physics students spent making complicated calculations. A working model was finished in 1942. Atanasoff's decisions—to use an electronic medium with vacuum tubes, the base-2 numbering system, and memory and logic circuits—set the direction for the modern computer. Ironically, Iowa State failed to patent the device and IBM, when contacted about the ABC, airily responded, "IBM will never be interested in an electronic computing machine." A 1973 federal court ruling officially credited Atanasoff with the invention of the automatic electronic digital computer. Courtesy of Iowa State University

1942: The First Computer, The ABC   During the years 1935 through 1938, Dr. Atanasoff had begun to think about a machine that could reduce the time it took for him and his physics students to make long, complicated mathematical calculations. The ABC was, in fact, born of frustration. Dr. Atanasoff later explained that one night in the winter of 1937, "nothing was happening" with respect to creating an electronic device that could help solve physics problems. His "despair grew," so he got in his car and drove for several hours across the state of Iowa and then across the Mississippi River. Finally, he stopped at an Illinois roadhouse for a drink. It was in this roadhouse that Dr. Atanasoff overcame his creative block and conceived ideas that would lay the foundation for the evolution of the modern computer. Courtesy of Iowa State University

1944: The Electromechanical Mark I Computer The first electromechanical computer, the *MARK I*, was completed by Harvard University professor Howard Aiken in 1944 under the sponsorship of IBM. A monstrous 51 feet long and 8 feet high, the *MARK I* was essentially a serial collection of electromechanical calculators and was in many ways similar to Babbage's analytical machine. (Aiken was unaware of Babbage's work, though.) The Mark I was a significant improvement, but IBM's management still felt electromechanical computers would never replace punched-card equipment. Courtesy of International Business Machines Corporation. Unauthorized use not permitted.

1946: The Electronic ENIAC Computer Dr. John W. Mauchly (middle) collaborated with J. Presper Eckert, Jr. (foreground) at the University of Pennsylvania to develop a machine that would compute trajectory tables for the U.S. Army. (This was sorely needed; during World War II, only 20% of all bombs came within *1000 feet* of their targets.) The end product, the first fully operational electronic computer, was completed in 1946 and named the *ENIAC* (Electronic Numerical Integrator and Computer). A thousand times faster than its electromechanical predecessors, it occupied 15,000 square feet of floor space and weighed 30 tons. The ENIAC could do 5000 additions per minute and 500 multiplications per minute. Unlike computers of today that operate in binary, it operated in decimal and required 10 vacuum tubes to represent one decimal digit.

The ENIAC's use of vacuum tubes signaled a major breakthrough. (Legend has it that the ENIAC's 18,000 vacuum tubes dimmed the lights of Philadelphia whenever it was activated.) Even before the ENIAC was finished, it was used in the secret research that went into building the first atomic bomb at Los Alamos. United Press International Photo

1951: The UNIVAC I and the First Generation of Computers The first generation of computers (1951–1959), characterized by the use of vacuum tubes, is generally thought to have begun with the introduction of the first commercially viable electronic digital computer. The Universal Automatic Computer (*UNIVAC I* for short), developed by Mauchly and Eckert for the Remington-Rand Corporation, was installed in the U.S. Bureau of the Census in 1951. Later that year, CBS News gave the UNIVAC I national exposure when it correctly predicted Dwight Eisenhower's victory over Adlai Stevenson in the presidential election with only 5% of the votes counted. Mr. Eckert is shown here instructing news anchor Walter Cronkite in the use of the UNIVAC I. Courtesy of Unisys Corporation

1954: The IBM 650 Not until the success of the UNIVAC I did IBM make a commitment to develop and market computers. IBM's first entry into the commercial computer market was the *IBM 701* in 1953. However, the *IBM 650* (shown here), introduced in 1954, is probably the reason IBM enjoys such a healthy share of today's computer market. Unlike some of its competitors, the IBM 650 was designed as a logical upgrade to existing punched-card machines. IBM management went out on a limb and estimated sales of 50—a figure greater than the number of installed computers in the entire nation at that time. IBM actually installed 1000. The rest is history. Courtesy of International Business Machines Corporation. Unauthorized use not permitted.

1907–1992: "Amazing" Grace Murray Hopper

Dubbed "Amazing Grace" by her many admirers, Dr. Grace Hopper was widely respected as the driving force behind COBOL, the most popular programming language, and a champion of standardized programming languages that are hardware-independent. In 1959 Dr. Hopper led an effort that laid the foundation for the development of COBOL. She also created a compiler that enabled COBOL to run on many types of computers. Her reason: "Why start from scratch with every program you write when a computer could be developed to do a lot of the basic work for you over and over again?"

To Dr. Hopper's long list of honors, awards, and accomplishments, add the fact that she found the first "bug" in a computer—a real one. She repaired the Mark II by removing a moth that was caught in Relay Number II. From that day on, every programmer has *debugged* software by ferreting out its *bugs*, or errors, in programming syntax or logic.
Official U.S. Navy photo

1963: The PDP-8 Minicomputer

During the 1950s and early 1960s, only the largest companies could afford the six- and seven-digit price tags of *mainframe computers*. In 1963 Digital Equipment Corporation introduced the *PDP-8* (shown here). It is generally considered the first successful minicomputer (a nod, some claim, to the playful spirit behind the 1960s miniskirt). At a mere $18,000, the transistor-based PDP-8 was an instant hit. It confirmed the tremendous demand for small computers for business and scientific applications. By 1971 more than 25 firms were manufacturing minicomputers, although Digital and Data General Corporation took an early lead in their sale and manufacture.   Courtesy of Digital Equipment Corporation

1959: The Honeywell 400 and the Second Generation of Computers

The invention of the transistor signaled the start of the second generation of computers (1959–1964). Transistorized computers were more powerful, more reliable, less expensive, and cooler to operate than their vacuum-tubed predecessors. Honeywell (its *Honeywell 400* is shown here) established itself as a major player in the second generation of computers. Burroughs, Univac, NCR, CDC, and Honeywell—IBM's biggest competitors during the 1960s and early 1970s—became known as the BUNCH (the first initial of each name).   Courtesy of Honeywell, Inc.

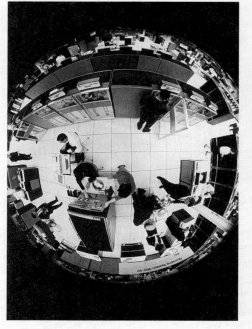

1964: The IBM System 360 and the Third Generation of Computers

The third generation was characterized by computers built around integrated circuits. Of these, some historians consider IBM's *System 360* line of computers, introduced in 1964, the single most important innovation in the history of computers. System 360 was conceived as a family of computers with *upward compatibility;* when a company outgrew one model it could move up to the next model without worrying about converting its data. System 360 and other lines built around integrated circuits made all previous computers obsolete, but the advantages were so great that most users wrote the costs of conversion off as the price of progress.   Courtesy of International Business Machines Corporation. Unauthorized use not permitted.

1964: BASIC—More than a Beginner's Programming Language

In the early 1960s, Dr. Thomas Kurtz and Dr. John Kemeny of Dartmouth College began developing a programming language that a beginner could learn and use quickly. Their work culminated in 1964 with BASIC. Over the years, BASIC gained widespread popularity and evolved from a teaching language into a versatile and powerful language for both business and scientific applications. From micros to mainframes, BASIC is supported on more computers than any other language. Courtesy of True BASIC, Inc.

1975: Microsoft and Bill Gates

In 1968, seventh grader Bill Gates and ninth grader Paul Allen were teaching the computer to play monopoly and commanding it to play millions of games to discover gaming strategies. Seven years later, in 1975, they were to set a course which would revolutionize the computer industry. While at Harvard, Gates and Allen developed a BASIC programming language for the first commercially available microcomputer, the MITS Altair. After successful completion of the project, the two formed Microsoft Corporation, now the largest and most influential software company in the world. Microsoft was given an enormous boost when its operating system software, MS-DOS, was selected for use by the IBM PC. Gates, now the richest man in America, provides the company's vision on new product ideas and technologies. Courtesy of Microsoft Corporation

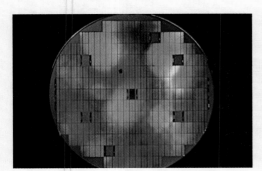

1971: Integrated Circuits and the Fourth Generation of Computers

Although most computer vendors would classify their computers as fourth generation, most people pinpoint 1971 as the generation's beginning. That was the year large-scale integration of circuitry (more circuits per unit of space) was introduced. The base technology, though, is still the integrated circuit. This is not to say that two decades have passed without significant innovations. In truth, the computer industry has experienced a mind-boggling succession of advances in the further miniaturization of circuitry, data communications, and the design of computer hardware and software. Courtesy of International Business Machines Corporation. Unauthorized use not permitted.

1977: The Apple II

Not until 1975 and the introduction of the Altair 8800 personal computer was computing made available to individuals and very small companies. This event has forever changed how society perceives computers. One prominent entrepreneurial venture during the early years of personal computers was the Apple II computer (shown here). Two young computer enthusiasts, Steven Jobs and Steve Wozniak (then 21 and 26 years of age, respectively), collaborated to create and build their Apple II computer on a makeshift production line in Jobs' garage. Seven years later, Apple Computer earned a spot on the Fortune 500, a list of the 500 largest corporations in the United States. Courtesy of Apple Computer, Inc.

1981: The IBM PC

In 1981, IBM tossed its hat into the personal computer ring with its announcement of the IBM Personal Computer, or IBM PC. By the end

of 1982, 835,000 had been sold. When software vendors began to orient their products to the IBM PC, many companies began offering IBM-PC compatibles or clones. Today, the IBM PC and its clones have become a powerful standard for the microcomputer industry.   Courtesy of International Business Machines Corporation. Unauthorized use not permitted.

1984: The Macintosh and Graphical User Interfaces

In 1984 Apple Computer introduced the Macintosh desktop computer with a very "friendly" graphical user interface—proof that computers can be easy and fun to use. Graphical user interfaces (GUIs) began to change the complexion of the software industry. They have changed the interaction between human and computer from a short, character-oriented exchange modeled on the teletypewriter to the now familiar WIMP interface—Windows, Icons, Menus, and Pointing devices. Courtesy of Apple Computer, Inc.

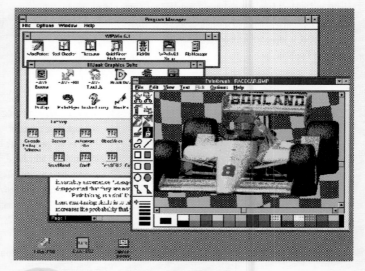

1982: Mitchell Kapor Designs Lotus 1-2-3

Mitchell Kapor is one of the major forces behind the microcomputer boom in the 1980s. In 1982, Kapor founded Lotus Development Company, now one of the largest applications software companies in the world. Kapor and the company introduced an electronic spreadsheet product that gave IBM's recently introduced IBM PC (1981) credibility in the business marketplace. Sales of the IBM PC and the electronic spreadsheet, Lotus 1-2-3, soared.

1985 to present: Microsoft Windows

Microsoft introduced Windows, a GUI for IBM-PC–compatible computers in 1985; however, Windows did not enjoy widespread acceptance until 1990 with the release of Windows 3.0. Windows 3.0 gave a huge boost to the software industry because larger, more complex programs could now be run on IBM-PC compatibles. Subsequent releases, including Windows 95, Windows NT, and Windows 98 make personal computers even easier to use, fueling the PC explosion of the 1990s.

Inside the Computer

- Describe how data are stored in a computer system.
- Demonstrate the relationships among bits, bytes, characters, and encoding systems.
- Understand the translation of alphanumeric data into a format for internal computer representation.
- Explain and illustrate the principles of computer operations.
- Distinguish processors by their word size, speed, and memory capacity.
- Identify and describe the relationships between the internal components of a personal computer.

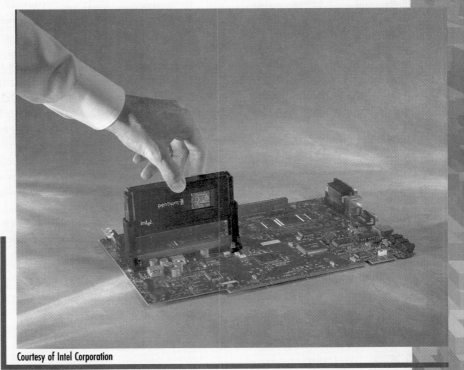

Courtesy of Intel Corporation

LET'S TALK

Can you follow this conversation? It includes computing concepts presented in this chapter. Read it now, then reread it once you've had an opportunity to study the chapter.

The Scene Travis is visiting a high school friend, Deb, at her house.

TRAVIS (entering Deb's game room): What are you doing, Deb?

DEB: Yo, Trav. I'm taking the cover off my PC.

TRAVIS: How come?

DEB: It's a long story, but here's the short version. I just bought the new Intergalactic Invaders game, but my motherboard didn't meet the system requirements.

TRAVIS: Why? What does it need?

DEB: Well, my Pentium II microprocessor's got the umph at 400 MHz and plenty of cache memory, but I'm short on RAM. Invaders works better with 64 megabytes, so I bought 32 MB on a DIMM to get me up to speed *(inserting the RAM on the motherboard).*

TRAVIS: What's that expansion card over there?

DEB: It's a new 56-kilobit fax modem. Since I paid for the SIMM, I appealed to my parents to pay for the fax modem.

TRAVIS: Wow! Are they always this generous?

DEB: No, but they wanted the fax modem so they could get America Online. Let's put it right here in the last PCI local bus expansion slot on my system board *(inserting it carefully in the only available slot).*

TRAVIS: All right! Let's put the cover on and take off!

2–1 Data Storage: A Bit About the Bit

**Monthly Technology Update
Chapter 2**

A computer can have seemingly limitless capabilities. It's an entertainment center with hundreds of interactive games. It's a virtual school or university providing interactive instruction and testing in everything from anthropology to zoology. It's a painter's canvas. It's a video telephone. It's a CD player. It's a home or office library giving ready access to the complete works of Shakespeare or interactive versions of corporate procedures manuals. It's a television. It's the biggest marketplace in the world. It's a medical instrument capable of monitoring vital signs. It's the family photo album. It's a print shop. It's a wind tunnel that can test experimental airplane designs. It's a voting booth. It's a calendar with a to-do list. It's a recorder. It's an alarm clock that can remind you to pick up the kids. It's an encyclopedia. It can perform thousands of specialty functions that require specialized skills: preparing taxes, drafting legal documents, counseling suicidal patients, and much more.

In all of these applications, the computer deals with everything as electronic signals. Electronic signals come in two flavors—**analog** and **digital.** Analog signals are *continuous* wave forms in which variations in frequency and amplitude can be used to represent information from sound and numerical data. The sound of our voice is carried by analog signals when we talk on the telephone. With digital signals, everything is described in two states: the circuit as either *on* or *off.* Generally, the *on* state is expressed or represented by the number 1 and the *off* state by the number 0. Computers are digital and, therefore, require digital data. To make the most effective use of computers and automation, most everything in the world of electronics and communication is *going digital.*

Going Digital

A by-product of the computer revolution is a trend toward "going digital" whenever possible. For example, the movement in the recording industry has been away from analog recording on records and toward digital recording on CD. One reason for this move is that analog signals cannot be reproduced exactly. If you have ever duplicated an analog audiotape, you know that the copy is never as good as the source tape. In contrast, digital CDs can be copied onto other CDs over and over without deterioration. When CDs are duplicated, each is an exact copy of the original.

Digital sound information is stored temporarily in the RAM chips on this circuit board (center) which enables stereo sound output from a PC. Sound information can be stored permanently on magnetic disk or optical laser disk (left). ATI Technologies Inc.

So how do you go digital? You simply need to **digitize** your material. To digitize means to convert data, analog signals, images, and so on into the discrete format (1s and 0s) that can be interpreted by computers. For example, Figure 2–1 shows how music can be digitized. Once digitized, the music recording, data, image, shape, and so on can be manipulated by the computer. For example, old recordings of artists from Enrico Caruso to the Beatles have been digitized and then digitally reconstructed on computers to eliminate unwanted distortion and static. Some of these reconstructed CDs are actually better than the originals!

Binary Digits: On-Bits and Off-Bits

It's amazing, but the seemingly endless potential of computers is based on the two digital states—*on* and *off*. The electronic nature of the computer makes it possible to combine these two electronic states to represent letters, numbers, colors, sounds, images, shapes, and much more—even odors. An "on" or "off" electronic state is represented by a **bit,** short for *b*inary dig*it*. In the **binary** numbering system (base 2), the *on-bit* is a 1 and the *off-bit* is a 0.

Vacuum tubes, transistors, and integrated circuits characterize the generations of computers. Each of these technologies enables computers to distinguish between on and off and, therefore, to use binary logic. Physically, these states are achieved in a variety of ways.

- In RAM, the two electronic states often are represented by the presence or absence of an electrical charge.
- In disk storage, the two states are made possible by the magnetic arrangement of the surface coating on magnetic tapes and disks (see Figure 2–2).

FIGURE 2–1   Going Digital with Compact Discs
The recording industry has gone digital. To create a master CD, analog signals are converted to digital signals that can be manipulated by a computer and written to a master CD. The master is duplicated and the copies are sold through retail channels.

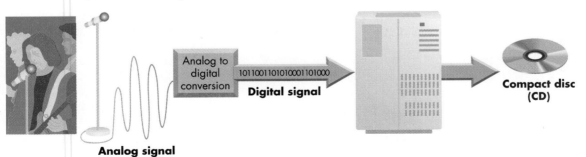

Analog signal · Analog to digital conversion · 1011001101010001101000 · Digital signal · Compact disc (CD)

FIGURE 2-2 Bits on the Surface of a Magnetic Disk This highly magnified area of a magnetic disk-face surface shows elongated information bits recorded serially along 8 of the disk's 1774 concentric tracks. One square inch of this disk's surface can hold 22 million bits of information. *Courtesy of International Business Machines Corporation. Unauthorized use not permitted.*

- In CDs and CD-ROMs, digital data are stored permanently as microscopic pits.
- In fiber optic cable, binary data flows through as pulses of light.

Bits may be fine for computers, but human beings are more comfortable with letters and decimal numbers (the base-10 numerals 0 through 9). We like to see colors and hear sounds. Therefore, the letters, decimal numbers, colors, and sounds that we input into a computer system while doing word processing, graphics, and other applications must be translated into 1s and 0s for processing and storage. The computer translates the bits back into letters, decimal numbers, colors, and sounds for output on monitors, printers, speakers, and so on.

Data in a Computer

To manipulate stored data within a computer system, we must have a way of storing and retrieving it. Data are stored *temporarily* during processing in random-access memory (RAM). RAM is also referred to as **primary storage.** Data are stored *permanently* on **secondary storage** devices such as magnetic tape and disk drives. We discuss primary storage (RAM) in detail in this chapter, as well as how data are represented electronically in a computer system and on the internal workings of a computer.

2-2 Encoding Systems: Bits and Bytes

Computers do not speak to one another in English, Spanish, or French. They have their own languages, which are better suited to electronic communication. In these languages, bits are combined according to an **encoding system** to represent letters (**alpha** characters), numbers (**numeric** characters), and special characters (such as *, $, +, and &), collectively referred to as **alphanumeric** characters.

INTERNET BRIDGE

Encoding

ASCII and ANSI

ASCII (*American Standard Code for Information Interchange*—pronounced "*AS-key*") is the most popular encoding system for PCs and data communication. In ASCII, alphanumeric characters are *encoded* into a bit configuration on input so that the computer can interpret them. This coding equates a unique series of on-bits and off-bits with a specific character. Just as the words *mother* and *father* are arbitrary English-language character strings that refer to our parents, 1000010 is an arbitrary ASCII code that refers to the letter *B*. When you tap the letter *B* on a PC keyboard, the *B* is transmitted to the processor as a coded string of binary digits (for example, 1000010 in ASCII), as shown in Figure 2-3. The characters are *decoded* on output so we can interpret them. The combination of bits used to represent a character is called a **byte** (pronounced "bite"). Figure 2-4 shows the binary value (the actual bit configuration) of commonly used characters in ASCII.

FIGURE 2-3 Encoding When you tap the B key on the keyboard, a binary representation of that *B* is sent to the processor. The processor sends the encoded *B* to the monitor, which interprets and displays a **B.**

The 7-bit ASCII code can represent up to 128 characters (2^7). Although the English language has considerably fewer than 128 printable characters, the extra bit configurations are needed to represent additional common and not-so-common special characters (such as - [hyphen]; @ [at]; | [a broken vertical bar]; and ~ [tilde]) and to signal a variety of activities to the computer (such as ringing a bell or telling the computer to accept a piece of datum).

ASCII is a 7-bit code, but the PC byte is 8 bits. There are 256 (2^8) possible bit configurations in an 8-bit byte. Hardware and software vendors accept the 128 standard ASCII codes and use the extra 128 bit configurations to represent control characters or noncharacter images to complement their hardware or software product. For example, the IBM-PC version of **extended ASCII** contains the characters of many foreign languages (such as *ä* [umlaut] and *é* [acute]) and a wide variety of graphic images that can be combined on a text screen to produce larger images (for example, the box around a window on a display screen).

Microsoft Windows uses the 8-bit **ANSI** encoding system (developed by the *A*merican *N*ational *S*tandards *I*nstitute) to enable the sharing of text between Windows applications. As in IBM, extended ASCII, the first 128 ANSI codes are the same as the ASCII codes, but the next 128 are defined to meet the specific needs of Windows applications.

Unicode: 65,536 Possibilities

A consortium of heavyweight computer industry companies, including IBM, Microsoft, and Sun Microsystems, is sponsoring the development of **Unicode,** a uniform 16-bit encoding system. Unicode will enable computers and applications to talk to one another more easily and will accommodate most languages of the world (including Hebrew ‫ש‬, Japanese ⽊, and upper- and lower-case Greek ψ). ASCII, with 128 (2^7) character codes, is sufficient for the English language but falls far short of the Japanese language requirements. Unicode's 16-bit code allows for 65,536 characters (2^{16}). The consortium is proposing that Unicode be adopted as a standard for information interchange throughout the global computer community. Universal acceptance of the Unicode standard would help facilitate international communication in all areas, from monetary transfers between banks to e-mail. With Unicode as a standard, software could be created more easily to work with a wider base of languages.

Unicode, like any advancement in computer technology, presents conversion problems. The 16-bit Unicode demands more memory than do traditional 8-bit codes. An *A* in Unicode takes twice the RAM and disk space of an ASCII *A*. Currently, 8-bit encoding systems provide the foundation for most software packages and existing databases. Should Unicode be adopted as a standard, programs would have to be revised to work with Unicode, and existing data would need to be converted to Unicode. Information processing needs have simply outgrown the 8-bit standard, so conversion to Unicode or some other standard is inevitable. This conversion, however, will be time-consuming and expensive.

Character	ASCII Code
A	100 0001
B	100 0010
C	100 0011
D	100 0100
E	100 0101
F	100 0110
G	100 0111
H	100 1000
I	100 1001
J	100 1010
K	100 1011
L	100 1100
M	100 1101
N	100 1110
O	100 1111
P	101 0000
Q	101 0001
R	101 0010
S	101 0011
T	101 0100
U	101 0101
V	101 0110
W	101 0111
X	101 1000
Y	101 1001
Z	101 1010
0	011 0000
1	011 0001
2	011 0010
3	011 0011
4	011 0100
5	011 0101
6	011 0110
7	011 0111
8	011 1000
9	011 1001
Space	010 0000
.	010 1110
(	010 1000
+	010 1011
&	010 0110
$	010 0100
*	010 1010
)	010 1001
;	011 1011
,	010 1100
-	101 1111
?	011 1111
:	011 1010
=	011 1101

Creating text for a video display calls for a technology called "character generation." An 8-bit encoding system, with its 256 unique bit configurations, is more than adequate to represent all of the alphanumeric characters used in the English language. The Chinese, however, need a 16-bit encoding system, like Unicode, to represent their 13,000 characters. Courtesy of Dynatech Corporation

FIGURE 2–4 ASCII Codes This figure shows the ASCII codes for upper-case letters, numbers, and several special characters. The ASCII codes for upper-case and lower-case letters are similar. Replace the second binary digit with a 1 to get the lowercase equivalent (*A* is 1000010 and *a* is 1100010).

2–3 Analyzing a Computer System, Bit by Bit

The processor runs the show and is the nucleus of any computer system. Regardless of the complexity of the hundreds of different computers sold by various manufacturers, each processor, sometimes called the **central processing unit** or **CPU,** has only two fundamental sections: the *control unit* and the *arithmetic and logic unit.* These units work together with random-access memory (RAM) to make the processor—and the computer—go. Let's look at their functions and the relationships among them.

RAM: Random-Access Storage

RAM TECHNOLOGY: SDRAM AND RDRAM   RAM, a *read-and-write memory,* enables data to be both read and written to memory. RAM (primary storage) is electronic circuitry with no moving parts. Electrically charged points in the RAM chips represent the bits (1s and 0s) that comprise the data and other information stored in RAM. With no mechanical movement, data can be accessed from RAM at electronic speeds. Over the past two decades, researchers have given us a succession of RAM technologies, each designed to keep pace with ever-faster processors. Existing PCs have FPM RAM, EDO RAM, SRAM, DRAM, BEDO RAM, and other types of memory. However, most new PCs are being equipped with **synchronous dynamic RAM (SDRAM)**. SDRAM is able to synchronize itself with the processor, enabling data transfer at more than twice the speed of previous RAM technologies. With the next generation of processors, we'll probably move to **Rambus DRAM (RDRAM)**, which is six times faster than SDRAM.

A state-of-the-art **SDRAM** memory chip, smaller than a postage stamp, can store about 128,000,000 bits, or more than 12,000,000 characters of data! Physically, memory chips are installed on **single in-line memory modules**, or **SIMMs,** and on the newer **dual in-line memory modules**, or **DIMMS**. SIMMS are less expensive, but have only a 32-bit data path to the processor, whereas DIMMs have a 64-bit data path.

There is one major problem with RAM storage: It is **volatile memory.** That is, when the electrical current is turned off or interrupted, the data are lost. Because RAM is volatile, it provides the processor only with *temporary* storage for programs and data. Several **nonvolatile** memory technologies have emerged, but none has exhibited the qualities necessary for widespread use as primary storage (RAM). Although much slower than RAM, nonvolatile memory is superior to SDRAM for use in certain computers because it is highly reliable, it is not susceptible to environmental fluctuations, and it can operate on battery power for a considerable length of time. For example, it is well suited for use with industrial robots.

READIN', 'RITIN', AND RAM CRAM   *All programs and data must be transferred to RAM from an input device (such as a keyboard) or from secondary storage (such as a disk) before programs can be executed and data can be processed.* Therefore, RAM space is always at a premium. Once a program is no longer in use, the storage space it occupied is assigned to another program awaiting execution. PC users attempting to run too many programs at the same time face *RAM cram,* a situation in which there is not enough memory to run the programs.

Programs and data are loaded to RAM from secondary storage because the time required to access a program instruction or piece of datum from RAM is significantly less than from secondary storage. Thousands of instructions or pieces of data can be accessed from RAM in the time it would take to access a single piece of datum from disk storage. RAM is essentially a high-speed holding area for data and programs. In fact, *nothing really happens in a computer system until the program instructions and data are moved from RAM to the processor.*

Nonvolatile memory is frequently the memory of choice for computer-controlled systems that operate in harsh environments, such as this automobile window systems manufacturing facility.
Rockwell/David Perry

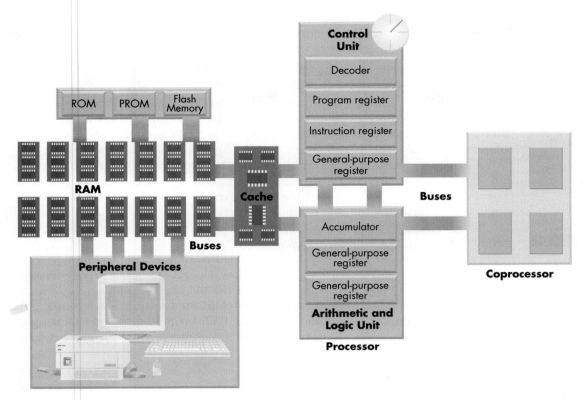

FIGURE 2–5 Interaction between Computer System Components
During processing, instructions and data are passed between the various types of internal memories, the processor's control unit and arithmetic and logic unit, the coprocessor, and the peripheral devices over the common electrical bus. A system clock paces the speed of operation within the processor and ensures that everything takes place in timed intervals. Refer back to this figure as you read about these components throughout the remainder of this chapter.

Figure 2–5 illustrates how all input/output (I/O) is "read to" or "written from" RAM. Programs and data must be "loaded," or moved, to RAM from secondary storage for processing. This is a **nondestructive read** process; that is, the program and data that are read reside in both RAM (temporarily) and secondary storage (permanently).

The data in RAM are manipulated by the processor according to program instructions. A program instruction or a piece of datum is stored in a specific RAM location called an **address.** RAM is analogous to the rows of boxes you see in post offices. Just as each P.O. box has a number, each byte in RAM has an address. Addresses permit program instructions and data to be located, accessed, and processed. The content of each address changes frequently as different programs are executed and new data are processed.

CACHE MEMORY To facilitate an even faster transfer of instructions and data to the processor, computers are designed with **cache memory** (see Figure 2–5). Cache memory is used by computer designers to increase computer system throughput. **Throughput** refers to the rate at which work can be performed by a computer system.

Like RAM, cache is a high-speed holding area for program instructions and data. However, cache memory uses internal storage technologies, such as SDRAM, that are much faster (and much more expensive) than conventional RAM. With only a fraction of the capacity of RAM, cache memory holds only those instructions and data that are *likely* to be needed next by the processor. Cache memory is effective because,

Inside the Computer Explorer

MEMORY BITS

Internal Storage

- Volatile memory
  —Synchronous Dynamic RAM (SDRAM)
  —Rambus DRAM (RDRAM)
  —Cache
  —Registers
- Nonvolatile memory
  —ROM and PROM
  —Flash memory

in a typical session, the same data or instructions are accessed over and over. The processor first checks cache memory for needed data and instructions, thereby reducing the number of accesses to the slower SDRAM.

ROM, PROM, AND FLASH MEMORY   A special type of internal memory, called *read-only memory (ROM)*, cannot be altered by the user (see Figure 2–5). The contents of ROM (rhymes with *"mom"*), a nonvolatile technology, are "hard-wired" (designed into the logic of the memory chip) by the manufacturer and can be "read only." When you turn on a microcomputer system, a program in ROM automatically readies the computer system for use and produces the initial display-screen prompt.

A variation of ROM is **programmable read-only memory (PROM).** PROM is ROM into which you, the user, can load read-only programs and data. Generally, once a program is loaded to PROM, it is seldom, if ever, changed. ROM and PROM are used in a variety of capacities within a computer system.

Flash memory is a type of PROM that can be altered easily by the user. Flash memory is a feature of many new processors, I/O devices, and storage devices. The logic capabilities of these devices can be upgraded by simply downloading new software from a vendor-supplied disk to flash memory. Upgrades to early processors and peripheral devices required the user to replace the old circuit board or chip with a new one. The emergence of flash memory has eliminated this time-consuming and costly method of upgrade. Look for nonvolatile flash memory to play an increasing role in computer technology as its improvements continue to close the gap between the speed and flexibility of CMOS RAM.

The Processor: Nerve Center

INTERNET BRIDGE

Chips

THE CONTROL UNIT   Just as the processor is the nucleus of a computer system, the **control unit** is the nucleus of the processor. It has three primary functions:

1. To read and interpret program instructions
2. To direct the operation of internal processor components
3. To control the flow of programs and data in and out of RAM

During program execution, the first in a sequence of program instructions is moved from RAM to the control unit, where it is decoded and interpreted by the **decoder.** The control unit then directs other processor components to carry out the operations necessary to execute the instruction.

The control unit contains high-speed working storage areas called **registers** that can store no more than a few bytes (see Figure 2–5). Registers handle instructions and data at a speed about 10 times faster than that of cache memory and are used for a variety of processing functions. One register, called the **instruction register,** contains the instruction being executed. Other general-purpose registers store data needed for immediate processing. Registers also store status information. For example, the **program register** contains the RAM address of the next instruction to be executed. Registers facilitate the movement of data and instructions between RAM, the control unit, and the arithmetic and logic unit.

THE ARITHMETIC AND LOGIC UNIT   The **arithmetic and logic unit** performs all computations (addition, subtraction, multiplication, and division) and all logic operations (comparisons). The results are placed in a register called the **accumulator.** Examples of *computations* include the payroll deduction for social security, the day-end inventory, and the balance on a bank statement. A *logic* operation compares two pieces of data, either alphabetic or numeric. Based on the result of the comparison, the program "branches" to one of several alternative sets of program instructions. For example, in an inventory system each item in stock is compared to a reorder point at the end of each day. If the inventory level falls below the reorder point, a sequence of program instructions is executed that produces a purchase order.

Should PC Ownership Be an Entrance Requirement for Colleges?

As THE JOB MARKET TIGHTENS, COLLEGES ARE LOOKING TO give their students a competitive edge. With computer knowledge becoming a job prerequisite for many positions, hundreds of colleges have made the purchase of a personal computer a prerequisite for admission. Personal computers are versatile in that they can be used as stand-alone computers or they can be linked to the college's network, the Internet, or other personal computers. At these colleges, PCs are everywhere—in lounges, libraries, and other common areas.

Wouldn't it be great to run a bibliographic search from your dorm room or home? Make changes to a report without retyping it? Run a case search for a law class? Use the computer for math homework calculations?

Instead of making hard copies of class assignments, some instructors key in their assignments, which are then "delivered" to each student's electronic mailbox. Students can correspond with their instructors through their computer to get help with assignments. They can even "talk" to other students at connected colleges.

Discussion: If your college does not require PC ownership for admission, should it? If it does, should the policy be continued?

Extended Classroom At some colleges, owning a computer has been made a prerequisite for admission. Courtesy of International Business Machines Corporation. Unauthorized use not permitted.

Buses: The Processor's Mass Transit System

Just as big cities have mass transit systems that move large numbers of people, the computer has a similar system that moves millions of bits a second. Both transit systems use buses, although the one in the computer doesn't have wheels. All electrical signals travel on a common electrical bus. The term **bus** was derived from its wheeled cousin because passengers on both buses (people and bits) can get off at any stop. In a computer, the bus stops are the control unit, the arithmetic and logic unit, internal memory (RAM, ROM, flash, and other types of internal memory), and the **device controllers** (small computers) that control the operation of the peripheral devices (see Figure 2–5).

The bus is the common pathway through which the processor sends/receives data and commands to/from primary and secondary storage and all I/O peripheral devices. Bits traveling between RAM, cache memory, and the processor hop on the **address bus** and the **data bus.** Source and destination addresses are sent over the address bus to identify a particular location in memory, then the data and instructions are transferred over the data bus to or from that location.

Making the Processor Work

We communicate with computers by telling them what to do in their native tongue—the machine language.

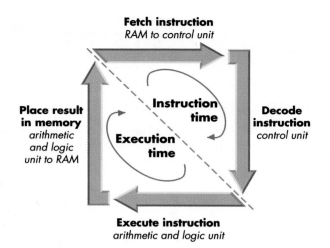

Fetch instruction
RAM to control unit

Instruction
time

Execution
time

Decode
instruction
control unit

Place result
in memory
*arithmetic
and logic
unit to RAM*

Execute instruction
arithmetic and logic unit

FIGURE 2–6 The Machine Cycle

THE MACHINE LANGUAGE You may have heard of computer programming languages such as Visual BASIC and C++. There are dozens of these languages in common usage, all of which need to be translated into the only language that a computer understands—its own **machine language.** Can you guess how machine-language instructions are represented inside the computer? You are correct if you answered as strings of binary digits.

THE MACHINE CYCLE: MAKING THE ROUNDS Every computer has a **machine cycle.** The speed of a processor is sometimes measured by how long it takes to complete a machine cycle. The timed interval that comprises the machine cycle is the total of the **instruction time,** or **I-time,** and the **execution time,** or **E-time** (see Figure 2–6). The following actions take place during the machine cycle (see Figure 2–6):

Instruction time

- *Fetch instruction.* The next machine-language instruction to be executed is retrieved, or "fetched," from RAM or cache memory and loaded to the instruction register in the control unit.
- *Decode instruction.* The instruction is decoded and interpreted.

Execution time

- *Execute instruction.* Using whatever processor resources are needed (primarily the arithmetic and logic unit), the instruction is executed.
- *Place result in memory.* The results are placed in the appropriate memory position or the accumulator.

Processor Design: There Is a Choice

CISC AND RISC: MORE IS NOT ALWAYS BETTER Most processors in mainframe computers and personal computers have a **CISC** (*complex instruction set computer*) design. A CISC computer's machine language offers programmers a wide variety of instructions from which to choose (add, multiply, compare, move data, and so on). CISC computers reflect the evolution of increasingly sophisticated machine languages. Computer designers, however, are rediscovering the beauty of simplicity. Computers designed around much smaller instruction sets can realize significantly increased throughput for certain applications, especially those that involve graphics (for exam-

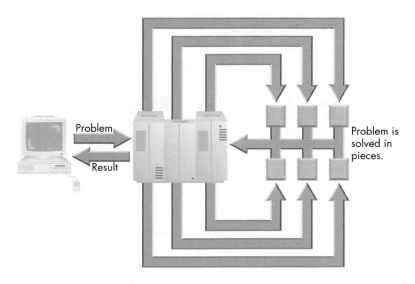

FIGURE 2–7 Parallel Processing
In parallel processing, auxiliary processors solve pieces of a problem to enhance system throughput.

ple, computer-aided design). These computers have **RISC** (*reduced instruction set computer*) design. The RISC processor shifts much of the computational burden from the hardware to the software. Proponents of RISC design feel that the limitations of a reduced instruction set are easily offset by increased processing speed and the lower cost of RISC microprocessors.

PARALLEL PROCESSING: COMPUTERS WORKING TOGETHER In a single processor environment, the processor addresses the programming problem sequentially, from beginning to end. Today, designers are building computers that break a programming problem into pieces. Work on each of these pieces is then executed simultaneously in separate processors, all of which are part of the same computer. The concept of using multiple processors in the same computer is known as **parallel processing.** In parallel processing, one main processor examines the programming problem and determines what portions, if any, of the problem can be solved in pieces (see Figure 2–7). Those pieces that can be addressed separately are routed to other processors and solved. The individual pieces are then reassembled in the main processor for further computation, output, or storage. The net result of parallel processing is better throughput.

Computer designers are creating mainframes and supercomputers with thousands of integrated microprocessors. Parallel processing on such a large scale is referred to as **massively parallel processing (MPP).** These super-fast supercomputers have sufficient computing capacity to attack applications that have been beyond that of computers with traditional computer designs. For example, researchers can now simulate global warming with these computers.

2–4 Describing the Processor: Distinguishing Characteristics

How do we distinguish one computer from the other? Much the same way we'd distinguish one person from the other. When describing someone we generally note gender, height, weight, and age. When describing computers or processors we talk about *word size, speed,* and the *capacity* of their associated RAM (see Figure 2–8). For example, a computer might be described as a 64-bit, 450-MHz, 256-MB PC. Let's see what this means.

Word Size: 16-, 32-, and 64-Lane Bitways

Just as the brain sends and receives signals through the central nervous system, the processor sends and receives electrical signals through its common electrical bus a

INTERNET BRIDGE
Serendipitous Surfing: Popular Culture

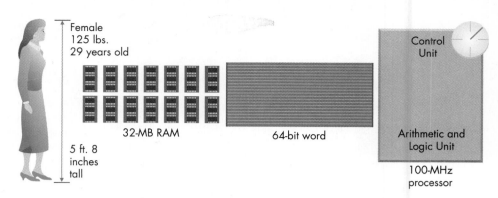

FIGURE 2–8 Describing a Computer
We describe computers much like we would a person, but we use different characteristics (word size, speed, and RAM capacity).

Female
125 lbs.
29 years old

5 ft. 8 inches tall

32-MB RAM

64-bit word

Control Unit

Arithmetic and Logic Unit

100-MHz processor

word at a time. A **word** describes the number of bits that are handled as a unit within a particular computer system's bus or during internal processing.

Twenty years ago, a computer's word size applied both to transmissions through the electrical *bus* and to *all internal processing*. This is no longer the case. In some of today's computers, one word size defines pathways in the bus and another word size defines internal processing capacity. Internal processing involves the movement of data and commands between registers, the control unit, and the arithmetic and logic unit (see Figure 2–5). Many popular computers have 64-bit internal processing but only a 32-bit path through the bus. For certain input/output-oriented applications, a 64-bit computer with a 32-bit bus may not realize the throughput of a full 64-bit computer.

The word size of modern microcomputers is normally 64 bits (eight 8-bit bytes). Early PCs had word sizes of 8 bits (one byte) and 16 bits (two bytes). Workstations, mainframes, and supercomputers have 64-bit word sizes and up.

Processor Speed: Warp Speed

A tractor can go 12 miles per hour (mph), a minivan can go 90 mph, and a slingshot drag racer can go 240 mph. These speeds, however, provide little insight into the relative capabilities of these vehicles. What good is a 240-mph tractor or a 12-mph minivan? Similarly, you have to place the speed of computers within the context of their design and application. Generally, PCs are measured in *MHz*, workstations and mainframes are measured in *MIPS*, and supercomputers are measured in *FLOPS*.

MEGAHERTZ: MHz The PC's heart is its *crystal oscillator* and its heartbeat is the *clock cycle*. The crystal oscillator paces the execution of instructions within the processor. A micro's processor speed is rated by its frequency of oscillation, or the number of clock cycles per second. Most modern personal computers are rated between 300 and 600 **megahertz,** or **MHz** (millions of clock cycles). The elapsed time for one clock cycle is 1/frequency (1 divided by the frequency). For example, the time it takes to complete one cycle on a 400-MHz processor is 1/400,000,000, or 0.000000025 seconds, or

Many field sales representatives carry notebook PCs when they call on customers. This Merck Human Health-U.S. representative uses computer-based detailing to make a presentation on cholesterol reducer to a cardiologist. Computer data help her better target information to physicians. Her notebook has a 64-bit processor with a speed of 300 MHz and a RAM capacity of 128 MB. Courtesy of Merck & Co., Inc.

The CRAY T90 supercomputer is the most powerful general-purpose computer ever built. General purpose computers are capable of handling a wide range of applications. The system is capable of crunching data at a peak rate of 64 GFLOPS (gigaflops). One GFLOP equals one billion floating point logic operations per second.   Courtesy of E-Systems, Inc.

2.5 nanoseconds (2.5 billionths of a second). Normally several clock cycles are required to fetch, decode, and execute a single program instruction. The shorter the clock cycle, the faster the processor.

To properly evaluate the processing capability of a computer, you must consider both the processor speed and the word size. A 64-bit computer with a 450-MHz processor has more processing capability than does a 32-bit computer with a 450-MHz processor.

MIPS   Processing speed may also be measured in **MIPS,** or *m*illions of *i*nstructions *p*er *s*econd. Although frequently associated with workstations and mainframes, MIPS is also applied to high-end PCs. Computers operate in the 20- to 1000-MIPS range. A 100-MIPS computer can execute 100 million instructions per second.

FLOPS   Supercomputer speed is measured in **FLOPS**—*f*loating point *o*perations *p*er *s*econd. Supercomputer applications, which are often scientific, frequently involve floating point operations. Floating point operations accommodate very small or very large numbers. State-of-the-art supercomputers operate in the 500-**GFLOPS** to 3-**TFLOPS** range. (A GFLOPS, gigaflops, is one billion FLOPS; a TFLOPS, or teraflops, is one trillion FLOPS.)

RAM Capacity: Megachips

The capacity of RAM is stated in terms of the number of bytes it can store. Memory capacity for most computers is stated in terms of **megabytes (MB).** One megabyte equals 1,048,576 (2^{20}) bytes. Memory capacities of modern PCs range from 32 MB to 512 MB. Memory capacities of early PCs were measured in **kilobytes (KB).** One kilobyte is 1024 (2^{10}) bytes of storage.

Some high-end mainframes and supercomputers have more than 8000 MB of RAM. Their RAM capacities are stated as **gigabytes (GB)**—about one billion bytes. It's only a matter of time before we state RAM in terms of **terabytes (TB)**—about one trillion bytes. GB and TB are frequently used in reference to high-capacity secondary storage. Occasionally you will see memory capacities of individual chips stated in terms of **kilobits (Kb)** and **megabits (Mb).** Figure 2–9 should give you a feel for KBs, MBs, GBs, and TBs.

Compare the number of characters in the Gettysburg Address to 1 KB (Kilobyte)

Compare the number of characters in this book to 1 MB (Megabyte)

Compare the number of people in China to 1 GB (Gigabyte)

Compare the number of gallons of water consumed each day in North America to 1 TB (Terabyte)

FIGURE 2–9   How Much Is a KB, an MB, a GB, and a TB?

EMERGING TECHNOLOGY

Computers: The Enabling Technology for the Disabled

COMPUTER TECHNOLOGY IS HAVING A PROFOUND EFFECT ON physically challenged people. With the aid of computers they now are better prepared to take control of their environments.

On the Move

Paraplegic Walks A little over a decade ago, Nan Davis stunned the world. A paraplegic since an automobile accident on the night of her high school graduation, she walked to the podium to receive her college diploma—with the help of a rehabilitative tool that uses FES, or functional electrical stimulation.

FES uses low-level electrical stimulation to restore or supplement the minute electrical currents the nervous system generates to control different parts of the body. This electrical stimulation is controlled by a microprocessor—a computer—that uses feedback from the body to adjust the electrical stimulation's length and intensity.

In Nan's case, FES took the form of electrodes to stimulate her leg muscles; a sensory feedback system; and a small, portable computer. The sensory feedback system tells the computer the position and movement of the legs so that it knows which muscles it must electrically stimulate next to produce a coordinated gait.

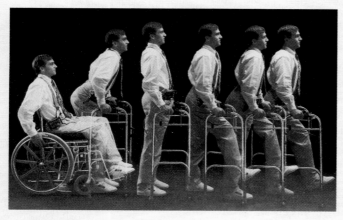

Paraplegic Walks The Parastep® System is a microcomputer controlled functional neuromuscular stimulation (FNS) device enabling standing and walking by people paralyzed with spinal cord injuries. This system comes from the medical engineering sciences known as neuroprosthetics.

The Parastep stimulator generates sequences of electrical pulses passed to target peripheral nerves through electrodes placed over muscles and nerves of the lower extremities. The user controls stimulation through a key pad on the stimulator unit or with control switches on the walker. Courtesy of Sigmedics, Inc.

FES Comes of Age Although the use of FES to restore one's ability to stand, walk, and use the arms and hands is still in the experimental stage, many other FES applications are accepted medical practice. The best-known application is the cardiac pacemaker that is attached directly to a faulty heart with electrodes. FES can also be used to control chronic pain, correct spinal deformities, improve auditory defects, and pace the rise and fall of the diaphragm during breathing.

Grasping the Technology This person, whose hands are paralyzed due to a spinal cord injury, uses an implanted FES system that causes her finger muscles to contract and allows her to grasp the telephone. Courtesy of MetroHealth Medical Center, Cleveland, Ohio

FES can also be used as a therapeutic tool to strengthen muscles idled by paralysis. Without exercise, muscles atrophy, circulation becomes sluggish, cardiovascular fitness declines, and pressure sores develop. These FES devices, which look like high-tech exercise bicycles, use a microprocessor to coordinate a system of electrodes and feedback sensors, allowing the user to push the pedals and turn a hand crank. Like anyone who engages in a regular exercise program, users of the FES devices report noticeable improvements in muscle tone, mass, and cardiovascular fitness. These devices cannot restore function, of course, but they can help the paralyzed to maintain their bodies while researchers continue to seek ways to help them walk again. In the meantime, many are thrilled just to see their bodies move again.

Scaling the Barriers at Work

For most disabled workers—especially those with physical impairments—the barriers to gainful employment have been as steep as the stairs flanking many public buildings. This is changing thanks to federal legislation and revolutionary advances in computer hardware and software.

The Americans with Disabilities Act of 1990

This legislation prohibits discrimination that might limit employment or access to public buildings and facilities. In fact, many call the law a bill of rights for people with physical limitations, mental impairments, and chronic illnesses. The legislation promises to benefit the nation, too. Of the approximately 43 million disabled workers, only about 28% hold full- or part-time jobs at a time when experts are projecting labor shortages and a shrinking pool of *skilled* workers.

Enabling Technology

Under the law, employers cannot discriminate against any employee who can perform a job's "essential" responsibilities with "reasonable accommodations." Increasingly, these "accommodations" take the form of a personal computer with special peripherals and software. All told, almost 20,000 technology-based products are available for the disabled.

For example, getting a complete impression of the contents of a computer screen is a problem for the visually impaired, as is the ability to maneuver around such features as pull-down windows and click-on icons. The partially sighted can benefit from adaptive software packages that create large-type screen displays, while voice syn-

Personal Reader This personal reader allows visually impaired people to "hear" books and typewritten material. An optical scanner reads the words into the computer system, where they are converted into English speech using a speech synthesizer (a device that produces electronic speech). Users can request any of nine different voices (including male, female, and child).   Xerox Imaging Systems/Kurzweil, a Xerox Company

thesizers can let the blind "read" memos, books, and computer screens.

For the hearing impaired, voice mail and a computer's beeps can be translated into visual cues, such as a screen display of text or flashing icons. Advancing communications and video technologies have made it possible for users to sit in front of their respective computer screens and have sign language conversations.

Virtually any type of physical movement can be used to input commands and data to a computer. This is good news for people with limited use of their arms and hands. Alternative input devices can range from a standard trackball (instead of a mouse) to the relatively slow sip-and-puff devices to faster voice-recognition systems. There are even software programs which allow keystroke combinations to be entered one key at a time.

Several studies, including ones by the U.S. Department of Labor and private firms, concluded that 80% of all accommodations would cost less than $500 per employee. Text-to-speech software, for example, can be purchased for as little as $150. More sophisticated PC-based accommodations are more costly, of course. The leading speech-recognition system, for example, costs about $9000, while a PC modified for a blind word processor can cost about $8000 (versus $2000 for a standard PC). Still, the prices of these technologies, like the prices of PCs themselves, continue to drop. The cost of a "reading" device, for example, fell from $40,000 to $2000 in about a decade. Furthermore, employers who provide "assistive technologies" to their employees are eligible for tax incentives. Employers benefit, too, by gaining highly motivated and productive workers. A study at a major chemical company found that workers with and without disabilities were equal or closely matched on safety and performance.

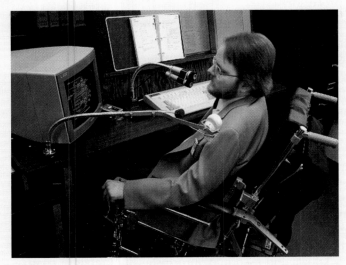

At Work The nature of the work and the availability of specially designed workstations have made computer careers particularly inviting to the physically disabled. The man in the photo works as a database administrator at a computer services company.   Boeing Computer Services

Differences in Processor Personality

Word size, speed, and *RAM capacity* are the primary descriptors of processors. However, computers, like people, have their own "personalities." That is, two similarly described computers might possess attributes that give one more capability than the other. For example, one 64-bit, 450-MHz, 256-MB PC might permit the connection of four peripheral devices and another eight peripheral devices. Just remember when you buy a PC that the basic descriptors tell most but not all of the story.

2–5 Inside the PC

Now that you have had an opportunity to see what happens inside computers in general, let's take a closer look inside a personal computer.

The Microprocessor: Computer on a Chip

What is smaller than a postage stamp and found in wristwatches, sewing machines, and CD players? The answer: a **microprocessor.** The processor component of personal computer systems is a microprocessor, or simply a small processor. The microprocessor, which is a product of the microminiaturization of electronic circuitry, it is literally a "computer on a chip." We use the term *chip* to refer to any self-contained integrated circuit. The size of chips, which are about 30 thousandths of an inch thick, vary in area from fingernail size (about $\frac{1}{4}$-inch square) to postage-stamp size (about 1-inch square). Microprocessors have been integrated into thousands of mechanical and electronic devices— even elevators, band saws, and ski-boot bindings. In a few years virtually everything mechanical or electronic will incorporate microprocessor technology into its design.

The System Board: The Mother of All Boards

The **system board,** or **motherboard,** is the physical foundation of the PC. In a personal computer, the following are attached to the system board, a single circuit board:

- Microprocessor (main processor)
- Support electronic circuitry (for example, one chip handles input/output signals from the peripheral devices)
- Memory chips (RAM, ROM, flash memory, cache memory, and so on)
- Bus (the path through which the processor communicates with memory components and peripheral devices)
- Expansion slots for linking other circuit boards and peripheral devices to the processor

Before being attached to the system board, the microprocessor and other chips are mounted onto a **carrier.** Carriers have standard-sized pin connectors that allow the chips to be attached to the system board.

What's on the system board, the "guts" of a microcomputer, defines the PC's speed and capacity. The central component of the system board, the microprocessor, is generally not made by the manufacturers of PCs. It is made by companies that specialize in the development and manufacture of microprocessors. Although the Motorola and Intel chips are the most widely known and used microprocessors, a number of companies make PC microprocessors.

MOTOROLA MICROPROCESSORS   Motorola manufactures two prominent families of microprocessors: the M680X family and the **PowerPC** family. The M680X family (MC68000, MC68020, MC68030, MC68040, and MC68060) has been the processor for the Apple line of computers and for hundreds of electronic devices from microwave

Dell Computer Corporation, founded in 1984, is the world's leading direct-sales computer-systems company. Shown here is one of the company's manufacturing facilities, where they make the Dell OptiPlex® desktop computers. The OptiPlex®, which is widely used in Corporate America, is designed primarily for the multiuser networked environment. Courtesy of Dell Computer Corporation

ovens to automobiles. However, Apple and others are adopting the newer PowerPC technology.

Because the PowerPC line of microprocessors is a product of an alliance between three of the computer industry's most powerful players (Motorola, Apple, and IBM), it has emerged as a formidable force in the PC industry. The PowerPC family includes the PowerPC 600 series and the 700 series. The first three are designed for use in PCs, including those manufactured by Apple and IBM. The PowerPC 620 is designed for use with everything from high-end workstations to supercomputers. The PowerPC provides users with tremendous flexibility in that it can run all major industry-standard **platforms.** A platform is defined by a combination of hardware and control software, for which additional software applications are developed. The most popular platforms in state-of-the-art PCs are the *PowerPC with Apple's Mac OS* control software and the *Intel microprocessors with Microsoft Windows 95, Microsoft Windows 98,* or *Microsoft Windows NT* control software.

INTEL MICROPROCESSORS   The system board for the original IBM PC, the IBM PC/XT, and most of the *IBM-PC–compatible* microcomputers manufactured through 1984, used the Intel 8088 microprocessor chip. The Intel 8088 chip is a slower version of the Intel 8086, which was developed in 1979. At the time of the introduction of the IBM PC (1981), the Intel 8086 was thought to be too advanced for the emerging PC market. Ironically, the more powerful Intel 8086 chip was not used in PCs until the introduction of the low-end models of the IBM PS/2 series in 1987. The 8086 is considered the base technology for all microprocessors used in IBM-PC–compatible and the IBM PS/2 series computers.

The IBM PC/AT (Advanced Technology), which was introduced in 1984, employed an Intel 80286 microprocessor. As much as six times faster than the 8088, the 80286 provided a substantial increase in PC performance. The more advanced Intel 80386 and 80486 chips offered even greater performance for IBM-PC–compatible PCs, which usually are called simply *PC compatibles.* When someone talks about a "286," "386," or "486" machine, he or she is referring to a PC that uses Intel 80286, 80386, or 80486 chip technology. Successor Intel microprocessors to the 486 fall in the **Pentium**™, **Pentium Pro**™, and **Pentium II**™ family of microprocessors. The Pentium chips are designed to better accommodate multimedia applications that involve sound and motion video. Figure 2–10 illustrates relative performance (speed in MIPS) of past, present, and future Intel microprocessors.

Motorola's PowerPC family of microprocessors (top) can run all major industry standard platforms. Intel Corporation's Pentium II™ is the microprocessor found in most new PC-compatible computers.   Courtesy of International Business Machines Corporation. Unauthorized use not permitted.   Courtesy of Intel Corporation

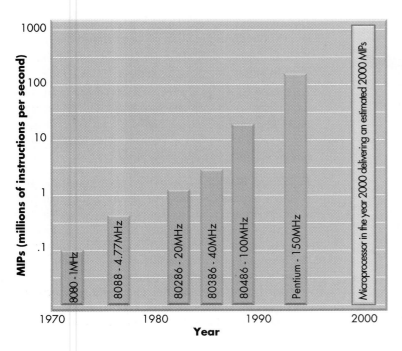

FIGURE 2–10   The Intel Family of Processors
The Intel family of processors have been installed in 9 of every 10 of the about 200 million PCs in use today. This chart is an approximation of the relative speeds of popular Intel processors. It also compares these to one that reflects anticipated technology at the turn of the century. This processor will have about 10,000 times the speed of the Intel 8088 (2000 MIPs to .2 MIPs), the processor that ushered in the age of personal computing.

Connecting Peripheral Devices: Putting It Together

The system board, with its processor and memory, is ready for work. Alone, though, a system board is like a fish without water. The system board must be linked to I/O, storage, and communication devices to receive data and return the results of processing.

PORTS OF CALL   In a PC, external peripheral devices (such as a printer and a mouse) come with a cable and a multipin connector. To link a device to the PC, you plug its connector into a receptacle in much the same way you plug a lamp cord into an electrical outlet. The receptacle, called a **port,** provides a direct link to the PC's common electrical bus.

External peripheral devices can be linked to the processor via cables through either a **serial port** or a **parallel port.** The system board is normally designed with at least one of each plus a dedicated keyboard port. Newer PCs have a dedicated port for the mouse.

- *Serial ports.* Serial ports facilitate the *serial transmission* of data, *one bit at a time* (see Figure 2–11). The mouse is usually connected to a serial port. The standard for PC serial ports is the 9-pin or 25-pin (male or female) **RS-232C connector.** One of the 9 or 25 lines carries the serial signal to the peripheral device, and another line carries the signal from the device. The other lines carry control signals.

- *Parallel ports.* Parallel ports facilitate the *parallel transmission* of data; that is, several bits are transmitted simultaneously. Figure 2–11 illustrates how 8-bit bytes travel in parallel over 8 separate lines. Extra lines carry control signals. Parallel ports use the same 25-pin RS-232C connector or the 36-pin **Centronics connector.** These ports provide the interface for such devices as high-speed printers, magnetic tape backup units, and other computers.

- *SCSI port.* The **SCSI port** enables faster data transmission than serial and parallel ports. Also, up to 15 peripheral devices can be daisy-chained to a single SCSI port (connected along a single cable).

- *USB port.* The **USB port** (Universal Serial Bus port) is the most recent innovation in high-speed device interfaces. Up to 127 peripheral devices can be daisy-chained to a single USB port.

- *Dedicated keyboard port.* The keyboard's dedicated serial port has a unique 5-pin or 7-pin round connector.

- *Dedicated mouse port.* Most new system boards have a built-in serial port for the mouse.

- *IrDA port.* The **IrDA port, infrared port,** transmits data via infrared light waves. Many PCs and devices, such as printers, come with IrDA ports. As long as the devices are within a few feet, data can be transferred without the use of cables.

A FLEET OF BUSES   The system board includes several empty **expansion slots** (see Figure 2–12) that provide direct connections to the common electrical bus that services the processor and RAM. These slots enable a PC owner to expand the capabilities of a basic PC by plugging in a wide variety of special-function **expansion boards,** also called **expansion cards.** These add-on circuit boards contain the electronic circuitry for many supplemental capabilities, such as extra ports or video capture capability. Expansion boards are made to

Inside the Computer Explorer

FIGURE 2–11   Serial and Parallel Data Transmission
In serial transmission, outgoing and incoming bits flow one-at-a-time through a single line. In parallel transmission, bytes flow together over eight separate lines.

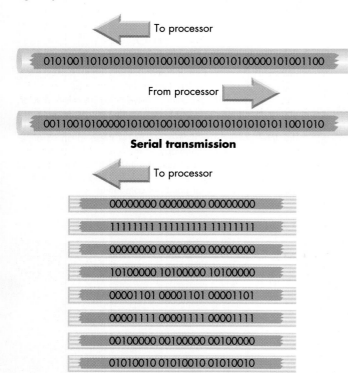

fit a particular type of bus. The more popular types of buses for PC compatibles are introduced here.

ISA buses. The most common PC expansion boards plug into an ISA (Industry Standard Architecture) **expansion bus.** The expansion bus, an extension of the common electrical bus, accepts the expansion boards that control the video display, disks, and other peripherals. For almost a decade, expansion bus technology stood still while processor and peripheral performance skyrocketed. As a result, we have bumper-to-bumper traffic on the interstate (high-speed data streams) exiting onto a single-lane covered bridge (the antiquated ISA bus). The ISA bus is slow, moving data in 16-bit words (compared to 32 bits within the processor) and at a much slower rate (8 MHz versus up to 100 MHz). A slow expansion bus forces the processor into a wait state, thereby causing a decrease in throughput.

PCI local bus. Recent innovations in bus technology have resulted in linking expansion boards directly to the system's common bus, sometimes referred to as the **local bus.** The local bus offers channels that transfer data at the processor speeds (for example, 32 bits at 100 MHz). Intel Corporation's **PCI local bus** addresses the data stream bottleneck in PCs. Local bus operation improves performance for today's high-speed peripherals, especially for graphics applications using high-resolution monitors. As a result, most new system boards are designed to accommodate a mix of expansion boards. Modern system boards normally include the popular ISA bus and the PCI (Peripheral Component Interconnect) local bus.

SCSI buses. The **SCSI bus,** or "scuzzy" bus, provides an alternative to the expansion bus. Up to fifteen SCSI (Small Computer System Interface) peripheral devices can be daisy-chained to a SCSI interface expansion card via the SCSI port, which means that the devices are connected along a single cable with multiple SCSI connectors. Components within the processor unit (perhaps a CD-ROM drive and tape backup unit) are daisy-chained on an internal cable, and others (perhaps a printer and a scanner) are linked to the external cable (see Figure 2–13). Users who are running out of serial and parallel ports are looking to the SCSI bus for expansion. It's not unusual to find a CD-ROM drive, a tape backup unit, a printer, and perhaps an image scanner daisy-chained on a SCSI bus.

Universal Serial Buses. The **Universal Serial Bus (USB)** is a relatively new bus standard developed by seven industry leaders, including Compaq, Microsoft, and IBM. The new bus will permit up to 127 peripheral devices to be connected to a USB port. The USB will eliminate the hassle of installing expansion cards. PC peripheral devices are designed to connect to the Uniform Serial Bus. The USB **hot plug** feature allows peripheral devices to be connected to or removed from the USB port while the PC is running.

PC Growth: Adding Capabilities

EXPANSION: SLOTS FOR BOARDS The *expansion slots* associated with the expansion buses (ISA) and local buses (PCI), and the *SCSI adapter* let you enhance processor functionality by adding *expansion boards*. The number of available expansion slots

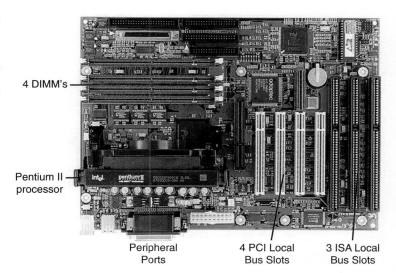

4 DIMM's

Pentium II processor

Peripheral Ports   4 PCI Local Bus Slots   3 ISA Local Bus Slots

FIGURE 2–12 A System Board This system board contains a 333-MHz Intel Pentium II processor, 512K of cache memory, and eight expansion slots (three ISA bus slots, four PCI local bus slots, and on AGP slot for video) for adding additional capabilities, such as a fax modem. The system board has four DIMMs that can accept of the 512 MB of SDRAM. It also has mouse and keyboard ports, two serial ports, one parallel port, two USB ports, and an Infrared (IrDA) port. Courtesy of Advanced Integration Research, Inc.

INTERNET BRIDGE

Serendipitous Surfing Online Shopping

FIGURE 2–13 SCSI Bus

Two external devices, a printer and a scanner, are daisy-chained on the SCSI's external cable. Two internal devices, the CD-ROM and the tape backup unit, are daisy-chained on the SCSI's internal cable. Terminators are attached at the end of each cable to denote the end of the chain.

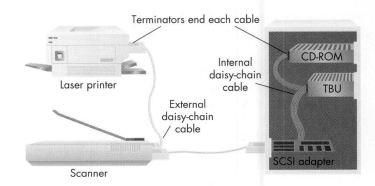

Terminators end each cable

CD-ROM

TBU

Internal daisy-chain cable

Laser printer

External daisy-chain cable

SCSI adapter

Scanner

Expansion Boards

varies from computer to computer (see Figure 2–12). Keep in mind that an expansion board and/or peripheral device is designed for use with a particular type of expansion bus (ISA, SCSI, and so on). There are literally hundreds of expansion boards from which to choose. You will find these on most PCs.

- *Graphics adapter.* These adapters permit interfacing with video monitors. The VGA (video graphics array) board and the newer **AGP (accelerated graphics port)** board enables the interfacing of high-resolution monitors with the processor.

- *Sound.* The sound card, which is included on most new PCs, makes two basic functions possible. First, it enables sounds to be captured and stored on disk. Second, it enables sounds, including music and spoken words, to be played through external speakers. The sound card can add realism to computer games with stereo music and sound effects, and it allows us to insert spoken notes within our word processing documents. The typical sound card will have receptacles for a microphone, a headset, an audio output, and a joystick.

- *Fax modem.* A **modem** permits communication with remote computers via a telephone-line link. The **fax modem** performs the same function as a regular modem plus it has an added capability—it enables a PC to emulate a **facsimile** or **fax** machine. Fax machines transfer images of documents via telephone lines to another location. A different type of modem, the **cable modem,** is connected to the TV cable.

Depending on your applications needs, you might wish to augment your system with some of these expansion boards:

- *Peripheral device interface.* The aforementioned graphics adapter is the device interface for the monitor. Other peripheral devices, such as scanners (devices that capture images on hard-copy documents), very high-resolution printers, plotters (devices that provide precision plots of graphs), and external magnetic disk drives sometimes are sold with an interface card, as well as a cable. To install one of these devices you will need to insert its interface card into an empty expansion slot (see Figure 2–12), then connect the device's cable to the card. Devices with interface cards do not require the use of one of the PC's serial or parallel ports.

- *Serial and parallel ports.* Installation of this board provides access to the bus via auxiliary serial and parallel ports.

- *Network interface.* The network interface card (NIC) facilitates and controls the exchange of data between the microcomputers in a PC *network* (several PCs linked together). Each PC in a network must be equipped with an NIC. The cables that link the PCs are physically connected to the NICs.

- *SCSI interface card.* The SCSI bus can be built into the system board or installed as an expansion board.

- *Video capture.* This card enables full-motion color video with audio to be captured and stored on disk. Once on disk storage, video information can be integrated with text, graphics, and other forms of presentation.

Online users are often frustrated as they wait for applications to build or files to be downloaded. Cable modems (shown here) may put an end to this frustration, offering online services at speeds hundreds of times faster than traditional telephone-based modems. For example, a 45-minute file download over a traditional modem would take only 3 seconds over a cable modem. The cable modem is here now, but you may have to wait a year or so for your cable TV provider to upgrade its facilities. The cable modem hooks directly to your TV cable. Photo courtesy of Hewlett-Packard Company

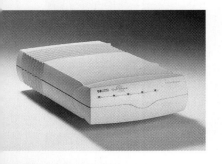

Most expansion boards are *multifunction*, which means that they include two or more capabilities. For example, one popular **multifunction expansion board** comes with a serial port and a fax modem.

PC CARDS: PCMCIA TECHNOLOGY The **PCMCIA card,** sometimes called **PC card,** is a credit-card–sized removable expansion module that is plugged into a external PCMCIA expansion slot. Functionally, the PC card is like an expansion board in that it offers a wide variety of capabilities. PC cards can be expanded RAM, programmable nonvolatile flash memory, network interface cards, SCSI adapters, fax modems, sound cards, hard-disk cards, and much more. For example, one PC card comes in the form of a Mobile GPS (global positioning system). The Mobile GPS card can be used to pinpoint the latitude and longitude of the user within a few feet, anywhere on or near earth. Business travelers use GPS cards in conjunction with computer-based road maps to help them get around in unfamiliar cities.

Virtually all new portable computers are equipped with a PCMCIA-compliant interface. PDAs (personal digital assistants) and notebook PCs do not have enough space for as many expansion slots as do their desktop cousins. Interchangeable PC cards let laptop users insert capabilities as they are needed. For example, a user can insert a fax modem PC card to send e-mail, then do a *hot swap* (PC remains running) with a sound PC card to give a presentation.

Notebook PCs, because of their compact size, have fewer expansion slots than desktop PCs. For this reason, notebook PCs are designed with PCMCIA expansion slots. PC cards are plugged into PCMCIA expansion slots to give the system-added capability. This U.S. Robotics PC card includes a fax modem.
U.S. Robotics Mobile Communications Corporation

Why It's Important to Know What's Inside Your PC

If you want to take advantage of ever-advancing PC technology, get the most for your PC dollar, and allow your PC to grow with your capabilities, you need to know what's inside your PC. You need to know because personal computing is very personal. You are the decision maker. A little knowledge about what's inside can save you big bucks and make you a more effective user. Someday we won't have to worry about what's inside a PC. That day, however, will not be any time soon.

INTERNET BRIDGE

Interactive Study Guide
Chapter 2

IMPORTANT TERMS AND SUMMARY OUTLINE

2–1 DATA STORAGE: A BIT ABOUT THE BIT The two kinds of electronic signals are **analog** and **digital.** To make the most effective use of computers and automation, the electronics world is going digital. The music industry **digitizes** the natural analog signals that result from recording sessions, then stores the digital version on CDs. Computers are digital and, therefore, work better with digital data.

The two digital states of the computer—on and off— are represented by a **bit,** short for *binary digit*. These electronic states are compatible with the **binary** numbering system. Letters and decimal numbers are translated into bits for storage and processing on computer systems.

Data are stored temporarily during processing in **primary storage** (RAM) and permanently on **secondary storage** devices such as magnetic tape and disk drives.

2–2 ENCODING SYSTEMS: BITS AND BYTES Alphanumeric (**alpha** and **numeric**) characters are represented in computer storage by unique bit configurations. Characters are translated into these bit configurations, also called **bytes,** according to a particular coding scheme, called an **encoding system.**

The 7-bit **ASCII** encoding system is the most popular encoding system for PCs and data communication. The various versions of **extended ASCII,** an 8-bit encoding system, offer 128 more codes. Microsoft Windows uses the 8-bit **ANSI** encoding system.

Unicode, a uniform 16-bit encoding system, will enable computers and applications to talk to one another more easily and will accommodate most of the world's languages.

2–3 ANALYZING A COMPUTER SYSTEM, BIT BY BIT The processor is the nucleus of any computer system. A processor, which is also called the **central processing unit** or **CPU,** has only two fundamental sections, the **control unit** and the **arithmetic and logic unit,** which work together with RAM to execute programs. The control unit reads and interprets instructions and directs the arithmetic and logic unit to perform computation and logic operations.

RAM, or random-access memory, provides the processor with temporary storage for programs and data. Physically, memory chips are installed on **single in-line memory modules** (**SIMMs**) and on **dual in-line memory modules** (**DIMMS**). Most new PCs are being equipped with **synchronous dynamic RAM** (**SDRAM**); however, an even faster RAM, **Rambus DRAM** (**RDRAM**) may be the de facto standard in the near future.

In RAM, each datum is stored at a specific **address.** Most of today's computers use SDRAM technology for RAM. SDRAM is **volatile memory** (contrast with **non-volatile memory**); that is, the data are lost when the electrical current is turned off or interrupted. All input/output, including programs, must enter and exit RAM. Programs are loaded to RAM from secondary storage in a **nondestructive read** process. Other variations of internal storage are ROM, **programmable read-only memory** (**PROM**), and **flash memory,** a nonvolatile memory.

Some computers employ **cache memory** to increase **throughput** (the rate at which work can be performed by a computer system). Like RAM, cache is a high-speed holding area for program instructions and data. However, cache memory holds only those instructions and data likely to be needed next by the processor. During execution, instructions and data are passed between very high-speed **registers** (for example, the **instruction register,** the **program register,** and the **accumulator**) in the control unit and the arithmetic and logic unit.

The **bus** is the common pathway through which the processor sends/receives data and commands to/from primary and secondary storage and all I/O peripheral devices. Like the wheeled bus, the bus provides data transportation to all processor components, memory, and **device controllers.** Source and destination addresses are sent over the **address bus,** then the data and instructions are transferred over the data bus.

Every **machine language** has a predefined format for each type of instruction. During one **machine cycle,** an instruction is "fetched" from RAM, decoded by the **decoder** in the control unit, and executed, and the results are placed in memory. The machine cycle time is the total of the **instruction time (I-time)** and the **execution time (E-time).**

Most mainframes and PCs use **CISC** (*c*omplex *in*struction *set* *c*omputer) architecture. Those using **RISC** (*r*educed *i*nstruction *set* *c*omputer) architecture realize increased throughput for certain applications.

In **parallel processing**, one main processor examines the programming problem and determines what portions, if any, of the problem can be solved in pieces. Those pieces that can be addressed separately are routed to other processors, solved, then recombined in the main processor to produce the result. Parallel processing on a large scale is referred to as **massively parallel processing (MPP)**.

2–4 DESCRIBING THE PROCESSOR: DISTINGUISHING CHARACTERISTICS A processor is described in terms of its word size, speed, and RAM capacity.

A **word** is the number of bits handled as a unit within a particular computer system's common electrical bus or during internal processing.

Microcomputer speed is measured in **megahertz (MHz).** High-end PC, workstation, and mainframe speed is measured in **MIPS.** Supercomputer speed is measured in **FLOPS, GFLOPS,** and **TFLOPS.**

Memory capacity is measured in **kilobytes (KB), megabytes (MB), gigabytes (GB),** and **terabytes (TB).** Chip capacity is sometimes stated in **kilobits (Kb)** and **megabits (Mb).**

2–5 INSIDE THE PC The **microprocessor**, a product of the microminiaturization of electronic circuitry, is literally a "computer on a chip." The processor in a microcomputer is the microprocessor. It, the electronic circuitry for handling input/output signals from the peripheral devices, and the memory chips are mounted on a single circuit board called a **system board**, or **motherboard**. Before being attached to the system board, the microprocessor and other chips are mounted onto a **carrier**.

Motorola manufactures two prominent families of microprocessors—the M680X family and the **PowerPC** fam-ily. The PowerPC lets users run all major industry-standard **platforms.** Most PCs in use today have an Intel 80486 **Pentium**, **Pentium Pro**, or **Pentium II** microprocessor.

In a PC, external peripheral devices come with a cable and a multipin connector. A **port** provides a direct link to the PC's common electrical bus. External peripheral devices can be linked to the processor via cables through either a **serial port, parallel port, SCSI port, USB port**, or **IrDA (infrared) port**. The standard for PC serial ports is the **RS-232C connector**. The RS-232C and **Centronics connectors** are used with parallel ports.

The system board includes several empty **expansion slots** so you can purchase and plug in optional capabilities in the form of **expansion boards**, or **expansion cards**.

The most common PC expansion boards plug into a 16-bit ISA **expansion bus**. The expansion bus accepts the expansion boards that control the video display, disks, and other peripherals. Recent innovations have resulted in linking expansion boards directly to the system's **local bus**. The **PCI local bus** offers a local bus solution to the data stream bottleneck in PCs. The **SCSI bus**, or "scuzzy" bus, allows up to 15 SCSI peripheral devices to be daisy-chained to a SCSI interface expansion card. The **Universal Serial Bus (USB)** permits up to 127 USB peripheral devices to be **hot plugged** to the PC.

Popular expansion boards include graphics adapters, such as the **AGP** or **Accelerated Graphics Port board**, sound, **modem** (permits communication with remote computers via a telephone-line link), **fax modem** (enables emulation of a **facsimile** or **fax** machine), **cable modem**, peripheral device interface, serial and parallel ports, network interface, SCSI interface card, and video capture. Most are **multifunction expansion boards**.

The **PCMCIA card**, sometimes called **PC card**, provides a variety of interchangeable add-on capabilities in the form of credit-card–sized modules. The PC card is especially handy for the portable environment.

REVIEW EXERCISES

Concepts

1. Distinguish between RAM, ROM, PROM, and flash memory.
2. How many ANSI bytes can be stored in a 32-bit word?
3. Which two functions are performed by the arithmetic and logic unit?
4. List examples of alpha, numeric, and alphanumeric characters.
5. Write your first name as an ASCII bit configuration.
6. What are the functions of the control unit?
7. We describe computers in terms of what three characteristics?
8. What is the basic difference between SDRAM technology and nonvolatile memory technology?
9. For a given computer, which type of memory would have the greatest capacity to store data and programs: cache or RAM? RAM or registers? registers or cache?
10. Name two types of registers.
11. What do the *I* in *I-time* and the *E* in *E-time* stand for?

12. What is the relationship between a microprocessor, a motherboard, and a microcomputer?
13. List five functional enhancements that can be added to a microcomputer by inserting one or more optional expansion boards into expansion slots.
14. Why are some microcomputers sold with empty expansion slots?
15. Describe a hot swap as it relates to a PCMCIA-compliant interface.
16. Name two buses used with for PC-compatible computers.
17. Order the following Intel microprocessors by performance: 80486, 8088, 80386, and Pentium II.
18. Source and destination addresses sent to identify a particular location in a computer's memory are sent to which bus?

Discussion and Problem Solving

19. Create a five-bit encoding system to be used for storing upper-case alpha characters, punctuation symbols, and the apostrophe. Discuss the advantages and disadvantages of your encoding system in relation to the ASCII encoding system.
20. Compute the time it takes to complete one cycle on a 200-MHz processor in both seconds and nanoseconds.
21. List at least 10 products that are smaller than a toaster oven and use microprocessors. Select one and describe the function of its microprocessor.
22. Explain how internal and external devices are linked to a PC via a SCSI adapter.
23. Convert 5 MB to KB, Mb, and Kb. Assume a byte contains eight bits.

SELF-TEST (BY SECTION)

2–1 **a.** What are the two kinds of electronic signals: (a) analog and digital, (b) binary and octal, or (c) alpha and numeric? *A*
　　 b. *Bit* is the singular of *byte*. (T/F) *F*
　　 c. The base of the binary number system is: (a) 2, (b) 8, or (c) 16? *A*
　　 d. Data are stored permanently on secondary storage devices, such as magnetic tape. (T/F) *T*

2–2 **a.** The combination of bits used to represent a character is called a _____. *byte*
　　 b. The proposed 16-bit encoding system is called _____. *unicode*

2–3 **a.** Data are loaded from secondary storage to RAM in a nondestructive read process. (T/F) *T*
　　 b. The _____ is that part of the processor that reads and interprets program instructions. *control unit*
　　 c. The arithmetic and logic unit controls the flow of programs and data in and out of main memory. (T/F) *F*
　　 d. Put the following memories in order based on speed: cache, registers, and RAM. *Ram, Cache, reg*
　　 e. The timed interval that comprises the machine cycle is the total of the _instruction_ time and the _____ time. *execution*
　　 f. The rate at which work can be performed by a computer system is called _through put_

2–4 **a.** The word size of all microcomputers is 64 bits. (T/F) *F*
　　 b. *MIPS* is an acronym for "millions of instructions per second." (T/F) *T*
　　 c. _____ is a common measure of supercomputer processor speed. *Flops or G Flops*
　　 d. Which has the most bytes: (a) a kilobyte, (b) a gigabyte, or (c) a megabyte? *b*

2–5 **a.** The processing component of a motherboard is a _____. *micro processor*
　　 b. The Intel _____ and the Motorola _____ are prominent microprocessors used in PCs. *Pentium, Power PC*
　　 c. The RS-232C connector provides the interface to a port. (T/F) *T*
　　 d. Peripheral devices are _____ along a cable to a SCSI interface expansion card. *daisy chained*
　　 e. PC components are linked via a common electrical _____. *bus*
　　 f. Which local bus solution addresses the data stream bottleneck in PCs: (a) ISA, (b) PCI local bus, or (c) PCM local bus? *b*

Self-test Answers. **2–1 (a)** a; **(b)** F; **(c)** a; **(d)** T. **2–2 (a)** byte; **(b)** Unicode. **2–3 (a)** T; **(b)** control unit; **(c)** F; **(d)** from the slowest to the fastest memory: RAM, cache, registers; **(e)** instruction, execution; **(f)** throughput. **2–4 (a)** F; **(b)** T; **(c)** FLOPS or GFLOPS; **(d)** b. **2–5 (a)** microprocessor; **(b)** Pentium (or Pentium II), PowerPC; **(c)** T; **(d)** daisy-chained; **(e)** bus **(f)** b.

Focus on IT

The Computer on a Chip

The invention of the light bulb in 1879 symbolized the beginning of electronics. Electronics then evolved into the use of vacuum tubes, then transistors, and now integrated circuits. Today's microminiaturization of electronic circuitry is continuing to have a profound effect on the way we live and work.

Current technology permits the placement of hundreds of thousands of transistors and electronic switches on a single chip. Chips already fit into wristwatches and credit cards, but electrical and computer engineers want them even smaller. In electronics, smaller is better. The ENIAC, the first full-scale digital electronic computer, weighed 50 tons and occupied an entire room. Today, a computer far more powerful than the ENIAC can be fabricated within a single piece of silicon the size of a child's fingernail.

Chip designers think in terms of nanoseconds (one billionth of a second) and microns (one millionth of a meter). They want to pack as many circuit elements as they can into the structure of a chip. High-density packing reduces the time required for an electrical signal to travel from one circuit element to the next—resulting in faster computers. Circuit lines on the initial Intel processors (early 1980s) were 6.5 microns wide. Today's are less than .5 microns. The latter holds 35 million transistors and is 550 times as powerful as the initial one. By the turn of the century, researchers expect to break the .2 micro barrier.

Chips are designed and manufactured to perform a particular function. One chip might be a microprocessor for a personal computer. Another might be for primary storage or the logic for a talking vending machine. Cellular telephones use semiconductor memory chips.

The development of integrated circuits starts with a project review team made up of representatives from design, manufacturing, and marketing. This group works together to design a product the customer needs. Next, team members go through prototype wafer manufacturing to resolve potential manufacturing problems. Once a working prototype is produced, chips are manufactured in quantity and sent to computer, peripheral, telecommunications, and other customers.

The manufacturing of integrated circuits involves a multistep process using various photochemical etching and metallurgical techniques. This complex and interesting process is illustrated here with photos, from silicon to the finished product. The process is presented in five steps: design, fabrication, packaging, testing, and installation.

DESIGN

1. Using CAD for Chip Design Chip designers use computer-aided design (CAD) systems to create the logic for individual circuits. Although a chip can contain up to 30 layers, typically there are 10 to 20 patterned layers of varying material, with each layer performing a different purpose. In this multilayer circuit design, each layer is color-coded so the designer can distinguish between the various layers. Photo courtesy of Micron Semiconductor, Inc.

Chips

2. Creating a Mask The product designer's computerized drawing of each circuit layer is transformed into a *mask*, or *reticle*, a glass or quartz plate with an opaque material (such as chrome) formed to create the pattern. The number of layers depends on the complexity of the chip's logic. The Pentium™ processor, for example, contains 20 layers. When all these unique layers are combined, they create the millions of transistors and circuits that make up the architecture of the processor. Photo courtesy of Micron Semiconductor, Inc.

FABRICATION

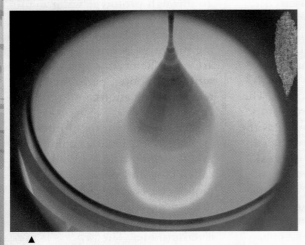

3. Creating Silicon Ingots Molten silicon is spun into cylindrical ingots. Because silicon, the second most abundant substance, is used in the fabrication of integrated circuits, chips are sometimes referred to as "intelligent grains of sand." © M/A-COM, Inc.

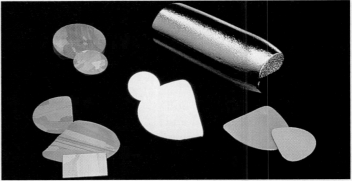

4. Cutting the Silicon Wafers The ingot is shaped and prepared prior to being cut into silicon wafers. Once the wafers are cut, they are polished to a perfect finish. © M/A-COM, Inc.

6. Keeping a Clean House Clean air continuously flows from every pore of the ceiling and through the holes in the floor into a filtering system at the manufacturing plant. A normal room contains some 15 million dust particles per cubic foot, but a clean room contains less than 1 dust particle per cubic foot. All of the air in a "clean room" is replaced seven times every minute.

Portions of the micro chip manufacturing process are performed in yellow light because the wafers are coated with a light-sensitive material called "photoresist" before the next chip pattern is imprinted onto the surface of the silicon wafer. Courtesy of Intel Corporation

5. Wearing Bunny Suits To help keep a clean environment, workers wear semi-custom-fitted Gortex® suits. They follow a hundred-step procedure when putting the suits on. Courtesy of Intel Corporation

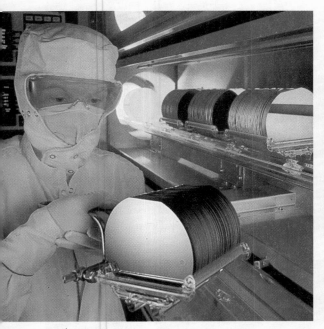

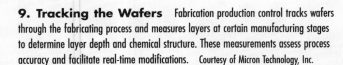

8. Etching the Wafer A photoresist is deposited onto the wafer surface creating a film-like substance to accept the patterned image. The mask is placed over the wafer and both are exposed to ultraviolet light. In this way the circuit pattern is transferred onto the wafer. The photoresist is developed, washing away the unwanted resist and leaving the exact image of the transferred pattern. Plasma (superhot gases) technology is used to etch the circuit pattern permanently into the wafer. This is one of several techniques used in the etching process. The wafer is returned to the furnace and given another coating on which to etch another circuit layer. The procedure is repeated for each circuit layer until the wafer is complete. AT&T Technologies

7. Coating the Wafers Silicon wafers that eventually will contain several hundred chips are placed in an oxygen furnace at 1200 degrees Celsius. In the furnace each wafer is coated with other minerals to create the physical properties needed to produce transistors and electronic switches on the surface of the wafer. Gould Inc.

9. Tracking the Wafers Fabrication production control tracks wafers through the fabricating process and measures layers at certain manufacturing stages to determine layer depth and chemical structure. These measurements assess process accuracy and facilitate real-time modifications. Courtesy of Micron Technology, Inc.

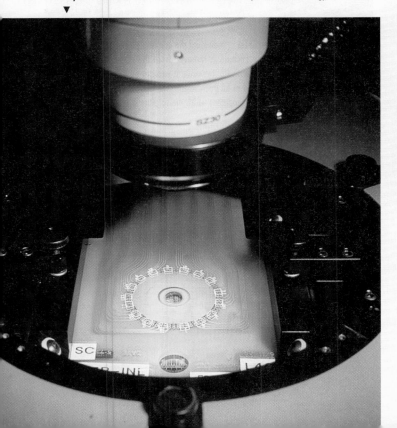

10. Drilling the Wafers It takes only a second for this instrument to drill 1440 tiny holes in a wafer. The holes enable the interconnection of the layers of circuits. Each layer must be perfectly aligned (within a millionth of a meter) with the others. Courtesy of International Business Machines Corporation. Unauthorized use not permitted.

PACKAGING

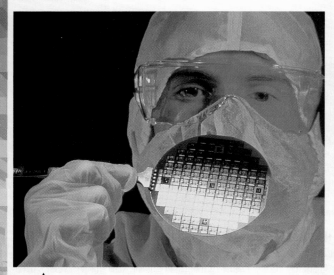

▲
11. Removing the Etched Wafers The result of the coating/etching process is a silicon wafer that contains from 100 to 400 integrated circuits, each of which includes millions of transistors.   National Semiconductor Corporation

▲
13. Dicing the Wafers A diamond-edged saw, with a thickness of a human hair, separates the wafer into individual processors, known as die, in a process called *dicing*. Water spray keeps the surface temperature low. After cutting, high-pressure water rinses the wafer clean. In some situations, special lasers are used to cut the wafers.   Courtesy of Micron Technology, Inc.

15. Packaging the Chips The chips are packaged in protective ceramic or metal carriers. The carriers have standard-sized electrical pin connectors that allow the chip to be plugged conveniently into circuit boards. Because the pins tend to corrode, the pin connectors are the most vulnerable part of a computer system. To avoid corrosion and a bad connection, the pins on some carriers are made of gold.   Courtesy of International Business Machines Corporation. Unauthorized use not permitted.

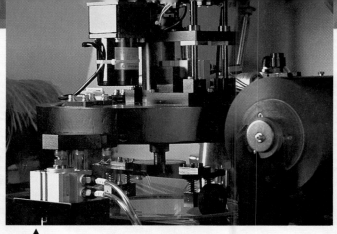

▲
12. Mounting the Wafers Each wafer is vacuum mounted onto a metal-framed sticky film tape. The wafer and metal frame are placed near the tape; then all three pieces are loaded into a vacuum chamber. A vacuum forces the tape smoothly onto the back of the wafer and metal frame.   Courtesy of Micron Technology, Inc.

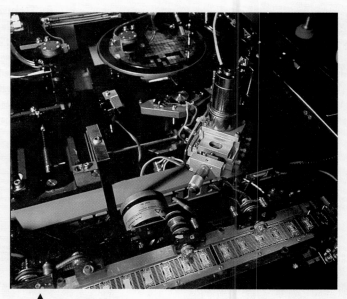

▲
14. Attaching the Die Individual die are attached to silver epoxy on the center area of a lead frame. Each die is removed from the tape with needles plunging up from underneath to push the die while a vacuum tip lifts the die from the tape. Lead frames are then heated in an oven to cure the epoxy. The wafer map created in probe tells the die-attach equipment which die to place on the lead frame.
Courtesy of Micron Technology, Inc.

▶

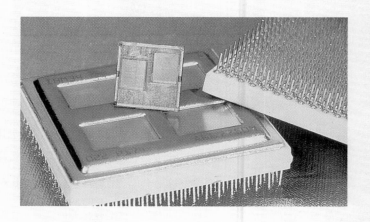

TESTING

◄ 16. Testing the Chips Each chip is tested to assess functionality and to see how fast it can store or retrieve information. Chip speed (or access time) is measured in nanoseconds (a billionth, 1/1,000,000,000th of a second). The precision demands are so great that as many as half the chips are found to be defective. A drop of ink is deposited on defective chips.   Courtesy of Micron Technology, Inc.

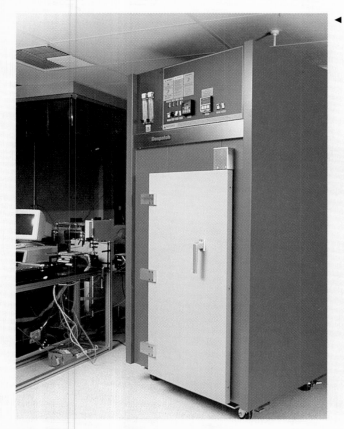

◄ 17. Burning In This burn-in oven runs performance tests on every chip simulating actual usage conditions. Each chip is tested by feeding information to the chip and querying for the information to ensure the chip is receiving, storing, and sending the correct data.   Courtesy of Micron Technology, Inc.

18. Scanning All chips are scanned, using optics or lasers, to discover any bent, missing, or incorrectly formed leads.   Courtesy of Micron Technology, Inc.

▼

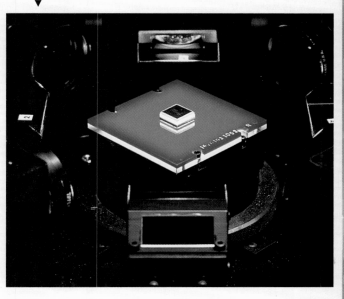

INSTALLATION

◄ **19. Creating Circuit Boards** Pick and place equipment precisely positions various chips on the solder and contacts. Completed boards are then heated in the reflow ovens, allowing the lead coating and solder to melt together, affixing the chip to the printed circuit board. Courtesy of Micron Technology, Inc.

20. Installing the Finished Chips ►
The completed circuit boards are installed in computers and thousands of other computer-controlled devices.
Courtesy of E-Systems

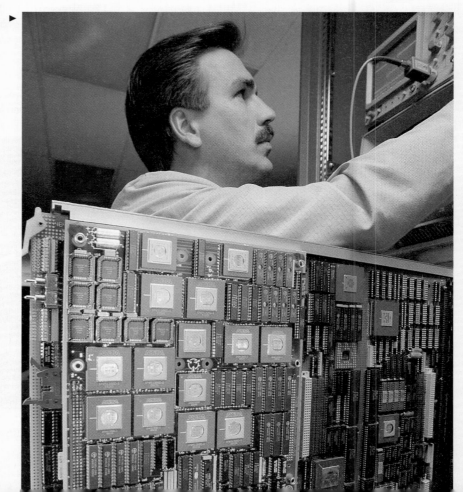

INTERNET BRIDGE

Serendipitous Surfing

Software: Telling Computers What to Do

LEARNING OBJECTIVES

- Understand common system software concepts.
- Detail the purpose and objectives of an operating system.
- Understand the relationship between computers and programming languages.
- Distinguish between several different types of programming languages.
- Describe the capabilities of visual programming languages and natural languages.
- Describe what constitutes a platform.
- Grasp concepts related to the effective use of computers and software.
- Describe various keyboard, mouse, and data entry conventions.

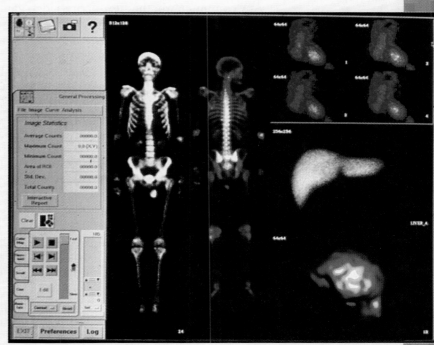

Courtesy of GE Medical Systems

LET'S TALK

Can you follow this conversation? It includes computing concepts presented in this chapter. Read it now, then reread it once you've had an opportunity to study the chapter.

The Scene The boss (Celeste), a certified cyberphobic, is seeking advice and compassion from her secretary (Jo Ellen).

CELESTE: I'm beginning to feel out of sync now that we've linked the PCs in a local area network and standardized on the Windows NT platform. Other managers are passing information and making decisions with the help of applications software for workgroup computing. . .

JO ELLEN: And you want in the loop?

CELESTE: You bet I do.

JO ELLEN: Two months ago I didn't know the difference between the foreground and the background. I suffered a mild case of cyberphobia but overcame it by learning a little something new each day. Now it's a snap to click and drag icons around the GUI. Today, I'm even learning to write macros in the Lotus 1-2-3 macro language.

CELESTE: You're so at ease with the computer. What's your secret?

JO ELLEN: No secret—I just used my manuals, the online help commands, and Rick, the guy at the help desk.

CELESTE: I think I'm ready to enter cyberland. Will you help me, Jo Ellen?

JO ELLEN: Sure, let's go in your office and boot your system.

(a couple of minutes later)

JO ELLEN: Let's begin with the main menu and call up a few dialog boxes to fine-tune your default options. Tomorrow we'll go over the basics: the menu bar, scrolling, cursor movement, and so on. How about I block out 30 minutes each morning for the next month on your electronic calendar?

CELESTE: Maybe a month from now I'll be keeping my own calendar!

3–1 Software in Perspective

**Monthly Technology Update
Chapter 3**

Any computer, whether it supports video games or an enterprise-wide information system, does nothing until given exact, step-by-step instructions by a human. We provide these instructions in the form of a computer *program*. How many instructions fit into a program? The program in a wristwatch has about 1000 instructions. The programs that control the space shuttle during flight have about the same number of instructions as those for a cash register—about 400,000. Word processing and spreadsheet programs have over a million instructions.

Most people commonly use the term *software* to refer to computer programs. Let's put software into perspective. Suppose you are sick in bed and you ask a friend to get you a glass of ice water. Your friend then instinctively goes to the kitchen, opens the cabinet door and selects a glass, opens the refrigerator, gets some ice, turns on the tap, fills the glass with water, returns to your bedside, and hands you the water. Now imagine making the same request to a computer. You would have to tell the computer not only where to get the water but also how to get there, which end of the glass to fill, when to shut off the water, and much, much more. Now you know why software has to have so many instructions!

Software alone won't make computers do what we want them to do. Instead, we interact with software to direct the overall activities within a computer system. For example, if you wish to print a spreadsheet, you choose *Print* from your spreadsheet software's menu of options. The print-routine program is executed, performing the internal operations needed to print your spreadsheet.

At the Olympic Games in Atlanta, Georgia, a vast network of computers and terminals gave officials and the media up-to-the-minute information on every competition at every venue. Officials and media personnel had immediate access to profiles of all the athletes as well as graphic illustrations that described all aspects of their sports and venues. Shown here are an image from an information kiosk and the press corps box at the cycling venue. Communications software (a type of system software) facilitated the transfer of information within the Olympics network. Applications software enabled people to get the information they need to do their jobs.   Courtesy of International Business Machines Corporation (Allsport/Jamie Squire). Unauthorized use not permitted.

At this point on your journey toward computer competency, you probably are feeling more comfortable with general computer hardware concepts than you were when you started. *Hardware*, however, is useless without *software*, and vice versa. This chapter should raise your comfort level with software.

Applications Explorer

3–2 System Software: Maintaining Control

Software refers to any program that tells the computer system what to do. Of course, there are many different types of software. The more you understand about the scope and variety of available software, the more effective you will be as a user. Actually, understanding software is a lot like being in a big house—once you know its layout, you're able to move about the house much easier.

The House of Software

Once but a cottage, the house of software is now a spacious eight-room house (by the turn of the century, it will be a mansion). Figure 3–1 shows the blueprint for today's house of software, with the rooms arranged by function. We'll visit every room in the house by the time you finish this book. In Chapter 1, we peeked in all of the rooms except one—system software. In this chapter, we'll relax in the system software room for a while. An understanding of the scope and function of system software will make your visits to the other rooms more enjoyable and fruitful.

System Software in Perspective: Behind the Scenes

The entryway in the house of software consists of **system software** (see Figure 3–1). When you turn on the computer, the first actions you see are directed by system software. It takes control of the PC on start up, then plays a central role in all interactions with the computer.

The *operating system* and the *graphical user interface (GUI)*, both system software, are at the heart of the software action (see Figure 3–2). All of the software in the

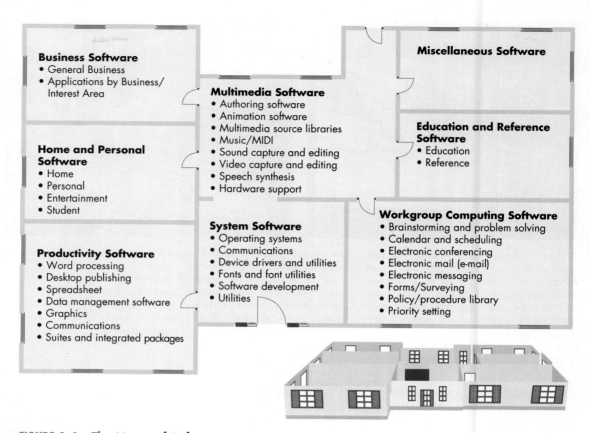

FIGURE 3–1 The House of Software
This blueprint shows the layout of the house of software. The rooms are laid out to feature software in eight major areas.

other rooms of the house depend on and interact with the **operating system,** the software that controls everything that happens in a computer, and its **graphical user interface (GUI),** which provides a user-friendly interface to the operating system. The software from the other rooms, collectively known as **applications software,** is designed and created to perform specific personal, business, or scientific processing tasks, such as word processing, tax planning, or interactive gaming. Figure 3–2 illustrates examples of and the relationship between system and applications software.

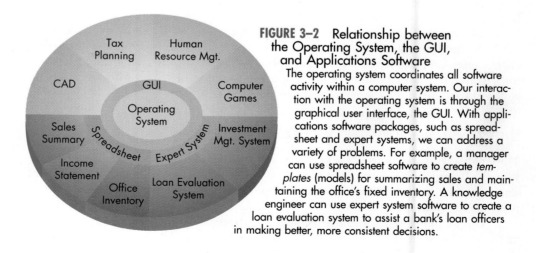

FIGURE 3–2 Relationship between the Operating System, the GUI, and Applications Software
The operating system coordinates all software activity within a computer system. Our interaction with the operating system is through the graphical user interface, the GUI. With applications software packages, such as spreadsheet and expert systems, we can address a variety of problems. For example, a manager can use spreadsheet software to create *templates* (models) for summarizing sales and maintaining the office's fixed inventory. A knowledge engineer can use expert system software to create a loan evaluation system to assist a bank's loan officers in making better, more consistent decisions.

When we go out to a movie, we see only a few of those responsible for making the film—the actors. We don't see the director, the producers, the writers, the editors, and many others. Perhaps it's because of this visual link that we, the audience, tend to become adoring fans of glamorous actors. We tend to forget the others involved in the film, even the director, the person who ties it all together and makes it happen. It's much the same with software. As software users, we tend to shower our praise on that which we see most often—the *applications software.* However, *system software,* like the film director, stays in the background and ties it all together. We'll discuss the most prominent of these behind-the-scenes players, the operating system.

3–3 The Operating System: Directing the Action

Just as the processor is the nucleus of the computer system, the *operating system* is the nucleus of all software activity (see Figure 3–2). The operating system is actually a family of *system software* programs that monitor and control all I/O and processing activities within a computer system. These programs are usually, although not always, supplied by the computer system vendor when you buy a computer. One of the operating system programs, often called the **kernel,** loads other operating system and applications programs to RAM as they are needed. The kernel is loaded to RAM on system start up and remains *resident*—available in RAM—until the system is turned off.

Operating Systems

All hardware and software are under the control of the operating system. It determines how valuable RAM is apportioned to programs, sets priorities for handling tasks, and manages the flow of information to and from the processor. To be an effective PC or workstation user, you will need a working knowledge of your system's operating system.

Operating System Objectives and Orientation

The operating system is what gives a *general-purpose computer,* such as a PC or a corporate mainframe, its flexibility to tackle a variety of jobs. (Most *dedicated computers,* such as those that control appliances and arcade games, are controlled by a single-function program and do not need a separate operating system.) Windows 98, Windows NT, and Mac OS are popular operating systems for PCs and workstations. These and other operating systems are discussed in Section 3–5. The use and functionality of the Windows 98 operating system is discussed in more detail in the Appendix, "The Windows Environment."

One of the best ways to understand an operating system is to understand its objectives. All operating systems are designed with the same basic objectives in mind. These objectives are listed and explained in Figure 3–3. The operating system objectives in Figure 3–3 apply to all computer systems. However, mainframe and PC operating systems differ markedly in complexity and orientation. On the mainframe, *multiuser operating systems* coordinate a number of special-function processors and monitor interaction with hundreds, even thousands, of terminals in a network. Most PC operating systems are designed primarily to support a *single user on a single micro,* that may or may not be linked to a network.

Living on a Budget: Allocating Computer Resources

We all must live within our means, and the same goes for computers. A conscientious shopper can stretch the value of a dollar and a good operating system can get the most from its limited resources. Any computer system's most precious resource is its processor. Operating systems get the most from their processors through multitasking. **Multitasking** is the *concurrent* execution of more than one program at a time. Actually, a single computer can execute only one program at a time. However, its internal processing speed is so fast that several programs can be allocated "slices" of

OPERATING SYSTEM OBJECTIVES

1. To facilitate communication between the computer system and the people who run it.	The interface through which users issue system-related commands is part of the operating system.
2. To facilitate communication among computer system components.	The operating system facilitates the movement of internal instructions and data between peripheral devices, the processor, programs, and the computer's storage.
3. To maximize throughput.	The operating system coordinates system resources to maximize throughput, the amount of processing per unit of time.
4. To minimize the time needed to execute a user command.	In today's interactive systems, even small decreases in user wait time pay big dividends in user efficiency.
5. To optimize the use of computer system resources.	The operating system is continually looking at what tasks need to be done and what resources (processor, RAM, and peripheral devices) are available to accomplish these tasks. The incredible speed of a computer system dictates that resource-allocation decisions be made at computer speeds. Each millisecond the operating system makes decisions about what resources to assign to which tasks.
6. To keep track of all files in disk storage.	The operating system and its file and disk management utility programs enable users to perform such tasks as making backup copies of work disks, erasing disk files that are no longer needed, making inquiries about the number and type of files on a particular disk, and preparing new disks for use. The operating system also handles many file- and disk-oriented tasks that are *transparent* (invisible) to the end user. For example, operating systems keep track of the physical location of disk files so that we, as users, need only refer to them by name (for example, myfile or year-end-summary) when loading them from disk to RAM.
7. To provide an envelope of security for the computer system.	The operating system can allow or deny user access to the system as a whole or to individual files. Specific security measures, such as passwords, are discussed later in the book.
8. To monitor all systems capabilities and alert the user of system failure or potential problems.	The operating system is continually checking system components for proper operation. Any problems are brought immediately to the attention of the user.

FIGURE 3–3 Objectives of an Operating System
The operating system is continually checking system components for proper operation. Any problems are brought immediately to the attention of the user.

computer time in rotation, making it appear that several programs are being executed at once.

The great difference in processor speed and the speeds of the peripheral devices makes multitasking possible. The speed of a 22-page-per-minute printer does not even come close to the speed of a low-end PC. The computer's processor is continually waiting for peripheral devices to complete such tasks as retrieving a record from disk storage or printing a report. During these waiting periods, the processor just continues processing other programs. The operating system ensures that the most appropriate resources are allocated to competing tasks in the most efficient manner.

In a multitasking environment, programs running concurrently are controlled and assigned priorities by the operating system. For example, you can prepare a graphics presentation on CorelDRAW, while sending an Excel spreadsheet document over the fax modem and backing up the hard disk to a tape. The **foreground** is that part of RAM containing the active or current program (CorelDRAW in the example) and is usually given priority by the operating system. Other lower-priority programs, such as the fax transmittal and the backup in the example, are run in the **background** part of RAM. The operating system rotates allocation of the processor resource between foreground and background programs, with the foreground programs receiving the lion's share of the processor's attention.

The Graphical User Interface: Goodie "Gooie"

To appreciate the impact and significance of graphical user interfaces, you need to understand what preceded them.

TEXT-BASED SOFTWARE Through the 1980s, the most popular microcomputer operating system, **MS-DOS,** was strictly *text-based, command-driven* software. That is, we issued commands directly to DOS (the MS-DOS nickname) by entering them on the keyboard, one character at a time. For example, if you had wished to issue a command to copy a word processing document from one disk to another for your friend, you might have entered "copy c:\myfile a:\yourfile" via the keyboard at the DOS prompt, "C:\ > ".

C:\ > copy c:\myfile a:\yourfile

When using command-driven, text-based software you must be explicit. In the previous example, you could not just enter "copy" or even "copy MYFILE". You would have to enter the command that tells the PC where to find MYFILE and where to make the copy. If you omitted necessary information in a command or the format of the command was incorrect, an error message would be displayed and/or an on-screen prompt would request that you reenter the command. Command-driven DOS, in particular, demanded strict adherence to command **syntax,** the rules for entering commands, such as word spacing, punctuation, and so on.

GRAPHICS-BASED SOFTWARE Today, relatively few computers run with purely text-based operating systems. For the past decade, the trend in microcomputer operating systems has been toward a user-friendly, graphics-oriented environment—the graphical user interface, or GUI (pronounced *"G-U-I"* or *"gooie"*). Graphical user interfaces rely on graphics-based software, which permits the integration of text with graphic images (see Figure 3–4).

All modern operating systems, including the *Windows 95* and *Windows 98* operating systems, provide GUIs. GUI users interact with the operating system and other software packages by using a pointing device (for example, a mouse) and a keyboard to issue commands. Rather than enter a command directly, as in a command-driven interface, the user chooses from options displayed on the screen. The equivalent of a syntax-sensitive operating system command is entered by pointing to and choosing one or more options from menus or by pointing to and choosing a graphics image, called an **icon.**

FIGURE 3–4 Icons
Each of the icons in this Microsoft Windows 95 display represents an available program. To run a program, simply use the mouse to point to and click on the desired icon.

An icon is a graphic rendering that represents a processing activity. For example, the file folder icon or the file cabinet icon generally represents processing activities associated with file management. Users might choose the "trash can" icon to delete a file from disk storage. Figure 3–4 shows a screen with a variety of symbolic icons from the Windows 95 operating system, which is discussed in more detail in the Appendix.

GUIs have effectively eliminated the need for users to memorize and enter cumbersome commands. For example, GUIs permit a file to be copied from one disk to another disk by repositioning the file's icon from one area on the screen to another.

3–4 Programming Languages: Computertalk

Programming

The instructions in programs are logically sequenced and assembled through the act of **programming. Programmers,** people who write programs, use a variety of **programming languages,** such as C++, Visual BASIC, and Java, to communicate instructions to the computer. Twenty years ago, virtually all programmers were computer specialists. Today, office managers, management consultants, engineers, politicians, and people in all walks of life write programs to meet business and domestic needs. And, some people do it for fun. Unless you plan on becoming a computer professional, it is unlikely that you will write programs in support of an enterprise-wide information system. You may, however, write programs to perform many personal tasks, such as preparing graphs from spreadsheet data and sequencing displays for multimedia presentations. As you develop expertise and confidence you may tackle more challenging programming tasks.

Many languages have emerged over thousands of years of spoken communication. Although computers have existed for only a short while, there are already as many programming languages as there are spoken languages. In this section, we will sort out these languages and explain what they mean to you.

Programming has come a long way in 50 years. Early programmers had to set hundreds of switches manually to enter a program. To run another program, they had to reset the switches. Today, the technology assists us in the programming effort while providing us with a user-friendly interface.
Photo courtesy of Hewlett-Packard Company/Courtesy of International Business Machines Corporation. Unauthorized use not permitted.

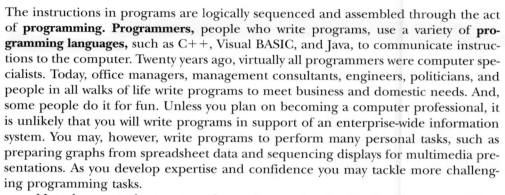

Computer Programs: The Power of Logic

We use programming languages to write programs. A single program addresses a particular problem—to compute grades, to monitor a patient's heart rate, and so on. In effect, when you write a program, you are solving a *problem*, which requires you to use your powers of *logic* to develop a procedure for solving the problem. Creating a program is like constructing a building. Much of the brainwork involved in the construction goes into the blueprint. The location, appearance, and function of a building are determined long before the first brick is laid. With programming, the design of a program, or its *programming logic* (the blueprint), is completed before the program is written.

Each programming language has an instruction set with several instructions in each of the following *instruction classifications*.

- *Input/output instructions* direct the computer to "read from" or "write to" a peripheral device (for example, a printer or disk drive).
- *Computation instructions* direct the computer to perform arithmetic operations (add, subtract, multiply, divide, and raise a number to a power). For example, PAY = HOURS * RATE computes gross earnings for hourly employees.
- *Control instructions* can alter the sequence of the program's execution or terminate execution. For example, in an accounts receivable program, different sequences of instructions are executed for customers who pay on time and for those who pay after the due date.
- *Assignment instructions* transfer data internally from one RAM location to another.
- *Format instructions* are used in conjunction with input and output instructions (for example, where data are placed on a page).

The traditional computer program consists of a sequence of instructions that are executed in order unless the order is altered by a control instruction. With these few instruction sets, you can create software to model almost any business or scientific procedure, whether it be sales forecasting or guiding rockets to the moon.

Types of Programming Languages

We "talk" to computers within the framework of a particular programming language, and the selection of a programming language depends on who is doing the talking and the nature of the "conversation." For example, we use one language to create enterprise-wide information systems and another to prepare a dynamic sales presentation. There are many different types of programming languages in use today.

MACHINE LANGUAGE: NATIVE TONGUE In Chapter 2 we learned that all programs are ultimately executed in machine language, the computer's native language. Creating programs in machine language is a cumbersome process, so we write programs in more programmer-friendly programming languages. However, our resulting programs must be translated into machine language before they can be executed.

PROCEDURE-ORIENTED LANGUAGES The introduction of more user-friendly programming languages (in 1955) resulted in a quantum leap in programmer convenience. Programmers could write a single instruction instead of several cumbersome machine-language instructions. These early languages were **procedure-oriented languages,** which require programmers to solve programming problems using traditional programming logic. That is, programmers code, or write, the instructions in the sequence in which they must be executed to solve the problem. Examples of procedure-oriented languages include *COBOL* (see Figure 3–5) and *FORTRAN*, both introduced in late 1950s but still popular today.

```
0100   IDENTIFICATION DIVISION.
0200   PROGRAM-ID.              PAYPROG.
0300   REMARKS.        PROGRAM TO COMPUTE GROSS PAY.
0400   ENVIRONMENT DIVISION.
0500   DATA DIVISION.
0600   WORKING-STORAGE SECTION.
0700   01 PAY DATA.
0800        05 HOURSPIC 99V99.
0900        05 RATE PIC 99V99.
1000        05 PAY         PIC 9999V99.
1100   01 LINE-1.
1200        03 FILLER     PIC X(5).      VALUE SPACES.
1300        03 FILLER     PIC X(12).     VALUE "GROSS PAY IS."
1400        03 GROSS-PAY  PIC $$$$9.99.
1500   01 PRINT-LINE.     PIC X(27).
1600   PROCEDURE DIVISION.
1700   MAINLINE-PROCEDURE.
1800        PERFORM ENTER-PAY.
1900   PERFORM COMPUTE-PAY.
2000   PERFORM PRINT-PAY.
2100   STOP RUN.
2200   ENTER-PAY.
2300        DISPLAY "ENTER HOURS AND RATE OF PAY."
2400        ACCEPT HOURS, RATE.
2500   COMPUTE-PAY.
2600        MULTIPLY HOURS BY RATE GIVING PAY ROUNDED.
2700   PRINT PAY.
2800        MOVE PAY TO GROSS-PAY.
2900        MOVE LINE-1 TO PRINT-LINE.
3000        DISPLAY PRINT-LINE.
```

Enter hours and rate of pay
43, 8.25
                    Gross pay is $354.75

FIGURE 3–5   A COBOL Program
This COBOL program accepts the number of hours worked and the pay rate for an hourly
wage earner, then computes and displays the gross pay amount. The interactive session below
the program listing shows the input prompt, the values entered by the user, and the result.

OBJECT-ORIENTED LANGUAGES AND OOP   In procedure-oriented languages, the
emphasis is on *what* is done (the procedure). In **object-oriented languages,** the emphasis is on the *object* of the action. The structure of **object-oriented programming
(OOP)** makes programs easier to design and understand. Also, OOP (rhymes with
"*hoop*") handles images, videos, and sound better than do procedure-oriented languages. Examples of object-oriented languages include *Smalltalk* and *C++*.

THE FOURTH GENERATION: 4GLs   Most of the programming in procedure- and
object-oriented languages is done by computer specialists. Programming in user-
friendly **fourth-generation languages (4GLs)** is done by computer specialists and also
a growing legion of end users. Users write 4GL programs to query (extract information from) a database and to create personal or departmental information systems.

   Fourth-generation languages use high-level English-like instructions to retrieve
and format data for inquiries and reporting. Most of the procedure portion of a 4GL
program is generated automatically by the computer and the language software. That
is, for the most part the programmer specifies what to do, *not* how to do it.

   Fourth-generation languages are effective tools for generating responses to a variety of requests for information. A few simple 4GL instructions are all that are needed
to respond to the following typical management requests:

- Which employees have accumulated more than 20 sick days since May 1?

- Which deluxe single hospital rooms, if any, will be vacated by the end of the
  day?

- List departments that have exceeded their budgets alphabetically by the department head's name.

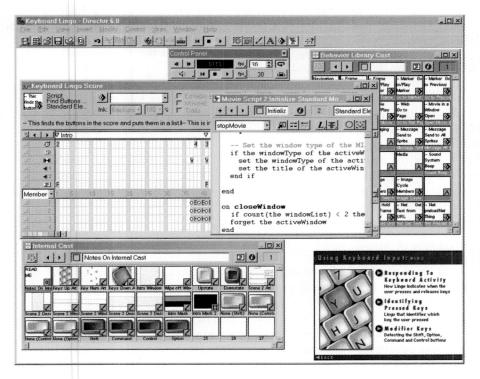

FIGURE 3–6 Visual Programming
Macromedia Director 6 "movies," which are interactive multimedia images, are the result of a scripting program. A variety of Director visual programming enables the creation of the program (see center of example). When played, the resulting "Using Keyboard Input" (lower right) demonstrates interactively, with sound and motion, the use of a keyboard. The Score window (top left) graphically illustrates the sequencing and play attributes of the elements in the Director "movie." The Internal Cast window (bottom left) shows the members of the cast (elements under program control). Members of the cast can be assigned a particular type of behavior using the Behavior Library Cast window.

VISUAL LANGUAGES: ICONS FOR WORDS   Programming for today's applications with their GUIs is far more complex than programming for the text-based applications of the 1970s and 1980s. Switching to the efficiency of object-oriented programming (OOP) helped programmers keep pace for a while, but the sheer volume of instructions needed to create GUI-based software can be overwhelming. Enter visual programming. As they say, a picture is worth a thousand words, and so it is in programming. **Visual programming** takes object-oriented programming to the next level, replacing text-based instructions with symbolic icons, each of which represents an object or a common programming function (see Figure 3–6). Microsoft's **Visual BASIC** is one of the most popular visual languages for both the casual user and the professional software developer (see Figure 3–7).

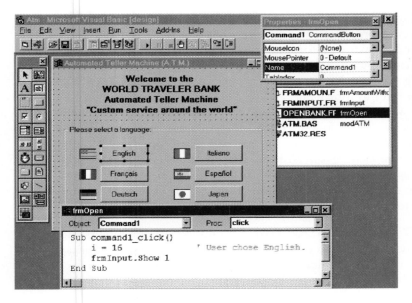

FIGURE 3–7 Visual BASIC
Microsoft Visual BASIC, shown here, offers an easy-to-learn visual development environment. A Visual BASIC programmer used visual programming capabilities to create the interface for an ATM (automatic teller machine). This screen asks the user to select a language to be used during the ATM interaction. The screen was created by moving appropriate objects to the form. Separate windows show programming code and properties for the highlighted "English" button.

NATURAL LANGUAGES: THE ULTIMATE PROGRAMMING LANGUAGE **Natural languages** refer to software that enables computer systems to accept, interpret, and execute instructions in the native, or "natural," language of the end user—typically, English. The premise behind a natural language is that the programmer or user needs little or no training. The programmer simply writes, or perhaps speaks, processing specifications without regard for instruction syntax (the rules by which instructions are formulated). In theory, people using natural languages are not constrained by the instruction syntax inherent in traditional programming languages. In practice, however, there are limitations.

The state of the art of natural languages is still somewhat primitive. Researchers are currently working to develop pure natural languages that permit an unrestricted dialogue between us and a computer. Although the creation of such a language is difficult to comprehend, it is probably inevitable.

Programming and You

As you continue to gain experience with PCs and PC software, you, like so many before you, will probably begin to seek greater speed, power, and efficiency from your PC and its software. To gain speed and power, you will need to upgrade your hardware with the latest technology. To improve efficiency, you might wish to consider learning to write programs—yes, programs. You do not have to be a professional programmer—most people who program are not. They are users who write programs to accomplish personal processing objectives. Many users who write programs get hooked on the benefits of programming by using time-saving macros.

The Java language, created by Sun Microsystems, is a programming environment for the Internet. Java is designed for programmers who wish to develop new publishing and interactive multimedia applications for the Internet. Java enables both the professional and the casual programmer to create dynamic multimedia-based online applications.   Courtesy of Sun Microsystems, Inc.

MACROS: PAST AND PRESENT   As end users, we issue commands and initiate operations by selecting activities to be performed from a *hierarchy of menus*. A **menu** is simply a list of options for the user. When we choose an item on a menu, that operation is performed and the applications software causes the system to wait for further commands. We select operations (menu items) one at a time until we have accomplished what we wish to do. This one-at-a-time approach to system interaction is fine for one-time jobs, such as preparing and printing a sales summary bar chart. However, what if you prepare the same charts from an updated spreadsheet at the end of each week? Then, you might wish to consider creating a macro to do the job automatically. A **macro** is a sequence of frequently used operations or keystrokes that can be recalled as needed. A macro is actually a *short program*, containing a sequence of instructions to be performed.

The original macro concept grew from a need to automate repetitive interactions with applications software. The first macros (for spreadsheet and word processing software) simply recorded command interactions for replay at a later time. *Record-and-play macros* are handy for performing interactions that are done over and over. Straightforward macros can be created easily by recording operations as they are entered, then storing their sequence on disk for later recall. To **invoke,** or execute, the macro, you simply refer to it by name.

Today's users want more than record-and-play macros. For example, they want to be able to play macros that include user-defined conditions. In response to this need, software vendors began distributing their software with **macro languages.** Most of today's office software (word processing, spreadsheet, database, and so on) have their own powerful macro language. These languages are like procedure-oriented languages, except each is designed to support a particular piece of software. Users can write programs to do simple tasks or to create comprehensive office information systems (see Figure 3–8).

THE TREND IS SET: PROGRAM YOUR OWN   Professional programmers and system developers focus their energies on enterprise-wide information systems. Perhaps more companies should make programmers available to end users to assist users with personal processing objectives, but, in reality, few do. In general, if you want to create a macro or write a macro program, you will need to do it yourself. There are literally millions of PC users who routinely play macros and run their own programs, most of whom never dreamed they would write a program. It's not unusual to talk with users who attribute savings of two to fifteen hours a week to the programs they wrote.

3–5 Platforms: Homes for Software

A **platform** defines a standard for which software packages are developed. Specifically, a platform is defined by two key elements:

- The processor (for example, Intel Pentium II or PowerPC)
- The operating system (for example, Mac OS or Windows NT)

Generally, software created to run on one platform is not compatible with any other platform.

The typical computer system, large or small, runs under a single platform. However, some can be configured to run several platforms. A multiplatform computer runs its native platform and *emulates* other platforms. Although emulation adds flexibility, programs running in emulation mode run more slowly than they do if run on the real thing.

INTERNET BRIDGE

Serendipitous Surfing: Travel

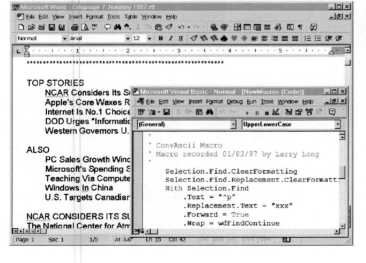

FIGURE 3–8 Microsoft Word 97 Macro Programming Language
The macro programming language for Microsoft Office 97 applications, including Word 97, is Visual BASIC. This partially displayed macro in the Visual BASIC window converts basic text files to a format that is more compatible with word processing.

The selection of a platform is important because it establishes boundaries for what you can and cannot do with your computer system. Before choosing a platform consider the following:

- Availability of appropriate commercial applications software for the platform
- Compatibility of platform with existing hardware, software, and expertise (a heavy investment in one platform often deters people from switching to another)

PC Platforms

In the mainframe environment, choosing a platform is the responsibility of computer specialists. Typically, in the PC environment, you—the individual user—are responsible for selecting the platform. The following discussion will provide some insight into that decision process. Our discussion will focus on the most common personal computing environments, one characterized by PC-compatible computers and the other by the Apple Macintosh series of computers. The following platforms are designed for use by a single user.

MS-DOS AND WINDOWS WITH PC-COMPATIBLES The PC-compatible platforms of the modern era are the Microsoft Windows family of operating systems: Windows 95, Windows 98, Windows NT, and Windows CE. However, two other operating systems ruled the PC-compatible environment for 15 years: *MS-DOS* and *Windows*. Through 1990, the platform of choice for the majority of PC users was defined by PCs that are functionally compatible with the 1984 IBM PC-AT architecture (the Intel family of microprocessors) and run under MS-DOS. Although the wide popularity of the modern Windows family and its user-friendly graphical user interface has all but eliminated the use of MS-DOS for modern computing, there are still a few loyal DOS fans.

The original Microsoft's **Windows,** which introduced the GUI to the PC-compatible environment, was introduced in 1987 and made obsolete with the introduction of Windows 95 in 1995 (see Figure 3–9). It, however, is still used by many individuals and companies who have chosen not to make the upgrade. Windows runs within MS-DOS. Think of Windows as a subplatform running under the MS-DOS platform. MS-DOS programs that do not conform to Windows standards can still be run within Windows, though. These programs, called *non-Windows* programs, are no less effective when run within Windows, but they cannot take full advantage of the Windows capabilities.

FIGURE 3–9 The Windows 98 Operating System
The popular Microsoft Windows 98 platform has a user-friendly graphical user interface (GUI). The programs currently open in this image include (clockwise) Outlook 98 (calendar, e-mail, journal, address book, and so on), Macromedia Director (multimedia development tool), Hijaak Pro (graphics viewing and conversion) and PointCast (online news service). Both Windows 98 and its predecessor, Windows 95, are widely used.

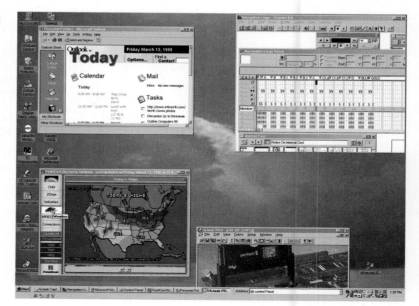

THE PC/WINDOWS PLATFORMS: 95, 98, NT, AND CE   Windows 95, 98, NT, and CE have almost, but not quite, replaced MS-DOS and the original Windows in the PC-compatible environment. Windows 95, a truly user-friendly operating system, has an interface that strikes a balance between usability for the novice and power for the expert. Unlike its predecessor, Windows 95 does not need the antiquated MS-DOS operating system to run.

The PC/Windows platforms offer many advantages over their predecessors, including **plug-and-play** capability. Plug-and-play refers to making a peripheral device or an expansion board immediately operational by simply plugging it into a port or an expansion slot. Users no longer have to juggle limited system resources, such as I/O ports, to eliminate system-level conflicts. Another major advantage of Windows 95 is its ability to run 32-bit programs; that is, programs that use the full 32-bit data paths in the processor. (MS-DOS and the original Windows are 16-bit operating systems.) Windows 95 features and functionality are discussed in the Appendix. All members of the PC/Windows family have a similar look and feel.

Each member of the Windows family of operating systems plays an important role in Microsoft's strategy for the future of personal computing. The following descriptions for the family members should provide some insight into the roles they play.

- *Windows 95 and Windows 98.* **Windows 95** and **Windows 98** are operating systems designed to bridge the technology gap between the original Windows and Windows NT. Most individuals and companies were not technologically prepared or willing to jump directly to Windows NT, the most sophisticated of the Windows family of operating systems. Bill Gates, the founder of Microsoft, has made it clear that ". . . Windows 95 was a milestone, not a destination." The primary difference between Windows 95 and Windows 98 is that the latter integrates the Internet into the operating system. After Windows 98, users will be expected to upgrade to Windows NT.

- *Windows NT.* **Windows NT** is the future of the PC/Windows family of operating systems. Windows NT is a powerful client/server operating system that is emerging as the choice for businesses doing client/server computing. Windows NT has two components: **Windows NT Workstation,** the client-side operating system, and **Windows NT Server,** the server-side portion of the operating system (runs on the server computer). The two work together to enable client/server computing. Windows NT Workstation has the look and feel of Windows 98, but it has a number of additional features, most of which have to do with security and networking. The Windows NT Workstation system's requirements are greater than those for Windows 95 and Windows 98. A high-end PC is needed to run Windows NT Workstation.

   Windows NT is among the new wave of client/server platforms supporting LAN-based **workgroup computing.** Workgroup computing allows people on a network to use the network to foster cooperation and the sharing of ideas and resources. **Groupware,** such as electronic messaging, calendar, brainstorming, and scheduling, is developed to run under workgroup platforms.

- *Windows CE.* The **Windows CE** operating system is designed for handheld and pocket PCs. Its look and feel are similar to the other members of the family. Windows CE users can share information with other Windows-based PCs. And, they can connect to the Internet.

The Cassiopeia Handheld PC comes with a ROM-based Windows CE operating system for mobile computing. The Cassiopeia can run up to 20 hours on two "AA" batteries.   Courtesy of Casio, Inc.

THE MACINTOSH/MAC OS PLATFORM   The Apple family of microcomputers (including the Macintosh and Powerbook computers) and its operating system, **Mac OS** (see Figure 3-10), define another major platform. About one in every 10 PCs runs under this platform. The Apple line of microcomputers is based on the Motorola family of microprocessors. One inviting feature of Apple's Mac OS is that it can be adjusted to fit the user's level of expertise.

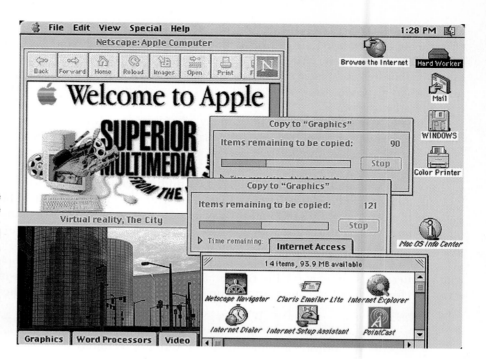

FIGURE 3–10 The Mac OS
Apple Computer Company introduced the GUI concept almost 15 years ago, and the Mac OS operating system (shown here) continues the GUI tradition. Apple has adopted a dual-operating system strategy that offers customers the choice of staying with the Mac OS or transitioning to their new "industrial strength" Rhapsody operating system. The new operating system will run on the new line Macintosh PCs, plus it will run on Intel-based PCs, as well.   Courtesy of Apple Computer, Inc.

PC PLATFORM OPTIONS: WHICH TO CHOOSE?   Several personal computing platform options, including **UNIX** (another popular operating system), await new and existing PC users; but which one is right for you? Your choice depends on your circumstances (knowledge, compatibility with office PCs, existing configuration, budget, and so on) and personal preferences.

Platform Problems: Interoperability and Cross-Platform Technologies

Many companies purchase and maintain a fleet of automobiles for use by employees. Companies routinely exchange entire fleets of Chevys for Fords (and vice versa) without any loss of functionality. Employees simply come to work in a Chevy and drive away in a Ford. It's not unusual for companies to rotate between major manufacturers every couple of years. The decision to go with Chrysler or Toyota doesn't commit a company over the long term. The choice of a computer platform, however, involves substantial commitment.

When you decide on a particular platform, you begin to purchase and create resources for that platform. The investment required in selecting a platform demands a long-term commitment—at least five years. This type of commitment makes choosing a platform at the individual or company level a very important decision.

All companies have platform problems, although some to a lesser extent than others. Those that standardized on platforms can enjoy the benefits of easily shared resources (from data to printers). Those that did not must do some work to achieve interoperability. **Interoperability** refers to the ability to run software and exchange information in a **multiplatform environment** (a computing environment of more than one platform). Enabling technologies that allow communication and the sharing of resources between different platforms are called **cross-platform technologies.** Multiplatform organizations use cross-platform technologies, both hardware and software, to link PCs, workstations, LANs, mainframes, and so on. Multiplatform environments are more the rule than the exception in medium-sized and large organizations. Whenever possible, companies try to minimize the number of platforms represented in the company. The fewer the number of platforms, the less the hassle and expense associated with installing and maintaining cross-platform technologies.

This airport management system software helps operators control gate scheduling, security, baggage handling, and other operations for this international airport. The chart in the background graphically depicts the activity throughout the airport. Trouble spots or conflicts are highlighted.
Courtesy of Harris Corporation

3–6 Interacting with the PC and Its Software

The thesaurus lists these synonyms for the word *interact: blend, associate, hobnob, mingle, combine, mix, stir,* and *socialize.* To some extent we do all of these, even socialize, when we *interact* with PCs and their software. Most of us will interact directly with a personal computer or a workstation that may or may not be linked to a network or the Internet. Or we will interact with a terminal linked to a mainframe or a supercomputer in a remote location. The look and feel of a modern terminal is very much like that of the PC, except that the actual processing is done on a remote computer.

To interact effectively with a computer and its software, you need to be knowledgeable in four areas.

1. General software concepts
2. The operation and use of the hardware over which you have control
3. The function and use of the computer's operating system and/or its graphical user interface (GUI), both of which provide a link between you, the computer system, and the various applications programs
4. The specific applications programs you are using

The first three areas are *prerequisites* to the fourth. That is, you will need a working knowledge of software concepts, hardware, and the operating system and/or a GUI before you can make effective use of Quicken (accounting), PowerPoint (presentation graphics), Paradox (database), or any of the thousands of software packages on the market today.

Computer Operation: Getting Started

Who operates computers? Probably you do. End users, especially those of PCs and workstations, routinely do everything from unpacking boxes of hardware to installing and using the software.

INSTALLING HARDWARE AND SOFTWARE When you purchase a computer system, typically you will receive several boxes containing the various components of the system. Unless it is a portable computer, your system will come in several pieces: a keyboard, a mouse, a monitor, a printer, and a processor unit that houses the magnetic disk drives. Normally you can complete the installation of the hardware simply by link-

EMERGING TECHNOLOGY

Tailoring PCs to the Needs of Mobile Workers

Electronic Fashion Statement

THOUSANDS OF MOBILE WORKERS COULD benefit from using a computer—if only the computer were lighter, freed their hands, and didn't tether them to a desk or a power outlet. Now a new generation of wearable computers promises to extend the trend begun by laptop, notebook, and pen-based computers.

Prototypes of wearable computers, long a staple of science fiction, are already being promoted by Japan's NEC Corporation. In an effort to create truly personal computers that meld a computer and its user, NEC designers have divided the PC's components into cable-connected modules that fit into headsets, drape across shoulders, hang around the neck, and fasten around the waist, forearm, or wrist. Lightweight (about two pounds or less), the components would be covered in soft plastic and strapped on with Velcro.

Many of these prototypes combine existing or emerging technologies to create customized PCs for specific types of workers. The TLC (Tender Loving Care) PC for paramedics is a good example. At an accident scene, speech-recognition software would let the paramedic dictate symptoms and vital signs into a slender microphone hanging from a headset. The computer, draped across the medic's shoulders like a shawl, would compare this data to a CD-ROM medical directory in the shoulder unit. The computer would then project possible diagnoses and suggested treatments onto the headset's goggle-type display. The TLC unit would also improve upon the two-way radio medics now use to communicate with emergency-room doctors. Instead of

The Future of PCs? At NEC a handful of engineers and designers are creating what they believe to be the future of PCs—wearable PCs. Their objective is to blend the machine with the body. Courtesy NEC Corporation, Tokyo, Japan

describing symptoms over a two-way radio, medics could use a trackball-operated video camera and body sensor strapped to their palm to *show* doctors the patients' condition. The video and additional data would be beamed to the doctors by a satellite link on the medics' back. Headphones would let the medics get feedback and additional advice from the waiting doctors.

Wearable Computers and Body Nets

Given the industry's ongoing success in miniaturizing electronics and developing more powerful but lightweight batteries, we should expect a range of commercially viable wearable PCs to appear by the late 1990s. However, GRiD Systems Corporation, pioneer of the pen-based computer, isn't waiting. It has already introduced the Palmpad, a rugged 2.8-pound computer designed to be worn on a belt, slung over a shoulder, or strapped to a wrist. MIT's Media Lab has produced another wearable computer. This one is worn as a pair of eyeglasses. In it are a tiny computer and screen that you wear over one eye to read news feeds automatically downloaded throughout the day.

Perhaps the most intriguing concept in wearable computers is the Body Net. The Body Net will be a network of wearable computers strategically located over the body. For example, the shoe-based computer might detect your location, then transmit appropriate location-specific information for viewing on your eyeglasses computer. Perhaps by the twenty-first century, the PC will become as much an essential part of one's wardrobe as an indispensable business tool.

ing the pieces of the system with the various types of cables. A computer, however, does nothing without software.

Many new PCs are sold with the operating system and, perhaps, a few applications already installed (stored on the hard disk and ready to run). If not, you must install the software—first the operating system, then any applications software you intend to run. Even if your new system includes some software, you will likely install other software as well. **Software installation** involves copying the program and data files from the vendor-supplied master disks or CD-ROMs to the permanently installed hard disk. Software installation is a two-step process for the operating system and all applications software packages.

Software installation step 1: Install or set up software. Most new commercial software is distributed on *CD-ROM* (some of the smaller programs are available on $3\frac{1}{2}$-inch diskettes). This normally straightforward installation process can take up to an hour depending on the complexity of the software, the distribution media, and the speed of the PC. Installing programs from CD-ROM is a relatively standard and straightforward procedure.

- Insert the CD-ROM. If installing within Windows 95, enter *d:setup* or *d:install* (where *d* is the letter of the CD-ROM drive) at the Run command line (click on the Start button, then select Run). The software is installed on hard-disk Drive C unless you indicate otherwise.

- Depending on the software, you may be asked to respond to several questions. For example, you may be asked to confirm certain sound card options.

Many CD-ROM–based applications, especially games, are designed to be run entirely, or at least in part, from the CD-ROM. However, because CD-ROM is relatively slow, critical programs are loaded to the hard disk during installation to speed up the running of the overall software package. Most business programs, such as word processing, presentation graphics, and so on, are copied in their entirety to hard disk.

Software installation step 2: Set system information. Applications software is installed to accommodate the "typical" PC. You may need to revise some of the standard settings to better fit your PC's specific configuration. You may be prompted to make some of these changes automatically during software installation. Also, you may wish to customize an application to better meet your processing needs. If so, you will probably need to revise certain **default options** (standard settings), such as location of data files, display colors, and so on.

HELP! If you run into a problem after installation, help is never farther away than your keyboard. A handy feature available on nearly all modern software packages is the **help command.** When you find yourself in need of a more detailed explanation or instructions on how to proceed, tap the *Help* key, often assigned to Function Key 1 (F1), or choose *Help* from the main menu. The resulting explanation relates to what you were doing when you entered the command because help is usually context-sensitive. When you are finished reading the help information, the system returns you to your work at the same point you left it.

POWER UP/SHUT DOWN Computers are similar to copy machines, toasters, and other electrical devices—you must turn them on by applying electrical power. The power-on procedure on almost any computer is straightforward—flip the on/off switch on the processor unit to *on.* Some input/output devices, such as the monitor and the printer, may have separate on/off switches. It is good practice to turn on needed input/output devices before turning on the processor.

When you **power up,** or add electrical power to a computer system, you also **boot** the system. The booting procedure is so named because the computer "pulls itself up by its own bootstraps" (without the assistance of humans). When you boot the system, a ROM (read-only memory) program performs a **system check,** readies the computer for processing, and loads the operating system to RAM (see Figure 3–11).

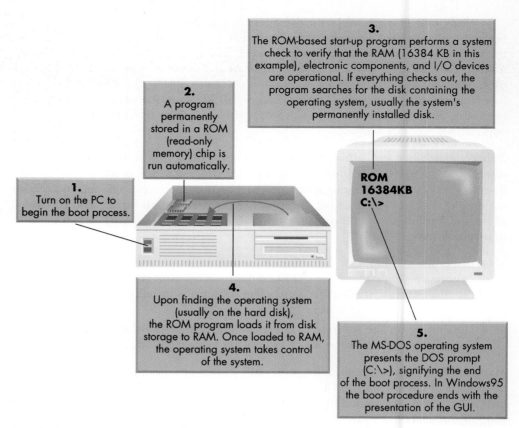

3.
The ROM-based start-up program performs a system check to verify that the RAM (16384 KB in this example), electronic components, and I/O devices are operational. If everything checks out, the program searches for the disk containing the operating system, usually the system's permanently installed disk.

2.
A program permanently stored in a ROM (read-only memory) chip is run automatically.

1.
Turn on the PC to begin the boot process.

4.
Upon finding the operating system (usually on the hard disk), the ROM program loads it from disk storage to RAM. Once loaded to RAM, the operating system takes control of the system.

5.
The MS-DOS operating system presents the DOS prompt (C:\>), signifying the end of the boot process. In Windows95 the boot procedure ends with the presentation of the GUI.

ROM
16384KB
C:\>

FIGURE 3–11   The Boot Procedure

Although the boot procedure officially ends with the display of the **system prompt** (for example, C:\ > for MS-DOS) or the Windows 95 desktop, the operating system may execute predefined user instructions. Frequently, these instructions load an applications program, such as Excel, so your first interaction with the system may be with an application, not at the system prompt.

Unlike electrical appliances, computers should not simply be turned off when you are done using them. You must **shut down** your computer in an orderly manner. Shutting down involves a normal exit from all active applications programs before shutting off the power. All applications programs have an **exit routine** that, when activated, returns you to a GUI, an operating system prompt, or a higher-level applications program. *Exit routines perform some administrative processing that, if bypassed, can result in loss of user data and problems during subsequent sessions.*

Entering Commands and Data: Computers Can Be Very Picky

Computers do *exactly* what you tell them to do—no more, no less. If you tell a computer to compute an employee's pay by adding hours worked to rate of pay (PAY = HOURS-WORKED+RATE), then that is what it does. The computer knows only what you tell it, not that you have given it an erroneous command to add (+) rather than multiply (*). All computers can do is interpret and do what you tell them to do.

Generally, if you make a mistake, the worst that can happen is that you get an error message or inaccurate results. Fortunately, most software packages have built-in safeguards that ask for confirmation before executing a command that might significantly alter or erase your work.

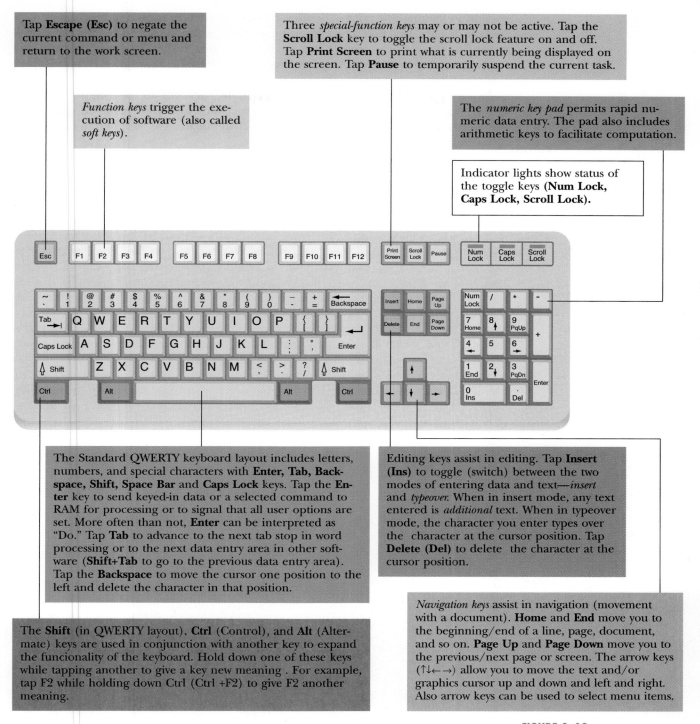

Tap **Escape (Esc)** to negate the current command or menu and return to the work screen.

Function keys trigger the execution of software (also called *soft keys*).

Three *special-function keys* may or may not be active. Tap the **Scroll Lock** key to toggle the scroll lock feature on and off. Tap **Print Screen** to print what is currently being displayed on the screen. Tap **Pause** to temporarily suspend the current task.

The *numeric key pad* permits rapid numeric data entry. The pad also includes arithmetic keys to facilitate computation.

Indicator lights show status of the toggle keys (**Num Lock, Caps Lock, Scroll Lock**).

The Standard QWERTY keyboard layout includes letters, numbers, and special characters with **Enter, Tab, Backspace, Shift, Space Bar** and **Caps Lock** keys. Tap the **Enter** key to send keyed-in data or a selected command to RAM for processing or to signal that all user options are set. More often than not, **Enter** can be interpreted as "Do." Tap **Tab** to advance to the next tab stop in word processing or to the next data entry area in other software (**Shift+Tab** to go to the previous data entry area). Tap the **Backspace** to move the cursor one position to the left and delete the character in that position.

Editing keys assist in editing. Tap **Insert (Ins)** to toggle (switch) between the two modes of entering data and text—*insert* and *typeover*. When in insert mode, any text entered is *additional* text. When in typeover mode, the character you enter types over the character at the cursor position. Tap **Delete (Del)** to delete the character at the cursor position.

The **Shift** (in QWERTY layout), **Ctrl** (Control), and **Alt** (Alternate) keys are used in conjunction with another key to expand the funcionality of the keyboard. Hold down one of these keys while tapping another to give a key new meaning . For example, tap F2 while holding down Ctrl (Ctrl +F2) to give F2 another meaning.

Navigation keys assist in navigation (movement with a document). **Home** and **End** move you to the beginning/end of a line, page, document, and so on. **Page Up** and **Page Down** move you to the previous/next page or screen. The arrow keys (↑↓←→) allow you to move the text and/or graphics cursor up and down and left and right. Also arrow keys can be used to select menu items.

FIGURE 3–12
A Representative PC Keyboard

Input and Control: Keyboards and Point-and-Draw Devices

The primary input devices found on all PCs, workstations, and many VDTs are the *keyboard* and a *point-and-draw device*. The function and use of these critical input devices are discussed in this chapter, but most other optional input devices are discussed in Chapter 5.

THE KEYBOARD   The *keyboard* is the primary input and control device, and you can use it to enter data and issue commands. Figure 3–12 shows the keyboard commonly used by PC-compatible micros. Besides the standard lettered and numbered keys, most keyboards have **function keys.** When tapped, these function keys trigger the execution of software. For example, tapping Function Key 4, the F4 key, might cause the last action to be repeated. Function keys are numbered and assigned different functions in different software packages. HELP (context-sensitive user assistance) is often assigned to F1 (Function Key 1). Some software packages are distributed with **keyboard templates** that you can put on your keyboard to designate which commands are assigned to which function keys. The plastic templates are designed to fit adjacent to the function keys.

Most keyboards are equipped with a *numeric key pad* and *cursor-control keys* (see Figure 3–12). The key pad permits rapid numeric data entry and is normally positioned to the right of the standard alphanumeric keyboard. Space limitations preclude keyboards on portable PCs from having a separate numeric key pad. The cursor-control keys, or "arrow" keys, can be used to select options from a menu. The arrow keys also allow you to move the **text cursor** *up* (↑) and *down* (↓), usually a line at a time, and *left* (←)and *right* (→), usually a character at a time. The text cursor always shows the location of where the next keyed-in character will appear on the screen. The text cursor can appear as several shapes depending on the application, but frequently you will encounter a blinking vertical line (|). To move the text cursor rapidly about the screen, simply hold down the appropriate arrow key.

For many software packages, you can use the arrow keys to move through a document or worksheet to view parts that extend past the bottom, top, or sides of the screen. This movement is known as **scrolling.** Use the up and down arrow keys(↑↓) to scroll vertically and the left and right keys (←→) to scroll horizontally. For example, if you wish to scroll vertically through a word processing document, move the up or down arrow key to the edge of the current screen and continue to press the key to view more of the document, one line at a time. Figure 3–13 illustrates vertical and horizontal scrolling in a spreadsheet.

FIGURE 3–13 Scrolling
When a spreadsheet does not fit on a single screen, you can scroll horizontally (to the right as shown in the figure) and vertically (down in the figure) to view its other portions.

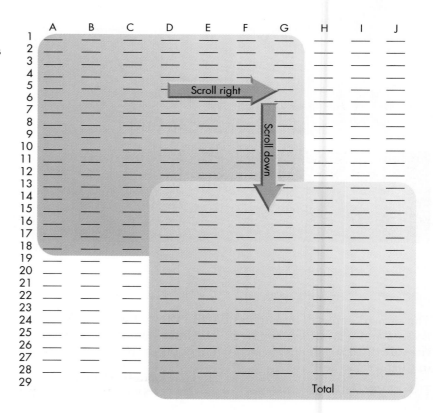

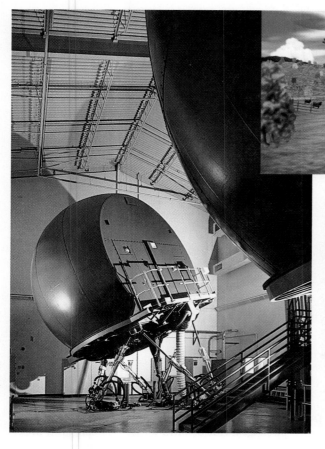

Our interaction with computers is not always with a keyboard and mouse. Helicopter pilots at Camp Pendleton, California, training facility might think they are flying a helicopter when they enter these domed flight simulators. They are actually flying a computer. The flight simulators combine a joystick, an actual instrument panel, a high-resolution visual system, and a motion system to give pilots the feeling of actual flight. Courtesy of Evans & Sutherland Computer Corporation

In summary, the keyboard provides three basic ways to enter commands:

- *Key in* the command using the alphanumeric portion of the keyboard.
- Tap a *function key.*
- Use the *arrow keys* to select a *menu option* from the displayed menu. (Menus are discussed in detail in the next section.)

Other important keys common to most keyboards are illustrated and described in Figure 3–12.

POINT-AND-DRAW DEVICES   The handheld mouse, or something like it, is a must-have item on any PC or workstation. The mouse is a small device that, when moved across a desktop, moves the **graphics cursor** accordingly. The graphics cursor, which can be positioned anywhere on the screen, is displayed as a bracket ([), an arrow (←), a crosshair (+), or a variety of other symbols (for example, ☞). Depending on the application, the text and graphics cursors may be displayed on the screen at the same time. The graphics cursor is used to *point* and *draw.*

The mouse is either attached to the computer by a cable (the mouse's "tail") or linked via a wireless remote connection. All movements of the mouse are reproduced by the graphics cursor on the screen. For example, when you move a mouse up and to the right, the graphics cursor moves toward the top right-hand corner of the screen. Use the mouse for quickly positioning the graphics cursor (for example, over a menu item, an icon, or a word in a word processing document). When positioned at a menu item or an icon, the graphics cursor is said to *point* to that item.

Mice and other point-and-draw devices (discussed in Chapter 5) have one or more buttons. The Macintosh mouse has one button, and the PC-compatible mouse normally has a left and right button (see Figure 3–14). You tap, or **click,** the left but-

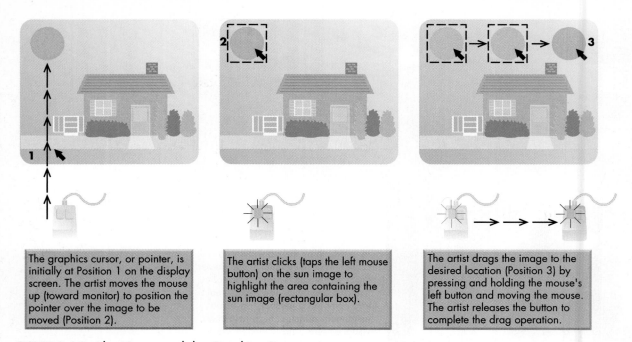

The graphics cursor, or pointer, is initially at Position 1 on the display screen. The artist moves the mouse up (toward monitor) to position the pointer over the image to be moved (Position 2).

The artist clicks (taps the left mouse button) on the sun image to highlight the area containing the sun image (rectangular box).

The artist drags the image to the desired location (Position 3) by pressing and holding the mouse's left button and moving the mouse. The artist releases the button to complete the drag operation.

FIGURE 3–14 The Mouse and the Graphics Cursor
In the example, a computer artist moves the sun image from the left to the right side of the screen.

ton to select a menu item or a program represented by an icon. The function of the right button varies between software packages, but often it is used to call up a menu of options germane to the current activity. A **double-click,** which is tapping a button twice in rapid succession, gives each button a different meaning. Some software packages permit a **simultaneous click,** or tapping both buttons simultaneously, to give the mouse added functionality.

Press and hold a button to **drag** the graphics cursor across the screen. When using a graphics software program, you drag the graphics cursor across the screen to create the image. When using a word processing program, you highlight a block of text by dragging the graphics cursor from the beginning to the end of the block. In a GUI, you can point to an object, perhaps an icon, then drag it to a new position.

Click and drag operations are demonstrated in Figure 3–14 within the context of a graphics software package. In the example, a computer artist uses a mouse to reposition the sun in the drawing.

Menus and Button Bars

Software designers continue to create new and more efficient ways for us to issue commands and initiate operations. These include a variety of menus and button bars.

MENUS Traditionally, we tell computers what we wish to do by selecting activities to be performed from a *hierarchy of menus.*

Menu trees. Menu hierarchies are sometimes called **menu trees.** When you select an item from the **main menu,** you are often presented with another menu of activities, which can then yield another menu, and so on. Depending on the items you select, you may progress through as few as one and as many as eight levels of menus before processing is started for the desired activity.

Let's use presentation graphics software to illustrate how you might use a hierarchy of menus. Consider the following main menu.

| CREATE CHART | EDIT CHART | GET/SAVE | PRINT CHART | EXIT |

Notice that two of the options in the main menu are dimmed. **Dimmed** options, which are usually gray, are disabled or unavailable. The current circumstance dictates whether an option is dimmed. In this example, there is no active chart to be edited or printed, so these options are dimmed.

One option on the main menu of the example graphics software package is *Create Chart*.

| CREATE CHART | EDIT CHART | GET/SAVE | PRINT CHART | EXIT |

If you select the *create chart* option, you are presented with another menu and an opportunity to choose one of five types of charts.

| BAR | PIE | LINE | TEXT | ORGANIZATION |

If you select the *text* option, another menu asks you to choose from three available types of text charts.

| TITLE CHART | SIMPLE LIST | BULLET LIST |

If you select the *bullet list* option, you are presented with the bullet list work screen, on which you would enter the text for your bullet points.

Menu formats. Menus are presented in five basic formats.

- *Menu bar.* The main menu is frequently presented as a **menu bar** at the top of the application window. The menu bar provides a *horizontal list* of menu options, usually at the top of the screen (see Figure 3–15).
- *Pull-down menu.* The result of a menu selection from a menu bar at the top of the screen may be a subordinate menu bar or a **pull-down menu** (see Figure 3–15). The subordinate pull-down menu is "pulled down" from the selected menu bar option and displayed as a *vertical list* of menu options. The entire pull-down menu is shown in a box directly under the selected menu bar option and over whatever is currently on the screen (see Figure 3–15).

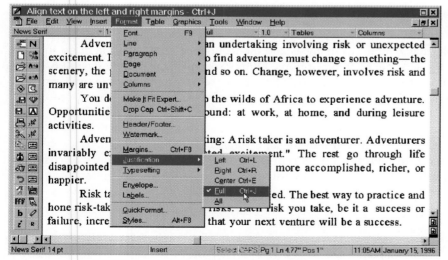

FIGURE 3–15 Menus
The WordPerfect for Windows main menu is presented in a menu bar above the user work area. In the example, the *Format* option in the bar menu is selected and the pull-down menu is presented. Selecting the *Justification* option results in a pop-out menu of justification options.

- *Pop-up menu.* Like the pull-down menu, the **pop-up menu** is superimposed on the current screen in a window. Context-sensitive pop-up menus are often available by clicking the right mouse button.

- *Pop-out menu.* The **pop-out menu** is displayed next to the menu option selected in a higher-level pull-down or pop-up menu. The pop-out menu becomes the active menu, but the higher-level menu continues to be displayed (see Figure 3–15).

- *Floating menu.* You can activate a special-function menu such that it *floats* over the work area until you no longer need it. A menu that "floats" can be dragged with a mouse to any position on the work area. Floating menus streamline interaction with the software because you do not have to work through the main menu to get to a frequently used subordinate menu.

Most software packages provide users with three ways to select an item from a menu.

1. Use the left/right ($\leftarrow \rightarrow$) or up/down ($\uparrow \downarrow$) arrow keys to highlight the desired menu option and tap *Enter.*
2. Enter the **mnemonic** (pronounced *"neh MON ik"*) of the desired item. A letter or number within the text of the menu item is noted as its mnemonic, which means memory aid. The mnemonic is usually the first letter in the first word of the option unless there is another option with the same first letter. Examine the underlined mnemonics in the menu bar in Figure 3–15 (File, Edit, View, Insert, Format, Table, and so on).
3. Use the mouse (or other point-and-draw device) to point to the desired option and click the left button.

Parameters and dialog boxes. Once you have progressed through a series of menus to the option you wanted to choose, you are usually asked to enter the specifications, perhaps the location of the data to be graphed (graphics software) or the orientation of output on the printer paper (word processing software). These specifications are presented as parameters. **Parameters** are variables whose values must be defined by the user before the current command can be executed. Parameters are normally entered and revised in a dialog box. The text in a pop-up **dialog box** gives the user an opportunity to change default options or enter further information. Dialog boxes are discussed further in the Appendix, "The Windows Environment."

Menu summary. All software, whether applications or system, is designed such that at any given point in a work session, the processing options are either displayed somewhere on the screen or can be displayed by tapping a key or clicking a mouse. So, if you are ever confused about what to do next or what can be done, the options usually are right in front of your nose.

BUTTON BARS A software package's main menu is but the tip of a hierarchy of menus that may contain as many as 200 menu item options. You might go for years and not choose some of these options. Others you might use every day. Button bars have been created to give you ready access to these frequently used menu items. **Button bars** contain a group of rectangular graphics that represent a menu option or a command (see Figure 3–16). To execute a particular command, simply click on the button. The graphics on the buttons are designed to represent actions of the command. For example, a button showing a person running represents the *run* command, and a button with a printer image represents the *print* command. You can customize your button bars to meet your processing needs.

INTERNET BRIDGE

Interactive Study Guide
Chapter 3

FIGURE 3–16 Button Bar
This PROCOMM PLUS for Windows (a communications program) button bar contains buttons for frequently used menu options.

IMPORTANT TERMS AND SUMMARY OUTLINE

3–1 SOFTWARE IN PERSPECTIVE We interact with software, which refers to programs, to direct the overall activities within a computer system.

3–2 SYSTEM SOFTWARE: MAINTAINING CONTROL Software falls into two major categories: **system software** and **applications software**. System software, such as the **operating system**, takes control of the PC on start up, then plays a central role in all interactions with the computer via the **graphical user interface (GUI)**. Applications software is designed and created to perform specific personal, business, or scientific processing tasks.

3–3 THE OPERATING SYSTEM: DIRECTING THE ACTION The operating system is the nucleus of all software activity. One of the operating system programs, called the **kernel**, loads other operating system and applications programs to RAM as they are needed.

All operating systems are designed with the same basic objectives in mind. Perhaps the most important objectives are to facilitate communication between the computer system and the people who run it and to optimize the use of computer system resources.

Operating systems get the most from their processors through **multitasking**, the concurrent execution of more than one program at a time. High-priority programs run in the **foreground** part of RAM and the rest run in the **background**.

Through the 1980s, the most popular microcomputer operating system, **MS-DOS**, was strictly *text-based, command-driven* software that required strict adherence to command **syntax**. The trend now is to GUIs that use graphical **icons**. All modern operating systems have adopted the GUI concept.

3–4 PROGRAMMING LANGUAGES: COMPUTER-TALK The instructions in programs are assembled through the act of **programming**. **Programmers** use a variety of **programming languages** to communicate instructions to the computer. The design of a program, or its *programming logic*, is completed before the program is written. Each language uses several types of instructions, including *input/output instructions, computation instructions, control instructions, assignment instructions*, and *format instructions*.

All programming languages are ultimately translated into *machine language* in order to be executed. In **procedure-oriented languages**, programmers code the instructions in the sequence in which they must be executed to solve the problem. COBOL and FORTRAN are examples.

Object-oriented languages, such as Smalltalk and C++, emphasize the *object* of the action. The hierarchical structure of **object-oriented programming (OOP)** makes programs easier to design and understand.

In **fourth-generation languages (4GLs)**, the programmer need only specify *what* to do, not *how* do to it. One feature of 4GLs is the use of English-like instructions.

In **visual programming**, text-based instructions are replaced with symbolic icons, each of which represents a common programming function. **Visual BASIC** is an example.

Natural languages are programs that permit a computer to accept instructions without regard to format or syntax in the native language of the end user.

As end users, we can issue commands and initiate operations by selecting activities to be performed from a hierarchy of **menus**. A **macro** can also be used. To **invoke** the macro, you simply refer to it by name. Most of today's office software have their own **macro language**.

3–5 PLATFORMS: HOMES FOR SOFTWARE

MS-DOS is *text-based, command-driven* software that requires strict adherence to command syntax. The original Microsoft **Windows,** with its GUI, was made obsolete with the introduction of Windows 95. PC-compatibles with MS-DOS and/or Windows was the platform of choice through 1990. A **platform** defines a standard for which software packages are developed. The modern PC/Windows platforms include PC-compatible computers with **Windows 95**, **Windows 98**, **Windows NT**, and **Windows CE**. These PC/Windows platforms offer many advantages, including **plug-and-play** capability and an ability to run 32-bit programs. The Windows 95 and Windows 98 operating systems are designed to bridge the technology gap between the original Windows and Windows NT. Windows NT is a powerful client/server operating system for client/server computing. Windows NT has two components: **Windows NT Workstation** (for the client side) and **Windows NT Server** (for the server side). **Windows CE** is designed for handheld and pocket PCs.

Workgroup computing allows people on a network to use the network to foster cooperation and the sharing of ideas and resources. **Groupware**, such as electronic messaging, runs under workgroup platforms.

The Apple family of microcomputers and **Mac OS** define another major platform.

Those companies that do not standardize on a platform must work to achieve **interoperability**, which refers to the ability to run software and exchange information in a **multiplatform environment**. Enabling technologies that allow communication and the sharing of resources between different platforms are called **cross-platform technologies**.

Another personal computing platform is **UNIX**.

3–6 INTERACTING WITH THE PC AND ITS SOFTWARE

The effective user will understand general computer software concepts, how to operate and use the hardware, the operating system and/or a graphical user interface (GUI), and one or more applications programs.

When you purchase a computer system, you receive several components. Hardware installation involves linking the pieces of the system with the various types of cables. **Software installation** involves copying the program and data files from the vendor-supplied CD-ROM (or diskettes) to the permanently installed hard disk. Software installation is a two-step process for the operating system and all applications software packages: Copy files to the permanently installed hard disk; and set system information, revising **default options** (standard settings) as needed. Use the **help command**, which is usually context-sensitive, when you need assistance.

When you **power up** a computer, you **boot** the system. First, a program in read-only memory (ROM) initializes the system and runs a **system check**. Next, the operating system is loaded to random-access memory (RAM), takes control of the system, and presents the user with a **system prompt** or a GUI screen full of options. RAM provides temporary storage of data and programs during processing.

To **shut down** in an orderly manner, perform the **exit routine** from all active applications programs prior to shutting off the power.

When entering a command the user must be explicit. The primary input devices found on all PCs, workstations, and many VDTs are the *keyboard* and a *point-and-draw device*. In addition to the standard typewriter keyboard, most keyboards have **function keys**. Tapping a function key might present the user with a menu. Some software packages are distributed with **keyboard templates** that designate which commands are assigned to which function keys. Most keyboards are equipped with a numeric key pad and cursor-control keys. Use the cursor-control keys to position the **text cursor** and for **scrolling**.

The *mouse*, when moved across a desktop, moves the **graphics cursor** accordingly. The graphics cursor is used to *point* and *draw*. Use point-and-draw devices for quick positioning of the graphics cursor. Typically, you would **click** the mouse's left button to select a menu item. The **double-click** and **simultaneous click** give the mouse added functionality. You would press and hold a button to **drag** the graphics cursor across the screen.

Menu hierarchies are sometimes called **menu trees**. When you select an item from the **main menu**, you are often presented with another menu of activities. A menu can appear as a **menu bar**, a **pull-down menu**, a **pop-up menu**, or a **pop-out menu.** Menu options that are unavailable or disabled are **dimmed**.

Software packages provide users with three ways to select an item from a menu: Use the left/right or up/down arrow keys; enter the **mnemonic**; or use the mouse to position the graphics cursor at the desired option. Most menus present users with default options in a pop-up **dialog box**. User specifications needed for processing are presented in the form of **parameters**.

Button bars, which can be customized, contain a group of rectangular graphics that represent a menu option or command.

REVIEW EXERCISES

Concepts

1. Give two examples each of applications and system software.
2. What defines a platform?
3. Does the current program run in RAM's foreground or background?
4. Briefly describe two platforms for microcomputers.
5. Give an original example of a computation instruction.
6. Name two object-oriented programming languages.
7. What is the trademark of 4GLs?
8. What is the name given the software entities that provide the foundation for OOP?
9. What kind of programming languages use symbolic icons to represent common programming functions?
10. What is the purpose of function keys? Of cursor-control keys?
11. Contrast a menu bar with a pull-down menu.
12. Briefly describe two ways you can use a keyboard to enter commands to a software package.
13. During a software session, which key would you commonly press to move to the beginning of the work area? To negate the current command?
14. How is a pop-out menu displayed?
15. What does "booting the system" mean?
16. What must be accomplished to shut down in an orderly manner?

17. Which key is tapped to toggle between insert and typeover modes?
18. The help command is often assigned to which function key?

Discussion and Problem Solving

19. If each new generation of programming languages enhances interaction between programmers and the computer, why not write programs using the most recent generation of languages?
20. What is a macro and how can using macros save time? Give an example.
21. Explain in general terms what a natural language would do with the following command: "List all fixed inventory items in the purchasing department purchased prior to 1985." Give an example of what a response to the request might look like. Fixed inventory items would include items such as desks, chairs, lamps, and so on.
22. People have been saying that DOS is dead since 1990, but it clings to life. Will Windows NT be the last nail in the MS-DOS coffin?
23. Multitasking allows PC users to run several programs at a time. Describe a PC session in which you would have at least two applications running at the same time.

SELF-TEST (BY SECTION)

3–1   The term *software* commonly is used to refer to computer programs. _T_

3–2 a. _____ software takes control of the PC on start up. _System_

   b. Which type of software is designed to perform specific personal, business, or scientific processing tasks: (a) system, (b) applications, or (c) GUI? _b_

3–3 a. The concurrent execution of more than one program at a time is called _____. _multi tasking_

   b. GUIs are: (a) text-based, (b) graphics-based, or (c) label-based? _b_

   c. MS-DOS is a mainframe-based operating system. (T/F) _F_

3–4 a. When programming in a procedure-oriented language, you tell the computer what to do and how to do it. (T/F) _T_

   b. Programmers use a variety of _____ _____ to communicate instructions to the computer. _Programming Languages_

c. C++ is: (a) a procedure-oriented language, (b) a problem-oriented language, or (c) an object-oriented language? *c*

d. To _____, or execute, a macro, you refer to it by name. *Invoke*

3–5 a. Which of the following is not in the PC/Windows platform family: (a) Windows 98, (b) Windows TN, or (c) Windows CE? *b*

b. The Macintosh family of PCs is unique in that it does not need an operating system. (T/F) *F*

c. UNIX is a subset of Windows NT, a more sophisticated operating system. (T/F) *F*

d. A computing environment that runs more than one platform is called a _____ environment. *multiplatform*

3–6 a. Both the operating system and/or a _____ provide a link between the user, the computer system, and the applications programs. *graphical user interface*

b. A computer user must "kick the system" to load the operating system to RAM prior to processing. (T/F) *F*

c. The MS-DOS operating system displays a system _____ to signal the user that it is ready to accept a user command. *prompt*

d. Help commands are rarely context-sensitive. (T/F) *F*

e. Use the _____ for rapid numeric data entry. *numeric keypad*

f. Menu hierarchies are sometimes called menu charts. (T/F) *F*

g. Press and hold a mouse button to _____ the graphics cursor across the screen. *drag*

h. Which is not considered a common menu format: (a) floating; (b) pop-over; or (c) pop-up? *b*

Self-test Answers. **3–1** T. **3–2 (a)** System; **(b)** b. **3–3 (a)** multitasking; **(b)** b; **(c)** F. **3–4 (a)** T; **(b)** programming languages; **(c)** c; **(d)** invoke. **3–5 (a)** b; **(b)** F; **(c)** F; **(d)** multiplatform. **3–6 (a)** graphical user interface (GUI); **(b)** F; **(c)** prompt; **(d)** F; **(e)** numeric key pad; **(f)** F; **(g)** drag; **(h)** b.

Storing and Retrieving Information: Disks and Tape Backup Units

LEARNING OBJECTIVES

- Distinguish between primary and secondary storage.
- Describe how data are stored and retrieved in computer systems.
- Understand the fundamental principles of sequential and random access.
- Distinguish between secondary storage devices and secondary storage media.
- Describe the principles of operation, methods of data storage, and use of magnetic disk and magnetic tape drives.
- Know the different types and sources of computer virus.
- Describe procedures for backing up disk files to data cartridge or diskette.
- Discuss the applications and use of optical laser disk storage.

Courtesy of Seagate Technology

LET'S TALK

Can you follow this conversation? It includes computing concepts presented in this chapter. Read it now, then reread it once you've had an opportunity to study the chapter.

The Scene The executive director of the State University Alumni Association (Max) is meeting in his office with an analyst from the University Computer Center (Leah) and the president of the Alumni Association (Scottie).

SCOTTIE: Our membership is disappointed with the Annual Alumni Directory. They don't like the $50 price tag, and they're complaining that it's out of date.

MAX: And they're right! I say we go electronic with it. Can we do it, Leah?

LEAH: Well, all the university administrators already have direct access to the entire database, which now has over 140,000 records on magnetic disk. Technically, providing greater access to it is not a problem, but you guys will have to address the security and privacy issues.

MAX: Let's assume we can overcome these concerns. Is our current database complete?

SCOTTIE: In this era of multimedia, our members may want more than name-and-address ASCII files. I suggest we give them the flexibility to attach their own graphics files, audio files, and even video files to their record.

MAX: Great idea! I'd love to listen to my old friends and see some family photos.

LEAH: If we do that, we'll need to go to optical laser disk storage to make this economically feasible. It sounds neat. Think about it—alums could change messages and their photos with the seasons.

SCOTTIE: People want their databases on a computer, not in a book. Let's do the annual directory on CD-ROM.

LEAH: You know, with CD-R coming down in price, we could do our own CD-ROM publishing right here in the Alumni Office. With a little file compression and a CD production station, we could provide a great service for the alumni.

SCOTTIE: And, our members would love to be able to import selected portions of the alumni database on the Internet to their spreadsheet files.

MAX: I'm excited! Forget the printed directory. What do you say we explore these options further?

4–1 Secondary Storage and Files: Data Keepers

Monthly Technology Update
Chapter 4

Did you ever stop to think about what happens behind the scenes when you

- Request a telephone number through directory assistance?
- Draw money from your checking account at an ATM?
- Check out at a supermarket?
- Download a file on the Internet?

Needed information—such as telephone numbers, account balances, item prices, or stock summary files on the Internet—is retrieved from rapidly rotating disk-storage media and loaded to random-access memory (RAM) for processing. Untold terabytes (trillions of characters) of information, representing millions of applications, are stored *permanently* for periodic retrieval in **secondary storage,** such as magnetic disk. There they can be retrieved in milliseconds. For example, as soon as the directory assistance operator keys in the desired name, the full name and number are retrieved from disk storage and displayed. Moments later, a digitized version of voice recordings of numbers is accessed from disk storage and played in response to the caller's request: "The number is five, zero, one, two, two, four, nine."

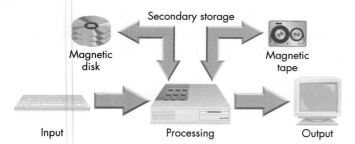

FIGURE 4–1 RAM Secondary Storage
Programs and data are stored permanently in secondary storage and temporarily in RAM.

Storage Technologies: Disk and Tape

Within a computer system, programs and information in all forms (text, image, audio, video) are stored in both *RAM* and *secondary storage* (see Figure 4–1). Programs and information are retrieved from secondary storage and stored *temporarily* in high-speed RAM (primary storage) for processing. In this section we examine two common types of secondary storage, magnetic disk and tape.

Over the years, manufacturers have developed a variety of permanent secondary storage devices and media. Today the various types of **magnetic disk drives** and their respective storage media are the state of the art for permanent storage. **Magnetic tape drives** complement magnetic disk storage by providing inexpensive *backup* capability and *archival* storage. The rest of this chapter will discuss these drives as well as **optical laser disk** drives, a rapidly emerging alternative to magnetic disk and magnetic tape storage. First, let's take a look at the files stored on these drives.

The Many Faces of Files

We have talked in general about the *file* in previous chapters. The **file** is simply a recording of information. It is the foundation of permanent storage on a computer system. To a computer, a file is a string of 0s and 1s (digitized data) that are stored and retrieved as a single unit.

TYPES OF FILES: ASCII TO VIDEO   There are many types of files, most of which are defined by the software that created them (for example, a word processing document or spreadsheet). Popular files are listed here.

- *ASCII file*. An **ASCII file** is a text-only file that can be read or created by any word processing program or text editor.
- *Data file*. A **data file** contains data organized into records.
- *Document file*. All word processing and desktop publishing **document files** contain text, and many document files contain both text and images.
- *Spreadsheet file*. A **spreadsheet file** contains rows and columns of data.
- *Source program file*. A **source program file** contains high-level instructions to the computer. These instructions must be translated to machine language prior to program execution.
- *Executable program file*. An **executable program file** contains executable machine language code.
- *Graphics file*. A **graphics file** contains digitized images.

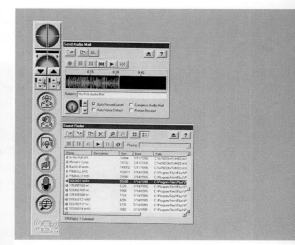

There could be no better example of a graphics file than this drawing, called "Porsche," by Jay Roth. A digitized version of this image is maintained on magnetic disk storage.   Electric Image, Inc.

Midisoft Sound Bar software works with audio files, giving users immediate control over every aspect of PC sound. It lets users add voice-recorded messages (audio files) to e-mail and other business communications.   Courtesy of Midisoft Corporation

- *Audio file*. An **audio file** contains digitized sound.
- *Video file*. A **video file** contains digitized video frames that when played rapidly (for example, 30 frames per second) produce motion video.

FILES AND PARKING LOTS   Secondary storage is much like a parking lot for files. In a parking lot, a variety of vehicles—cars, buses, trucks, motorcycles, and so on—are put in parking places to be picked up later. Similarly, all sorts of files are "parked" in individual spots in secondary storage, waiting to be retrieved later. To help you find your vehicle, large parking lots are organized with numbered parking places in lettered zones. The same is true with files and secondary storage. Files are stored in numbered "parking places" on disk for retrieval. Fortunately, we do not have to remember the exact location of the file. The operating system does that for us. All we have to know is the name of the file. We assign user names to files, then recall or store them by name. Filenames in the MS-DOS/Windows environment can be up to eight characters long, with an optional three-character extension (LETTER.DOC, PLAYGAME.EXE). Windows 95, Apple's System 7, and several other operating systems allow descriptive filenames of up to 255 characters. "MAN_CP_3" in Windows 3.1 could be extended to "Operations Manual Chicago Plant ver 3" in Windows 95. The latter makes a lot more sense and is easier to understand.

WHAT TO DO WITH A FILE   Everything we do on a computer involves a file and, therefore, secondary storage. But what do we do with files?

- *We create, name, and save files*. We create files when we name and save a letter, a drawing, a program, or some digital entity (an audio clip) to secondary storage.
- *We copy files, move files, and delete files*. We copy files from CD-ROMs and diskettes to a hard disk to install software. We move files during routine file management activities. When we no longer need a file, we delete it.
- *We retrieve and update files*. We continuously retrieve and update our files (such as when we update the entries in a spreadsheet or revise a memo).
- *We display, print, or play files*. Most user files that involve text and graphics can be displayed and printed. Audio and video files are played.
- *We execute files*. We execute program files to run our software. In the MS-DOS/Windows environment, executable filenames end in EXE, COM, BAT, and PIF (Windows only).
- *We download and upload files*. We download useful files from the Internet to our PCs. We sometimes work on, then upload updated files to our company's mainframe computer.
- *We export/import files*. The *file format*, or the manner in which a file is stored, is unique for each type of software package. For example, Word for Windows and WordPerfect for Windows are both word processing programs, but the format of their files is different. For a Word user to read a WordPerfect file, the WordPerfect file must be converted to the Word file format. To do this the user must **import** the WordPerfect document to a Word file format. When we import a file, we convert it from its foreign format to a format that is compatible with the current program. Figure 4–2 illustrates how an Excel for Windows 97 spreadsheet can be imported into a Word for Windows 97 document. When we **export** a file, we convert a file in the current program to a format needed by another program.
- *We compress files*. When the air is squeezed out of a sponge, it becomes much smaller. When you release it, the sponge returns to its original shape—nothing changes. **File compression** works in a similar fashion. File formats for most software packages are inefficient, resulting in wasted space on secondary storage when you save files. Using file compression, a repeated pattern, such as the word *and* in text documents, might be replaced by a one-byte descriptor in a compressed file, saving two bytes for each occurrence of *and*. One technique used

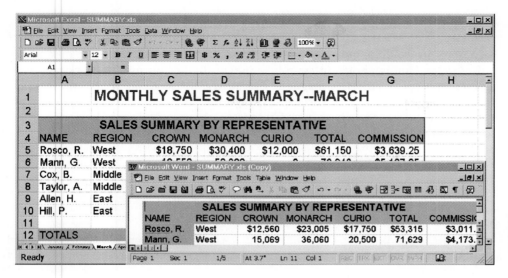

FIGURE 4–2 Importing Files
An Excel 97 spreadsheet is imported into a Word 97 document.

when compressing graphics files replaces those portions of an image that are the same color with a brief descriptor. Depending on the type and content of the file, file compression can create a compressed file that takes 10% to 90% less secondary storage (average is about 50%). Compressed files are decompressed when loaded to RAM for processing.

● *We protect files.* We can protect sensitive files by limiting access to authorized persons. For example, the human resources manager would want to limit access to the personnel file containing salaries and other employee information.

4–2 Sequential and Random Access: New Terms for Old Concepts

An important consideration in both the design of an information system and the purchase of a computer system is the way that data and files are accessed. Magnetic tape can be used for *sequential access* only. Magnetic disks have *random-* or *direct-access* capabilities as well as sequential-access capabilities. You are quite familiar with these concepts, but you may not realize it. Operationally, magnetic tape is the same as the tape used in home and automobile audiotape decks. The magnetic disk can be compared to a compact disk (CD).

Suppose you have Paul Simon's album, *The Rhythm of the Saints,* on CD. The first four songs on this CD are: (1) "The Obvious Child," (2) "Can't Run But," (3) "The Coast," and (4) "Proof." Now suppose you also have this album on a tape cassette. To play the third song on the cassette, "The Coast," you would have to wind the tape forward and search for it sequentially. To play "The Coast" on the CD, all you would have to do is select track number 3. This simple analogy demonstrates the two fundamental methods of storing and accessing data—*sequential* and *random.*

Magnetic disk drives are secondary storage devices that provide a computer system with **random-** *and* **sequential-processing** capabilities. In random processing, the desired programs, data, and files are accessed *directly* from the storage medium. In sequential processing, the computer system must search the storage medium, from the beginning, to find the desired programs, data, or files. Magnetic tapes have only sequential-processing capabilities. Today's online information systems and Internet services demand immediate and direct access to information; therefore, virtually all active files and databases are maintained on media that permit random processing—primarily magnetic disk and optical laser disk. Magnetic tape is mainly a backup and archival storage medium.

4-3 Magnetic Disks: Round and Round

Magnetic Disk

Because of its random- and sequential-processing capabilities, magnetic disk storage is the overwhelming choice of computer users, whether on micros, workstations, or supercomputers. A variety of magnetic disk drives, the *hardware device,* and magnetic disks, the *medium* (the actual surface on which the information is stored), are manufactured for different business requirements.

Hardware and Storage Media

Peripheral Explorer

There are two fundamental types of magnetic disks: interchangeable and fixed.

- **Interchangeable magnetic disks** can be stored offline and loaded to the magnetic disk drives as they are needed.
- **Fixed magnetic disks,** also called *hard disks,* are permanently installed, or fixed. All hard disks are rigid and are usually made of aluminum with a surface coating of easily magnetized elements, such as iron, cobalt, chromium, and nickel. Today's integrated systems and databases are stored on hard disk, especially those used in workgroup computing. Such systems and databases require all data and programs to be *online* (accessible to the computer for processing) at all times.

Figure 4-3 shows the different types of interchangeable magnetic disks and fixed disks. As you can see, the drives for the various magnetic disk media are available in a wide variety of shapes and storage capacities. The type you (or a company) should use depends on the volume of data you have and the frequency with which those data are accessed.

FIGURE 4-3 Magnetic Disk Drives and Media
Shown here (*clockwise*) are the popular $3\frac{1}{2}$-inch diskette and drive, the 100-MB Zip diskette and drive, a 3.1-GB hard disk (3 disk platters) and a 420-MB hard drive on a PCMCIA card that can be inserted in a PCMCIA slot on a PC.

Courtesy of International Business Machines Corporation. Unauthorized use not permitted.

Courtesy of Iomega Corporation

Courtesy of Integral Peripherals

Courtesy of Western Digital Corporation/

PC MAGNETIC DISK DRIVES AND MEDIA Virtually all PCs sold today are configured with at least one hard disk drive and one interchangeable disk drive. Having two disk drives increases system flexibility and throughput. The interchangeable disk drive provides a means for the distribution of data and software and for backup and archival storage. The high-capacity hard-disk storage has made it possible for today's PC users to enjoy the convenience of having their data and software readily accessible at all times.

The diskette. Three types of interchangeable disk drives are commonly used on PCs. These disk drives accept interchangeable magnetic disks such as the traditional *diskette* and the new high-capacity *SuperDisk* and *Zip disk.*

- *Diskette and SuperDisk.* The traditional $3\frac{1}{2}$-inch diskette, or *floppy disk*, is a thin, mylar disk that is permanently enclosed in a rigid plastic jacket. The traditional diskette comes in two capacities—720 **KB** (**kilobytes** or about 1000 bytes) and 1.44 MB. A modern version, called the **SuperDisk,** can store 120 MB of information. Both the diskette and the SuperDisk are the same size but have different disk densities. **Disk density** refers to the number of bits that can be stored per unit of area on the disk-face surface. In contrast to a hard disk, a diskette and SuperDisk are set in motion only when a command is issued to read from or write to the disk. The 120 MB SuperDisk combines floppy and hard disk technology to read and write to specially formatted floppy-size disks. The SuperDisk drive reads and writes to the traditional diskette as well.

- *Zip Disk.* The **Zip drive** reads and writes to 100-MB **Zip disks.** The Zip disk and SuperDisk have storage capacities of 70 and 83 floppy diskettes, respectively.

The diskette-based floppy disk is still standard equipment on PCs and will remain so during this transition period to a new higher-density interchangeable disk, such as the Zip disk or the SuperDisk.

The hard disk: permanently installed and interchangeable. Hard disk manufacturers are working continuously to achieve two objectives: to put more information in less disk space and to enable a more rapid transfer of that information to/from RAM. Consequently, hard-disk storage technology is forever changing. There are two types of hard disk, those that are permanently installed and those that are interchangeable.

- *Permanently installed hard disks.* Generally, the 1- to $5\frac{1}{4}$-inch permanent PC-based hard disks have storage capacities from about 2 GB (gigabytes) to 20 GB. A 20-GB hard disk can store as much data as thirteen thousand $3\frac{1}{2}$-inch high-density diskettes. That's a stack of floppies almost 150 feet high!

  A hard disk contains several disk platters stacked on a single rotating spindle. Data are stored on all *recording surfaces.* For a disk with four platters, there are eight *recording surfaces* on which data can be stored (see Figure 4–4). The disks spin continuously at a high speed (from 3600 to 6000 revolutions per

---

MEMORY BITS

Characteristics of Magnetic Disk

Media	Fixed (hard) and interchangeable disks
Type access	Random (direct) or sequential
Data representation	Serial
Storage scheme	Sector on tracks

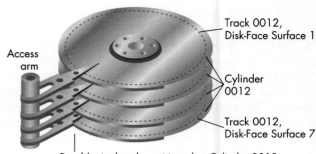

FIGURE 4–4 Fixed Hard Disk with Four Platters and Eight Recording Surfaces
A cylinder refers to similarly numbered concentric tracks on the disk-face surfaces. In the illustration, the read/write heads are positioned over Cylinder 0012. At this position, the data on any one of the eight tracks numbered 0012 are accessible to the computer on each revolution of the disk. The read/write heads must be moved to access data on other cylinders.

Track 0012, Disk-Face Surface 1

Access arm

Cylinder 0012

Track 0012, Disk-Face Surface 7

Read/write heads positioned at Cylinder 0012

The Jaz drives and disks are an ideal solution for storing, transporting, and playing multimedia applications. You can store up to 1 gigabyte on each removable disk. Courtesy of Iomega Corporation

minute) within a sealed enclosure. The enclosure keeps the disk-face surfaces free from contaminants, such as dust and cigarette smoke. This contaminant-free environment allows hard disks to have greater density of data storage than the interchangeable diskettes.

The rotation of a magnetic disk passes all data under or over a **read/write head,** thereby making all data available for access on each revolution of the disk (see Figure 4–4). A fixed disk will have at least one read/write head for each recording surface. The heads are mounted on **access arms** that move together and literally float on a cushion of air over (or under) the spinning recording surfaces. The tolerance is so close that a particle of smoke from a cigarette will not fit between these "flying" heads and the recording surface!

● *Interchangeable hard disks.* The majority of hard disks are permanently installed in the same physical unit as the processor and diskette drive. This, however, is changing with the introduction of interchangeable hard disks, such as Iomega's **Jaz drive.** The $3\frac{1}{2}$-inch **Jaz cartridge,** which can store up to 1 GB of information, is inserted and removed as easily as the $3\frac{1}{2}$-inch floppy. The Jaz cartridges are about the size of a stack of four floppies. The Jaz drive's performance is almost as good as that of a permanently installed hard disk.

PC MAGNETIC DISK ORGANIZATION The way in which data and programs are stored and accessed is similar for both hard and interchangeable disks. Both media have a thin film coating of one of the easily magnetized elements (cobalt, for example). The thin film coating on the disk can be magnetized electronically by the read/write head to represent the absence or presence of a bit (0 or 1).

Tracks and sectors: A disk floor plan. Data are stored in concentric **tracks** by magnetizing the surface to represent bit configurations (see Figure 4–5). Bits are recorded using *serial representation;* that is, bits are aligned in a row in the track. The number of tracks varies greatly between disks, from as few as 40 on some diskettes to several thousand on high-capacity hard disks. The spacing of tracks is measured in **tracks per inch,** or **TPI.** The $3\frac{1}{2}$-inch diskettes are rated at 135 TPI. The TPI for hard disks can be in the thousands. The *track density* (TPI) tells only part of the story. The *recording density* tells the rest. Recording density, which is measured in *bits per inch,* refers to the number of bits (1s and 0s) that can be stored per inch of track.

Microcomputer disks use **sector organization** to store and retrieve data. In sector organization, the recording surface is divided into pie-shaped **sectors.** The number of sectors depends on the density of the disk. The surface of the diskette in Figure 4–5 is logically divided into 15 sectors. Typically, the storage capacity of each sector on a particular track is a multiple of 512 (for example, 512, 1024, or 4096), regardless of the number of sectors per track. The disk sectors are all numbered, and the *sector number* and *track number* comprise the **disk address** on a particular disk-face surface. The disk address represents the physical location of a particular file or set of data on a specific disk-face surface. To read from or write to a disk, an access arm

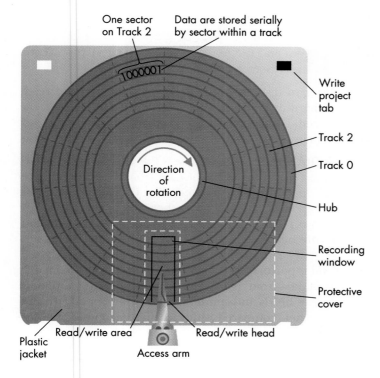

One sector on Track 2

Data are stored serially by sector within a track

1000001

Write project tab

Track 2

Track 0

Direction of rotation

Hub

Recording window

Protective cover

Plastic jacket

Read/write area

Access arm

Read/write head

FIGURE 4–5 Cutaway of a $3\frac{1}{2}$-Inch Diskette
The access arm on this $3\frac{1}{2}$-inch disk drive is positioned at a particular track (Track 2 in the example). Data are read or written serially in tracks within a given sector.

containing the read/write head is moved, under program control, to the appropriate *track* (see Figures 4–4 and 4–5). When the sector containing the desired data passes under or over the read/write head, the data are read or written.

Cylinders: Tracks on tracks. Each of the high-density disk-face surfaces of a hard disk may have several thousand tracks, numbered consecutively from outside to inside. A particular **cylinder** refers to the same-numbered tracks on each recording surface (for example, Track 0012 on each recording surface—see Figure 4–4). When reading from or writing to a hard disk, all access arms are moved to the appropriate *cylinder*. For example, each recording surface has a track numbered 0012, so the disk has a cylinder numbered 0012. If the data to be accessed are on Recording Surface 01, Track 0012, then the access arms and the read/write heads for all eight recording surfaces are moved to Cylinder 0012.

In Figure 4–4 the access arm is positioned over Cylinder 0012. In this position, data on any of the sectors on the tracks in Cylinder 0012 can be accessed without further movement of the access arm. If data on Surface 5, Track 0145 are to be read, the access arm must be positioned over Cylinder 0145 until the desired data pass under the read/write head.

Fortunately, software automatically monitors the location, or address, of our files and programs. We need only enter the name of the file to retrieve it for processing. In the case of a personnel master file with individual records, we simply enter the employee's name to retrieve his or her personnel record. The computer system searches the disk address associated with that person's record, locates it, and loads it to RAM for processing. Although the addressing schemes vary considerably between disks, the address normally will include the *cylinder (or track)*, the *recording surface*, and the *sector number.*

FORMATTING: PREPARING A DISK FOR USE Every PC user is eventually confronted with preparing a new diskette or hard disk for use. A new disk is coated with a surface that can be magnetized easily to represent data. However, before the disk can be used, it must be **formatted.** The formatting procedure causes the disk to be initialized with a recording format for your operating system. Specifically, it:

- Creates *sectors* and *tracks* into which data are stored.
- Sets up an area for the file allocation table. The **file allocation table (FAT)** tells the system where to find the files and file folders (groups of files) you eventually store on the disk—that is, what sectors and tracks to look in.

If you purchased a PC today, the hard disk probably would be formatted and ready for use. However, if you added a hard disk or upgraded your existing hard disk, the new disk would need to be formatted. Diskettes can be purchased as formatted or unformatted. Unformatted diskettes cost less, but they must be formatted prior to use.

DISK ACCESS TIME: SEEK AND TRANSMIT **Access time** is the interval between the instant a computer makes a request for the transfer of data from a disk-storage device to RAM and the instant this operation is completed. The read/write heads on the access arm in the illustration of Figure 4–4 move together. Some hard disks have multiple access arms, some with two read/write heads per disk-face surface. Having multiple access arms and read/write heads results in less mechanical movement and faster access times.

The access of data from RAM is performed at electronic speeds—approximately the speed of light. But the access of data from disk storage depends on the movement of mechanical apparatus (read/write heads and spinning disks) and can take from 6 to 15 milliseconds—still very slow when compared with the microsecond-to-nanosecond internal processing speeds of computers.

DISK CACHING: SPEED BOOST The **data transfer rate** is the rate at which data are read from (written to) secondary storage to (from) RAM. Even though the data transfer rate from magnetic disk to RAM may be millions of bytes per second, the rate of transfer between one part of RAM to another is much faster. **Disk caching** (pronounced *"cashing"*) is a technique that improves system speed by taking advantage of the greater transfer rate from RAM. With disk caching, programs and data that are *likely* to be called into use are moved from a disk into a separate disk-caching area of RAM. When an application program calls for the data or programs in the disk cache area, the data are transferred directly from RAM rather than from magnetic disk. Updated data or programs in the disk cache area eventually must be transferred to a disk for permanent storage. All state-of-the-art PCs come with software that takes full advantage of the potential of disk caching.

DISKETTE CARE: DO'S AND DON'TS A blank interchangeable disk has a very modest value. But once you save your files on it, its value, at least to you, increases greatly. Such a valuable piece of property should be handled with great care. Following are a few guidelines for handling interchangeable disks.

Do's

- *Do* store disks at temperatures between 50 and 125 degrees Fahrenheit.
- *Do* keep a backup of disks containing important data and programs.
- *Do* remove disks from disk drives before you turn off the computer.
- *Do* clean diskette drive read/write heads periodically with a diskette cleaning kit (available at most computer retailer locations).
- *Do* slide the *write-protect tab* to its open position on all important $3\frac{1}{2}$-inch disks intended for read-only use (see Figure 4–5).

Don'ts

- *Don't* force a disk into the disk drive. It should slip in with little or no resistance.
- *Don't* touch the disk surface.
- *Don't* place disks near a magnetic field, such as magnetic paper-clip holders, tape demagnetizers, telephones, or electric motors.

Ethical Issues and Concerns

Accessibility to E-mail Archives

E-MAIL MAY BE THE CORPORATE ACHILLES HEEL WHEN IT comes to lawsuits. Attorneys can subpoena e-mail archives on disk or tape relative to pending lawsuits. Among the thousands of e-mail messages sent each day in a typical medium-sized company, attorneys are likely to find statements that support their cause. People tend to be conversational when writing e-mail messages. People don't write e-mail with the thought that it might be shown as evidence in a court of law. To avoid the potential for litigation, many companies routinely purge e-mail archives.

Discussion: Should companies save e-mail? If so, for how long? Should attorneys be allowed to subpoena e-mail archives?

- *Don't* expose disks to direct sunlight for a prolonged period.
- *Don't* insert or remove a disk from a disk drive if the "drive active" light is on.

Magnetic Disks: The Mainframe Environment

Direct-access storage devices (DASDs), such as magnetic disks, are necessary for all mainframe information systems in which the data must be online and accessed directly. For example, an airline reservation system needs direct-access capability to retrieve the record for any flight at any time from any reservations office. The data must be current, or flights may be under- or overbooked.

Mainframes and supercomputers use a wide variety of hard-disk media. The differences are primarily the size of the platter (up to 14 inches in diameter), the number of platters per disk drive, and the density at which data are recorded. Current technology enables a single mainframe disk drive to store more than several hundred gigabytes of data. The way data and files are organized on mainframe disk systems is similar to that on microcomputer disk systems.

Computer Viruses: The Plague of Magnetic Disks

Computers can get sick just like people. A variety of highly contagious "viruses" can spread from computer to computer, much the way biological viruses do among human beings. Just as a virus can infect human organs, a **computer virus** can infect programs and databases. It can also hide duplicates of itself within legitimate programs, such as an operating system or a word processing program. These viruses, which are programs, reside on and are passed between magnetic disks.

Most people who write and propagate virus programs fall into two groups. The first group uses viruses to demonstrate their programming cleverness to a small group of peers. Their intent is seldom destructive. The second, and far more dangerous group, creates viruses with malicious intent. These people want their viruses to result in property damage and cause human suffering.

TYPES OF COMPUTER VIRUSES: BAD AND WORSE There are many types of viruses. Some act quickly by erasing user programs and files on disk. Others grow like a cancer, destroying small parts of a file each day. Some act like a time bomb. They lay dormant for days or months but eventually are activated and wreak havoc on any software on the system. Many companies warn their PC users to back up all software prior to every Friday the thirteenth, a favorite date of those who write virus programs.

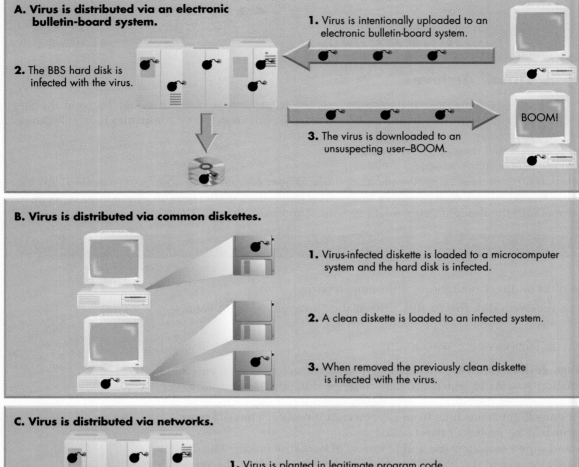

A. Virus is distributed via an electronic bulletin-board system.

1. Virus is intentionally uploaded to an electronic bulletin-board system.

2. The BBS hard disk is infected with the virus.

3. The virus is downloaded to an unsuspecting user–BOOM.

BOOM!

B. Virus is distributed via common diskettes.

1. Virus-infected diskette is loaded to a microcomputer system and the hard disk is infected.

2. A clean diskette is loaded to an infected system.

3. When removed the previously clean diskette is infected with the virus.

C. Virus is distributed via networks.

1. Virus is planted in legitimate program code.

2. Virus is transmitted via data communications to another node on the network.

3. Virus propagates itself to other nodes on the network.

FIGURE 4–6   How Viruses Are Spread

Some viruses attack the hardware and have been known to throw the mechanical components of a computer system, such as disk-access arms, into costly spasms.

SOURCES OF COMPUTER VIRUSES: BBSS, DISKS, AND COMPUTERS   In the microcomputer environment, there are three primary sources of computer viruses (see Figure 4–6).

- *Electronic bulletin-board systems.* The most common source of viral infection is the public electronic bulletin board on which users exchange software. Typically, a user logs on to the bulletin board and downloads a game, a utility program, or some other enticing piece of freeware, but gets the software with an embedded virus instead.

- *Diskettes.* Viruses are also spread from one system to another via common diskettes. For example, a student with an infected application disk might unknowingly infect several other laboratory computers with a virus, which, in turn, infects the applications software of other students. Software companies have unknowingly distributed viruses with their proprietary software products.

- *Computer networks.* Viruses can spread from one computer network to another.

How serious a problem are viruses? They have the potential of affecting an individual's career and even destroying companies. (A company that loses its accounts receivables records—records of what the company is owed—could be a candidate for bankruptcy.) Antiviral programs, also called *vaccines,* exist, but they can be circumvented by a persistent (and malicious) programmer. The best way to cope with viruses is to recognize their existence and to take precautionary measures. Your chances of living virus free are greatly improved if you periodically check for viruses and are careful about what you load to your system's hard disk. If you catch a virus, your best chance of surviving is backing up all important data and programs.

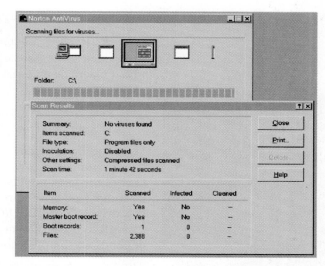

Symantec Corporation's Norton AntiVirus program scans the hard disk for computer viruses; and if any are detected, they are removed.

4–4 Magnetic Tape: Ribbons of Data

Magnetic Tape and PCs

During the 1950s and 1960s, the foundation of many information systems was *sequential processing* using *magnetic tape* master files. Today, magnetic tape storage is no longer used for routine processing; however, it has three other important functions.

- *Protection against loss of valuable files.* Magnetic tape is used primarily as a backup medium for magnetic disk storage.

- *Archiving files.* Important files no longer needed for active processing can be archived to magnetic tape. For example, banks archive old transactions (checks and deposits) for a number of years.

- *File portability between computers.* Large amounts of information can be transferred between computers by writing to magnetic tape at the source site and reading from the tape at the destination site.

A magnetic tape medium, such as the **magnetic tape cartridge,** can be loaded conveniently to a tape drive (the hardware device) for processing. Once loaded to a tape drive, the magnetic tape is online; that is, the data and programs on the tape are accessible to the computer system. When processing is complete, the tape is removed for offline storage until it is needed again for processing.

The magnetic tape cartridge, which is also called a **data cartridge,** is self-contained and is inserted into and removed from the tape drive in much the same way you would load or remove a videotape from a VCR. Like the videotape, the supply and the take-up reels are encased in a plastic shell.

Because the majority of us, as PC users, will use magnetic tape cartridges designed for use with PCs, our discussion of tape devices and media will focus on magnetic tape in the PC environment.

Magnetic Tape

Peripheral Explorer

Principles of Operation

MAGNETIC TAPE MEDIA   The mechanical operation of a magnetic tape drive is similar to that of an audiocassette tape deck. The tape, a thin polyester ribbon coated with a magnetic material on one side, passes under a *read/write head*, and the data are either

1. Read and transferred to RAM, or
2. Transmitted from RAM and written to the tape.

Magnetic tape media come in several widths, up to $\frac{1}{2}$ inch, and many different lengths, some over 2000 feet. The tape format describes the characteristics of the tape. One of the most popular PC tape cartridge formats is the *QIC minicartridge*. The minicartridge tape drive normally is housed in the same physical unit as the processor and disk drives. The QIC (*QIC* stands for *quarter-inch cartridge*) minicartridge can hold from 250 MB to 8 GB of data. The actual amount of data a given tape cartridge can store depends on the precision of the magnetic tape drive and its length.

THE TBU: TAPE BACKUP UNIT   The $\frac{1}{4}$-inch cartridges (QIC) used with PCs record data in a continuous stream. Drives for $\frac{1}{4}$-inch tape cartridges, often called **tape backup units (TBUs),** record data using **serial representation;** that is, the bits are aligned in a row, one after another, in tracks. The tracks run the length of the tape (see Figure 4–7). A tape cartridge can be formatted to have from 4 to 128 tracks, depending on the precision of the tape drive. The read/write head reads or writes data to one, two, or four tracks at a time. Figure 4–7 illustrates how data are written two tracks at a time. In the figure, data are written serially on the top two tracks for the entire length of the tape or until the data are exhausted. The tape is reversed, the read/write head is positioned over the next two tracks, and writing continues in a similar manner. If more backup capacity is needed, the computer operator must insert a clean tape before writing continues.

A tape drive is rated by its *storage capacity* and its *data transfer rate.* You might recall that the data transfer rate is the rate at which data are read from (written to) secondary storage to (from) RAM. For example, a tape backup unit might have a 4-GB capacity with a data transfer rate of about 18 MB per minute.

4–5 Backup: Better Safe than Sorry

At the Skalny Basket Company, in Springfield, Ohio, Cheryl Hart insisted on daily backups of the small family-owned company's accounts receivables files. The backups were inconvenient and took 30 minutes each day. Cheryl took the backup home each

This robotic tape storage and retrieval unit holds up to 258 high-density tape cartridges, each with a capacity of 25 GB (gigabytes). The tape cartridges are automatically loaded and unloaded to a tape drive as they are needed for processing. Corporations, such as E-Systems, use tape storage and retrieval systems to back up massive master files on magnetic disk storage.   *Courtesy of E-Systems, Inc.*

FIGURE 4–7   Cross-Section of a Magnetic Tape
Data are recorded serially on this eight-track tape, two tracks at a time.

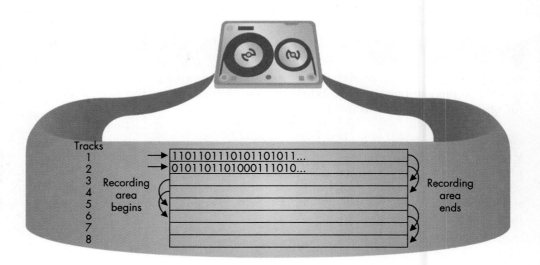

day in her briefcase, just in case. On December 23, she packed her briefcase and left for the Christmas holidays. Five days later, Skalny Basket Company burned to the ground, wiping out all inventory and its computer system. The company was up in smoke, all except for a tape cassette that contained records of its $600,000 accounts receivables. Cheryl said, "We thought we were out of business. Without the tape, we couldn't have rebuilt."

Safeguarding the content of your disks may be more important than safeguarding hardware. After all, you can always replace your computer, but you often cannot replace your lost files. The first commandment in computing, at any level, is

BACK UP YOUR FILES.

When you create a document, a spreadsheet, or a graph and you wish to recall it at a later time, you *store* the file on disk. You can, of course, store many files on a single disk. If the disk is in some way destroyed (scratched, demagnetized, burned, and so on) or lost, you have lost your files unless you have a backup.

If your system is configured with a tape backup unit, then you easily can back up all files on a system. However, if you do not have a TBU, you still can back up critical files to diskettes.

Back Up to Magnetic Tape

If your backup requirements exceed 10 MB per day, you are a candidate for a tape backup unit. Anything under 10 MB can be handled with diskettes. The relatively inexpensive TBU is a good investment for the active PC user and for all administrators of local area networks (LANs).

BACKUP METHODS You can choose from three common backup methods.

Full backup	A full backup copies all files on a hard disk to magnetic tape.
Selective backup	Only user-selected files are backed up to magnetic tape.
Modified files, only, backup	Only those files that have been modified since the last backup are backed up to magnetic tape.

FIGURE 4–8 Tape Backup Rotation: Six Tapes
This six-tape backup rotation is common in small businesses and with individuals whose files have high volatility. Two total backups are done every Monday, one of which is taken to an off-site location. Only files that are modified on a given day are backed up for each of the other weekdays. If all files are lost on Friday, the total backup from Monday is restored to the hard disk, then modified backups are restored for Tuesday through Thursday.

The frequency with which files are backed up depends on their *volatility*, or how often you update the files on the disk. If you spend time every day working with files, you should back them up each day. Others should be backed up no more often than they are used. Figure 4–8 illustrates a six-tape backup rotation.

At one time or another, just about everyone who routinely works with computers has experienced the trauma of losing work for which there was no backup. It is no fun seeing several days (or weeks) of work disappear, but it does emphasize the point that it is well worth the effort to make backup copies of your work.

RESTORING FILES If you lose your data or programs, you will need to restore the backed-up file to disk. If you use a backup system similar to the one shown in Figure 4-8, then some updating will occur between total backup runs. To re-create your files, then, you need to use the last total backup and incorporate all subsequent partial backups. For example, assume a virus wiped your hard drive clean at the end of a Thursday.

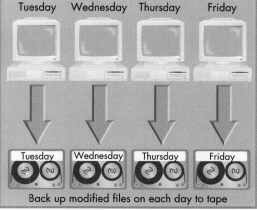

To restore the backup files, you would restore the full backup tape from Monday, then the modified backup from Tuesday, and finally the modified backup tape from Wednesday. Then you would need to redo any processing that was done on Thursday prior to the virus striking.

Backup to Interchangeable Disks

What if you do not have a tape backup unit? If you do not have a TBU (which is usually the case), then you will need to back up your files to diskettes, available on every PC, or to Zip disks. Backing up a complete hard disk to diskette is impractical because it would require hundreds, perhaps thousands, of diskettes. However, you should back up critical files to diskette. If you have a Zip disk drive, then you can back up your entire system to 100-MB Zip disks. For the casual PC user, Zip disks provide an excellent alternative to tape backup units.

Figure 4–9 illustrates and explains a backup procedure for critical files that are used daily. The procedure is the same whether your critical files are maintained on a hard disk or on one or more diskettes. In the figure, two generations of backup are

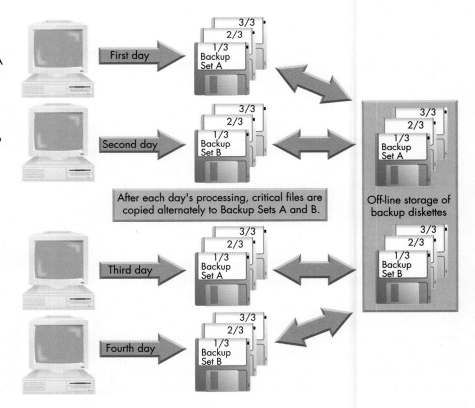

FIGURE 4–9 Diskette Backup Rotation: Two Backup Sets
After each day's processing, critical disk files are copied alternately to Backup Sets A and B. In this manner, one backup set (possibly several diskettes) is always current within a day's processing. If the critical work files and the most recent backup are accidentally destroyed, a third backup is current within two days' processing. Backup Sets A and B are alternated as the most current backup.

maintained on Backup Sets A and B. Critical disk files are copied alternately to Backup Sets A and B each day. This technique is popular with individual users, especially those in an office setting.

4–6 Optical Laser Disks: High-Density Storage

Some industry analysts have predicted that *optical laser disk* technology eventually may make magnetic disk and tape storage obsolete. With this technology, the read/write head used in magnetic storage is replaced by two lasers. One laser beam writes to the recording surface by scoring microscopic *pits* in the disk, and another laser reads the data from the light-sensitive recording surface. A light beam is easily deflected to the desired place on the optical disk, so a mechanical access arm is not needed.

Optical Storage

Optical technology opens the door to new and exciting applications. Already, this technology is leading the way to the library of the future. Because the world's output of knowledge is doubling every four years, the typical library is busting at the seams with books and other printed materials. With library budgets declining, it may be impractical to continue to build structures to warehouse printed materials. Perhaps the only long-term solution for libraries is to move away from storing printed materials and toward storing information in electronic format—possibly some form of optical disk. Perhaps in the not-too-distant future we will check out electronic "books" by downloading them from a library's optical disk to our personal optical disk. In such a library of the future, knowledge will be more readily available and complete. In theory, the library of the future could have every book and periodical ever written. And, a "book" would never be out on loan.

Optical laser disks are becoming a very inviting option for users. These disks are less sensitive to environmental fluctuations, and they provide more direct-access storage at a much lower cost than does the magnetic disk alternative. Optical laser disk technology is still emerging and has yet to stabilize. At present there are three main categories of optical laser disks: *CD-ROM and DVD, WORM disks,* and *rewritable optical disks.*

CD-ROM and DVD: *Moby Dick*, Mozart, and *Cinemania*

HISTORY: AUDIO TO VIDEO Introduced in 1980 for stereo buffs, the extraordinarily successful CD, or compact disk, is an optical laser disk designed to enhance the reproduction of recorded music. To make a CD recording, the analog sounds of music are translated into their digital equivalents and stored on a 4.72-inch optical laser disk. Seventy-four minutes of music can be recorded on each disk in digital format in 2 billion bits. (A bit is represented by the presence or absence of a pit on the optical disk.) With its tremendous storage capacity per square inch, computer industry entrepreneurs immediately recognized the potential of optical laser disk technology. In effect, anything that can be digitized can be stored on optical laser disk: data, text, voice, still pictures, music, graphics, and motion video.

CD-ROM AND DVD: THE TECHNOLOGY *CD-ROM,* a spinoff of audio CD technology, stands for *compact disk–read-only memory.* The name implies its application. Once inserted into the *CD-ROM drive,* the text, video images, and so on can be read into RAM for processing or display. However, the data on the disk are fixed—*they cannot be altered.* This is in contrast, of course, to the read/write capability of magnetic disks.

Peripheral Explorer

What makes CD-ROM so inviting is its vast capacity to store data and programs. The capacity of a single CD-ROM is up to 680 MB—about that of 477 DS/HD $3\frac{1}{2}$-inch diskettes. To put the density of CD-ROM into perspective, the words in every book ever written could be stored on a hypothetical CD-ROM that is eight feet in diameter.

EMERGING TECHNOLOGY

CD-ROM Publishing: A New Approach to Publishing

A SINGLE CD-ROM CAN HOLD A MASSIVE AMOUNT OF INFORMATION, all of which is readily available to the user. A CD-ROM costs less to produce than does a single newspaper, yet it can hold the information in a year's worth of newspapers. A CD-ROM can provide information in an interactive microcomputer format. This inexpensive mass-storage medium that offers interactivity with pizazz has not been overlooked by publishers.

CD-ROM Publishing Saves Money

Shearson Lehman Brothers, Inc. discovered it was paying more than $1 million using its PCs to access online financial information services that charge $20 to $400 an hour. The company needed the data, though. An investment banker's recommendations are only as good as the data backing up those recommendations. But wasn't there a cheaper way to gather it? For Shearson Lehman and an increasing number of companies, research centers, universities, and libraries, CD-ROM publishing was the answer.

CD-ROM publishing refers to the collection and distribution of large financial, scientific, technical, legal, medical, and bibliographic databases, as well as reference works, catalogs, and manuals, on CD-ROM disks. Shearson Lehman's solution was to order a $30,000 subscription to One Source, a CD-ROM–based financial, business, and reference database from Lotus Development Corporation, which is updated weekly.

Information Service Offerings

One Source is just one of the more than 4000 databases offered on CD-ROM disks, often by the same information services that operate the online databases. Dialog Information Services, Inc., for example, offers many of its 400 databases both online and on CD-ROM. Other offerings include regularly updated databases on engineering developments, cancer research, and environmental issues surrounding pollution and hazardous wastes. Some of the databases contain bibliographic citations only; others contain the full text of articles, sometimes including all illustrations.

At many public libraries, the dogeared *Reader's Guide to Periodical Literature* has been replaced by workstations that sport a CD-ROM drive, an ink-jet printer, and InfoTrac, a service from Information Access Company. InfoTrac is a collection of CD-ROM–based indexes for more than 1100 popular magazines and journals; about 800 business, management, and trade journals; and such leading newspapers as *The New York Times* and *The Wall Street Journal*. Other InfoTrac CD-ROM disks let users retrieve financial and investment data.

CD-ROM–based databases are also available for specific industries. One example is Sabrevision, a national database for travel agencies that is updated quarterly.

Government Data on CD-ROM

CD-ROM publishing is proving invaluable to the U.S. government, which collects, maintains, and distributes the world's largest storehouse of information. Consider just one example from the U.S. Geological Survey's Geological Division, which maintains vast databases of satellite images of the earth for use by its scientists and by the public. The division once stored the database on 125-MB tapes; the price to the public was $2000 for each tape. The CD equivalent offers 680 MB of data for only $32 per disk.

Other government data available on CD-ROM disks include complete demographic data (from the U.S. Bureau of the Census); high-resolution displays of sonar-scanned oceanographic data (the product of a cooperative project between the U.S. Geological Survey, NOAA, and NASA); as well as CD-ROM disks on aquaculture, the Agent Orange defoliant, and acid rain (from the National Agricultural Library). And, over at the Library of Congress, the American Memory project is developing CD-ROM disks of sound recordings, book excerpts, manuscripts, photographs, and other primary source material that is organized around specific themes.

Magazines, Manuals, Catalogs, and Software

Magazines take on a new look when reformatted for multimedia. With a built-in audience, computer magazines, such as *PC Magazine* and *Computerworld,* are leading the way into this new medium. Look for other mainline magazines to follow suit.

Consulting and accounting firms have made the same discovery. Instead of sending auditors and consultants out with 20 pounds of printed, hard-to-search manuals, the firms now issue their staff CD-ROMs that can be used with multimedia-equipped laptop computers. The new systems cut printing costs as well as reduce the risk of mistakes that could lead to lawsuits.

Shop manuals and parts catalogs also lend themselves to CD-ROM publishing. The catalog from Intel Corporation, the major semiconductor manufacturer, delivers some 25,000 pages of technical data, wiring diagrams, schematics, and photographs to 300,000 design engineers worldwide. The massive amount of data can be stored on just two CD-ROM disks. Automobile and truck manufacturers also are providing parts catalogs to dealers on CD-ROM; the dealers find using the disks faster and easier than going online to access a central mainframe. Retailers like CD-ROM–based catalogs because they can employ multimedia presentations to present their products.

Many new commercial programs are also being shipped on CD-ROM disks to reduce the sheer number of magnetic disks required to deliver sophisticated programs. For example, CorelDraw, Windows 95 Office, and Hijaak Pro are distributed on CD-ROM drive.

Reference Works

A representative title here is the *New Grolier Electronic Encyclopedia,* which packs all 21 volumes of *Grolier's Academic American Encyclopedia* onto a single CD-ROM disk. Like other CD-ROM titles, the encyclopedia includes audio excerpts, such as excerpts from famous speeches, musical passages, and the sounds of animals and birds. CD-ROMs that contain reference material are being created and updated every day. Reference CD-ROMs are available on a wide range of topics, including case law, pharmaceuticals, and the cinema. Whatever your special interest or occupation, there is a good chance that someone is planning on providing you with a reference CD-ROM to support it.

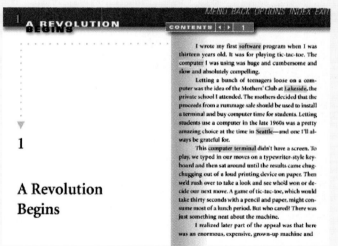

The Next Dimension in Publishing Traditional publishing (books) is sequential—one page after another. Publishing via CD-ROM lets the reader choose what comes next. The *PC Magazine CD*, shown here, is distributed each quarter. It contains the complete text of all issues of *PC Magazine* published during the past year. The CD-ROM also contains motion video, animation, and much more. Bill Gates's book, *The Road Ahead,* has been published traditionally and on CD-ROM. The CD-ROM version includes the complete text with hundreds of hypertext links to further details (shown here) or multimedia presentations, a multimedia view of the future, an "Ask Bill" section, and much more.

The CD-ROM is the foundation technology for an explosion of multimedia applications. Multimedia kiosk information centers are popping up everywhere (*left*). The information provided by the interactive kiosks is frequently stored on CD-ROM. CD-ROMs have made it possible for us to enjoy motion video, audio, and sophisticated animation on our home PC (*right*). Courtesy of International Business Machines Corporation. Unauthorized use not permitted.

Magnetic disks store data in concentric tracks, each of which is divided into sectors (see Figure 4–5). The sectors on the inside tracks hold the same amount of information as those on the outside tracks, even though the sectors on the outside tracks take up more space. In contrast, CD-ROMs store data in a single track that spirals from the center to the outside edge (see Figure 4–10). The ultrathin track spirals around the disk thousands of times.

Data are recorded on the CD-ROM's reflective surface in the form of *pits* and *lands*. The pits are tiny reflective bumps that have been burned in with a laser. The lands are flat areas separating the pits. Together they record read-only binary (1s and 0s) information that can be interpreted by the computer as text, audio, images, and so on. Once the data have been recorded, a protective coating is applied to the reflective surface (the non-label side of a CD-ROM).

Popular CD-ROM drives are classified simply as 24X, 32X, and 40X. These spin at 24, 32, eight, and 40 times the speed of the original CD standard. The speed at which a given CD-ROM spins depends on the physical location of the data being read. The data pass over the movable laser detector at the same rate, no matter where the data are read. Therefore, the CD-ROM must spin more quickly when accessing data near the center.

The laser detector is analogous to the magnetic disk's read/write head. The relatively slow spin rates make the CD-ROM access time much slower than that of its magnetic cousins. A CD-ROM drive may take 10 to 50 times longer to ready itself to read the information. Once ready to read, the transfer rate also is much slower.

The introduction of *multidisk CD-ROM player/changers* enables ready access to vast amounts of online data. This device is like a CD audio player/changer in that the desired CD-ROM can be loaded to the CD-ROM disk drive under program control. These CD-ROM player/changers, sometimes called **jukeboxes,** can hold from 6 to more than 100 CD-ROMs.

Just as CD-ROMs become mainstream equipment, **DVDs** are poised to replace them. The DVD (**digital videodisk**) looks like the CD and the CD-ROM, but it can store from seven to fourteen times as much information (up to about 10 gigabytes). A DVD can store the video for a full-length movie. DVD drives are

FIGURE 4–10 CD-ROM Organization
A laser beam detector interprets pits and lands, which represent bits (1s and 0s), located within the sectors in the spiraling track on the CD-ROM reflective surface.

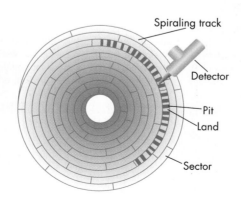

Spiraling track

Detector

Pit

Land

Sector

backwards compatible; that is, they can play all of your CD-ROMs and CDs. DVDs probably will replace videotapes and CDs in a few years.

CD-ROM AND DVD APPLICATIONS The tremendous amount of low-cost direct-access storage made possible by optical laser disks has opened the door to many new applications. Currently, most of the thousands of commercially produced CD-ROM disks contain reference material. This number is growing rapidly every year. CD-ROM is also the backbone of multimedia applications. Multimedia applications involve the integration of text, sound, graphics, motion video, and animation. Multimedia is discussed in detail in Chapter 10, "Graphics and Multimedia: Tickling Our Senses." The following is a sampling of available CD-ROM disks.

- *The Grolier Multimedia Encyclopedia* (including text, thousands of still photos, motion video sequences, and sounds)
- *The Oxford English Dictionary*
- *Microsoft Bookshelf 98 for Windows* (dictionary, thesaurus, almanac, atlas, book of facts, and more)
- The 1990 U.S. Census (county level)
- The text of 450 titles (including *Moby Dick,* the *King James version of the Bible, Beowulf, The Odyssey,* and many more)
- Multilingual dictionaries (one disk contains translation dictionaries for 12 languages)
- Scientific writings for the Apple Macintosh
- *Cinemania* (thousands of movie reviews from 1914 to present, actor biographies, movie stills, and more)
- *Great Cities of the World* (narratives, facts, photos, hotel and transportation information)
- *Space Quest* (space adventure game)
- Sound effects (thousands of sound clips)
- The Animals (multimedia zoo with 225 animals)
- World Atlas (thousands of maps and graphs, flags, audio of anthems, and more)
- *Desert Storm: The War in the Persian Gulf* (chronological multimedia presentation)

The cost of commercially produced CD-ROMs varies considerably from as little as $10 to several thousand dollars. Sales of commercial CD-ROM titles are doubling each year.

CREATING CD-ROMS FOR MASS DISTRIBUTION Most CD-ROMs and DVDs are created by commercial enterprises and sold to the public for reference and multimedia applications. Application developers gather and create source material, then write the programs needed to integrate the material into a meaningful application. The resulting files are then sent to a mastering facility, often via magnetic tape. The master copy is duplicated, or "pressed," at the factory, and the copies are distributed with their prerecorded contents (for example, the complete works of Shakespeare or *Gone with the Wind*). Depending on the run quantity, the cost of producing and packaging a CD-ROM for sale can be less than a dollar apiece! CD-ROM is a very inexpensive way to distribute applications and information.

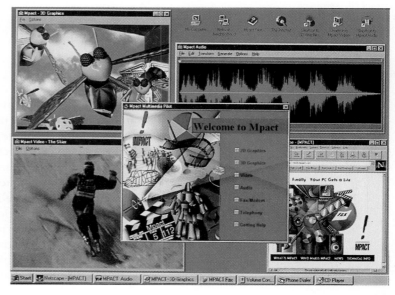

High-capacity CD-ROM and DVD drives open the door to exciting multimedia applications with audio, video, graphics, and more.   Courtesy of Chromatic Research, Inc.

CD-R: CREATING CD-ROMS LOCALLY Already, more than half the world's PCs have CD-ROM drives. This rapid and universal acceptance of CD-ROM has given rise to another technology—**CD-R, compact disk-recordable.** A few years ago, the capability to record on CD-ROM media cost over $100,000 dollars. CD-R, at around $300, brings that capability into small businesses and homes.

Locally produced CD-R disks, which will play in any CD-ROM drive, are created on CD writers. **CD writers** are peripheral devices that can write once to a CD-R disk to create an audio CD or a CD-ROM. CD writers offer a low-cost alternative to the mastering of CD-ROMs. For under $1000, commercial enterprises can expand the capabilities of a PC to create one-of-a-kind CDs or CD-ROMs at a fraction of the cost of low-volume pressed disk manufacturing. A growing number of organizations are using CD-R and CD writers to create their own CD-ROMs, primarily for internal reference applications and for archiving. Already there is a trend among manufacturing companies to replace their printed sales manuals with CD-ROM–based manuals. Sales manuals, which can span thousands of pages, are compressed to a single CD-ROM that can be easily updated each quarter. Relatively inexpensive low-volume **CD production stations** are used to duplicate locally produced CD-ROMs.

FIRST THE CD-ROM, THEN CD-R, NOW CD-RW People are still celebrating the arrival of CD-R and a new CD technology is introduced, **CD-ReWritable (CD-RW).** This technology goes one step further, allowing users to rewrite to the same CD media, just as is done on magnetic disk media. The manufacturers believe that the new CD-RW will replace the CD-ROM drives that are currently installed on most new PCs. With the cost of CD-R and CD-RW technologies converging, CD-R may disappear as people opt to pay a few dollars more for rewrite capability.

WORM Disks

Write once, read many optical laser disks, or **WORM disks,** are used by end user companies to store their own proprietary information. As with CD-ROMs, once the data have been written to the medium, they can only be read, not updated or changed. **WORM disk cartridges** can store greater volumes of information than can a CD-ROM. Typically, WORM applications involve image processing or archival storage. A single mainframe-based 200-gigabyte (GB) WORM disk can store more than 3 million digitized images the size of this page. A good example of an image processing application is an "electronic catalog." The retailer digitizes images of items for sale and stores these images for ready access on WORM disks. A customer can see the item while reading about it when perusing a retailer's Internet-based electronic catalog. And, with a few keystrokes, the customer can order the item as well. The Library of Congress is using WORM technology to help alleviate a serious shelf-space problem and to make more material available over the Internet.

Rewritable Optical Disks

Economically-priced CD-RW is relatively new, but other types of **rewritable optical disks** have been around for a while. They use several technologies, including **magneto-optical technology** (MO technology), to integrate optical and magnetic disk technology to enable read-*and*-write storage. A $5\frac{1}{4}$-inch rewritable disk cartridge can store up to 5 GB. However, the technology must be improved before these optical disks can be considered as a direct alternative to magnetic media. At present, rewritable optical disk drives are more expensive and less reliable than are magnetic media. In addition, the disk access times for rewritable optical disks are slow relative to magnetic media. For these reasons, most traditional information systems continue to rely on magnetic disks.

Rewritable optical disks have their niche, though. Applications that call for large volumes of storage with relatively little update activity are made to order for rewritable optical disks. Also, applications that require hardware to operate in harsh environ-

The HP SureStore CD-Writer 4020i is an internal compact disc record-once system that comes with a complete software suite for creating custom CDs, along with the necessary media, cards, and cables to begin recording immediately. Photo courtesy of Hewlett-Packard Company

Writable CD Media
(about $.02/MB)

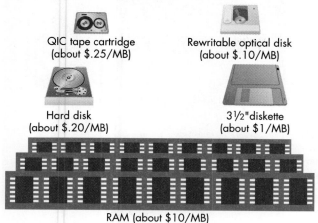
QIC tape cartridge
(about $.25/MB)

Rewritable optical disk
(about $.10/MB)

Hard disk
(about $.20/MB)

3½"diskette
(about $1/MB)

RAM (about $10/MB)

FIGURE 4-11 Relative Cost of Storage Media
This infographic compares the relative cost of popular secondary storage media and RAM. Cost, though, is only one consideration. For example, RAM cost many times more per magabyte than CD-ROM but it is much faster.

ments may be candidates for rewritable optical disks. MO technology is very durable, able to withstand shock, magnetic fields, and a wide range of temperatures, from below freezing to 100 degrees Fahrenheit. Magnetic storage media may malfunction under less-than-ideal conditions. As optical laser disk technology matures to offer reliable, cost-effective read/write operation, it eventually may dominate secondary storage in the future, as magnetic disks and tape do today.

Let's Compare: Space and $

The choice of which technologies to choose for a system or an application is often a trade-off between storage capacity and cost (dollars per megabyte). You can never compare apples to apples when comparing storage media because one might have an advantage in access time, portability, random access, nonvolatility, and so on. However, we can give you a feel for relative capacities and storage costs for representative storage technologies. Figure 4-11 compares costs of the storage media. These costs do not include the cost of the disk and tape drives, except for the hard disk, which is fixed. RAM is not only very expensive, it's volatile; thus the need for secondary storage. Figure 4-12 compares capacities of the storage media. The capacity of DVD is fixed, but the capacities of the other media vary. Those sizes shown are in common usage.

4–7 Storage Forecast: Is There a Disk in Your Future?

Storage is like money: No matter how much you have, you always want more. Each year, improvements are made in existing secondary storage devices as the storage industry strives to meet our craving for more storage.

Some scientists believe that holographic technology may give users everything they want in a storage device. Holographic memory systems enable the stacking of data on the recording surface. The different layers are read by changing the angle of the laser beam used for reading the data. Holographic memory systems will enable the entire *Encyclopedia Britannica* to be stored in a space the size and thickness of a penny.

Rotating storage media may go the way of the steam engine when low-cost solid-state memory (RAM) can store as much in less space. If nonvolatile chip technology continues to improve at the current pace, the entire *Encyclopedia Britannica* will fit into 8 tiny memory chips in the near future. Already, flash memory chips are being de-

3½"diskette
(1.44/MB)

RAM
(32/MB)

Rewritable optical disk
(7 GB)

QIC tape cartridge
(7 GB)

Hard disk
(3 GB)

DVD
(10 GB)

FIGURE 4-12 Relative Capacity of Storage Media
This infographic compares the relative capacity of popular secondary storage media and RAM. Capacity, though, is only one consideration. For example, QIC tape cartridges do not offer random access to data.

This researcher at Merck's Clinical & Regulatory Development (CARD) department displays a compact disk. Disks equivalent to four inches in height can store documentation that (if stacked) would be 2.5 times the height of the World Trade Center. CARD is supporting the use of the electronic medium as a means of both a faster delivery and review of their drug submissions to regulatory agencies and as a better use of Merck resources.   Courtesy of Merck & Co., Inc.

veloped that will have 16 times more storage capacity than the largest flash chips currently available. The 30-MB flash memory chips could be used in place of hard drives in portable PCs. Perhaps someday the only moving parts on PCs will be the keys on the keyboard and the cooling fan. If chip companies can make 1-GB flash memory chips by the end of the decade, which is entirely possible, rotating storage may very quickly be relegated to archival storage.

What does being able to store more information in less space mean to you? It means videophones that can be worn like wristwatches. It means that you can carry a diskette-sized reader and all your college "textbooks" in your front pocket. We can expect at least one big leap in storage technology by the end of the century. That leap will forever change much of what we do and how we do it.

Interactive Study Guide
Chapter 4

IMPORTANT TERMS AND SUMMARY OUTLINE

4–1 SECONDARY STORAGE AND FILES: DATA KEEPERS

Data and programs are stored in **secondary storage** for permanent storage. **Magnetic disk drives** and **magnetic tape drives** are the primary devices for secondary storage. **Optical laser disk** technology is emerging as an alternative to magnetic disks and magnetic tapes.

The **file** is the foundation of permanent storage on a computer system. Popular file types include the **ASCII file, data file, document file, spreadsheet file, source program file, executable program file, graphics file, audio file,** and **video file.**

In the MS-DOS/Windows environment, filenames can include up to eight characters with an optional three-character extension (for example, *myphoto.bmp*).

Everything we do on a computer has to do with a file and, therefore, secondary storage. We can create, copy, move, delete, retrieve, print, execute, download, **export, import,** compress, and protect files. **File compression** is used to economize on storage space.

4–2 SEQUENTIAL AND RANDOM ACCESS: NEW TERMS FOR OLD CONCEPTS

Data are retrieved and manipulated either sequentially or randomly. Magnetic disk drives enable **random-** and **sequential-processing** capabilities. Magnetic tapes have only sequential-processing capabilities.

4–3 MAGNETIC DISKS: ROUND AND ROUND

Popular types of **interchangeable magnetic disks** include the $3\frac{1}{2}$-inch **diskette,** also called a **floppy disk,** the **SuperDisk,** and the 100-MB **Zip disk,** which is inserted into a **Zip drive.** The disks are about the same size but have different **disk densities.**

There are two types of hard disk, those that are permanently installed and those that are interchangeable. Permanently installed **fixed magnetic disks** contain several disk platters stacked on a single rotating spindle. The rotation of a magnetic disk passes all data under or over a **read/write head,** which is mounted on **access arms.** The **Jaz drive** uses an interchangeable **Jaz cartridge.**

In **sector organization,** the recording surface is divided into pie-shaped **sectors,** and each sector is assigned a number. Data are stored via serial representation in **tracks** on each recording surface. The spacing of tracks is measured in **tracks per inch,** or **TPI.** A particular **cylinder** refers to every track with the same number on all recording surfaces. A particular set of data stored on a disk is assigned a **disk address** that designates its physical location (disk-face surface, track, sector).

Before a disk can be used, it must be **formatted.** Formatting creates *sectors* and *tracks* into which data are stored and establishes an area for the **file allocation table (FAT).**

The **access time** for a magnetic disk is the interval between the instant a computer makes a request for transfer of data from a disk-storage device to RAM and the instant this operation is completed.

The **data transfer rate** is the rate at which data are read from (written to) secondary storage to (from) RAM. **Disk caching** improves system speed.

Apply the dictates of common sense to the care of diskettes (avoid excessive dust, avoid extremes in temperature and humidity, and so on).

In the mainframe environment, **direct-access storage devices (DASDs)** are the prerequisite for virtually all information systems that demand direct-access processing.

A **computer virus** is a program that "infects" other programs and databases upon contact. Three primary sources of computer viruses are electronic bulletin-board systems, diskettes, and computer networks. Antiviral programs, also called *vaccines,* exist to help fight viruses.

4–4 MAGNETIC TAPE: RIBBONS OF DATA

Today, magnetic tape storage is no longer used for routine processing; however, it has three other important functions. It is used for backup, for archiving files, and for file portability between computers.

A **magnetic tape cartridge** (also called **data cartridge**) is loaded to a tape drive, where data can be read or written. The physical nature of the magnetic tape results in data being stored and accessed sequentially.

One of the most popular PC tape cartridge formats is the *QIC minicartridge.* A tape drive is rated by its *storage capacity* and its *data transfer rate.*

Drives for $\frac{1}{4}$-inch tape cartridges are often called **tape backup units (TBUs).** Data are recorded in tracks using **serial representation.**

4–5 BACKUP: BETTER SAFE THAN SORRY

The frequency with which a work disk is backed up depends on its volatility. It is common practice to maintain two generations of backup. Three common backup methods are full backup, selective backup of files, or backup of modified files only.

4–6 OPTICAL LASER DISKS: HIGH-DENSITY STORAGE

Optical laser disk storage is capable of storing vast amounts of data. The three main categories of optical laser disks are CD-ROM and DVD, WORM disk, and rewritable optical disk.

A CD-ROM is inserted into the CD-ROM drive for processing. Most of the commercially produced read-only CD-ROM disks contain reference material or support multimedia applications. Multidisk player/changers are called **jukeboxes.**

The **DVD (digital videodisk)** looks like the CD and the CD-ROM, but it can store up to about 10 gigabytes. DVD drives can play CD-ROMs and CDs.

A blank **compact disk-recordable (CD-R)** disk looks like a CD-ROM and once information is recorded on it, it works like a CD-ROM. Locally produced CD-R disks are created on **CD writers.** Relatively inexpensive low-volume **CD production stations** are used to duplicate locally produced CD-ROMs. **CD-ReWritable (CD-RW)** allows users to rewrite to the same CD media.

WORM disks are used by end user companies to store their own proprietary information. **WORM disk car-** tridges can store greater volumes of information than can a CD-ROM. WORM applications involve image processing or archival storage.

Rewritable optical disks use **magneto-optical technology** to integrate optical and magnetic disk technology to enable read-*and*-write storage.

The choice of which technologies to choose for a system or an application is often a trade-off between storage capacity and cost (dollars per megabyte).

4–7 STORAGE FORECAST: IS THERE A DISK IN YOUR FUTURE? Each year, improvements are made in existing secondary storage devices as the storage industry strives to meet our craving for more storage.

REVIEW EXERCISES

Concepts

1. Which disk has the greatest capacity, the traditional floppy or the Zip disk?
2. Name and briefly describe four types of files.
3. What advantages will the Windows 95 operating system have over MS-DOS/Windows with respect to naming files?
4. Describe file compression and why it might be used.
5. CD-ROM is a spinoff of what technology?
6. A program issues a "read" command for data to be retrieved from a magnetic tape. Describe the resulting movement of the data.
7. Why must hard disks and diskettes be formatted?
8. What are the three main categories of optical laser disks?
9. What is the width of the magnetic tape in the QIC minicartridge?
10. List three content topic areas available on CD-ROM.
11. What name is given to programs intended to damage the computer system of an unsuspecting victim? Name three sources of these.
12. Although magnetic tape storage is no longer used for routine processing, list two other functions it may serve.

Discussion and Problem Solving

13. A floppy disk does not move until a read or write command is issued. Once it is issued, the floppy begins to spin. It stops spinning after the command is executed. Why is a hard disk not set in motion in the same manner? Why is a floppy not made to spin continuously?
14. Every Friday night a company makes backup copies of all master files and programs. Why is this necessary? The company has both tape and disk drives. Which storage medium would you suggest for the backup? Why?
15. Describe the potential impact of optical laser disk technology on public and university libraries. On home libraries.
16. How many 1-GB QIC minicartridges would be needed to back up the contents of a 4-GB hard disk?
17. Describe at least two applications where rewritable optical laser disk would be preferred over hard disks for storage.
18. Briefly describe the primary difference between CD-R and CD-RW.

SELF-TEST (BY SECTION)

4–1 a. Data are retrieved from temporary secondary storage and stored permanently in RAM. (T/F) ~~F~~

b. An _____ file is a text-only file that can be read or created by any word processing program or text editor. *ASCII*

c. A *file* is to *secondary storage* as a *vehicle* is to a *parking lot.* (T/F) *T*

d. WINTER.SALES and .ADD are valid filenames in the MS-DOS/Windows environment. (T/F) *F*

e. When we _____ a file, we convert a file in the current program to a format needed by another program. *export*

4–2 Magnetic disks have both _____- and _____-access capabilities. *Random sequential*

4–3 a. The _____ drive uses optical technology together with magnetic technology to read and write to 100-MB disks. *Zip*

b. In a disk drive, the read/write heads are mounted on an access arm. (T/F) *T*

c. Interchangeable disks cannot be stored offline. (T/F) *F*

d. The standard size for magnetic diskettes is _____ inches. *3½*

e. What percentage of the data on a magnetic disk is available to the system with each complete revolution of the disk: (a) 10%, (b) 50%, or (c) 100%? *c*

f. The _____ _____ denotes the physical location of a particular file or set of data on a magnetic disk. *disk address*

4–4 a. When activated, which tape backup unit feature results in increased capacity on the data cartridge: (a) data compression, (b) data reduction, or (c) tape stretching? *A*

b. Tape backup units store data on tape cartridges _____ in tracks. *serially*

4–5 The frequency with which a work disk is backed up depends on its volatility. (T/F) *T*

4–6 a. _____ _____ _____ storage technology uses laser beams to write to the recording surface. *optical laser disk*

b. CD-ROM is read-only. (T/F) *T*

c. Disks that use magneto-optical technology are: (a) rewritable, (b) read-only, or (c) write-only? *A*

d. CD writers are peripheral devices that can write once to a WORM disk. (T/F) *F*

Self-test Answers. **4–1 (a)** F; **(b)** ASCII; **(c)** T; **(d)** F; **(e)** export. **4–2** random, sequential. **4–3 (a)** Zip; **(b)** T; **(c)** F; **(d)** $3\frac{1}{2}$; **(e)** c; **(f)** disk address. **4–4 (a)** a; **(b)** serially. **4–5** T. **4–6 (a)** Optical laser disk; **(b)** T; **(c)** a; **(d)** F.

Input/Output: Computers in Action

- Explain alternative approaches to and devices for providing input to a system.
- Describe the operation and application of common output devices.
- Describe the use and characteristics of the different types of terminals.

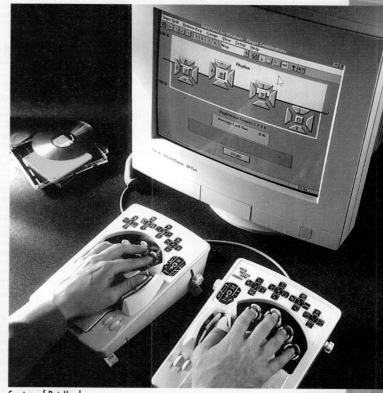

Courtesy of DataHand

LET'S TALK

Can you follow this conversation? It includes computing concepts presented in this chapter. Read it now, then reread it once you've had an opportunity to study the chapter.

The Scene A sales representative (Zeta) specializing in the sale of grocery store technology is calling on the vice president of operations (Paul) for an East Coast grocery chain.

PAUL: Hello, Zeta. We don't want any more speech synthesis devices!

ZETA: I know, Paul. The voice feedback at the cash registers didn't take off here or anywhere else. But what I have today is already in demand.

PAUL: Let's see it.

ZETA: Let's see *them*, Paul. I've got two new products. The first is a handheld scanner with a badge reader for use by customers in a hurry and by those who have trouble walking through the store. Customers insert their smart card for ID purposes. Then, rather than taking items off the shelves and putting them in shopping carts or baskets, shoppers simply scan the bar code of the desired item and continue shopping. On their way out, customers drop off their scanners, whose contents are entered into the system. How about that for source-data automation?

PAUL: But what about the groceries?

ZETA: Well, based on the scanner output, the customer's account is charged, and an aisle-by-aisle list is printed for one of your professional shoppers. The order is gathered and boxed for pickup or delivery.

PAUL: Sounds interesting. What's the other product?

ZETA: A multimedia kiosk that helps customers find what they need. Its easy-to-use touch screen monitor has 1280 by 1024 resolution and a .28 dot pitch. A quiet ink-jet printer provides hard-copy output, mainly shopping lists and coupons.

PAUL: So what's the value of the kiosk?

ZETA: For starters, the kiosk eliminates a thousand "Where is this?" questions each day, but it has many other benefits.

PAUL: You've got my attention; tell me more.

5-1 I/O Devices: Let's Interface

**Monthly Technology Update
Chapter 5**

Just about everyone routinely communicates directly or indirectly with a computer, even people who have never sat in front of a personal computer or video display terminal. Perhaps you have had one of these experiences.

- Have you ever been hungry and short of cash? No problem. Just stop at an automatic teller machine (ATM) and ask for some "lunch money." The ATM's keyboard and monitor enable you to hold an interactive conversation with the bank's computer. The ATM's printer provides you with a hard copy of your transactions when you leave. Some ATMs talk to you as well.

- Have you ever called a mail-order merchandiser and been greeted by a message like this: "Thank you for calling BrassCo Enterprises Customer Service. If you wish to place an order, press one. If you wish to inquire about the status of an order, press two. To speak to a particular person, enter that person's four-digit extension or hold and an operator will process your call momentarily." The message is produced by a voice-response system, which responds to the buttons you press on your telephone key pad.

How exactly are we managing to communicate with these computers? Through input/output devices. Input devices translate our data and communications into a form that the computer can understand. The computer then processes these data, and an

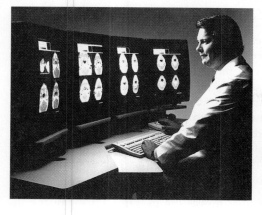

There are many ways to interact with a computer system. This doctor is surrounded by four high-resolution monitors. He uses a keyboard and trackball for input. GE's PACS Diagnostic and Clinical Display Workstation provides versatile, high-performance medical imaging display capabilities designed for diagnostic reading and clinical review of patient examinations.   Courtesy of GE Medical Systems

output device translates them back into a form that we can understand. In our two examples, the ATM's keyboard and monitor and the telephone key pad serve as input devices, and the ATM's printer and the voice-response system serve as output devices.

Input/output devices are quietly playing an increasingly significant role in our lives. The number and variety of I/O devices is expanding even as you read this, and some of these devices are fairly exotic. For example, AromaScan markets an electronic nose that can measure and digitally record smells. Perhaps the AromaScan smelling device will revolutionize aroma analysis in the food, drink, and perfume industries. Its cost, which is about the same as a BMW, may force us to do our sniffing the old-fashioned way. In this chapter we discuss *common* I/O devices and terminals with I/O capabilities.

5–2 Traditional Input Devices: Key, Point, and Draw

The Keyboard

All PCs, workstations, and VDTs have a keyboard, the most common device for transferring user input to the computer system. There are two basic types of keyboards: traditional alphanumeric keyboards and special-function keyboards.

ALPHANUMERIC KEYBOARDS: 12345 AND QWERTY   One of the most widely used types of keyboard is the 101-key keyboard with the traditional *QWERTY* key layout, 12 function keys, a key pad, a variety of special-function keys, and dedicated cursor-control keys. PC, workstation, and VDT keyboards vary considerably in appearance. Portable computers have a simple QWERTY keyboard with a minimum number of function keys. Desktop computers are frequently configured with a 124-key PC keyboard that includes an extended set of function keys and extra unlabeled keys that can be programmed to perform user-defined keystroke sequences (macros) when tapped. Chapter 3, "Software: Telling Computers What to Do," contains detailed information on working with keyboards.

Point-of-sale (POS) terminals at retail establishments, such as the one at this coffee specialty shop, are usually equipped with special-function keyboards that enable rapid processing of sales transactions as well as alphanumeric input.   Courtesy of International Business Machines Corporation. Unauthorized use not permitted.

SPECIAL-FUNCTION KEYBOARDS: TAP THE FRENCH FRY KEY   Some keyboards are designed for specific applications. For example, the cash-register-like terminals at most fast-food restaurants have special-purpose keyboards. Rather than key in the name and price of an order of French fries, attendants need only press the key marked "French fries" to record the sale. Such keyboards help shop supervisors, airline ticket agents, retail sales clerks, and many others interact more quickly with their computer systems.

Point-and-Draw Devices

Peripheral Explorer

The keyboard is too cumbersome for some applications, especially those that rely on a graphical user interface (GUI) or require the user to point or draw. The effectiveness of GUIs depends on the user's ability to make a rapid selection from a screen full of graphic icons or menus. In these instances the mouse can position the pointer (graphics cursor) over an icon quickly and efficiently. Computer artists use mice to create images. Engineers use them to "draw" lines that connect points on a graph. The mouse and its operation are discussed in Chapter 3.

For the moment, the mouse remains the most popular point-and-draw device. However, a variety of devices are available that move the graphics cursor to point and draw, and each has its advantages and disadvantages.

- *Joystick.* The **joystick** is a vertical stick that moves the graphics cursor in the direction the stick is pushed. Video arcade wizards are no doubt familiar with the joystick.

- *Trackball.* The **trackball** is a ball inset in a small external box or adjacent to and in the same unit as the keyboard. The ball is "rolled" with the fingers to move the graphics cursor. Some people find it helpful to think of a trackball as an upside-down mouse with a bigger ball on the bottom. Trackballs are sometimes configured with portable computers and workstations.

- *Mouse pen.* Like a mouse, the **mouse pen** is rolled across any smooth surface, but it is held like a pen.

- *Digitizer tablet and pen.* The **digitizer tablet and pen** are a pen and a pressure-sensitive tablet whose *X–Y* coordinates correspond with those on the computer's display screen. Some digitizing tablets also use a crosshair device instead of a pen. The movement of the pen or crosshair is reproduced simultaneously on the display screen. When configured with a PC, the digitizer tablet and pen enable the user to perform pen-based computing applications, such as drawing and entering handwritten data to the system.

- *Trackpoints.* **Trackpoints** are usually positioned in or near a laptop's keyboard. They function like miniature joysticks but are operated with the tip of the finger.

- *Trackpads.* The **trackpad** has no moving parts. Simply move your finger about a touch-sensitive pad to move the graphics cursor.

Figure 5–1 provides a visual overview of point-and-draw devices.

5–3 Source-Data Automation: Getting Closer to the Action

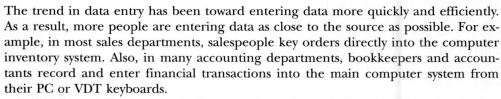

Input

The trend in data entry has been toward entering data more quickly and efficiently. As a result, more people are entering data as close to the source as possible. For example, in most sales departments, salespeople key orders directly into the computer inventory system. Also, in many accounting departments, bookkeepers and accountants record and enter financial transactions into the main computer system from their PC or VDT keyboards.

Until recently, data entry has been performed mainly through *keystrokes* and other key-driven methods. The keystroke will remain the standard of data entry for the foreseeable future, but the need for key-driven data entry has been eliminated in many applications. In the push toward speed and efficiency, data entry is relying more on **source-data automation,** or the elimination of key entries. For example, you have probably noticed the preprinted **bar codes** on consumer products. At checkout counters these bar codes have eliminated the need for most key entry. Checkers need only pass the product over the *laser scanner.* The price is entered into the store's computer system, and the shelf inventory is updated as well.

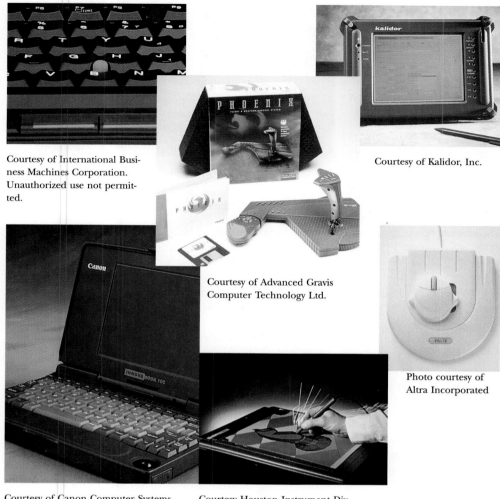

Courtesy of International Business Machines Corporation. Unauthorized use not permitted.

Courtesy of Kalidor, Inc.

Courtesy of Advanced Gravis Computer Technology Ltd.

Photo courtesy of Altra Incorporated

Courtesy of Canon Computer Systems, Inc.

Courtesy Houston Instrument Div. AMETEK, Inc.

FIGURE 5–1   Point-and-Draw Devices
This photo collage demonstrates the variety of ways we can point, draw, and click. The trackpoint is conveniently located within the keyboard. The digitizer tablet and pen are used by artists. The Phoenix Flight & Weapons Control System (joystick) is designed specifically for PC action games and flight simulation programs. Altra's Felix lets you move anywhere on the screen while moving its handle no more than an inch in any direction. The pen is used with this rugged Kalidor pen-based computer to enter information. This Canon notebook PC comes with a trackball.

Data entry is an area in which enormous potential exists for increases in productivity. The technology of data entry devices is constantly changing. New and improved methods of transcribing raw data are being invented and put on the market each month. These data entry methods and associated devices are discussed next.

Scanners: Making Hard Copy Soft

A variety of **scanners** read and interpret information on printed matter and convert it to a format that can be interpreted by a computer, primarily encoded alphanumeric characters and digitized images.

OCR AND BAR CODES: SEEING IS BELIEVING   What is it that scanners actually read? **OCR (optical character recognition)** is the ability to read printed information into a computer system. Some of them can even read your handwriting. More commonly, scanners read bar codes. Bar codes represent alphanumeric data by varying the size of adjacent vertical lines. There are a variety of bar-coding systems. Compare the POSTNET bar codes on metered mail with those on packing labels and with those on consumer products. One of the most visible bar-coding systems is the Universal Product Code (UPC). The UPC, originally used for supermarket items, is now being printed on other consumer goods.

The United States Postal Service relies on both OCR and bar code scanning to sort most mail. At the Postal Service, light-sensitive scanners read and interpret the

Courtesy of Norand Corporation

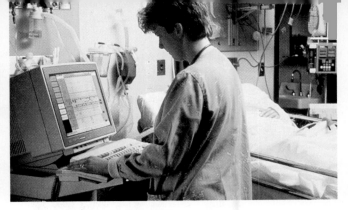

Photo courtesy of Hewlett-Packard Company.

The trend in data entry is to enter data as close to the source as possible. This store clerk enters inventory data directly to a handheld computer. The handheld computer is networked to the store's main computer via a wireless link. Bedside terminals enable doctors and nurses to enter patient data at the source. Doctors order blood tests, schedule operating rooms, and review medical records while interacting with the hospital's computer system.

Federal Express couriers and handlers use the SuperTracker, a handheld OCR data collection device, to track the progress of packages from source to destination. Package status information, such as pickup or delivery times, is transmitted directly to the company's centralized database through the DADS (Digitally Assisted Dispatch System) units in the courier vans and sorting facilities.   Courtesy of Federal Express Corporation. All rights reserved.

ZIP code and POSTNET bar code on billions of envelopes each day. The ZIP information is then sent to computer-based sorting machines that route the envelopes to appropriate bins for distribution.

Are there advantages to using OCR over bar codes or bar codes over OCR? The advantage of bar codes over OCR is that the position or orientation of the code being read is not as critical to the scanner. In a supermarket, for example, the UPC can be recorded even when a bottle of ketchup is rolled over the laser scanner.

OCR AND BAR CODE SCANNERS AND APPLICATIONS   Two types of OCR and bar code scanners—*contact* and *laser*—read information on labels and various types of documents. Both bounce a beam of light off an image, then measure the reflected light to interpret the image. Handheld contact scanners make contact as they are brushed over the printed matter to be read. Laser-based scanners are more versatile and can read data passed near the scanning area. Scanners of both technologies can recognize printed characters and various types of bar codes. Scanners used for OCR or bar code applications can be classified into three basic categories.

- *Handheld label scanners.* These devices read data on price tags, shipping labels, inventory part numbers, book ISBNs, and the like. Handheld label scanners, sometimes called **wand scanners,** utilize either contact or laser technology. You have probably seen both types used in libraries and various retail stores. Wand scanners also are used to read package labels in shipping and receiving and in inventory management.

- *Stationary label scanners.* These devices, which rely exclusively on laser technology, are used in the same types of applications as wand scanners. Stationary scanners are common in grocery stores and discount stores.

- *Document scanners.* Document scanners are capable of scanning documents of varying sizes. Document scanners read envelopes at the U.S. Postal Office, and they also read turnaround documents for utility companies. A **turnaround document** is *computer-produced output* that we can read and is ultimately returned as *computer-readable input* to a computer system. For example, when you pay your utility bills, you return a check and a stub for the invoice (the turnaround document). The stub is scanned, and payment information is entered automatically to the utility company's system.

Scanner technology has spawned an explosion of source-data automation applications. One of the more innovative uses of stationary scanners is along toll roads. Drivers who frequently use a particular toll road pay tolls in advance and receive labels for their cars. Stationary scanners along the toll road read the labels as cars pass at highway speeds. The electronic toll booths transmit the data directly to a central computer system. At the central site, the drivers' accounts are debited the amount of the toll.

Most retail stores and distribution warehouses, and all overnight couriers, are seasoned users of scanner technology. Salespeople, inventory management personnel, and couriers would much prefer to wave their "magic" wands than enter data one character at a time.

IMAGE SCANNERS AND PROCESSING   Source-data automation allows direct entry of graphic information, as well as text-based information, via scanners. An **image scanner** uses laser technology to scan and **digitize** an image. The hard-copy image is scanned and translated into an electronic format that can be interpreted by and stored on computers. The image to be scanned can be a photograph, a drawing, an insurance form, a medical record—anything that can be digitized. Once an image has been digitized and entered to the computer system, it can be retrieved, displayed, altered, merged with text, stored, sent via data communications to one or several remote computers, and even faxed. Manipulating and managing scanned images, known as **image processing,** is becoming increasingly important, especially with recent advances in optical storage technologies. Organizations everywhere are replacing space-consuming metal filing cabinets and millions of hard-copy documents, from tax returns to warrantee cards, with their electronic equivalents. Image processing's space saving incentive, along with its ease of document retrieval is making the image scanner a must-have peripheral in most offices.

Page and Hand Image Scanners.   Image scanners are of two types: *page* and *hand*. Either can be gray scale (the image is presented in shades of gray) or color. (Gray scale is discussed later in this chapter.) High-end *page image scanners* work like desktop duplicating machines. That is, the image to be scanned is placed face down on the scanning surface, covered, then scanned. The result is a high-resolution digitized image. Inexpensive page scanners weighing less than two pounds accept the document to be scanned in a slot. The *hand image scanner* is rolled manually over the image to be scanned. Because it must be guided across the image by the human hand, the resolution of a hand image scanner is not as high as that of a page image scanner. About five inches in width, hand image scanners are appropriate for capturing small images or portions of large images.

In addition to scanning photos and other graphic images, image scanners can also scan and interpret the alphanumeric characters on regular printed pages. People use page scanners to translate printed hard copy to computer-readable format. For applications that demand this type of translation, page scanners can minimize or eliminate the need for key entry. Today's image scanners and the accompanying OCR software are very sophisticated. Together they can read and interpret the characters from most printed material, such as a printed letter or a page from this book.

Image processing: Eliminating the paper pile.   Companies and even individuals are becoming buried in paper, literally. In some organizations, paper files take up most of the floor space. Moreover, finding what you want may take several minutes to hours. Or, you may never find what you want. Image processing applications scan and index thousands, even millions, of documents. Once these scanned documents are on the computer system, they can be easily retrieved and manipulated. For example, banks use image processing to archive canceled checks and to archive documents associated with mortgage loan servicing. Insurance companies use image processing in claims processing applications.

Images are scanned into a digital format that can be stored on disk, often optical laser disk because of its huge capacity. For example, decades worth of hospital medical records can be scanned and stored on a handful of optical laser disks that fit easily on a single shelf. The images are organized so they can be retrieved in seconds rather than minutes or hours. Medical personnel who need a hard copy can simply print one out in a matter of seconds.

Photo courtesy of Hewlett-Packard Company.

Courtesy of Epson America, Inc.

Courtesy of Caere Corporation.

Relatively inexpensive image scanners have given rise to a variety of image processing applications. Here (*top*), a graphic artist scans an image into the system on a page scanner. The Epson PhotoPlus Color Photo Scanner (*middle*) scans color photos and business cards right into your PC. In the bottom photo, a manager uses a hand scanner to convert text in a magazine into electronic text that can be inserted into a word processing document.

The State of Louisiana Department of Public Safety routinely supplies driver information to other state agencies and to outside organizations, such as insurance companies, and is a perfect example of how image processing can reduce the need for paper while making records more accessible. The department has the dual problem of keeping up with thousands of documents received each week and with servicing thousands of requests for driver information, mostly for problem drivers. The amount of paperwork involved could be staggering. However, because this department has gone to image processing for driver information, other state agencies have direct access to the image bank over communication lines, and the department has no trouble handling outside requests for information. The department's long-range plan calls for using image processing to minimize or eliminate paper and microfilm in as many applications as possible.

The real beauty of image processing is that the digitized material can be easily manipulated. For example, any image can be easily faxed to another location (without being printed). A fax is sent and received as an image. The content on the fax or any electronic image can be manipulated in many ways. OCR software can be used to translate any printed text on the stored image to an electronic format. For example, a doctor might wish to pull selected printed text from various patient images into a word processing document to compile a summary of a patient's condition. The doctor can even select specific graphic images (X-rays, photos, or drawings) from the patient's record for inclusion in the summary report.

This knowledge worker at Merck & Company works with an image processing application in which she scans images of case reports from clinical studies into a database. The application helps facilitate the FDA drug approval processes.   Courtesy of Merck & Co., Inc.

Magnetic Stripes and Smart Cards: Just Say Charge It

The magnetic stripes on the back of charge cards and badges offer another means of data entry at the source. The magnetic stripes are encoded with data appropriate for specific applications. For example, your account number and personal identification number are encoded on a card for automatic teller machines.

Magnetic stripes contain much more data per unit of space than do printed characters or bar codes. Moreover, because they cannot be read visually, they are perfect for storing confidential data, such as a personal identification number. Employee cards and security badges often contain authorization data for access to physically secured areas, such as the computer center. To gain access, an employee inserts a card or badge into a **badge reader.** This device reads and checks the authorization code before permitting the individual to enter a secured area. When badge readers are linked to a central computer, that computer can maintain a chronological log of people entering or leaving secured areas.

The enhanced version of cards with a magnetic stripe is called the **smart card.** The smart card, similar in appearance to other cards, contains a microprocessor that retains certain security and personal data in its memory at all times. Because the smart card can hold more information, has some processing capability, and is almost impossible to duplicate, smart cards may soon replace cards with magnetic stripes. Already, smart cards are gaining widespread acceptance in Europe and in the United States, especially smart cards with *stored value.* The dual-function stored-value smart card serves as a credit card and as a replacement for cash. Customers with these cards can go to automatic teller machines to transfer electronic cash from their checking or savings account to the card's memory. They are used like cash at the growing number of stores that accept stored-value cards. Each time the card is used, the purchase amount is deducted from the card's stored value. To reload the card with more electronic cash, the card's owner must return to an automatic teller machine. The stored-value smart card is another big step toward the inevitable elimination of cash.

Smart cards have a variety of applications, including banking, medical records, security, and more. Some smart cards allow access to information if they are given the correct password. In the photo a person is inserting his Gemplus smart card into a bank's ATM.   Courtesy of Gemplus

Speech Recognition: Getting on Speaking Terms with Computers

Speech recognition has been possible for over 20 years, but only when the words were spoken to an expensive, room-sized mainframe computer. The power of PCs has finally caught up with speech-recognition technology. With the modern speech-recognition software and a special microphone, the typical off-the-shelf PC is able to accept spoken words as input at speeds of up to 125 words a minute. Much of the manuscript for this book was dictated to a PC using IBM's VoiceType Dictation speech-recognition software. Quality-control personnel who must use their hands describe defects as they are detected. Physicians dictate patient summaries directly to the computer. Many executives now dictate, rather than keyboard, their e-mail messages.

Speech recognition is emerging as the newest *killer application*. In the PC world, a killer application has a profound impact on personal computing. The "killer app" handle places speech-recognition systems alongside some pretty good company: word processing, spreadsheet, database, and Internet browser applications.

If you were to purchase a **speech-recognition system** for your PC, you would receive software, a generic vocabulary database, and a high-quality microphone with noise-canceling capabilities. Successful speech recognition depends on a strong, clear signal from the microphone. Popular systems include IBM's VoiceType Dictation, Dragon System's DragonDictate, and Kurzweil Applied Intelligence's Kurzweil VOICE. The microphone, which is mounted on a headset, filters out general office noise, including ringing phones and slamming doors. The size of the vocabulary database ranges from 20,000 words for general dictation to more than 100,000 words for legal or medical dictation. Once you have installed the hardware and software, you are ready to speak to the computer. The system will accept most of your spoken words. However, you can *train* the system to accept virtually all of your words. It helps to train the system to recognize your unique speech patterns. We all sound different, even to a computer. To train the system, we simply talk to it for about an hour—the longer the better. Even if we say a word twice in succession, it will probably have a different inflection or nasal quality. The system uses artificial intelligence techniques to learn our speech patterns and update the vocabulary database accordingly. The typical speech-recognition system never stops learning, for it is always fine-tuning the vocabulary so it can recognize words with greater speed and accuracy. Each user on a given PC would need to customize his or her own vocabulary database. Some speech-recognition systems are smart enough to recognize different speakers and switch to each person's customized vocabulary database for speech interpretation. To further customize our personal vocabulary database, we can add words that are unique to our working environment.

Some speech-recognition systems are speaker independent; that is, they can accept words spoken by anyone. Such systems are restricted to accepting only a limited number of words and tasks. Despite its limitations, speaker-independent speech recognition has a number of applications. For example, salespeople in the field can enter an order simply by calling in to the company's computer and stating the customer number, item number, and quantity. Some telephone companies have implemented systems that permit customers to speak numbers and a few commands.

There are four basic steps involved in speech recognition (see Figure 5–2).

1. *Say the word.* Current speech-recognition systems require users to dictate or enter commands in *isolated* or *discrete speech.* That is, words must be spoken such that there is a split second of dead space separating each spoken word.
2. *Digitize the word.* The sounds in each frequency are digitized so they can be manipulated by the computer. Speech-recognition systems actually recognize *phonemes,* unique sounds that are the basic building blocks of speech. Speech-recognition software identifies the phonemes and groups them into words.

MEMORY BITS

Input Devices

- Keyboard
- Point-and-draw devices
- Scanners
- Image scanners (page and hand)
- Badge reader (for magnetic stripes and smart cards)
- Speech-recognition systems
- Vision-input systems
- Digital cameras
- Handheld data entry devices

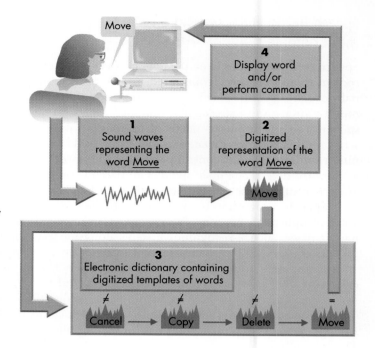

FIGURE 5–2 Speech Recognition

The sound waves created by the spoken word *Move* are digitized by the computer. The digitized template is matched against templates of other words in the electronic dictionary. When the computer finds a match, it displays a written version of the word.

3. *Match the word.* The digitized version of the word is matched against similarly formed *templates* in the system's electronic dictionary. The digitized template is a form that can be stored and interpreted by computers (in 1s and 0s).

4. *Display the word or perform the command.* When a match is found, the word is displayed within current application during dictation or, in command mode, the ap-

IBM's VoiceType Dictation is a flexible speech-recognition system that allows users to input text and control applications by speaking instead of typing. The software translates your spoken words into commands or dictated text. This caption and much of this book was dictated directly to the computer via VoiceType Dictation (*left*). The speech-recognition program displays a word list that contains its best guesses when a spoken word has several interpretations. In this example the only word not interpreted correctly was "guesses," which was interpreted as "dresses." Over time, the program adapts to a voice; that is, its guesses get better as you use it. Words can be dictated directly into spreadsheet, database, presentation graphics (*right*), and any other type of software that accepts text. In the PowerPoint 97 example the words "Information Services" were dictated directly into the title text box. When in command mode, VoiceType Dictation can assist users in navigating around the desktop, accepting commands like "start button," "delete to end of line," "clipboard," and so on. Courtesy of International Business Machines Corporation. Unauthorized use not permitted.

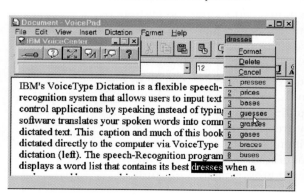

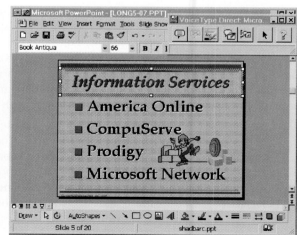

propriate command is performed (for example, "move" the marked text). In some cases, the word is displayed or repeated through the computer's sound system for confirmation. If no match is found, the speaker is asked to repeat the word.

It is only a matter of time before we all will be communicating with our PCs in spoken English rather than through time-consuming keystrokes. Already, thousands of attorneys, doctors, journalists, and others who routinely do dictation and write are enjoying the benefits of speech recognition. Speech recognition is also a tremendous enabling technology for the physically challenged.

Vision-Input Systems: Computer Eyes

Some data are best entered and processed visually. However, the simulation of human senses, especially vision, is extremely complex. A computer does not actually see and interpret an image the way a human being does. Computers need cameras for their "eyesight." To create a visual database, a vision system, via a camera, digitizes the images of all objects to be identified, then stores the digitized form of each image in the database. When the system is placed in operation, the camera enters each newly "seen" image into a digitizer. The system then compares the digitized image to be interpreted with the prerecorded digitized images in the computer's database, much like a speech-recognition system does with speech input. The computer identifies the image by matching the structure of the input image with those images in the database. This process is illustrated by the digital vision-inspection system in Figure 5–3.

As you can imagine, **vision-input systems** are best suited to very specialized tasks in which only a few images will be encountered. These tasks are usually simple, monotonous ones, such as inspection. For example, in Figure 5–3 a digital vision-inspection system on an assembly line rejects those parts that do not meet certain quality-control specifications. The vision system performs rudimentary gauging inspections, and then signals the computer to take appropriate action.

Vision input offers great promise for the future. Can you imagine traveling by car from your home

FIGURE 5–3 Digital Vision-Inspection System
In this digital vision-inspection system, the system examines parts for defects. If the digitized image of the part does not match a standard digital image, the defective part is placed in a reject bin.

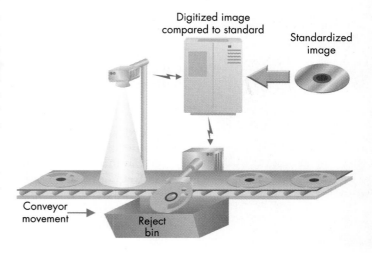

Digitized image compared to standard

Standardized image

Conveyor movement

Reject bin

We may be entering an era of filmless photography. With this Epson PhotoPC color digital camera, you can capture, view, print, store, and transmit almost any image. Up to 60 images can be recorded on a 2-inch floppy disk that is inserted in the camera. Once captured, images can be uploaded to a PC and used in countless applications, from the family photo album to training software. Courtesy of Epson America, Inc.

This handheld data entry device is actually a small PC that is worn on the hand and the arm. Workers at McKesson Corporation wear their 13-ounce PCs. The wearable PCs contain a small screen, a keypad, and a bar code scanner. This receiving clerk can read bar codes and enter data while keeping both hands free to lift and move shipping containers. Photo courtesy of McKesson Corporation

town to Charleston, South Carolina, without the burden of actually driving? Sound far-fetched? Not really. Mercedes-Benz, the German automobile maker, is actively developing a system that will allow you to do just that. The copilot system is a step up from cruise control, freeing the driver from both the accelerator pedal and the steering wheel. Like cruise control, the driver would remain behind the wheel, even when the system is operational. The foundation technology is vision input. When traveling down the German autobahn, the system "sees" the lines on either side of the lane and makes minor adjustments in direction to keep the automobile centered in the lane. This part of the system works well; however, Mercedes-Benz engineers have many hurdles to overcome (exit ramps, pedestrians, and so on) before you see this feature in showroom automobiles. Someday the safest drivers on the road won't be driving at all.

Digital Cameras: Look, No Film

Most of us take photographs in the traditional manner—with a camera and film. We drop off our rolls of film for developing, then enjoy the results in the form of prints and slides. Some people use image scanners to digitize photos for use in newspapers, magazines, and so on. This process may change forever as the price of **digital cameras** continues to plummet (currently priced from $400 to $7,000). When you take a picture with a digital camera, a digitized image goes straight to $3\frac{1}{2}$-inch diskette, CD-R, or onboard RAM. Once on disk or in RAM, it can be loaded to a computer and manipulated as you would other graphic images.

There are many applications for digital cameras, not the least of which is expanding the family photo album. As mentioned in Chapter 1, dermatologists use digital cameras to take close-up shots of lesions and skin disorders. Each time a patient comes in for an appointment, the doctor takes a file photo so that progress can be compared from visit to visit.

Handheld Data Entry Devices

Some close-to-the-source data entry tasks still require the use of some keystrokes and are best performed on handheld data entry devices. The typical *handheld data entry device,* which is actually a small computer, has the following:

- A limited external keyboard or a soft keyboard (displayed on a touch-sensitive screen)
- A small display that may be touch sensitive
- Some kind of storage capability for the data, usually solid-state nonvolatile random-access memory
- A scanning device, capable of optical character recognition

After the data have been entered, the portable data entry device is linked with a central computer and data are *uploaded* (transmitted from the data entry device to a central computer) for processing.

Stock clerks in department stores routinely use handheld devices to collect and enter reorder data. As clerks visually check the inventory level, they identify the items that need to be restocked. They first scan the price tag (which identifies the item), then enter the number to be ordered on the keyboard.

Handheld slate PCs and PDAs (personal digital assistants), introduced in Chapter 1, frequently are used as data entry devices. Slate PCs have pressure-sensitive writing pads that recognize hand-printed alphanumeric characters. Also, they permit the entering of graphic information. For example, police officers use slate PCs to document accidents, including recording the handwritten signatures of the participants.

5–4 Output Devices: Computers Communicate with Us

Output devices translate bits and bytes into a form we can understand. We discuss the most common "output only" devices in this section. These devices include monitors, printers, plotters, screen image projectors, and voice-response systems.

Monitors and Graphics Adapters

The output device we are all most familiar with is the televisionlike monitor, which displays alphanumeric and graphic output. We define monitors in terms of the following:

- *Graphics adapter* (the electronic link between the motherboard and the monitor)
- *Size* (diagonal dimension of the display screen)
- *Resolution* (detail of the display)
- *Color* (monochrome or color)
- *Display quality*

INTERNET BRIDGE

Output

GRAPHICS ADAPTERS The **graphics adapter** is the device controller for the monitor. Most graphics adapters are inserted into an expansion slot on the motherboard. Those, however, with AGP technology are built into the motherboard. The monitor cable is plugged into the graphics adapter board to link the monitor with the processor. All display signals en route to the monitor pass through the graphics adapter, where the digital signals are converted to analog signals compatible with the monitor's display capabilities.

Most existing graphics adapters have their own RAM, called **video RAM,** where they prepare monitor-bound images for display. The size of the video RAM is important in that it determines the number of possible colors and resolution of the display, as well as the speed at which signals can be sent to the monitor. A minimum of one megabyte (1 MB) of video RAM (**VRAM**) is recommended to accommodate the complexities of modern graphics-based software. The newer AGP graphics adapters enjoy much better performance by using the PC system's RAM directly.

MONITOR SIZE Display screens vary in size from 5 to 30 inches (measured diagonally). The monitor size for newly purchased desktop PCs has inched up from 9 inches to 15 inches over the past 10 years and is now moving toward 17 inches. Output on a monitor is *soft copy*, which means it is temporary and available to the end user only until another display is requested (as opposed to the permanent *hard-copy* output of printers).

MONITOR RESOLUTION: PIXELS AND DOT PITCH Monitors vary in their quality of output, or **resolution.** Resolution refers to the number of addressable points on the screen—the number of points to which light can be directed under program control. These points are sometimes called **pixels,** short for *picture elements.* Each pixel can be assigned a shade of gray or a color. The typical monitor is set to operate with 786,432 (1024 by 768) addressable points; however, most can be set at resolutions ranging from 640 by 480 to 1280 by 1024. Monitors used primarily for computer graphics and computer-aided design may have more than 16 million addressable points. Such high-resolution monitors project extremely clear images that look almost like photographs.

A monitor's resolution is also affected by its **dot pitch,** or the distance between the centers of adjacent pixels. Any dot pitch equal to or less than .28 mm (millimeters) provides a sharp image. The crispness of the image improves as the dot pitch gets smaller. When you have an opportunity, use a magnifying glass to examine the pixels and observe the dot pitch on your computer's monitor.

MONOCHROME AND COLOR MONITORS Monitor displays are either monochrome or color. Monochrome monitors display images in a single color, usually white, green, blue, red, or amber. A monochrome monitor can, however, display shades of

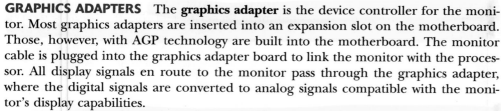

MEMORY BITS

Output Devices
- Monitors
- Described by graphics adapter, size, resolution (pixels and dot pitch), color (gray scales, RGB), and display quality
  - *Types of monitors:*
  - —Televisionlike
  - —Flat-panel
  - —Touch screen
- Printers
  - —Dot-matrix printers
  - —Page printers (color option)
  - —Ink-jet printers (color option)
  - —Multifunction peripheral
- Plotters
- Screen Image Projector
- Voice-Response Systems
  - —Recorded voice
  - —Speech synthesis

Peripheral Explorer

one color. The computer industry uses the term **gray scales** to refer to the number of shades of a color that can be shown on a monochrome monitor's screen. Monochrome monitors are seldom sold with PCs but are still very much a part of the technology landscape (for example, point-of-sale systems in retail stores, terminals at airline ticket counters, automatic teller machines).

Most color monitors mix red, green, and blue to achieve a spectrum of colors, and are called **RGB monitors.** The typical monitor, which can display images in brilliant color, is set up to display 256 colors. A monitor capable of displaying at least 65,536 colors is recommended for those who do desktop publishing and other graphics-intensive applications professionally.

DISPLAY QUALITY: BE FLICKER FREE   There are two more characteristics that affect the quality of the display—the *refresh rate* and whether the monitor is *interlaced*. The phosphor coating on a monitor's CRT (cathode-ray tube) must be repainted or refreshed 50 to over 100 times each second (Hz) to maintain clarity of the image. Generally, monitors with faster refresh rates have less flicker and are easier on the eyes. Interlacing will also affect screen flicker. Less expensive monitors are interlaced; that is, they paint every other horizontal line on the screen, then fill in the rest on a second pass (TVs are interlaced). Interlacing may result in some flicker. In contrast, *non-interlaced monitors* minimize flicker by painting the whole screen in one pass.

FLAT-PANEL MONITORS: THIN IS IN   Laptop PCs use space-saving **flat-panel monitors,** some less that $\frac{1}{2}$-inch thick. Flat-panel monitors use a variety of technologies, the most common being *LCD* (*l*iquid *c*rystal *d*isplay). LCD monitors are *active matrix* or *passive matrix*. Active matrix monitors have higher refresh rates and better contrast, making for a more brilliant display. Millions of transistors are needed for color active matrix LCD monitors. Color monitors need three transistors for each pixel: one each for red, green, and blue. Active matrix LCD displays are more expensive than passive matrix displays; therefore, active matrix LCD displays are usually associated with high-end notebook PCs.

TOUCH SCREEN MONITORS: NATURAL MONITORS   **Touch screen monitors** permit input as well as output. Pressure-sensitive overlays are placed over monitor screens that can detect pressure and the exact location of that pressure, right down to the pixel level. Users simply touch the desired icon or menu item with their finger (at least an ounce or more of pressure is needed). Educators realize that we are born with an ability to point and touch, and are beginning to use touch screen technology in the classroom to teach everything from reading to geography. Interactive touch screen systems are installed in shopping centers, zoos, airports, grocery stores, post offices, and many other public locations. Within a few years the information you need will be at your finger tips wherever you go.

Printers: Lots of Choices

Printers

Printers produce hard-copy output, such as management reports, cash register receipts, memos, payroll checks, and program listings. Hundreds of printers are produced by dozens of manufacturers. There is a printer manufactured to meet the hard-copy output requirements of any individual or company, and almost any combination of features can be obtained. You can specify its size (some weigh less than a pound), speed, quality of output, color requirements, flexibility requirements, and even noise level. PC printers sell for as little as a good pair of shoes or for as much as a minivan. Mainframe printers can cost as much as an upscale house.

Any person or company about to purchase a printer must consider:

● What's the budget?

● Is color needed or will black and white do?

Monitors are an integral component of virtually all computer-based applications. An engineer at E-Systems needs a large high-resolution monitor for computer-aided design (CAD) applications. His laptop PC has a LCD flat-panel monitor.   Courtesy of E-Systems

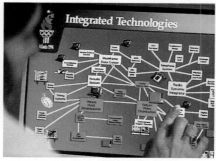

This Advanced Remote Control for Videoshow system enables the presentation of spectacular multimedia shows. The remote control includes a full-color LCD screen so that presenters can face their audience and still see what is on the big screen.   Courtesy General Parametrics Corporation

A growing number of public information kiosks use touch screen monitors. This kiosk at the 1996 Atlanta Olympics graphically illustrated how technology was used to circulate every form of information.   Courtesy of International Business Machines Corporation. Unauthorized use not permitted.

In video arcades, the action in Sega's Sonic and Knuckles (*shown here*) takes place on large, durable monitors.   Courtesy of Sega of America Inc.

- What will be the volume of output (pages per hour, day, or week)?
- How important is the quality of the output?
- What special features are needed (ability to print envelopes, on legal size paper, on multi-part forms, and so on)?
- If the printer is to be shared on a network, what do the other users want?

Think about these considerations as you read about various printer options. Keep in mind that color, additional features, and each increment in speed and quality of output add to the cost of the printer.

Printer technology is ever changing. Three basic technologies dominate the PC printer arena: dot matrix, page, and ink jet. The advantages and disadvantages of these technologies are summarized in Figure 5–4. All PC printers have the capability of printing graphs and charts and offer considerable flexibility in the size and style of print. All printers also can print in portrait or landscape format. **Portrait** and **landscape** refer to the orientation of the print on the page. Portrait format is like the page of this book—the lines run parallel to the shorter sides of the page. In contrast, landscape output runs parallel to the longer sides of the page. Landscape is frequently the orientation of choice for spreadsheet outputs with many columns.

DOT-MATRIX PRINTERS: WALKING INTO THE SUNSET   The **dot-matrix printer** forms images *one character at a time* as the print head moves across the paper. The dot-matrix printer is an *impact printer;* that is, it uses tiny *pins* to hit an ink ribbon and the

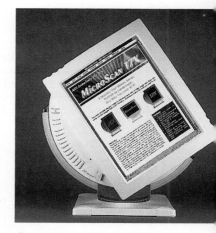

The Microscan 17X monitor is equipped with a pivoting capability. It's ideal for business professionals and computing enthusiasts who work with page-oriented document processing, over-sized spreadsheets, and graphics design applications. User can switch easily between landscape and portrait viewing.   Courtesy of ADI Systems, Inc.

	Dot-Matrix Printers	Page Printers	Ink-Jet Printers
Pros	• Inexpensive • Can print multi-part forms • Can print on narrow and wide fanfold paper • Low per page cost (less than a penny per page) • Energy efficient	• High-resolution output (up to 1200 dpi) • Fast (4 to 32 ppm–text only) • Quiet • Many choices from which to choose (from under $400 for low-speed home/office models up to $20,000 for sophisticated shared printers) • Low cost per page (1 to 4 cents)	• High-resolution output (but less than that of page) • Quiet • Small (footprint can be smaller than a sheet of paper) • Energy efficient • Many choices from which to choose (black and white from $150 to full 4-color for about $400)
Cons	• Noisy • Low-resolution output that gets worse as the ribbon ages • Slow (40 to 200 cps) • Poor quality graphics output • Requires add-on to handle cut sheets and envelopes • Limited font flexibility	• Cost • Limited to cut sheet media • Slow for graphics output	• Higher cost per page than page (2 to 8 cents) • Slower than page (1 to 3 ppm) • Special paper required for highest resolution output • Limited to cut sheet media
Color	Color ribbons can be used for highlighting.	Color page models produce high-resolution color output. At $.50 to $4.00 per color page, they can be expensive to operate.	Color ink-jet models may take over the low-end color market. Models under $400 are available that produce 720 dpi color output. Color output costs from $.10 to $1.20 per page.
Outlook	Dot-matrix technology is fading except for situations that require printing on multi-part forms.	High-speed, high-quality page printers will remain the mainstay of office printing for the foreseeable future. This is especially true for shared printers.	Ink-jet offers low-cost high-quality output. Home PC buyers with low volume output requirements may opt for color models in large numbers.

FIGURE 5–4   Printer Summary

FIGURE 5–5   Dot-Matrix–Printer Character Formation
Each character is formed in a matrix as the print head moves across the paper. The bottom pins are used for lowercase letters that extend below the line (for example, g and p). Notice how dots are overlapped to increase the density and, therefore, the quality of the image.

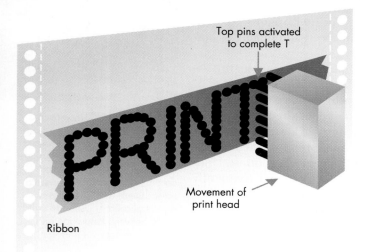

Top pins activated to complete T

Movement of print head

Ribbon

paper, much as a typewriter does. The dot-matrix printer arranges printed dots to form characters and all kinds of images in much the same way as lights display time and temperature on bank signs. Several vertical column pins are contained in a rectangular print head. Print heads may have from 9 to 24 pins. The pins are activated independently to form a dotted character image as the print head moves horizontally across the paper. The quality of the printed output increases with the number of dots in the letter matrix (a rectangular arrangement of dots). Figure 5–5 illustrates how the dots can form characters as a print head moves across the paper to create a letter. The better dot-matrix printers form characters that appear solid, and they can be used for business letters as well as for draft output. Dot-matrix printers print up to 200 cps (characters per second).

Most dot-matrix printers can accommodate both *cut-sheet paper* and *fanfold paper* (a continuous length of paper that is folded at perforations). If your output is mostly single sheet (for example, letters and envelopes), you may need to purchase an *automatic sheet*

By the mid-1990s, the price of color printers plummeted to the point that they were economically feasible for virtually all computing environments, including the home. Now users can add color to their everyday business (memos, reports, spreadsheets, graphs) and home (banners, invitations) printing needs. These Hewlett-Packard color notebook (*left*), color ink-jet (*middle*), and color laser (*right*) printers provide high-quality color output. The notebook printer allows wireless printing from up to three feet away from a PC.   Photos courtesy of Hewlett-Packard Company

feeder. The *tractor-feed* that handles fanfold paper is standard with most dot-matrix printers.

As long as people have a need to print on multi-part forms, there will be a need for impact dot-matrix printers. Impact printers, as opposed to nonimpact printers, touch the paper and can produce carbon copies along with the original. Those who do not print multi-part forms may opt for other types of printers in the future. The pros and cons of dot-matrix printers are summarized in Figure 5–4.

PAGE PRINTERS: A PAGE AT A TIME   Nonimpact **page printers** use laser, LED (*l*ight-*e*mitting *d*iode), LCS (*l*iquid *c*rystal *s*hutter), and other laserlike technologies to achieve high-speed hard-copy output by printing *a page at a time*. Page printers are also referred to simply as **laser printers.** The operation of a laser-based page printer is illustrated in Figure 5–6. The majority of laser printers print shades of gray; however, color laser printers are becoming increasingly popular as their price continues to drop.

Economically priced desktop page printers have become the standard for office printing. These printers, capable of print speeds up to 32 pages per minute (ppm), have redefined the hard-copy output potential of PCs. Automatic sheet feeders, which hold from 100 to 400 blank pages, are standard equipment on desktop page printers. Most page printers print on standard letter and legal paper; however, some models can print on paper up to 17 by 22 inches.

All desktop page printers are capable of producing high-quality text and graphics output. Some can produce *near-typeset-quality (NTQ)* text and graphics as well. The resolution (quality of output) of the low-end desktop page printer is *300 dpi* (dots per

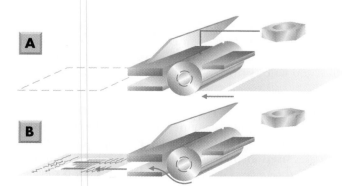

FIGURE 5–6   Desktop Page Printer Operation
The enclosure of a desktop page printer is removed to expose its inner workings. (a) Prior to printing, an electrostatic charge is applied to a drum. Then laser beam paths to the drum are altered by a spinning multisided mirror. The reflected beams selectively remove the electrostatic charge from the drum. (b) Toner is deposited on those portions of the drum that were affected by the laser beams. The drum is rotated and the toner is fused to the paper to create the image.

inch). High-end desktop page printers, which are sometimes called *desktop typesetters,* are capable of at least 1200 dpi. The dpi qualifier refers to the number of dots that can be printed per linear inch, horizontally or vertically. That is, a 600-dpi printer is capable of printing 360,000 (600 times 600) dots per square inch. Commercial typesetting quality is a minimum of 1200 dpi and is usually in excess of 2000 dpi. Desktop page printers are also quiet (an important consideration in an office setting). The emergence of desktop page printers has fueled the explosion of *desktop publishing* (discussed in detail in Chapter 8, "Making the Point: Word Processing, Desktop Publishing, and Presentation Software"). The pros and cons of page printers are summarized in Figure 5–4.

INK-JET PRINTERS: POPULAR IN SOHO   To the naked eye, there is little difference between the print quality of nonimpact **ink-jet printers** and page printers. Although the output quality of ink-jet printers is more in line with page printers, their mechanical operation is more like that of the dot-matrix printer because they have a print head that moves back and forth across the paper to write text and create the image. Instead of dot-matrix pins hitting the ribbon and paper, though, several independently controlled injection chambers squirt ink droplets on the paper. The droplets, which dry instantly as dots, form the letters and images. Because the ink droplets are much smaller than the area resulting from pin thrusts, the resolution is much better for ink-jet than it is for dot-matrix printers. Resolutions for the typical ink-jet printer approach that of a 300-dpi page printer. Some newer models boast resolutions in excess of 700 dpi.

   With a price tag about equal to a dot-matrix printer and a print quality close to that of a page printer, the ink-jet printer is emerging as the choice for budget-minded consumers. SOHO (small office/home office) buyers are opting for ink-jet printers by the millions. The high cost per page is not a deterrent for the low-volume output needs of the typical PC user. The pros and cons of ink-jet printers are summarized in Figure 5–4.

COLOR PRINTERS: OVER THE RAINBOW   A couple of years ago, color printers started at $7000. Today you can get a 720-dpi color ink-jet printer that produces near-photographic-quality output for under $300. The growing trend among printer consumers is to think (and usually buy) color. You can purchase a color page printer or a color ink-jet printer, and, generally, the more you pay the better and faster the output. Color page printers, which can cost up to $8,000 use one of three technologies. Color laser printers electrostatically adhere toner to the drum, then fuse toner to paper or transparencies. Thermal wax page printers melt wax-based inks that adhere to the paper or transparencies. Dye sublimation page printers press ink sheets against special paper, heating the color so they sink in. Ink-jet color printers use similar technologies for both black-and-white and color printers. Ink droplets are mixed to form the various colors.

THE MULTIFUNCTION PERIPHERAL: PRINT IT, FAX IT, SCAN IT, AND COPY IT
Traditionally, businesses have purchased separate machines to handle these paper-related tasks: computer-based printing, facsimile (fax), scanning, and copying. The considerable overlap in the technologies used in these machines has enabled manufacturers to create all-in-one *multifunction peripheral devices.* These multifunction devices

are becoming very popular in the small office/home office environments and in other setting where the volume for any of their functions is relatively low.

MAINFRAME-BASED PAGE PRINTERS Operating at peak capacity during an 8-hour shift, the fastest mainframe page printer can produce almost a quarter of a million pages—that's 50 miles of output. This enormous output capability is normally directed to people outside an organization. For example, large banks use mainframe page printers to produce statements for checking and savings accounts; insurance companies print policies on them; and electric utility companies use them to bill their customers.

This multifunction printer acts as a copier, a fax machine, and a printer, providing small office and home PC users with a range of capabilities. Photo courtesy of Hewlett-Packard Company

Plotters: Precision Instruments

Dot-matrix, page, and ink-jet printers are capable of producing page-size graphic output, but are limited in their ability to generate high-quality, perfectly proportioned graphic output. For example, on a blueprint, the sides of a 12-foot-square room must be exactly the same length. Architects, engineers, city planners, and others who routinely generate high-precision, hard-copy graphic output of widely varying sizes use another hard-copy alternative—**plotters.**

The two basic types of plotters are the *drum plotter* and the *flatbed plotter.* Both have one or more pens that move over the paper under computer control to produce an image. Several pens, selected and manipulated by the computer, are required to vary the width and color of the line. On the drum plotter, the pens and the drum move concurrently over different axes to produce the image. Drum plotters are used to produce continuous output, such as plotting earthquake activity, or for long graphic output, such as the structural view of a skyscraper. On some flatbed plotters, the pen moves in both axes while the paper remains stationary. However, on most desktop plotters, both paper and pen move concurrently in much the same way as on drum plotters.

Presentation Graphics: Be Persuasive

Business people have found that sophisticated and colorful graphics add an aura of professionalism to any report or presentation. This demand for *presentation graphics* has created a need for corresponding output devices. Com-

Many medium to large engineering, architectural, and mapping companies use PCs in a networked environment. This HP DesignJet 750C large-format color plotter is capable of a mechanical resolution of 0.0005 inches; that is, the output is accurate to within 5 ten-thousandths of an inch. Photo courtesy of Hewlett-Packard Company

Screen image projectors can fill a room with information. Courtesy of Proxima Corporation

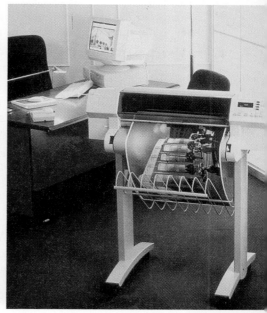

EMERGING TECHNOLOGY

The I-Book Reader: Textbook of the Future

BOOKS HAVEN'T CHANGED MUCH SINCE JOHANN GUTENBERG invented the printing press in the fifteenth century. The methods for producing books are, of course, far more sophisticated, but in the end, a book remains a sequential, static medium. This type of organization is made-to-order for novels, in which a story is read from page one to the end. The printed page, however, has its limits for just about any book or document that contains an index, including all varieties of reference books, encyclopedias, "how to" books, corporate manuals, and, of course, textbooks.

Over the next few years, the printed pages of college textbooks will begin their transformation to a technology-based presentation. Nobody knows for sure what the textbook of the future will look like. Most educators and publishers agree, however, that change is just over the horizon. Perhaps it's time to speculate on what that technology will look like and what it will bring to the classroom—or possibly the home, the office, the student union, the car. . .

The *interactive book,* or *i-book,* will offer many advantages over traditional books.

- Static figures will come alive with animation.
- Motion video will be available to demonstrate, elaborate, or clarify.
- More detailed information will be just a click or touch away.
- The i-book will help readers identify and overcome gaps in understanding.
- Readers will be able to click on or touch "active words" to display/play related material (for example, a definition, an exercise, or a demonstration).
- When linked to the Internet, readers of i-books will be given an opportunity to visit applicable Internet sites for further information and, possibly, animated demonstration.
- Margin notes can be written or spoken.
- Readers will be able to share information and thoughts via online communication with other readers.

The I-Book Reader

Any modern multimedia PC is ready to handle i-books, but PCs don't offer the flexibility of books. We can open books and begin reading immediately in any lighted location. To some extent, reading i-books on multimedia notebook PCs would give us this flexibility, but notebooks cost several thousand dollars. Further miniaturization of hardware components and inevitable price reductions will eventually lead us to the i-book reader. The adjacent figure shows the authors' concept of the i-book reader, essentially a small special-function computer. Here are some of the i-book's proposed features.

- *Lightweight.* The first i-book readers will weigh about the same as a college textbook.
- *Solid-state memory.* System software and user data are recalled from nonvolatile solid-state memory. The i-book reader will not need a hard disk.
- *DVD (digital videodisk) drive.* The multimedia-based i-books will require huge amounts of storage for programs, text, images, video, audio, animated figures, virtual reality presentations, and so on. I-books probably will be distributed on DVDs, the next generation of CD-ROMs (or something similar). A single DVD has a read-only capacity of 7 to 14 gigabytes, many times the capacity of a CD-ROM.
- *Detachable touch screen viewer.* The i-book reader is in two parts—the *base unit,* which contains the processor and storage, and the *viewer.* The detachable viewer, which is tethered to the base unit, will provide the student with the flexibility to study the i-book in class, under a tree, or in bed. The touch screen capability lets the student communicate with the i-book. With improved technology, the viewer's self-retracting tether may be eliminated and replaced with a wireless connection.
- *Speaker and microphone.* Both the speaker and the microphone are embedded in the detachable viewer. The student will have the option of playing sound through a headset.
- *Network interface cards.* The NICs in the base unit will accept twisted-pair telephone wire or coaxial cable so that the i-book reader can be linked to LANs and the Internet.
- *A serial/parallel port.* The port will enable a direct connection to the student's PC and its resources (printer, disk drives, and so on).
- *Touchpad.* The more sophisticated i-book readers will have extras, such as a touchpad to expedite interaction with the i-book.

- *Eyeglasses viewer.* Students who want hands-free viewing may purchase an optional eyeglasses viewer. This viewer, which has two tiny monitors, is worn like eyeglasses. Students use the touchpad to interact with the i-book.

I-Book Summary

A handful of CD-ROM–based i-books are beginning to dot the educational landscape. However, you must have access to and be at a multimedia PC to use them. This first generation of i-books have only a few of the features we'll find in the second- and third-generation i-books described earlier. The next generation of i-books will emerge when i-book readers move from the laboratory to the bookstore and authors have had an opportunity to gain experience in *3-D writing*.

Traditional books are written and presented in one dimension, along a straight line (page 1 to the end). In contrast, the cyberauthor must learn to write in three dimensions. The author must allow the reader to *jump forward or backward* (along the traditional book line), to *jump to either side for supplemental information* (for example, animated figures, supportive images and video, virtual reality presentations, and self-administered quizzes), and

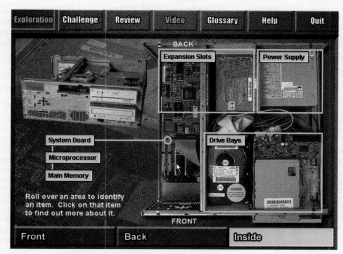

The IT Works CD-ROM that accompanies this book uses interactive methods to demonstrate computer concepts.

to *go into greater depth*—the third dimension (for example, greater conceptual detail, definitions, in-depth analysis, and links to applicable Internet sites).

Now for the big question. When will this all happen? Probably a lot sooner than you would think!

Shown here is the authors' concept of an i-book reader, a device that can be used to read interactive books.

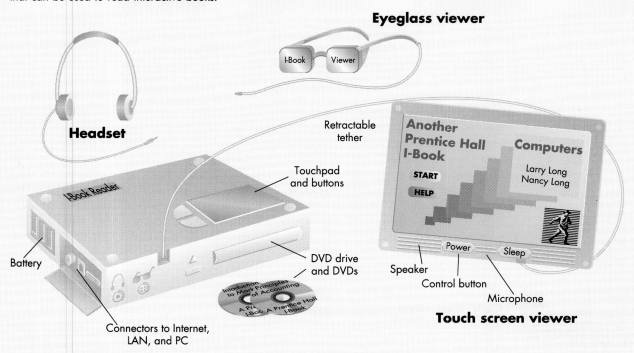

puter-generated graphic images can be re-created on paper and transparency acetates with printers. Graphic images also can be captured on 35-mm slides, displayed on a monitor, or projected onto a large screen.

The need for overhead transparencies and 35-mm slides is beginning to fade as presenters discover the ease with which they can create and deliver dynamic multimedia presentations. They do this with the help of **screen image projectors.** These output devices fall into two categories: *LCD panels* and *LCD projectors.* The LCD panels, which are about the size of a notebook PC, are used with overhead projectors. The LCD panels are placed directly on the overhead projector as you would a transparency acetate. The light from the overhead projector is directed through an LCD panel and whatever image is on its display is shown on a large screen for all to see. The LCD projectors use their own built-in lens and light source to project the image on the screen.

Voice-Response Systems: Say It with Bits

Anyone who has used a telephone has heard "If you're dialing from a touch-tone phone, press 1." You may have driven a car that advised you to "fasten your seat belt." These are examples of talking machines that use output from a voice-response system. There are two types of **voice-response systems:** One uses a *reproduction* of a human voice and other sounds, and the other uses **speech synthesis.** Like monitors, voice-response systems provide temporary, soft-copy output.

The first type of voice-response system selects output from user-recorded words, phrases, music, alarms, or anything you might record on audio tape, just as a printer would select characters. In these recorded voice-response systems, the actual analog recordings of sounds are converted into digital data, then permanently stored on disk or in a memory chip. When output occurs, a particular sound is converted back into analog before being routed to a speaker. Sound chips are mass-produced for specific applications, such as output for automatic teller machines, microwave ovens, smoke detectors, elevators, alarm clocks, automobile warning systems, video games, and vending machines, to mention only a few. When sounds are stored on disk, the user has the flexibility to update them to meet changing application needs.

Speech synthesis systems, which convert raw data into electronically produced speech, are more popular in the microcomputer environment. All you need to produce speech on a PC are a sound expansion board, speakers (or headset), and appropriate software. Such software often is packaged with the sound board. To produce speech, sounds resembling the phonemes (from 50 to 60 basic sound units) are combined to make up speech. The existing technology produces synthesized speech with only limited vocal inflections and phrasing, however. Despite the limitations, the number of speech synthesizer applications is growing. For example, a visually impaired person can use the speech synthesizer to translate printed words into spoken words. Translation systems offer one of the most interesting applications for speech synthesizers and speech-recognition devices. Researchers are making progress toward enabling conversations among people who are speaking different languages. A prototype system has already demonstrated that three people, each speaking a different language (English, German, and Japanese), can carry on a computer-aided conversation. Each person speaks and listens to his or her native language.

Terminals

5–5 Terminals: Input and Output

A variety of terminals enable both *input to* and *output from* a remote computer system. Interactions via a terminal form the foundation for a wide variety of applications.

The Tube and the Telephone

Terminals come in all shapes and sizes and have a variety of input/output capabilities. The two most popular general-purpose terminals are the *video display terminal (VDT)* and the *telephone*. The VDT is affectionately known as "the tube," short for **cathode-ray tube.** A VDT's primary input mechanism is usually a *keyboard,* and the output is usually displayed on a *monitor.*

DUMB TERMINALS Most terminals are dumb; that is, they have little or no intelligence (processing capability). The terminals you see in most hospitals or airports are dumb terminals. These terminals only display text and must be linked to a multi-user processor, such as a mainframe computer.

SMART X TERMINALS **X terminals** have processing capabilities and RAM comparable to some micros and workstations; however, they are not designed for stand-alone operation. The X terminal's processing capability enables the user to interact via a graphical user interface (GUI). All X terminals are configured with some type of point-and-draw device, such as a mouse, to permit efficient interaction with the GUI.

Dumb terminals support only text I/O within a single application. In contrast, the X terminal user can work with several applications at a time, any of which can display high-resolution graphics. Each application is displayed in its own window. Some X terminals can even run applications on different computers at the same time.

TELEPHONE TERMINALS AND TELEPHONY The telephone's widespread availability is causing greater use of it as a terminal. You can enter alphanumeric data on the touch-tone key pad of a telephone or by speaking into the receiver (voice input). You would then receive computer-generated voice output from a voice-response system. Salespeople use telephones as terminals for entering orders and inquiries about the availability of certain products into their company's mainframe computer. Brokerage firms allow their clients to tap into the firm's computers via telephone. After entering a password, clients can request a wide variety of services and information by working through a hierarchy of spoken menus. For example, they can request account balances and stock quotes. They can even request that a specific company's earnings report be sent to their fax machines.

The telephone by itself has little built-in intelligence; however, when linked to a computer, potential applications abound. **Telephony** is the integration of computers and telephones, the two most essential instruments of business. In telephony, the computer, perhaps a PC, acts in concert with the telephone. For example, a PC can analyze incoming telephone calls and take appropriate action (take a message, route the call to the appropriate extension, and so on). The telephone is a terminal, but with only 12 buttons. In effect, telephony augments these 12 buttons to include a PC-based GUI. Consider these telephony applications.

- A mail-order house keeps customer records by customer telephone number. When a customer calls to phone in an order, the system detects the customer's telephone number (caller ID), routes the call to an available salesperson (or the one with the shortest wait time), and, finally, displays the customer's record on the salesperson's monitor before anyone says hello. If the salesperson is busy, the customer is given an opportunity to enter the order directly from a telephone.

- A school district uses telephony to reschedule district events. Here is how it works. A computer system can announce a last-minute change of time for a school board meeting via the telephone system. Upon being prompted by a user, the system automatically announces the change to the participants and the me-

Terminals and PCs are taking on a new dimension as users interact not only with the computer but also with one another. The camera (on top of monitor) and microphone enable an audio-visual link that permits colleagues in different locations literally to talk with and see one another while viewing the same text or graphic information. Courtesy Harris Corporation

dia community. The telephony system even negotiates scheduling conflicts with participants to arrive at an acceptable time for all concerned—all automatically.

Telephony promotes efficient interactions and as it matures, look for many routine communications to be handled entirely by computers (for example, scheduling of meetings). Much of what has to be done in a typical business phone call can be accomplished between cooperating computers. If and when we are needed, we will be asked to join the conversation.

Special-Function Terminals: ATMs and POSs

The number and variety of special-function terminals are growing rapidly. Special-function terminals are designed for a specific application, such as convenience banking. You probably are familiar with the *automatic teller machine (ATM)* and its input/output capabilities (see Figure 5–7). A badge reader (magnetic stripe) and a key pad enable input to the system. A monitor and a printer (for printing transaction receipts) provide output. Some ATMs use voice response as a monitor backup to alert people when to perform certain actions (for example, "Take your receipt").

The ATM idea has caught on for other applications. A consortium of companies is installing thousands of ATM-like terminals that will let you order and receive a wide variety of documents on the spot. For example, you can now obtain an airline ticket, your college transcript, and an IRS form electronically, and many more applications are on the way.

Another widely used special-function terminal is the *point-of-sale (POS)* terminal. POS terminals are used by clerks and salespeople in retail stores, restaurants, and other establishments that sell goods and services. POS terminals have a key pad for input, at least one small monitor, and a printer to print the receipt. Some have other input/output devices, such as a badge reader for credit cards, a wand or stationary scanner to read price and inventory data, and/or a printer to preprint checks for customers.

During the late 1980s, a number of grocery stores had POS terminals with voice-response systems that verbally confirmed the price on each item. The unnecessary noise caused by these systems added confusion to the checkout process without any increase in value to the store or the customer. These systems are now a part of computing history. That's the way it is with technology, especially input/output. Sometimes you have to try it to see if it works. Over the next few years we'll be confronted with many I/O experiments.

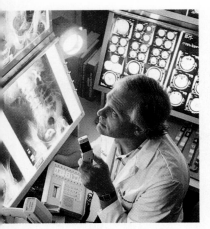

Terminals are being created to meet a variety of needs. This doctor at the Florida Hospital in Orlando is dictating into a dictation terminal. The terminal makes it easy for radiologists and other physicians to dictate findings into a central system.
Courtesy of Harris Corporation

INTERNET BRIDGE

Interactive Study Guide
Chapter 5

FIGURE 5–7 Terminals for Banking Customers: Automatic Teller Machines
The widely used automatic teller machine (ATM) supports a variety of input/output methods. The magnetic stripe on the ATM card contains identification and security information that, when read, is sent to the bank's computer system. The ATM responds with instructions via its monitor. The customer enters an identification number and data via a key pad. In the figure, the computer processes the customer's request, then provides instructions for the customer via the monitor and verbally with a voice-response unit.

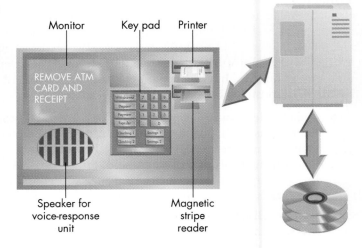

IMPORTANT TERMS AND SUMMARY OUTLINE

5–1 I/O DEVICES: LET'S INTERFACE   A variety of input/output (I/O) peripheral devices provide the interface between us and the computer.

5–2 TRADITIONAL INPUT DEVICES: KEY, POINT, and DRAW   There are two basic types of keyboards: traditional alphanumeric keyboard and special-function keyboards. A widely used keyboard layout is the 101-key keyboard with the traditional *QWERTY* key layout, 12 function keys, a key pad, a variety of special-function keys, and dedicated cursor-control keys. Some special-function keyboards are designed for specific applications. The mouse and its cousins enable us to point to objects on the screen and to draw. These include the **joystick, trackball, mouse pen, digitizer tablet and pen, trackpoint,** and **trackpad.**

5–3 SOURCE-DATA AUTOMATION: GETTING CLOSER TO THE ACTION   The trend in data entry has been toward **source-data automation.**

A variety of **scanners** read and interpret information on printed matter and convert it to a format that can be interpreted by a computer. **OCR (optical character recognition)** is the ability to read printed information into a computer system. **Bar codes** represent alphanumeric data by varying the size of adjacent vertical lines. Two types of OCR and bar code scanners—*contact* and *laser*—read information on labels and various types of documents. Scanners used for OCR or bar code applications can be classified into three basic categories—handheld label scanners (called **wand scanners**), stationary label scanners, and document scanners (which are often used with **turnaround documents**).

An **image scanner** uses laser technology to scan and **digitize** an image. Image scanners provide input for **image processing.** Image scanners are of two types: *page* and *hand.*

Magnetic stripes, **smart cards,** and badges provide input to **badge readers.**

Speech-recognition systems can be used to enter limited kinds and quantities of data by comparing digitized representations of words to similarly formed templates in the computer system's electronic dictionary.

Vision-input systems are best suited to very specialized tasks in which only a few images will be encountered.

Digital cameras are used to take photos that are represented digitally (already digitized).

Handheld data entry devices have a limited external keyboard or a soft keyboard; a small display that may be touch sensitive; nonvolatile RAM, and often a scanning device.

5–4 OUTPUT DEVICES: COMPUTERS COMMUNICATE WITH US   Output devices translate bits and bytes into a form we can understand. The most common "output only" devices include monitors, printers, plotters, screen image projectors, and voice-response systems.

Monitors are defined in terms of (1) their **graphics adapter** (which has **video RAM** or **VRAM**); (2) size; (3) **resolution** (number of **pixels**); (4) color capability; and (5) display quality.

A monitor's resolution is affected by its **dot pitch. Gray scales** are used to refer to the number of shades of a color that can be shown on a monochrome monitor's screen. **RGB monitors** mix red, green, and blue to achieve a spectrum of colors. The quality of the display is affected by the *refresh rate* and whether the monitor is *interlaced.*

Flat-panel monitors are used with laptop PCs, many of which use *LCD* technology. **Touch screen monitors** permit input as well as output.

Three basic PC printer technologies include dot-matrix, page and ink jet. Printers can print in **portrait** or **landscape** format. The **dot-matrix printer,** which is an impact printer, forms images *one character at a time* as the print head moves across the paper. Nonimpact **page printers (laser printers)** use laser, LED (light-emitting diode), LCS (liquid crystal shutter), and other laser-like technologies to achieve high-speed hard-copy output by printing *a page at a time.*

Nonimpact **ink-jet printers** have print heads that move back and forth across the paper squirting ink droplets to write text and create images. The ink-jet printer is emerging as the choice for budget-minded consumers.

The color option is available with most types of printers. Color ribbons are used for dot-matrix printers, ink droplets are mixed to form the various colors for ink-jet printers, and page printers use several technologies.

Multifunction peripheral devices are available that handle several paper-related tasks: computer-based printing, facsimile (fax), scanning, and copying. Mainframe-based page printers can have an enormous output capability.

Plotters, drum and flatbed, convert stored data into high-precision hard-copy graphs, charts, and line drawings.

The demand for *presentation graphics* has created a need for corresponding output devices, such as a **screen image projector.**

Voice-response systems provide recorded or synthesized audio output (via **speech synthesis**).

5–5 TERMINALS: INPUT AND OUTPUT Terminals enable interaction with a remote computer system. The general-purpose terminals are the *video display terminal (VDT)* and the *telephone.* The VDT is known as "the tube," short for **cathode-ray tube.** Terminals come in all shapes and sizes and have a variety of input/output capabilities.

Terminals that have little or no intelligence are called dumb terminals. **X terminals** with processing capabilities enable the user to interact via a graphical user interface. **Telephony** is the integration of computers and telephones.

A variety of special-function terminals, such as automatic teller machines and point-of-sale terminals, are designed for a specific application.

REVIEW EXERCISES

Concepts

1. Which output device, a plotter or a dot-matrix printer, generates graphs with the greatest precision?
2. What is isolated speech and why is it a requirement for dictation to a speech-recognition system?
3. List devices, other than key-driven, that are used to input data into a computer system.
4. A multifunction peripheral device has what four paper-related capabilities?
5. What is the relationship between a joystick and a graphics cursor?
6. Name a device other than a monitor that produces soft-copy output.
7. Which kind of printer is used to produce carbon copies?
8. Which type of OCR scanner is designed to read documents of varying sizes?
9. Name four types of point-and-draw devices.
10. Which monitor has the best resolution, one with .31 dot pitch or one with .25 dot pitch?
11. What is a turnaround document? Give an example.
12. Identify all input and output methods used by an automatic teller machine.
13. What is a smart card?
14. Describe two applications for bar codes.

Discussion and Problem Solving

15. Describe the input/output characteristics of a workstation/PC that would be used by engineers for computer-aided design.
16. Some department stores use handheld label scanners, and others use stationary label scanners to interpret the bar codes printed on the price tags of merchandise. What advantages does one scanner have over the other?
17. What input/output capabilities are available at your college or place of work?
18. Compare today's vision-input systems with those portrayed in such films as *2001* and *2010*. Do you believe we will have a comparable vision technology by the year 2001?
19. Four PCs at a police precinct are networked and currently share a 100-cps impact dot-matrix printer. The captain has budgeted enough money to purchase one page printer (12 ppm) or two more 100-cps dot-matrix printers. Which option would you suggest the precinct choose and why?
20. In the next generation of credit cards, the familiar magnetic stripe probably will be replaced by embedded microprocessors in smart cards. Suggest applications for this capability.

SELF-TEST (BY SECTION)

5-1 a. Input devices translate data into a form that can be interpreted by a computer. (T/F) *T*

  b. The primary function of I/O peripherals is to facilitate computer-to-computer data transmission. (T/F) *F*

5-2 a. Only those keyboards configured with VDTs have function keys. (T/F) *F*

  b. Which of the following is not a point-and-draw device: (a) joystick, (b) document scanner, or (c) trackpoint? *b*

5-3 a. Optical character recognition is a means of source-data automation. (T/F) *T*

  b. In speech recognition, words are _____ and matched against similarly formed _____ in the computer's electronic dictionary. *digitize templates*

  c. Vision-input systems are best suited to generalized tasks in which a wide variety of images will be encountered. (T/F) *F*

  d. The Universal Product Code (UPC) was originally used by which industry: (a) supermarket, (b) hardware, or (c) mail-order merchandising? *A*

  e. Image scanners are either page or _____ . *hand*

  f. The enhanced version of cards with a magnetic stripe is called a badge card. (T/F) *F*

5-4 a. The number of addressable points on the screen, called pixels, affects its _____ . *resolution*

  b. Most flat-panel monitors are used in conjunction with desktop PCs. (T/F) *F*

  c. Ink-jet printers are nonimpact printers. (T/F) *T*

  d. The tractor-feed on dot-matrix printers enables printing on what kind of paper: (a) cut-sheet paper, (b) fanfold paper, (c) both cut-sheet and fanfold paper? *b*

  e. What type of printers are becoming the standard for office microcomputer systems: (a) laser printers, (b) dot-matrix printers, or (c) multifunction duplicator systems? *A*

  f. _____ _____ systems convert raw data into electronically produced speech. *Speech synthesis*

  g. Another name for video RAM is SDRAM chip. (T/F) *F*

5-5 a. Which terminal permits system interaction via a GUI: (a) dumb terminal, (b) X terminal, or (c) text-based terminal? *b*

  b. _____ is the integration of computers and telephones. *telephony*

Self-test Answers. **5-1 (a)** T; **(b)** F. **5-2 (a)** F; **(b)** b. **5-3 (a)** T; **(b)** digitized, templates; **(c)** F; **(d)** a; **(e)** hand; **(f)** F. **5-4 (a)** resolution; **(b)** F; **(c)** T; **(d)** b; **(e)** a; **(f)** Speech synthesis; **(g)** F. **5-5 (a)** b; **(b)** Telephony.

Networks and Networking: Linking the World

- Describe the concept of connectivity.
- Demonstrate an understanding of data communications terminology and applications.
- Detail the function and operation of data communications hardware.
- Describe alternatives and sources of data transmission services.
- Illustrate the various kinds of network topologies.
- Describe a local area network and its associated hardware and software.

Courtesy of Harris Corporation

LET'S TALK

Can you follow this conversation? It includes computing concepts presented in this chapter. Read it now, then reread it once you've had an opportunity to study the chapter.

The Scene   Three techies (Herb, his wife Carol, and Art) and one nontechy (Art's fiancé, Jana) are talking during a candle-lit dinner at Chez O'bere's.

JANA: This atmosphere is perfectly romantic!

ART: I'll say. The waiters are taking orders on pocket computers with a wireless transceiver.

HERB: It looks like their radio signals are transmitted to that desktop PC in the corner. It's probably linked to the LAN server by way of a coaxial cable network bus.

CAROL: You know that digital convergence is imminent when your food orders are sent as messages from handheld PCs to a local net node in the kitchen.

JANA: Enough of this tech talk. Are we dining out or talking shop?

CAROL: You're right, Jana. It's difficult for people like us who work with telecommunications to overlook such a great application.

ART: I'm sorry, Jana. It's weird, but sometimes we find beauty in network topologies, especially those that enable cooperative processing.

JANA: Well, I hope the next time we come to Chez O'bere's, its technology won't overshadow the wonderful food and atmosphere.

HERB: Uh-oh, look at this note behind the pepper grinder. It says, "Coming Next Spring, Interactive Electronic Menus."

6–1 Our Weird, Wild, Wired World

**Monthly Technology Updates
Chapter 6**

Millions of people are knowledge workers by day and Internet surfers by night. As knowledge workers, we need ready access to information. In the present competitive environment, we cannot rely solely on verbal communication to get that information. Corporate presidents cannot wait until the Monday morning staff meeting to find out whether production is meeting demand. Field sales representatives can no longer afford to play telephone tag with headquarters personnel to get answers for impatient customers. The president, the field rep, and the rest of us now rely on *computer networks* to retrieve and share information quickly. Of course, we will continue to interact with our co-workers, but computer networks simply enhance the efficiency and effectiveness of that interaction.

As surfers, we surf the Internet, America Online, CompuServe, or any of scores of commercial information services. Once logged on to one of these networks, cybersurfers can chat with friends, strangers, and even celebrities. We can go shopping, peruse electronic magazines, download interesting photos and songs, plan a vacation, play games, buy and sell stock, send e-mail, and generally hang out. It's official: We now live in a weird, wild, wired world where computer networks are networked to one another. This chapter is devoted to concepts relating to computer networks and communications technology. Once you have a grasp of this technology, you will find it easier to understand the different uses and applications of networks.

Digital Convergence: Coming Together as Bits and Bytes

Serendipitous Surfing: Online Books

We are going through a period of **digital convergence.** That is, TVs, PCs, telephones, movies, college textbooks, newspapers, and much, much more are converging toward digital compatibility. For example, movies that are now frames of cellulose are in the

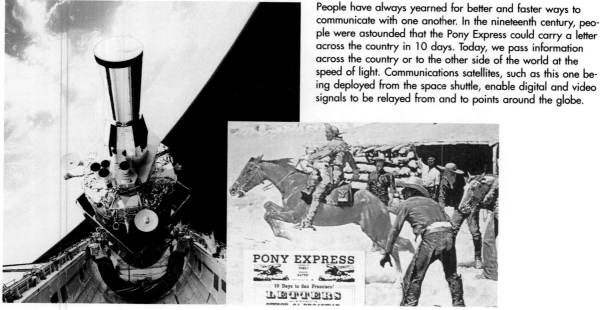

People have always yearned for better and faster ways to communicate with one another. In the nineteenth century, people were astounded that the Pony Express could carry a letter across the country in 10 days. Today, we pass information across the country or to the other side of the world at the speed of light. Communications satellites, such as this one being deployed from the space shuttle, enable digital and video signals to be relayed from and to points around the globe.

Courtesy NASA   AT&T Technologies

process of digital convergence. The 200,000 frames required for a full-length movie will converge to 16 billion bits on a single DVD. Already hundreds of movies have been released on DVD. Major components of this book's learning system are on CD-ROM and the Internet. Future editions will follow the trend toward digital convergence with an increasing portion of the material being distributed digitally.

Digital convergence, combined with an ever-expanding worldwide network of computers, will enable us all to take one giant leap into the future. Already the TV, PC, video game, stereo system, answering device, and telephone are on a collision course that will meld them into communications/information centers by the end of the century. We'll have video-on-demand such that we can view all or any part of any movie ever produced at any time, even in a window on our office PC. Instead of carrying a billfold, we might carry a credit-card-sized device that would contain all the typical billfold items such as money, credit cards, pictures, driver's license, and other forms of identification. These items will all be digital. When we buy a pizza in the future, we might simply enter a code into our electronic billfold to automatically order and pay for the pizza. The possibilities are endless.

Digital convergence is more than a convergence of technologies. It's also a convergence of industries. In a recent survey, 95 percent of the CEOs in the entertainment, telecommunications, cable, and computer industries agreed that their industries are converging.

With half the industrial world (and many governments) racing toward digital convergence, there is no question that we are going digital over the next few years. Our photo album will be digital. Our money will be digital. Already, digitized movies are being transmitted to theaters where they are shown via high-definition projection units.

Connectivity: Getting to the Information

All of this convergence is happening so that information will be more accessible to more people. To realize the potential of a universe of digital information, the business and computer communities are continually seeking ways to interface, or connect, a diverse set of hardware, software, and databases. This increased level of **connectivity** brings people from as close to the next room and as far as the other side of the world closer together.

The workstations and PCs at this hospital are linked to a server computer that is connected via a high-speed communications line. A computerized patient records system allows physicians to easily access up-to-date patient chart information from workstations throughout the hospital.   Courtesy of Harris Corporation.

- Connectivity means that a marketing manager can use a PC to access information in the finance department's database.
- Connectivity means that a network of PCs can route output to a shared page printer.
- Connectivity means that a manufacturer's server computer can communicate with a supplier's server.
- Connectivity means that you can send your holiday newsletter via e-mail.

Connectivity is implemented in degrees. We can expect to become increasingly connected to computers and information both at work and at home during the coming years. Thirty years ago there were tens of thousands of computers. Today there are tens of *millions* of them! Computers and information are everywhere. Our challenge is to connect them.

The Beginning of an Era: Cooperative Processing

We are living in an era of **cooperative processing.** Companies have recognized that they must cooperate internally to take full advantage of company resources, and that they must cooperate externally with one another to compete effectively in a world market. To promote internal cooperation, businesses are setting up *intra-company networking* (see Figure 6–1). These networks allow people in, say, the sales

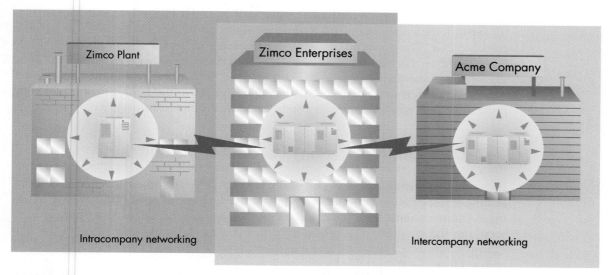

FIGURE 6–1 Intracompany and Intercompany Networking

department to know the latest information from the production department. Companies cooperate externally via *intercompany networking* (Figure 6–1) or, more specifically, via **electronic data interchange (EDI).** EDI relies on computer networks to transmit data electronically between companies. Invoices, orders, and many other intercompany transactions can be transmitted from the computer of one company to the computer of another. For example, at major retail chains, such as Wal-Mart, over 90% of all orders are processed directly between computers via EDI. Figure 6–2 contrasts the traditional interactions between a customer and supplier company with interactions via EDI.

FIGURE 6–2 Interactions between Customer and Supplier
In the figure, the traditional interaction between a customer company and a supplier company are contrasted with similar interactions via electronic data interchange (EDI).

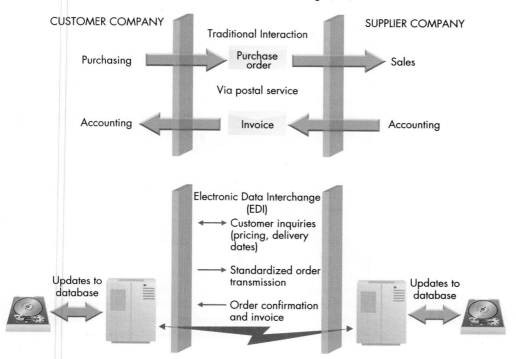

The phenomenal growth of the use of PCs in the home is causing companies to expand their information system capabilities to allow linkages with home and portable PCs. This form of cooperative processing increases system efficiency while lowering costs. For example, in many banks, services have been extended to home PC owners in the form of home banking systems. Subscribers to a home banking service use their personal computers as terminals linked to the bank's mainframe computer system to pay bills, transfer funds, and ask about account status.

6–2 Data Communications Hardware: Making It Happen

Data communications, or **telecommunications,** is the electronic collection and distribution of information between two points. Information can appear in a variety of formats—numeric data, text, voice, still pictures, graphics, and video. As we have already seen, raw information must be digitized before we can input it into a computer. For example, numerical data and text might be translated into their corresponding ASCII codes. Once the digitized information has been entered into a computer, that computer can then transfer the information to other computers connected over a network. Ultimately, all forms of digitized information are transmitted over the transmission media (for example, fiber optic cable) as a series of binary bits (1s and 0s).

Data communications hardware is used to transmit digital information between terminals and computers or between computers and other computers. These primary hardware components include the modem, the front-end processor, the multiplexor, and the router. Figure 6–3, which shows the integration of these devices with terminals and computer systems, is a representative computer network. Networks are like snowflakes—no two are alike. Unlike snowflakes, however, networks never melt. Once created, networks seem to have a life of their own, growing with the changing needs of the organization. There is a vast array of communications hardware and it's growing, especially with the trend to digital convergence. The more specialized devices, such as *switching hubs*, *bridges*, and *concentrators*, are beyond the scope of this book.

The Modem: Digital to Analog to Digital

Peripherals Explorer

If you have a PC, you can establish a communications link between it and any remote computer system in the world, assuming you have the authorization to do so. However, you must first have ready access to a telephone line, and your PC must be equipped with a *modem*. Most new PCs and many existing PCs are configured with modems.

Telephone lines were designed to carry *analog signals* for voice communication, not the binary *digital signals* (1s and 0s) needed for computer-based data communication. The modem (modulator-demodulator) converts *digital* signals into *analog* signals so data can be transmitted over telephone lines (see Figure 6–3). The digital electrical signals are modulated to make sounds similar to those you hear on a touch-tone telephone. Upon reaching their destination, these analog signals are demodulated into computer-compatible digital signals for processing. A modem is always required for two computers to communicate over a telephone line. It is not needed when the PC is wired directly to a computer network.

MODEMS: SOME ARE IN AND SOME ARE OUT There are two types of modems for PCs and terminals: *internal* and *external*. Most PCs and terminals have internal modems; that is, the modem is on an optional add-on circuit board that is simply plugged into an empty expansion slot in the PC's processor unit or the terminal's housing. Laptops with PCMCIA-compliant interfaces use modems on interchangeable PC cards. The external modem is a separate component, as illustrated in Figure 6–3, and is connected via a serial interface port. To make the connection with a telephone

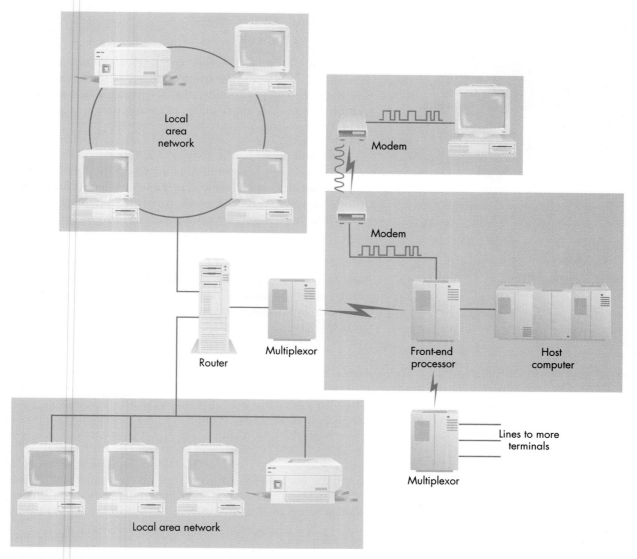

FIGURE 6–3 Hardware Components in Data Communications
Devices that handle the movement of data in a computer network are the modem, the front-end processor, the multiplexor, the router, and the host computer. Also in the figure, electrical digital signals are modulated (via a modem) into analog signals for transmission over telephone lines and then demodulated for processing at the destination. The lightening bolts indicate transmission between remote locations.

line and either type of modem, you simply plug the telephone line into the modem just as you would when connecting the line to a telephone.

FAX MODEMS: TWO FOR ONE The *fax modem* performs the same function as a regular modem, with an added capability—it enables a PC to simulate a *facsimile* or *fax* machine. Fax machines transfer images of hard-copy documents via telephone lines to another location. The process is similar to using a copying machine except that the original is inserted in a fax machine at one location and a hard copy is produced on a fax machine at another location. PCs configured with a fax modem (an add-on circuit board or a PC card) can fax text and images directly from an electronic file to a remote facsimile machine or to another similarly equipped computer. They can also receive faxes (a printable file) sent from a fax machine or another PC. The fax modem is considered a must-have item on new PCs.

Special-Function Processors: Help along the Line

In Figure 6–3, there is a *host computer,* or server computer, that is responsible for the overall control of the network and for the execution of applications (for example, a hotel reservation system). To improve the efficiency of a computer system, the *processing load* is sometimes *distributed* among several other special-function processors. The two communications-related processors in the network of Figure 6–3, the front-end processor and the multiplexor, are under the control of and subordinate to the host. In Figure 6–3, the host computer is a large server computer; however, the host could just as well be a PC, or a supercomputer, depending on the size and complexity of the network.

THE FRONT-END PROCESSOR The terminal or computer sending a **message** is the *source.* The terminal or computer receiving the message is the *destination.* The **front-end processor** establishes the link between the source and destination in a process called **handshaking.** The term *front-end processor* has evolved to a generic reference for a computer-based device that relieves the host computer of a variety of communications-related processing duties. These duties include the transmission of data to and from remote terminals and other computers. The host can instead concentrate on overall system control and the execution of applications software.

If you think of messages as mail to be delivered to various points in a computer network, the front-end processor is the post office. Each computer system and terminal/PC in a computer network is assigned a **network address.** The front-end processor uses these addresses to route messages to their destinations. The content of a message could be a prompt to the user, a user inquiry, a program instruction, an "electronic memo," or any type of information that can be transmitted electronically—even the image of a handwritten report.

THE MULTIPLEXOR The **multiplexor** is an extension of the front-end processor. It is located down-line from the host computer—at or near a remote site. The multiplexor collects data from several low-speed devices, such as terminals and printers. It then "concentrates" the data and sends them over a single communications channel (see Figure 6–4) to the front-end processor. The multiplexor also receives and distributes host output to the appropriate remote terminals.

The multiplexor is an economic necessity when several low-speed terminals are at one remote site. Using one high-speed line to connect the multiplexor to the host is considerably less expensive than is using several low-speed lines to connect each terminal to the host. For example, an airline reservation counter might have 10 terminals, and it would be very slow and very expensive to connect each directly to the host computer. Instead, each terminal would be connected to a common multiplexor, which in turn would be connected to the central host computer. An airline might have one or several multiplexors at a given airport, depending on the volume of passenger traffic.

Routers: Bridging the Gap

Computer networks are everywhere—in banks, in law offices, and in the classroom. In keeping with the trend toward greater connectivity, computer networks are themselves being networked and interconnected to give users access to a greater variety of applications and to more information. For example, the typical medium-to-large com-

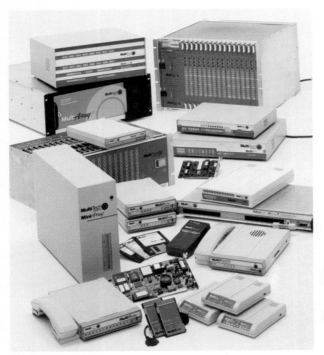

The applications of communications hardware are far more exciting than their appearance. Shown here are a wide variety of modems (internal, external, rack-mounted, PC card) and other communications hardware made by Multi-Tech Systems. Courtesy of Multi-Tech Systems, Inc.

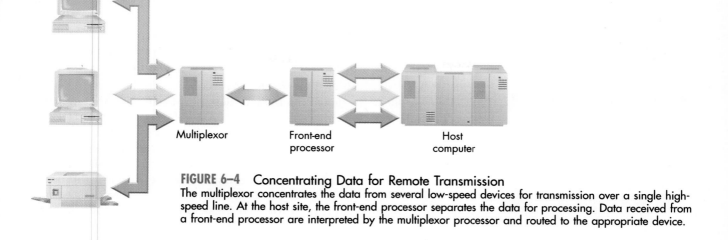

FIGURE 6–4 Concentrating Data for Remote Transmission
The multiplexor concentrates the data from several low-speed devices for transmission over a single high-speed line. At the host site, the front-end processor separates the data for processing. Data received from a front-end processor are interpreted by the multiplexor processor and routed to the appropriate device.

Multiplexor   Front-end processor   Host computer

pany links several PC-based networks to the company's enterprise-wide mainframe network. This enables end users on all networks to share information and resources.

Communications protocols are rules established to govern the way data are transmitted in a computer network. Because networks use a variety of communications protocols and operating systems, incompatible networks cannot "talk" directly to one another. The primary hardware/software technology used to help alleviate the problems of linking incompatible computer networks is the **router.** Routers help to bridge the gap between incompatible networks by performing the necessary protocol conversions to route messages to their proper destinations.

Organizations that are set up to interconnect computer networks do so over a **backbone.** The backbone is a collective term that refers to a system of routers and the associated transmission media (cables, wires, and wireless links) that link the computers in an organization.

Serendipitous Surfing: Government

6–3 The Data Communications Channel: Data Highways

A **communications channel** is the medium through which digital information must pass to get from one location in a computer network to the next. Most people refer to a communications channel simply as the *line.*

Transmission Media: Wires and Wireless

A variety of communication channels, some made up of wires and some without wires, carry digital signals between computers. Each is rated by its *channel capacity* or *bandwidth.* The channel capacity is the number of bits a channel can transmit per second. Channel capacities vary from 56,000 **bits per second (bps),** or 56 K bps (thousands of bits per second) to 622 M bps (megabits per second). In practice, the word **baud** is often used interchangeably with *bits per second.* Technically speaking, however, it is quite different. But if someone says *baud* when talking about computer-based communications, that person probably means bits per second.

TWISTED-PAIR WIRE: STILL GROWING IN CAPABILITY **Twisted-pair wire** is just what we think of as regular telephone wire. Each twisted-pair wire is actually two insulated copper wires twisted around each other. At least one twisted-pair line provides **POTS** (plain old telephone services) to just about every home and business in the

Transmission Media

United States. Telephone companies offer different levels of twisted-pair service. All companies offer voice-grade service. The other two services listed below may or may not be available in your area.

- *Voice-grade service.* When you call the telephone company and request a telephone line, it installs *voice-grade service.* This analog line permits voice conversations and digital transmissions with the aid of a modem. Traditional modem technology permits data transmission up to 56 K bps.

- *ISDN.* Some applications demand a higher channel capacity than that available over voice-grade lines. One alternative, which can be delivered over a POTS line, is **Integrated Services Digital Network (ISDN),** a digital service. The ISDN line terminates at an **ISDN modem,** sometimes called an *ISDN terminal adapter.* The ISDN modem is then connected to a port on the computer. The ISDN line enables data transmission at 128 K bps, more than twice the speed of the fastest analog modem. The ISDN modem allows the line's channel capacity to be split such that one channel can carry a voice conversation while the other supports an electronic link between computers. ISDN lines have become popular for telecommuters who work at home but need to be networked to their office's computer system.

- *ADSL.* A new technology, **Asymmetric Digital Subscriber Line (ADSL),** has made it possible to receive data over POTS lines at 1.5 to 9 M bps (the **downstream rate** in megabits per second). In a few years, the downstream rate will be 52 M bps. The **upstream rate** (sending) is 16 to 640 K bps. Like ISDN, ADSL requires a special modem. ADSL opens the door for some amazing applications to be delivered over POTS lines. Applications include support for full-motion video, very high-speed transfer of graphics, and real-time applications involving a group of online participants.

COAXIAL CABLE   Most people know coaxial cable as the cable in "cable television." **Coaxial cable** contains electrical wire (usually copper wire) and is constructed to permit high-speed data transmission with a minimum of signal distortion. It is laid along the ocean floor for intercontinental voice and data transmission and is also used to connect terminals and computers in a "local" area (from a few feet to a few miles). Coaxial cable has a very "wide pipe"; that is, it has a large channel capacity (up to 100 megabits per second).

FIBER OPTIC CABLE: LIGHT PULSE   Twisted-pair wire and coaxial cable carry data as electrical signals. **Fiber optic cable** carries data as laser-generated pulses of light. Made up of bundles of very thin, transparent, almost hair-like fibers, fiber optic cables transmit data more inexpensively and much more quickly than do copper wire transmission media. In fact, in the time it takes to transmit a single page of *Webster's Unabridged Dictionary* over twisted-pair copper wire (about 3 seconds), the entire dictionary could be transmitted over a single optic fiber!

Each time a communications company lays a new fiber optic cable, the world is made a little smaller. In 1956, the first transatlantic cable carried 50 voice circuits. Then, talking to someone in Europe was a rare and expensive experience. Today, a single fiber can carry over 32,000 voice and data transmissions, the equivalent of 2.5 billion bits per second. Nowadays, people call colleagues in other countries or link up with international computers as readily as they call home.

Another of the many advantages of fiber optic cable is its contribution to data security. It is much more difficult for a computer criminal to intercept a signal sent over fiber optic cable (via a beam of light) than it is over copper wire (an electrical signal).

HIGH-SPEED WIRELESS COMMUNICATION   Communications channels do not have to be wires or fibers. Data can also be transmitted via **microwave signals** or **ra-**

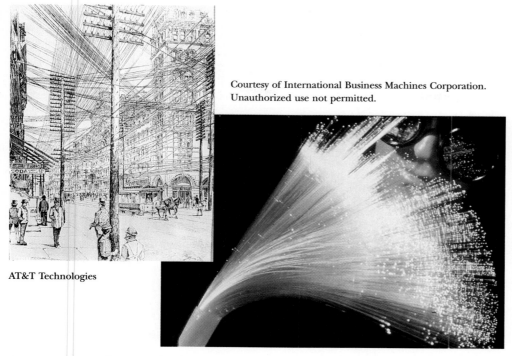

AT&T Technologies

At one time, New York City was laced with copper wire. Today, the more versatile fiber optic cable has re-placed the telephone poles and the wire. Laser-generated light pulses are transmitted through glass fibers. A pair of optic fibers can simultaneously carry 1344 voice conversations and interactive data communications sessions.

dio signals. Transmission of these signals is *line-of-sight;* that is, the signal travels in a straight line from source to destination.

Microwave signals are transmitted between transceivers. Because microwave signals do not bend around the curvature of the earth, signals may need to be relayed several times by microwave repeater stations before reaching their destination. Repeater stations are placed on the tops of mountains, tall buildings, and towers, usually about 30 miles apart. Microwave transmission is used when running a cable is difficult or too costly.

Satellites eliminate the line-of-sight limitation because microwave signals are bounced off satellites, avoiding buildings, mountains, and other signal obstructions. Satellites are routinely launched into orbit for the sole purpose of relaying data communications signals to and from earth stations. A satellite, which uses microwave signals and is essentially a repeater station, is launched and set in a **geosynchronous orbit** 22,300 miles above the earth. A geosynchronous orbit permits the communications satellite to maintain a fixed position relative to the earth's surface. Each satellite can receive and retransmit signals to slightly less than half of the earth's surface; therefore, three satellites are required to cover the earth effectively (see Figure 6–5). The main advantage of satellites is that data can be transmitted from one location to any number of other locations anywhere on (or near) our planet.

PCS COMMUNICATING WITHOUT WIRES   PCs in the office and on the road can be linked via wireless connections.

Wireless networks.   One of the greatest challenges and biggest expenses in a computer network is the installation of the physical links between its components. The **wireless transceiver** provides an alternative to running a permanent physical line (twisted-pair wire, coaxial cable, or fiber optic cable). Two PC-based wireless transceivers, each

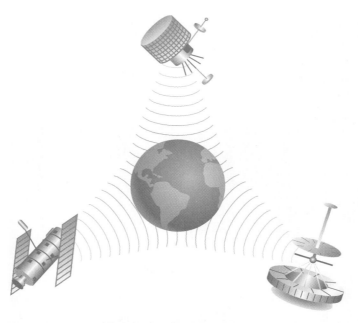

FIGURE 6–5 Satellite Data Transmission
Three satellites in geosynchronous orbit provide worldwide data transmission service.

about the size of a thick credit card, replace a physical line between any source and destination. For example, wireless communication is routinely used to link these devices:

- Desktop PC and laptop PC
- PC and local area network (LAN)
- PC and mainframe computer
- Terminal and multiplexor
- Laptop PC and page printer

This lightweight, easily transportable, satellite communications system ensures that military troops can stay in touch anywhere in the world.   Courtesy of Harris Corporation

This notebook PC is linked to a LAN via a wireless transceiver (*foreground*). Wireless communication lets users take the PC and the LAN link with them to the conference room, the boss's office, or wherever they want to go within the range of the wireless link.   Courtesy of Harris Corporation

The wireless transceiver hooks into a serial port or PCMCIA slot. Transceivers, which have a limited range (about 50 feet), link computers via omnidirectional (traveling in all directions at once) radio waves. You can really use transceivers only locally to connect computers in adjacent rooms or even on different floors.

When using transceivers, the source computer transmits digital signals to its transceiver, which, in turn, retransmits the signals over radio waves to the other transceiver. Transceivers provide users with tremendous flexibility in the location of PCs and terminals in a network; however, the flexibility advantage is offset by the transceivers' limited channel capacity (about 115 K bps). Also, the number of terminals/PCs that can be linked via transceivers is limited by the frequencies allotted for this purpose.

The 1998 Olympics in Nagano were the perfect venue for widespread use of wireless networks. Many sites at the games were temporary or difficult to wire and were thus made-to-order situations for wireless networks. Wireless networks allowed judges, statisticians, and journalists to move with the action within and between venues.

Anywhere, anytime network computing.   Most mobile workers use analog *Circuit-Switched Cellular (CSC)*. Any cellular subscriber with a PC and a modem can establish a link to his or her company's computer network from almost anywhere in the United States. The cellular user does this by dialing the number of the land-based network to make the two-way connection.

Common Carriers: Anything but Common

It is impractical for individuals and companies to string their own fiber optic cable between distant locations, such as Hong Kong and New York City. It is also impractical for them to set their own satellites in orbit, although some have. Therefore, most people and companies turn to communications **common carriers,** such as AT&T, MCI,

One of the services offered by common carriers is the facilitation of conferencing via telecommunications, called "teleconferencing." Here, corporate colleagues in the United States and Japan are able to communicate effectively with one another without having to fly halfway around the world to do so.   Photo courtesy of Hewlett-Packard Company

and Sprint to provide communications channels for data transmission. Organizations pay communications common carriers, which are regulated by the Federal Communications Commission (FCC), for *private* or *switched* data communications service.

A **private line** (or **leased line**) provides a dedicated data communications channel between any two points in a computer network. The charge for a private line is based on channel capacity (bps) and distance.

A **switched line** (or **dial-up line**) is available strictly on a time-and-distance charge, similar to a long-distance telephone call. You (or your computer) make a connection by "dialing up" a computer, then a modem sends and receives data. Switched lines offer greater flexibility than do private lines because they allow you to link up with any communications-ready computer. A regular telephone line is a switched line.

The number and variety of common carriers is expanding. For example, cable TV companies are entering the market. Most cable companies broadcast multiple television signals from one point (their office) to many points (our houses) over coaxial cable. Most, however, are planning to install switching mechanisms that will enable subscribers to establish a two-way data link to the Internet over the very same coaxial cable used to broadcast television signals. The 10 megabits per second channel capacity is very inviting to the millions of people now chugging along at 14.4 K bps to 56 K bps over voice-grade telephone lines. At present, this high-speed service is available only in a few cities in the United States. Look for this service to expand rapidly over the next few years, perhaps to your neighborhood.

Data rates offered by common carriers include voice-grade (up to about 56 K bps with a modem), 64 K bps (one channel ISDN), 128 K bps (2 channel ISDN), 1.5 to 9 M bps (ADSL), 44.7 M bps, 155.5 M bps, and the widest of all pipes, the massive 622 M-bps channel. The megabit-level services can handle data transmission requirements for hundreds, even thousands, of individual users over the same channel.

Data Transmission in Practice

A communications channel from Computer A in Seattle, Washington, to Computer B in Orlando, Florida (see Figure 6–6), usually would consist of several different transmission media. The connection between Computer A and a terminal in the same

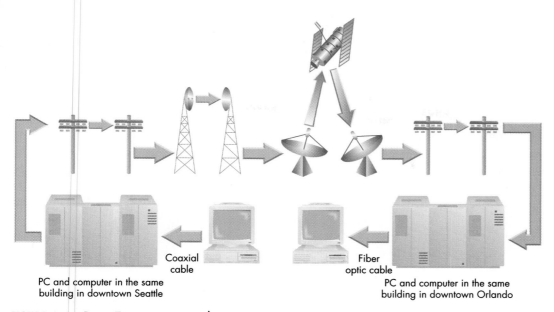

FIGURE 6–6 Data Transmission Path
It's more the rule than the exception that data are carried over several transmission media between source and destination.

PC and computer in the same building in downtown Seattle

Coaxial cable

Fiber optic cable

PC and computer in the same building in downtown Orlando

building is probably coaxial cable. The Seattle company might use a common carrier company such as AT&T to transmit the data. AT&T would then send the data through a combination of transmission facilities that might include copper wire, fiber optic cable, microwave signals, and radio signals.

6–4 Networks: Connecting Nodes

Each time you use the telephone, you use the world's largest computer network—the telephone system. A telephone is an endpoint, or a **node,** connected to a network of computers that routes your voice signals to any one of the 500 million telephones (other nodes) in the world. In a computer network the node can be a terminal, a computer, or any destination/source device (for example, a printer, an automatic teller machine, or even a telephone). Within an organization, computer networks are configured to meet the specific requirements of that organization. Some have five nodes; others have 10,000 nodes. We have already seen the hardware and transmission media used to link nodes in a network. In this section we put it all together and explain how networks are actually created and how they function.

Networks

Network Topologies: Star, Ring, and Bus

A **network topology** is a description of the possible physical connections within a network. The topology is the configuration of the hardware and shows which pairs of nodes can communicate. The basic computer network topologies—star, ring, and bus—are illustrated in Figure 6–7.

STAR TOPOLOGY The **star topology** involves a centralized host computer connected to several other computer systems, which are usually smaller than the host. The smaller computer systems communicate with one another through the host and usually share the host computer's database. The host could be anything from a PC to a supercomputer. Any computer can communicate with any other computer in the network. Banks often have a large home-office computer system with a star network of smaller mainframe systems in the branch banks.

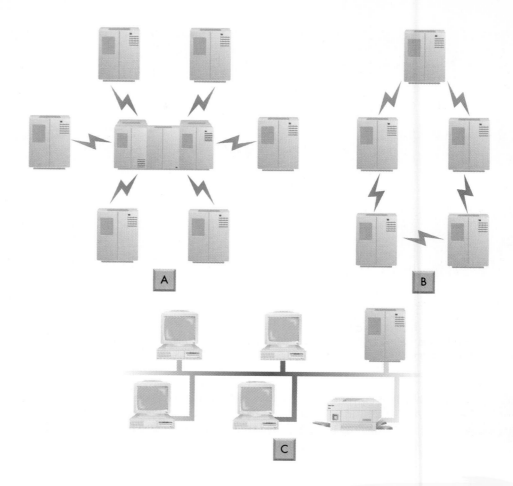

Network topologies include (a) star, (b) ring, and (c) bus.

RING TOPOLOGY The **ring topology** involves computer systems of approximately the same size, with no one computer system as the focal point of the network. When one system routes a message to another system, it is passed around the ring until it reaches its destination address.

BUS TOPOLOGY The **bus topology** permits the connection of terminals, peripheral devices, and microcomputers along a common cable called a **network bus.** The term *bus* is used because people on a bus can get off at any stop along the route. In a bus topology a signal is broadcast to all nodes, but only the destination node responds to the signal. It is easy to add devices or delete them from the network as devices are simply daisy-chained along the network bus. Bus topologies are most appropriate when the linked devices are physically close to one another. (See the discussion of local area networks that follows.)

HYBRID TOPOLOGY A pure form of any of these three basic topologies is seldom found in practice. Most computer networks are *hybrids*—combinations of these topologies.

Computer Systems Working Together: Client/Server Computing

Most computers, even PCs, exist as part of a network of computers. In this section we discuss the processing relationship between them.

CENTRALIZED COMPUTING: A BYGONE ERA Through the 1980s, mainframes performed most of the processing activity within a computer network. Back then, the shared use of a centralized mainframe offered the greatest return for the hard-

This is the nerve center of EDSNET, Electronic Data Systems Corporation's global communications system. EDSNET facilitates data, voice, and video communication among a quarter of a million sites on five continents. Here in Plano, Texas (near Dallas), more than 100 operators manage the system. Operators view 12- by 16-foot screens to keep abreast of system activity. Fourteen smaller screens provide detailed information for trouble-shooting situations, and 13 clocks display times from around the world. EDS photo by Steve McAlister

ware/software dollar. Today, though, PCs and workstations offer more computing capacity per dollar than do mainframe computers. This reversal of hardware economics has caused information technology professionals to rethink the way they design and use computer networks.

During the era of centralized mainframe computers, users communicated with a centralized host computer through dumb terminals with little or no processing capability. The mainframe performed the processing for all users, sometimes numbering in the thousands. Now, the trend in the design of computer networks is toward *client/server computing.*

DECENTRALIZING AND DOWNSIZING: A GROWING TREND In **client/server computing,** processing capabilities are distributed throughout the network, closer to the people who need and use them. A *server computer* supports many *client computers.*

- A **server computer,** which can be anything from a PC to a supercomputer, performs a variety of functions for its client computers, including the storage of data and applications software.

- The **client computer,** which is typically a PC or a workstation, requests processing support or another type of service (perhaps printing or remote communication) from one or more server computers.

In the client/server environment, both client and server computers perform processing to optimize application efficiency. For example, the client computer sys-

This company is moving toward a client/server–computing environment. The users at client PCs in this office access a common database on this Compaq ProLiant PC server computer (*foreground*). Reprinted with permission of Compaq Computer Corporation. All Rights Reserved.

tem might run a database application *locally* (on the client computer) and access data on a *remote* (not local) server computer system. In client/server computing, applications software has two parts—*the front end* and *the back end.*

- The client computer runs **front-end applications software,** which performs processing associated with the user interface and applications processing that can be done locally (for example, database and word processing).

- The server computer's **back-end applications software** performs processing tasks in support of its client computers. For example, the server might accomplish those tasks associated with storage and maintenance of a centralized corporate database.

In a client/server database application (see Figure 6–8), users at client PCs run front-end software to *download* (server-to-client) parts of the database from the server for processing. Upon receiving the requested data, perhaps sales data on customers in the mid-Atlantic region, the client user runs front-end software to work with the data. After local processing, the client computer may *upload* (client-to-server) updated data to the server's back-end software for processing. The server then updates the customer database. The database application is popular in client/server computing, but the scope and variety of applications are growing daily.

There is a mass migration *toward client/server computing* and *away from host-based networks.* Already more than 70% of all PCs are clients linked to at least one server computer, and most workstations are either clients or servers. Because client computers have their own software and processing capability, they request only needed data, resulting in reduced traffic over communications channels and increased speed and efficiency throughout the network. The trend toward client/server computing has resulted in companies downsizing their computers. **Downsizing** was coined to describe a policy that promotes increased reliance on smaller computers for *personal* and *enterprise-wide* processing tasks.

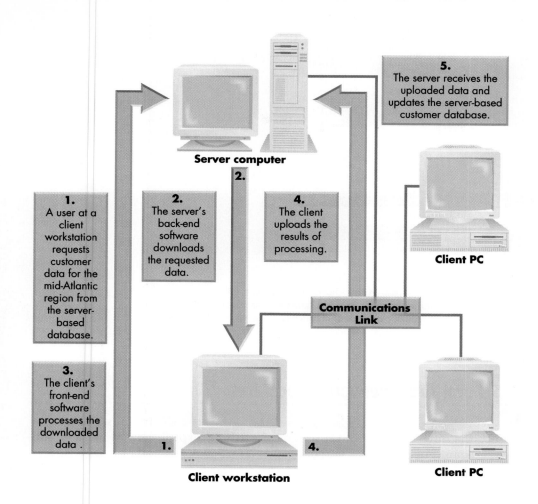

1.
A user at a client workstation requests customer data for the mid-Atlantic region from the server-based database.

2.
The server's back-end software downloads the requested data.

4.
The client uploads the results of processing.

5.
The server receives the uploaded data and updates the server-based customer database.

3.
The client's front-end software processes the downloaded data .

Server computer

Client PC

Communications Link

Client workstation

Client PC

FIGURE 6–8   A Walkthrough of a Client/Server Database Application

Network Line Control: Rules for Data Transmission

COMMUNICATIONS PROTOCOLS: TRANSMITTING BY THE RULES   *Communications protocols* describe how data are transmitted in a computer network. Communications protocols are defined in *layers,* the first of which is the physical layer. The physical layer defines the manner in which nodes in a network are connected to one another. Subsequent layers, the number of which vary between protocols, describe how messages are packaged for transmission, how messages are routed through the network, security procedures, and the manner in which messages are displayed. A number of different protocols are in common use.

ASYNCHRONOUS AND SYNCHRONOUS TRANSMISSION   Protocols fall into two general classifications: *asynchronous* and *synchronous* (see Figure 6–9). In **asynchronous transmission,** data are transmitted at irregular intervals on an as-needed basis. A modem is usually involved in asynchronous transmission. *Start/stop bits* are appended to the beginning and end of each message. The start/stop bits signal the receiving terminal/computer at the beginning and end of the message. In PC data communications, the message is a single byte or character. Asynchronous transmission, sometimes called *start/stop transmission,* is best suited for data communications involving low-speed I/O devices, such as serial printers and PCs functioning as remote terminals.

In **synchronous transmission,** the source and destination operate in timed synchronization to enable high-speed data transfer. Start/stop bits are not required in synchronous transmission. Data transmission between computers, routers, multiplexors, and front-end processors is normally synchronous.

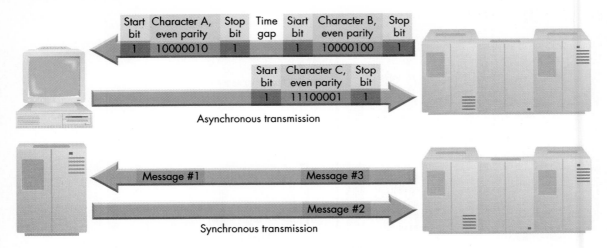

FIGURE 6–9 Asynchronous and Synchronous Transmission of Data
Asynchronous data transmission takes place at irregular intervals. In asynchronous transmission, the message is typically a single character. Synchronous data transmission requires timed synchronization between sending and receiving devices. The message is typically a block of characters.

6–5 Local Area Networks: Local Nets

Networks tend to be classified by the proximity of their nodes. In this section, we introduce the different network classifications and fully explain how to use and optimize the most popular network type, the LAN.

WANs, LANs, and TANs

A **WAN,** or **wide area network,** connects nodes in widely dispersed geographic areas, such as cities, states, and even countries. The WAN will normally depend on the transmission services of a common carrier to transmit signals between nodes in the network. In contrast, the *local area network (LAN),* or **local net,** connects nodes in close proximity, such as in a suite of offices or a building. The local net, including all data communications channels, is owned by the organization using it. Because of the proximity of nodes in local nets, a company can install its own communications channels (such as coaxial cable, fiber optic cable, or wireless transceivers). Therefore, LANs do not need common carriers. **TAN,** or **tiny area network,** is a term coined to refer to very small LANs, perhaps two, three, or four nodes. For example, TANs are popular in home computing. They enable households to share resources (printer, modem, files) among the kids' PC, the parents' PC, and perhaps a parent's laptop from the office. When we refer to WANs, LANs, and TANs, we refer to all hardware, software, and communications channels associated with them.

The focus of this section is the LAN. Strictly speaking, any type of computer can be incorporated within a LAN, but, in practice, PCs and workstations provide the foundation for local area networks. PCs in a typical LAN are linked to each other and share resources such as printers and disk storage. The distance separating devices in the local net may vary from a few feet to a few miles. As few as two and as many as several hundred PCs can be linked on a single local area network.

Companies are incorporating more PCs into local area networks to facilitate communication among knowledge workers and to enable the sharing of valuable computing resources. LANs make good business sense because these and other available resources can be shared:

A semiconductor chip set provides local area network (LAN) capabilities within an automobile, solving the problems created by increasingly complex, space-consuming electrical wiring.   Courtesy of Harris Corporation

- *Applications software.* The cost of a LAN-based word processing program (for example, Word for Windows) is far less than the cost of a word processing program for each PC in the LAN.
- *Links to mainframes.* The mainframe becomes an accessible resource. It is easier to link the mainframe to a single LAN than to many individual PCs.
- *Communications capabilities.* A dedicated outside telephone line or a fax modem can be shared by many users.
- *I/O devices.* With a little planning, a single page printer, plotter, or scanner can support many users on a LAN with little loss of office efficiency. In a normal office setting, a single page printer can service the printing needs of up to 10 LAN users.
- *Storage devices.* Databases on a LAN can be shared. For example, some offices make a CD-ROM–based national telephone directory available to all LAN users.
- *Add-on boards.* Add-on boards, such as a fax modem boards, can be shared by many PCs.

Like computers, automobiles, and just about everything else, local nets can be built at various levels of sophistication. At the most basic level, they permit the interconnection of PCs in a department so that users can send messages to one another and share files and printers. The more sophisticated local nets permit the interconnection of mainframes, PCs, and the spectrum of peripheral devices throughout a large but geographically constrained area, such as a cluster of buildings.

In the near future you will be able to plug a terminal or PC into a network just as you would plug a telephone line into a telephone jack. This type of data communications capability is being installed in the new "smart" office buildings.

LAN Hardware

The three basic hardware components in a PC-based LAN are the network interface cards, or NICs; the transmission media that connect the nodes in the network; and the servers. LANS may also have routers, modems, and other previously mentioned network hardware.

NETWORK INTERFACE CARDS   The **network interface card (NIC),** which we described briefly in Chapter 2, "Inside the Computer," is a PC add-on card or PCMCIA card that facilitates and controls the exchange of data between the PCs in a LAN. Each PC in a LAN must be equipped with an NIC. The cables or wireless transceivers that link the PCs are physically connected to the NICs. Whether as an add-on card or PCMCIA card, the NIC is connected directly to the PC's internal bus.

Only one node on a LAN can send information at any given time. The other nodes must wait their turn. The transfer of data and programs between nodes is controlled by the access method embedded in the network interface card's ROM. The two most popular access methods are *token* and *CSMA/CD.*

EMERGING TECHNOLOGY

Working@Home

TRADITIONALLY, PEOPLE GET UP IN THE MORNING, GET dressed, and fight through rush hour to go to the office because that's where their work is. Work, though, is moving out of the office. People who work at home have accounted for more than half of all new jobs since 1987. For many knowledge workers, work is really done at a PC or over the telephone, whether at the office or at home. PCs and communications technology make it possible for these people to access needed information, communicate with their colleagues and clients, and even deliver their work (programs, stories, reports, or recommendations) in electronic or hard-copy format. More and more people are asking: "Why travel to the office when I can telecommute?" Telecommuting is "commuting" to work via data communications. The trend toward PCs and networks has also fueled the growth of cottage industries where people work exclusively from their homes.

The Trend to Telecommuting

Millions of people are working at home full time: stockbrokers, financial planners, writers, editors, programmers, buyers, teachers (yes, some teachers work exclusively with online students), salespeople, and graphic artists, to mention a few. A larger group is working at home at least one day a week: engineers, lawyers, certified public accountants, company presidents, mayors, and plant managers, to mention a few. Anyone who needs a few hours, or perhaps a few days, of uninterrupted time to accomplish tasks that do not require direct personal interaction is a candidate for telecommuting.

Through the early 1990s, companies discouraged telecommuting. Management was reluctant to relinquish direct control of workers, worrying that workers would give priority to personal, not business, objectives. Now we know that telecommuters are not only more productive than office workers are, they also tend to work more hours. A recent Gartner Group study reported increases in productivity between 10% and 16% per telecommuter (as measured by employers). According to the study, each telecommuter experienced a two-hour increase in work time per day and saved the company about $4000 in annual facilities costs. It is only a matter of time before all self-motivated knowledge workers at all levels and in a variety of disciplines are given the option of telecommuting at least part of the time. Look at what companies are already doing.

- AT&T is encouraging its employees to telecommute on Tuesdays. Among other reasons, AT&T management is trying to support a more relaxed worker lifestyle.

- The Canadian government hopes to save taxpayers hundreds of millions of dollars by encouraging telecommuting for public servants. Those who participated in a government-sponsored telecommuting pilot project reported a 73% increase in productivity.

- Pacific Bell offered telecommuting to its workers in the aftermath of the 1994 earthquake in Los Angeles. Ninety percent of the workers who took advantage of the "telecommuting relief package" were still working at home nine months after the earthquake. Half of those who opted to telecommute had not considered it before. Now half of those work at home five days a week. More than half of those are managers.

Token access method. When a LAN with a *ring* topology uses the **token access method**, an electronic *token* travels around a ring of nodes in the form of a *header.* Figure 6–10 demonstrates the token-passing process for this type of LAN. The header contains control signals, including one specifying whether the token is "free" or carrying a message. A sender node captures a free token as it travels from node to node, changes it to "busy," and adds the message. The resulting *message frame* travels around the ring to the addressee's NIC, which copies the message and returns the message frame to the sender. The sender's NIC removes the message frame from the ring and circulates a new free token. When a LAN with a *bus* topology uses the token access method, the token is broadcast to the nodes along the network bus. Think of the token as a benevolent dictator who, when captured, bestows the privilege of sending a transmission.

The familiar surroundings of home inspire some people to do their best work. Others, however, are more comfortable working in a traditional office setting. *Courtesy of International Business Machines Corporation. Unauthorized use not permitted.*

Pros and Cons of Working at Home

Why Work at Home?   Everyone has a different reason for wanting to telecommute. A programmer with two school-age children says, "I want to say good-bye when the kids leave for school and greet them when they return." A writer goes into the office once a week, the day before the magazine goes to press. She says, "I write all of my stories from the comfort of my home. An office that puts out a weekly magazine is not conducive to creative thinking." A company president states emphatically, "I got sick and tired of spending nights up in my office. By telecommuting, I'm at least within earshot of my wife and kids."

These are the most frequently cited reasons for working at home.

- *Increased productivity.* Telecommuters get more done at home than they do at the office.
- *Greater flexibility.* Telecommuters can optimize the scheduling of life events. For example, they can work late on Monday and take off for a few hours to exercise on Tuesday.
- *Improved relations with family.* Telecommuters spend more time with or around their family.
- *No commute.* The average commuter in a major metropolitan area spends the equivalent of one working day a week traveling to and from work. Telecommuters get this time to themselves. They also eliminate transportation expenses associated with the commute.
- *More comfortable and cheaper clothes.* When telecommuting, men willingly trade ties for T-shirts and women prefer sneakers to heels.
- *Cleaner air.* Telecommuting results in significantly less pollution from car exhaust, especially in large cities.

Arguments against Working at Home   Working at home is not the answer for all workers. Some people are easily distracted and need the ready access to management and the routine of the office to maintain a business focus. Telecommuting is not possible when job requirements demand daily face-to-face meetings (for example, bank tellers and elementary school teachers). Telecommuters routinely interact with clients and colleagues over the telephone and e-mail. They even participate in online group meetings via groupware. However, those arguing against telecommuting say that this type of interaction does not permit "pressing of the flesh" and the transmittal of the nonverbal cues that are essential to personal interaction. These arguments, though valid, have done little to hamper the emergence of telecommuting as a mainstream business strategy.

CSMA/CD access method.   In the **CSMA/CD** (*Carrier Sense Multiple Access/Collision Detection*) **access method,** nodes on the LAN must contend for the right to send a message. To gain access to the network, a node with a message to be sent automatically requests network service from the network software. The request might result in a "line busy" signal. In this case the node waits a fraction of a second and tries again, and again, until the line is free. Upon assuming control of the line, the node sends the message and then relinquishes control of the line to another node. CSMA/CD LANs operate like a conversation between polite people. When two people begin talking at the same time, one must wait until the other is finished.

MOVING THE DATA: LAN TRANSMISSION MEDIA   Three kinds of cables can be connected to the network interface cards: twisted-pair wire (the same wire used to

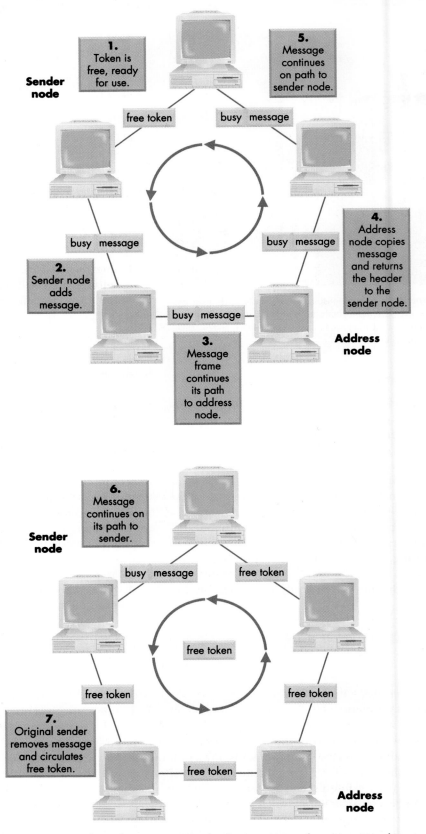

1. Token is free, ready for use.

Sender node

5. Message continues on path to sender node.

free token

busy message

2. Sender node adds message.

busy message

busy message

4. Address node copies message and returns the header to the sender node.

busy message

3. Message frame continues its path to address node.

Address node

6. Message continues on its path to sender.

Sender node

busy message

free token

free token

free token

free token

7. Original sender removes message and circulates free token.

free token

free token

Address node

FIGURE 6–10 The Token Access Method in a LAN with a Ring Topology

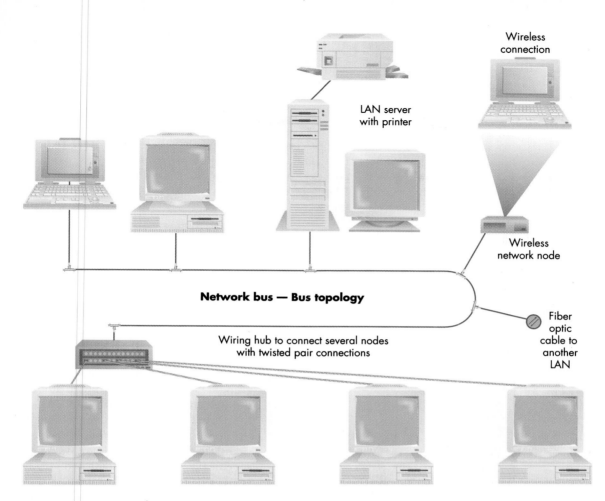

Wireless
connection

LAN server
with printer

Wireless
network node

Network bus — Bus topology

Fiber
optic
cable to
another
LAN

Wiring hub to connect several nodes
with twisted pair connections

FIGURE 6–11   LAN Links
In the figure, nodes in a LAN are linked via a bus topology. One of the nodes is linked to a wiring
hub that enables several PCs to be connected to the network bus. The wiring hub acts like a multiplexor, concentrating transmissions from several nodes. The LAN is linked to other LANs with fiber
optic cable.

connect telephones in a home), coaxial cable, and fiber optic cable. In wireless transmission, the cable runs from the transceiver to the NIC. Figure 6–11 illustrates how
nodes in a LAN are connected in a bus topology with a wiring hub at the end that allows several more nodes to be connected to the bus.

SERVERS: SERVING THE LAN   In a LAN, a *server* is a component that can be shared
by users on the LAN. The three most popular servers are the **file server,** the **print
server,** and the **communications server.**

The *file server* normally is a dedicated PC with a high-capacity hard disk for storing the data and programs shared by the network users. For example, the master customer file, word processing software, spreadsheet software, and so on would be stored
on the server disk. When a user wants to begin a spreadsheet session, the spreadsheet
software is downloaded from the file server to the user's RAM.

The *print server* typically is housed in the same dedicated PC as the file server.
The print server handles user print jobs and controls at least one printer. If needed,
the server *spools* print jobs; that is, it saves print jobs to disk until the requested printer
is available, then routes the print file to the printer.

The *communications server* provides communication links external to the LAN—
that is, links to other networks. To accomplish this service, the communications server
controls one or more modems, or perhaps access to an ISDN line.

MEMORY BITS

Networking
- Network topologies
  —Star
  —Ring
  —Bus
  —Hybrid
- Client/server computing
- Wide area network
  (WAN)
- Local area network
  (Also called LAN or
  local net)
  —Tiny area network
  (TAN)
  —Hardware compo-
  nents:
  NICs, transmission
  me-dia, and servers

The AllPoints™ Wireless PC Card slides into a PCMCIA slot on a laptop or palmtop computer. This PC card can be used to send and receive e-mail to and from any e-mail address, send faxes, page people, and send voice messages to telephones. It operates over a radio-based network in the United States and Canada.   U.S. Robotics Mobile Communications Corporation

These server functions may reside in a single PC or can be distributed among the PCs that make up the LAN. When the server functions are consolidated, the server PC usually is *dedicated* to servicing the LAN. Some PCs are designed specifically to be dedicated **LAN servers.** Until recently, you would purchase a traditional single-user PC and make it a dedicated server. Using a single-user PC continues to be an option with small- to medium-sized LANs, but not in large LANs with 100 or more users. Now, PC vendors manufacture powerful PCs designed, often with multiple processors, specifically as LAN servers. LAN servers are configured with enough RAM, storage capacity, and backup capability to handle hundreds of PCs.

LAN Software

In this section we explore LAN-based software, including LAN operating systems alternatives and a variety of applications software.

NETWORK OPERATING SYSTEMS   **LAN operating systems,** the nucleus of a local net, come in two formats: *peer-to-peer* and *dedicated server.* In both cases, the LAN operating system is actually several pieces of software. Each processing component in the LAN has a piece of the LAN operating system resident in its RAM. The pieces interact with one another to enable the nodes to share resources and communication.

The individual user in a LAN might appear to be interacting with an operating system, such as Windows 98. However, the RAM-resident LAN software *redirects* certain requests to the appropriate LAN component. For example, a print request would be redirected to the print server.

Peer-to-peer LANs.   In a **peer-to-peer LAN,** all PCs are peers, or equals. Any PC can be a client to another peer PC or any PC can share its resources with its peers. Peer-to-peer LANs are less sophisticated than those that have one or more dedicated servers. Because they are relatively easy to install and maintain, peer-to-peer LANs are popu-

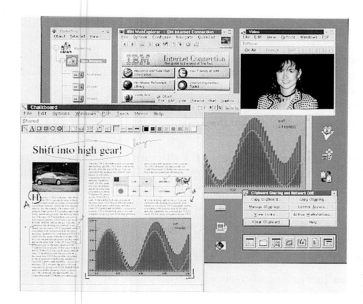

Users on a LAN can enjoy the benefits of workgroup computing. Here, users are speaking to one another about the page layout of a document while viewing the document and each other. Courtesy of International Business Machines Corporation. Unauthorized use not permitted.

lar when small numbers of PCs are involved (for example, from 2 to 20). PCs running the Windows 95, Windows 98, or Windows NT operating system can be linked together in a peer-to-peer LAN.

LANs with dedicated servers. In LANs with dedicated servers, the controlling software resides in the file server's RAM. LANs with dedicated servers can link hundreds of PCs in a LAN while providing a level of system security that is not possible in a peer-to-peer LAN. Control is distributed among the PCs in the LAN. Popular LAN operating systems are Novell's *NetWare* and Microsoft's *Windows NT Server.*

APPLICATIONS SOFTWARE FOR LANS LAN-based PCs can run all applications that stand-alone PCs can run plus those that involve electronic interaction with groups of people.

Shared applications software. LANs enable the sharing of general-purpose software, such as WordPerfect (word processing) and Excel (spreadsheet). LAN-based applications software is licensed for sharing. The PCs on the LAN with a dedicated central server interact with a file server to load various applications programs. When a LAN-based PC is booted, software that enables the use of the network interface card, communication with the file server, and interaction with the operating system is loaded from the PC's hard disk to RAM. Depending on how the LAN system administrator configured the LAN, you may see a graphical user interface that lists software options or you may see a prompt from the operating system. When you select a software package, it is downloaded from the LAN's file server to your PC's RAM for processing. You can then work with shared files on the file server or with your own local files (those stored on your PC).

Groupware: Software for the group. LANs have opened the door to applications that are not possible in the one-person, one-computer environment. For example, users linked together via a LAN can send electronic mail to one another. Scheduling meetings with other users on the LAN is a snap. This type of multi-user software designed to benefit a group of people is called groupware. Local area networks and groupware provide the foundation for *workgroup computing*. The breadth of workgroup computing encompasses any application that involves groups of people linked by a computer network. The following is a sampling of workgroup computing applications:

- *Electronic mail (e-mail).* E-mail enables people on a LAN to route messages to one another's electronic mailbox.
- *Calendar and scheduling.* People can keep online calendars and schedule meetings automatically. The scheduling software automatically checks appropriate users' electronic calendars for possible meeting times, schedules the meeting, and informs the participants via electronic mail.
- *Brainstorming and problem solving.* A LAN enables collaborative brainstorming and problem solving.
- *Shared whiteboarding.* Shared whiteboards permit a document or image to be viewed simultaneously by several people on the network. All people involved can make drawing or text annotations directly on the shared whiteboard. The annotations appear in the color associated with a particular participant.
- *Setting priorities.* Groupware is available that enables LAN users to establish priorities for projects through collective reasoning.
- *Electronic conferencing.* Conferencing groupware lets LAN users meet electronically.
- *Electronic forms.* American businesses and government spend over $400 billion each year to distribute, store, and update paper forms. Electronic forms groupware lets LAN users create forms for gathering information from other LAN users.

Interactive Study Guide Chapter 6

NETWORKS ON THE FLY The number and variety of workgroup computing applications can only increase. Already, notebook PC users are creating networks on the fly. That is, they bring their computers to the meeting and attach them to a common cable or activate their wireless transceivers to create a peer-to-peer LAN. In effect, we have progressed from the *portable computer* to the *portable network*. Once part of a LAN, users can enjoy the advantages of groupware.

IMPORTANT TERMS AND SUMMARY OUTLINE

6–1 OUR WEIRD, WILD, WIRED WORLD We rely on *computer networks* to retrieve and share information quickly; thus the current direction of **digital convergence. Connectivity** facilitates the electronic communication between companies and the free flow of information within an enterprise.

This is the era of **cooperative processing.** To obtain meaningful, accurate, and timely information, businesses have decided that they must cooperate internally and externally to take full advantage of available information. To promote internal cooperation, businesses are promoting intracompany and intercompany networking. An application of intercompany networking is **electronic data interchange (EDI).**

6–2 DATA COMMUNICATIONS HARDWARE: MAKING IT HAPPEN **Data communications** (also called **telecommunications**) is the electronic collection and distribution of information from and to remote facilities. Data communications hardware is used to transmit digital information between terminals and computers or between computers and other computers. These primary hardware components include the modem, the **front-end processor,** the **multiplexor,** and the **router.**

Modems, both internal and external, modulate and demodulate signals so that data can be transmitted over telephone lines. The fax modem acts as a modem and enables a PC to simulate a facsimile machine.

The front-end processor establishes the link between the source and destination in a process called **handshaking,** then sends the **message** to a **network address.** The front-end processor relieves the host computer of communications-related tasks. The multiplexor concentrates data from several sources and sends it over a single communications channel.

Communications protocols are rules established to govern the way data are transmitted in a computer network. The primary hardware/software technology used to enable the interconnection of incompatible computer networks is the router. A **backbone** is composed of one or more routers and the associated transmission media.

6–3 THE DATA COMMUNICATIONS CHANNEL: DATA HIGHWAYS A **communications channel** is the facility through which digital information must pass to get from one location in a computer network to the next. A channel's capacity is rated by the number of bits it can transmit per second (**bits per second** or **bps**). In practice, the word **baud** is often used interchangeably with *bits per second;* in reality, they are quite different.

A channel may be composed of one or more of the following transmission media: telephone lines of copper **twisted-pair wire, coaxial cable, fiber optic cable, mi-** crowave signals, radio signals, and wireless transceivers. Satellites are essentially microwave repeater stations that maintain a **geosynchronous orbit** around the earth. Three services are made available over POTS (plain old telephone services) using twisted-pair wire: voice-grade service, which is analog; **Integrated Services Digital Network (ISDN),** a digital service that requires an **ISDN modem;** and **Asymmetric Digital Subscriber Line (ADSL).**

Common carriers provide communications channels to the public, and lines can be arranged to suit the application. A **private,** or **leased, line** provides a dedicated communications channel. A **switched,** or **dial-up, line** is available on a time-and-distance-charge basis.

6–4 NETWORKS: CONNECTING NODES Computer systems are linked together to form a computer network. In a computer network the **node** can be a terminal, a computer, or any other destination/source device. The basic patterns for configuring computer systems within a computer network are **star topology, ring topology,** and **bus topology.** The bus topology permits the connection of nodes along a **network bus.** In practice, most networks are actually hybrids of these **network topologies.**

In **client/server computing,** processing is distributed throughout the network. The **client computer** requests processing or some other type of service from the **server computer.** Both client and server computers perform processing. The client computer runs **front-end applications software,** and the server computer runs the **back-end applications software.** The trend toward client/server computing has resulted in companies **downsizing** their computers.

Asynchronous transmission begins and ends each message with start/stop bits and is used primarily for low-speed data transmission. **Synchronous transmission** permits the source and destination to communicate in timed synchronization for high-speed data transmission.

6–5 LOCAL AREA NETWORKS: LOCAL NETS A **WAN,** or **wide area network,** connects nodes in widely dispersed geographic areas. The *local area network (LAN),* or **local net,** connects nodes in close proximity and does not need a common carrier. A **TAN,** or **tiny area network,** is a very small LAN. The three basic hardware components in a PC-based LAN are the **network interface cards (NICs),** the transmission media, and the servers. The physical transfer of data and programs between LAN nodes is controlled by the access method embedded in the network interface card's ROM, usually the **token** or **CSMA/CD access method.** The three most popular servers are the **file server,** the **print server,** and the **communications server.** These server functions may reside in a dedicated **LAN server.**

The **LAN operating system** is actually several pieces of software, a part of which resides in each LAN component's RAM. In a **peer-to-peer LAN,** all PCs are equals. Any PC can share its resources with its peers. In LANs with dedicated servers, the controlling software resides in the file server's RAM.

LANs and *groupware* provide the foundation for *workgroup computing*. The breadth of workgroup computing encompasses any application that involves groups of people linked by a computer network. Workgroup computing applications include electronic mail, calendar and scheduling, brainstorming and problem solving, shared whiteboarding, and others.

REVIEW EXERCISES

Concepts

1. Would EDI be more closely associated with inter-company networking or intracompany networking?
2. What is meant by *geosynchronous orbit,* and how does it relate to data transmission via satellite?
3. What is the unit of measure for the capacity of a data communications channel?
4. Expand the following acronyms: WAN, bps, and EDI.
5. What is the purpose of a multiplexor?
6. What is the relationship between a communications channel and a computer network?
7. What term describes the trend toward increased reliance on smaller computers?
8. List four workgroup applications.
9. What device converts digital signals into analog signals for transmission over telephone lines? Why is it necessary?
10. Why is it not advisable to increase the distance between microwave relay stations to 200 miles?
11. Name two pieces of hardware that might be configured with a host computer to improve the overall efficiency of the computer network.
12. Name the three basic computer network topologies.
13. Name two popular LAN access methods. Which one passes a token from node to node?
14. Name three types of LAN servers.
15. Briefly describe the function of a router.

Discussion and Problem Solving

16. Describe circumstances in which a leased line would be preferred to a dial-up line.
17. What is the relationship between EDI and connectivity?
18. Describe how information can be made readily accessible to many people in a company, but only on a need-to-know basis.
19. The five PCs in the purchasing department of a large consumer-goods manufacturer are used primarily for word processing and database applications. What would be the benefits and costs associated with connecting the PCs in a local area network?
20. The mere fact that a system uses data communications poses a threat to security. Why?
21. Suppose you are a systems analyst for a municipal government. In the current incident-reporting system, transactions are batched for processing on the city's mainframe at the end of each day. You have been asked to justify to the city council the conversion from the current system to a LAN-based on-line incident-reporting system. What points would you make?

SELF-TEST (BY SECTION)

6–1 **a.** We are going through a period of digital convergence. (T/F)
b. Using computers and data communications to transmit data electronically between companies is called: (a) EDI, (b) DIE, or (c) DEI?

6–2 **a.** The electronic collection and distribution of information between two points is referred to as _____ _____.

b. The modem converts _____ (digital or analog) signals to _____ (digital or analog) signals so that the data can be transmitted over telephone lines.
c. The terminal sending a message is the source and the computer receiving the message is the destination. (T/F)
d. Another name for a server is a multiplexor. (T/F)

e. _____ facilitate the interconnection of dissimilar networks. *Routers*

6–3 a. It is more difficult for a computer criminal to tap into a fiber optic cable than a copper telephone line. (T/F) *T*

b. A 56,000 bits-per-second channel is the same as a: (a) 56-kps line, (b) 56 K-bps line, or (c) dual 8000X2 K-bps line? *b*

c. The wireless transceiver replaces the physical link between the source and the destination in a network. (T/F) *T*

d. The two basic types of service offered by common carriers are a private line and a switched line. (T/F) *T*

e. The ISDN enables digital data transmission. (T/F) *T*

6–4 a. An endpoint in a network of computers is called a _____. *node*

b. The central cable called a network bus is most closely associated with which network topology: (a) ring, (b) star, or (c) bus?

c. The trend in the design of computer networks is toward: (a) distributed transmission, (b) client/server computing, or (c) CANs? *b*

d. Synchronous transmission is best suited for data communications involving low-speed I/O devices. (T/F) *F*

6–5 a. A LAN is designed for "long-haul" data communications. (T/F) *F*

b. Which of the following is not a popular LAN access method: (a) token, (b) CSMA/CD, or (c) parity checking? *c*

c. In a LAN with a dedicated server, the LAN operating system resides entirely in the server processor's RAM. (T/F) *F*

Self-test Answers. **6–1 (a)** T; **(b)** a. **6–2 (b)** data communications; **(b)** digital, analog; **(c)** T; **(d)** F; **(e)** Routers. **6–3 (a)** T; **(b)** b; **(c)** T; **(d)** T; **(e)** T. **6–4 (a)** node; **(b)** c; **(c)** b; **(d)** F. **6–5 (a)** F; **(b)** c; **(c)** F.

Going Online: The Net, Information Services, and More

- Understand the scope of features offered by online information services.
- Describe the Internet.
- Appreciate the scope of information, services, and applications made available over the Internet.
- Identify and describe common Internet capabilities.

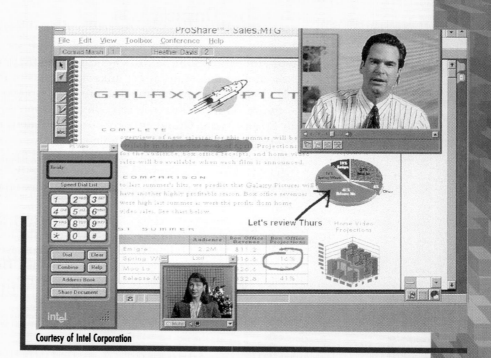

Courtesy of Intel Corporation

LET'S TALK

Can you follow this conversation? It includes computing concepts presented in this chapter. Read it now, then reread it once you've had an opportunity to study the chapter.

The Scene   The place is a private chat room on a commercial information service where a widow, IdaB (Ida's online name), in Austin, Texas, and a retired railroad supervisor, RailroadRoy (Roy's online name), in Kingfisher, Oklahoma, are enjoying a cyber-romance.

RAILROAD ROY: Good evening, Ida. How are you tonight?

IDA B: I have a cold. :-~) Worse, my 50-year-old son has left his good job in the city. :-(

RAILROAD ROY: Here's a dozen roses to pep you up. @—>—>— X12

IDA B: :-) Thanks. [*] Bill is taking a new job so he can telecommute. :-/   I'm a bit skeptical because I've never heard of Cyclometrics, his new company.

RAILROAD ROY: Me either, but I'll do some research. Let's log off now so I can get a PPP connection to the Cyclometrics Web site. Come back at 3:30 and I'll know more. TTYL

IDA B: Thanks, honey, bye now.***

(3:30)

RAILROAD ROY: Hi again, my little O :-). Check your e-mail. You'll find a file attached that contains

more than you'll ever want to know about Cyclometrics.

IDA B: Hi, sweetie. [*] How'd you do it?

RAILROAD ROY: I visited its World Wide Web site on the Internet at http://www.cyclometrics.com. The company's got a sound financial statement, some innovative products, and a bright future.

IDA B: How do you know all that?

RAILROAD ROY: I clicked on a few hypertext links and even listened to an audio message from its president. You might want to visit the site yourself. It's really informative.

IDA B: Thanks, triple R. I'm going surfin'. See you tomorrow—same time. [[[[****]]]]

7–1 The Online World

**Monthly Technology Updates
Chapter 7**

Your PC is a door to the online world. There are a variety of ways to open the door and enter the online world. One can enter using cable modems, ISDN, ADSL, wireless satellite links, and direct links via LANs, but most of us enter cyberspace by simply plugging the phone line into our PC's modem and running our communications software. Once online, you can talk (just as you would on the telephone) with friends in Europe, send Grandma a picture, schedule a meeting with your co-workers, pay your utility bill, play games with people you've never met, listen to a live audio broadcast of a sporting event, or conduct research for a report. Every day a growing number of online capabilities continue to change the way we live our lives. For example, each day more and more knowledge workers opt to **telecommute** to work over the digital highways.

The online world offers a vast network of resources, services, and capabilities. To go online, people with PCs generally subscribe to a commercial information service, such as America Online (AOL) and Microsoft Network, or open an account with a company that will provide access to the Internet. This chapter explores these and other online options and shows how you, too, can become a part of this global community.

7-2 Information Services: America Online, CompuServe, and Many More

Commercial information services have several powerful mainframe computer systems that offer a variety of online services, from hotel reservations to daily horoscopes. More and more PC users are subscribing to commercial information services, such as America Online (AOL), CompuServe (an AOL subsidiary), Microsoft Network (MSN), LEXIS-NEXIS, Dow Jones Business Information Service, and Dialog Web. The larger information services, such as America Online, already have several million subscribers each. In fact, information services have grown at a rate of 30% per year since 1990. Still, less than 30% of PC owners subscribe to an online information service, so there is plenty of room for these services to grow.

To take advantage of information services, you need a communications-equipped PC (that is, one with a modem and communications software) and a few dollars. Most services have a *monthly service charge*. The monthly service charge for the most popular services is usually a flat rate of $15 to $25 for unlimited usage. Some usage information services bill based on time online. The charges can be substantial for business-oriented services, perhaps as much as a dollar a minute for medical and legal services. Initially, you get:

- *Communications software.* Some information services, such as AOL and MSN, give you communications software packages designed specifically to interface with their information service network. Others rely on Internet **browsers** to deliver the service. Browsers are programs that let you view the various Internet resources.

- *A username and password.* To obtain authorization to connect with the online information service, you need to enter your username and a password.

- *A user's guide.* A user's guide provides an overview of services and includes telephone numbers that can be dialed to access the information service's private network. America Online is a worldwide network, something like the Internet but on a smaller scale. (Except for small towns, the AOL telephone number you dial is usually local.) Some information services deliver their services over the Internet.

Figure 7-1 takes you on a visual tour of America Online, one of the most popular information services. This walkthrough figure shows you a few of the well-traveled roads on this stretch of the information highway, but it does not begin to show the true breadth and scope of America Online (or any other major information service). If you were to spend every waking minute of the next year logged on to AOL, you would not be able to explore all of its features, bulletin boards, databases, download opportunities, and information services. In fact, you would probably fall behind. Existing services are updated and new services are added on AOL and all of the other information services every single day.

7-3 The Internet: A Worldwide Web of Computers and Information

America Online (AOL), the information service, is one of the many beautiful stars in cyberspace. Now imagine being able to explore an entire universe with millions of beautiful stars, each offering databases, forums for discussion, e-mail, files of every conceivable type, information services, and more. That's *the Internet*.

What Is the Internet?

The Internet (a worldwide collection of *inter*connected *net*works) is actually comprised of thousands of independent networks at academic institutions, military installations,

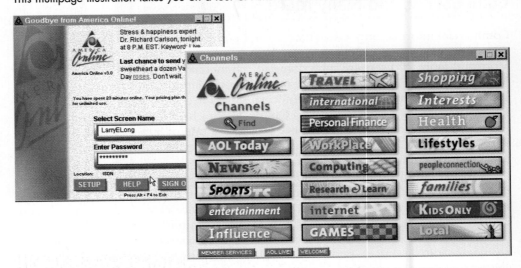

Sign On to America Online   Prior to going online with America Online (AOL), you must install the AOL program disk on your PC's hard disk. The program contains communications software and a graphical user interface that allows you to navigate among the many AOL services and channels (interest areas). To go online, run the AOL program and go through the "sign on" procedure (see example). First you enter your AOL *screen name*—your online persona. Some people use their real name, but most use an alias, like SkyJockey, CaptBart, PrincesLea, and so on. Once you enter your password, which appears as asterisks, the software dials the AOL number, makes the connection, and displays the AOL main menu (see example). The main menu is divided into channels (a name derived from the TV channel), most of which are discussed and illustrated in this figure.

Today's News   AOL's Today's News channel offers up-to-the-minute news in eight departments: *U. S. & World, Business, Sports, Politics, Life, Weather, local, Newstand,* and *Classified.* On-line news gives you both news highlights and in-depth coverage of the latest releases directly from the wire services. You can request general news or news about a specific topic. For example, you can request news about Australia, French politics, the plastics industry, or whatever interests you. In the example, the user chose to read an article on politics. You can also browse through an electronic version of the *New York Times* (click on the arrow) or request a short- or long-term weather forecast for any region in the world.

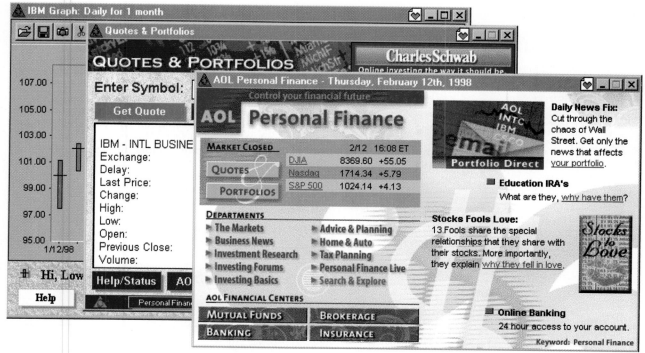

Personal Finance   Get up-to-the-minute quotes on stocks (see IBM quote), securities, bonds, options, and commodities. A wealth of financial information is available for the asking (see graph of daily IBM stock prices over a one-month period). You can also use this service to help you manage a securities portfolio and to keep tax records. You can even purchase and sell securities from your PC.

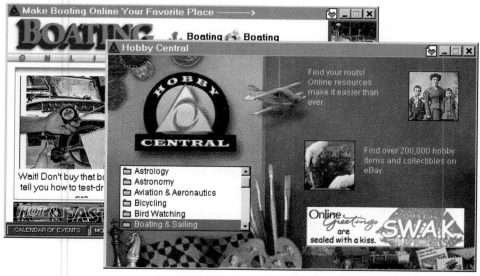

Interests   Of the millions of people who go online each day, many belong to the same clubs and have interests similar to yours. You can share notes with boating enthusiasts (see example). Or, you can talk with fellow homeowners, environmentalists, bikers, aviators, and so on. Whatever your interest, there is probably an online forum that offers an opportunity to interact and share information (health tips, recipes, travel deals, art, and so on). The AOL forum, which may be called an *area* or *club* on other information services, is a theme-based electronic area in which people can share ideas, information, and files that relate to the theme.

(**Figure 7–1** *continues on next page*)

FIGURE 7-1 (continued)

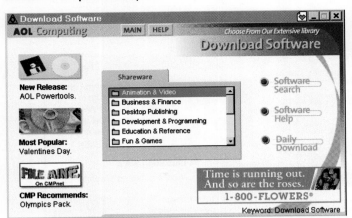

Computing On any information service, the computing channel is among the most active. PC enthusiasts can chat for hours about any subject relating to hardware or software. This AOL channel lets you download any of thousands of programs (shareware, freeware, and those programs uploaded by AOL members), in many different categories (see example). If you need help deciding what you want, AOL maintains a list of the most frequently downloaded software packages. Also, you can catch up on the latest technology news and talk directly with hardware and software vendors through the "Company Connection."

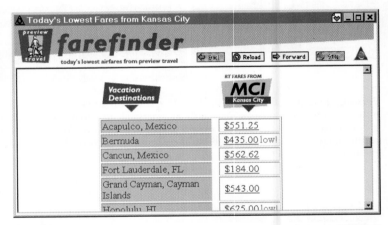

Travel You can plan your own vacation or business trip over AOL. All you have to do is check airline, train, and cruise schedules, then make your reservations. You can check the lowest airfares from many cities (Kansas City in the example) to many other cities, including those suitable for an impromptu mid-winter getaway. You can even charter a yacht in the Caribbean, locate the nearest bed-and-breakfast inn, or rent a lodge in the Rockies.

Shopping The AOL Shopping channel is the ultimate in one-stop shopping. You can get everything from pickup trucks to perfume (see example), often at discount prices. Electronic shopping adds a new dimension to shopping—information. For example, you can research financial services, telephone companies, car insurance agencies, or a particular product before buying. Photo-quality displays are available for many products.

Shop at your leisure. The online store is never closed, and there is no clerk rushing you to a decision. Online shopping helps you get the most for your money. It's easy to comparison shop or check out the recommendation of *Consumer Reports*. If you are in the market for a new automobile, you can find out exactly what the dealer paid for a particular model.

People Connection An online information service creates a community where people chat about cars (see examples), gather after work to relax at a virtual pub, go shopping, ask advice, and share stories, jokes, recipes, and so on. This electronic community, however, doesn't reflect society as a whole. Whether we will admit it or not, how we look, where we live, our economic status, and so on affects who we talk with and often the subject. This emerging electronic society allows people to set aside traditional social mores and interact freely regardless of race, creed, color, sex, age, appearance, ability, education, and so on. Cybersurfers have an opportunity to meet and converse with those who might be outside their social circle in real life. Members of the electronic society have talked openly with the President and Vice President of the United States. They have talked with the rich and famous. Even more importantly, they have talked with those who are younger or older, richer or poorer, or of different religions. In an electronic society, you are a player. For a few pennies, you can cross geographic, political, economic, and social boundaries and be heard by thousands, if not millions, of other players.

AOL offers a variety of ways for members to communicate, primarily *chat rooms*. People "enter" AOL chat rooms and talk with real people in real time. In the example, 23 people in the "car chat" chat room are talking about cars. It's like having a conference call, except the people involved key in their responses. You can "listen in" or be an active part of the electronic conversation. AOL sponsors three types of chat rooms: public (special-topic rooms defined by AOL), member (special-topic rooms defined by AOL members), and private (rooms created by members for private conversations). Chat rooms are found on all AOL channels, not just the People Connection.

AOL chat rooms have a couple of interesting features. You can send an instant message directly to a particular individual in the room. Your message appears on that individual's screen near the scrolling chat room conversation. Also, you can view the profile of a particular person in the room by clicking on that person's screen name (see the box in the upper-right corner in the "car chat" example). Most AOL members maintain an online member profile that contains basic information about the AOL member. If a member posts no profile, you have no way of knowing whether you're talking with a middle-aged woman, an elementary schoolboy, or an intelligent parrot.

Often, special guests are invited to auditoriums (a large chat room with slightly different rules) to meet with AOL members. When Vice President Al Gore participated in an online conference held over CompuServe, now an AOL subsidiary, 900 people "showed up" for the conference, of which over 300 got responses. During the conference, Gore noted that two-way interactive communication was far superior to the one-way communication of broadcast TV.

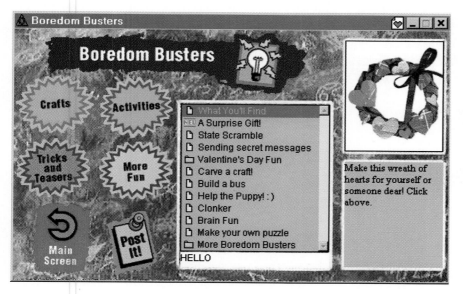

Family The AOL Family channel has seven departments: family ties, parenting, babies, newsstand, homebase, kids and teens, and parental controls. The online material in these departments includes a wide variety of family issues from effective parenting to how children can beat boredom blues (see example). Suggestions for the latter range from a dinosaur party to hand-shadow fun to radio theater.

(**Figure 7–1** *continues on next page*)

FIGURE 7–1 (continued)

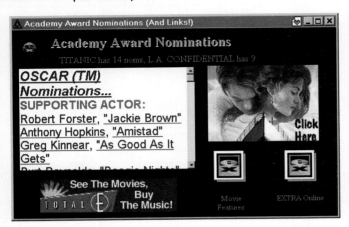

Entertainment The Entertainment Channel is just that—entertainment. You can learn about Academy Awards nominations (see example), or read reviews of these movies, as well as of videos, CDs, plays, and books. This channel offers pictures of movie and TV stars (see example), classic sound clips, a movie-talk chat room, and more. You can check out highlights of the day's TV programming or you can visit the Cartoon Network world.

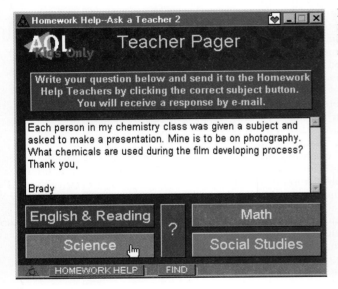

Research & Learn This channel is a potpourri of research/reference tools and of forums and activities associated with learning (careers, homework help, courses, reference desk, and so on). For example, students can get immediate help from teachers online. The education resources available to AOL members include encyclopedias, dictionaries, and a wide range of reference resources. You can take courses from the AOL Online Campus, including courses on law, business management, and writing. You can choose from a variety of educational packages, from learning arithmetic to preparing for the Scholastic Aptitude Test (SAT). You can even determine your IQ!

The information society is adopting a new approach to seeking information. The traditional approach involved finding print sources, then thumbing through them one-by-one. This approach is a bit cumbersome for today's knowledge worker. The research part of this channel allows users to search through dozens, even hundreds of books, documents, or databases in minutes. For example, if you are interested in learning more about a particular state, you can find many interesting facts and lots of information about that state (Hawaii in the example).

There are literally hundreds of databases that offer information in as many areas. For example, politicians can scan through various government publications on key words. You can recall articles on any conceivable subject from dozens of newspapers, trade periodicals, and newsletters. Lawyers have access to a complete law library online. No matter what your question, you can probably find an answer in the Research and Learn channel.

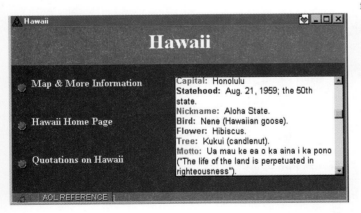

Sports On the Sports channel, you can get up-to-the-minute scores for college and professional sporting events or, in Olympic Games years, you can check in to keep up with Olympics gold (see example). Sports enthusiasts who revel in statistics need look no further—it's easy to find out who did what, when, and to whom. Sports fans can go to chat rooms and talk to one another about their favorite sport, team, or sports figure.

Kids Only Kids Only is KOOL (Kids Only OnLine), and kids love it. Kids Only is actually a hodgepodge of services from all AOL channels, but just for kids. The chat rooms in the "Tree House" are designed for kids, as are the reading materials, such as *Disney Adventure*. Kids can even create and post their own drawings (see example).

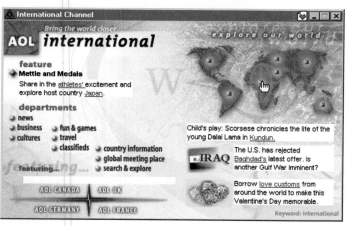

International and Other AOL Channels AOL has several other channels, including the International channel (see example). Other channels are AOL Today (miscellaneous service and features), Workplace (issues involving careers and the workplace), Local (information by region and city), Health, Internet (a gateway to the Internet), and Games.

(*text continues from page CORE 191*)

government agencies, commercial enterprises, and other organizations. Once on the Internet, cybersurfers can tap into a vast array of information resources, have access to millions of retrievable files, "talk" on thousands of worldwide newsgroups (similar to bulletin boards), send e-mail to any of millions of people, and take advantage of thousands of free and pay-for-use information services.

Just how big is the Internet? The Net, the Internet's nickname, links close to one million networks with over 35,000,000 Internet host server computers in almost every country in the world. Internet hosts are connected to the Internet 24 hours a day. Thousands more join this global network each month. The number of people using the Internet is expected to reach 180 million by the year 2000, up from an estimated 80 million in 1998.

From ARPANET to the Internet: Some Historical Perspective

A lot happened in 1969, including Woodstock and the first landing on the moon. Amidst all of this activity, the birth of what we now know as the Internet went virtually unnoticed. A small group of computer scientists on both coasts of the United States were busy creating a national network that would enable the scientific community to share ideas over communications links. At the time, this network was truly a giant leap because computers were viewed more as number crunchers than as aids to communication.

The Department of Defense's Advanced Research Project Agency (ARPA) sponsored the project, named ARPANET, to create a new community of geographically dispersed scientists who were united by technology. The first official demonstration linked UCLA with Stanford University, both in California. Ironically, this historic event had no reporters, no photographers, and no records. No one remembered the first message, only that it worked. By 1971, the ARPANET included more than 20 sites, including Harvard and MIT. By 1981, the ARPANET linked 200 sites. A few years later, this grand idea of interconnected networks caught on like an uncontrolled forest fire, spreading from site to site throughout the United States. Other countries wanted in on it, too.

ARPANET broke new ground. The diversity of computers and the sites forced ARPA to develop a standard protocol (rules of data communications) that would enable communication between diverse computers and networks. ARPANET eventually lost its reason to exist, as other special-interest networks took its place. In 1990, ARPANET was eliminated, leaving behind a legacy of networks that evolved into the Internet. At that time, commercial accounts were permitted access to what had been a network of military and academic organizations.

What we now know as the Internet is one of the federal government's success stories. Although the Internet, along with its policies and technologies, are now pushed along by market forces, the United States government remains active in promoting cooperation between communications, software, and computer companies. The current administration would like for the Internet to emerge as a *National Information Infrastructure (NII)* that may someday link schools, libraries, hospitals, corporations, agencies at all levels of government, and much more by the twenty-first century.

Who Governs the Internet?

We now know that the Internet wasn't always the Internet—it was first the ARPANET. When the ARPANET was conceived, one objective of its founders was to create a network in which communications could continue even if parts of the network crashed. To achieve this objective, it was designed with no central computer or network. This is still true today. The U.S. Internet *backbone,* the major communications lines and nodes to which thousands of host computers are connected, crisscrosses the United States with no node being the central focus of communications.

Unlike AOL, CompuServe, and other information services, the Internet is coordinated (not governed) by volunteers from many nations serving on various advisory boards, task groups, steering committees, and so on. There is no single authoritative organization. The volunteer organizations set standards for and help coordinate the global operation of Internet. Each autonomous network on the Internet makes its own rules, regulations, and decisions about which resources to make publicly available. Consequently, the Internet is being re-invented almost daily by the people who run these independent networks.

InterNIC, an organization funded by a cooperative agreement from the National Science Foundation, provides registration services for the Internet community. Any person or organization desiring to connect a computer to the Net must register its

The Internet

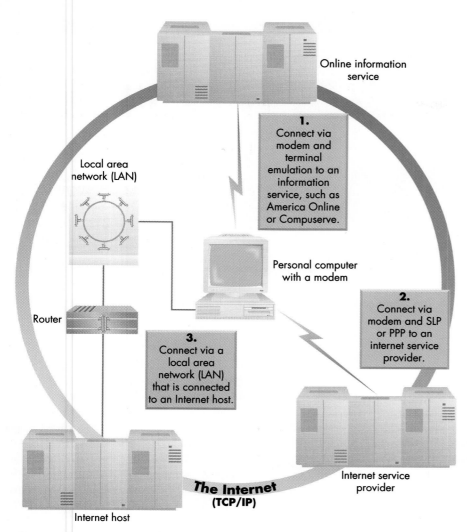

FIGURE 7–2 Ways to Connect to the Internet

computer with InterNIC. Besides keeping track of the computers connected to the Net (site names and addresses), it also provides assistance to users concerning policy and the status of their existing registrations. Registered Internet hosts must pay an amount based on Internet usage to support the Internet's backbone.

Making the Internet Connection

How do you get on the Internet? There are three levels at which you can connect your PC to the Internet (see Figure 7–2):

CONNECT VIA AN INFORMATION SERVICE GATEWAY One way to gain access to the Internet is to subscribe to a commercial information service, such as America On-line or Microsoft Network (MSN). This level one connection method is a popular choice for people working from their home or small businesses and for those who wish to link their home PC to the Internet. AOL and the other information services are themselves large self-contained networks. Each provides an electronic *gateway* to the Net. Figure 7–3 demonstrates interaction with the Internet through the America Online gateway.

FIGURE 7–3 The America Online Gateway to the Internet

CONNECT VIA AN INTERNET SERVICE PROVIDER At the second level of Internet service, you would make the connection via a *dialup connection* through an *Internet service provider*. This type of connection gives you full access to the Internet. A **dialup connection** is a temporary connection established using a modem to dialup the number (over a telephone line or a digital ISDN or ADSL line) for a line linked to a remote computer. An **Internet service provider (ISP)** is any company that provides individuals and organizations with access to, or presence on, the Internet. ISPs do not offer the extended information services offered by commercial information services, such as CompuServe, although some information services double as Internet service providers.

There are thousands of Internet service providers, ranging from a local elementary schools making unused line capacity available to students and parents to major communications companies, such as AT&T and Sprint. To use this kind of connection, you must have an account with a service provider and software that enables a direct link via **Transmission Control Protocol/Internet Protocol (TCP/IP).** Communications over the Net are built around this two-layer protocol. A protocol is a set of rules computers use to talk to each other.

The *Transmission Control Protocol* (the TCP of the TCP/IP) sets the rules for the packaging of information into the **packets** (strings of bits) that are routed over different paths on the Internet. The computer at their destination reassembles the packets. The *Internet Protocol* (the IP of the TCP/IP) handles the address, such that each packet is routed to its proper destination. Here is how it works. When you request a file from an Internet server computer, the TCP layer divides the file into one or more packets, numbers the packets, and then routes them one-by-one through the IP layer. Each packet has the same destination *IP address,* but they may take different paths through the Internet to their destination. At the destination, the TCP layer waits until all the packets arrive, reassembles them, and then forwards them to users as a single file.

Each **point-of-presence** (POP) on the Internet has a unique address with four numbers separated by periods (for example, 206.28.104.10). A **POP** is an access point to the Internet. An ISP may have many POPs so that subscribers can dial local telephone numbers to gain access. A POP for an ISP may be a leased router or server owned by a common carrier, such as Sprint or AT&T.

When you dialup an ISP's local POP, your dialup connection is made through a *SLIP* (Serial Line Internet Protocol) or *PPP* (Point-to-Point Protocol) connection to an Internet host. Generally, choose the PPP option if given a choice when setting up your Internet software. A "Slip" connection is slower and does not offer the same level of error protection. Once a TCP/IP connection is established, you are on the Internet, not an information service gateway. The TCP/IP protocol is different from the protocol used within the AOL network, the CompuServe network, and other information service networks. Their Internet gateways enable communication between the information services' native communications protocols and TCP/IP.

DIRECT VIA NETWORK CONNECTION A level three direct connection to the Internet is preferable to a dialup link (levels one and two above) because these normally enable faster interaction with the Internet. At this level, your PC is wired directly into the Internet, usually via a local area network (LAN). A LAN will normally have a high-speed digital link to the Internet, which is shared by the users on the LAN. Depending on the size of the LAN and the extent of Internet usage, the LAN may be connected to an ISDN (128 K bps), an ADSL line (up to 9 M bps [megabits per second]), a **T-1 line** (1.544 M bps), or a **T-3 line** (44.736 M bps) line. A faster connection means you do not have to wait so long to retrieve information, execute commands, or just connect to the Internet. A dialup connection can take from 15 seconds to about 45 seconds to establish, where a direct connection via a LAN is almost immediate, and it's available 24 hours a day. To have a direct connection, your PC must be configured with TCP/IP software and be connected to a LAN that is linked directly to an Internet host. This is the case with most businesses and many college computer labs.

READY ACCESS TO THE INTERNET Do you want to be a **newbie**? Newbies are what seasoned Internet surfers (those who regularly travel or "surf" from Internet site to Internet site) call novice Internet users. If you do, there is a good chance that your college or company's computer network is linked to the Internet. Obtaining access may be as easy as asking your boss, instructor, or the network administrator to assign you an Internet address (username) and password.

Retrieving and Viewing Information

Once you have established an Internet connection, you're ready to explore the wonders of the Internet—almost. To do so you need to open a *client program* that will enable you to retrieve and view Internet resources. A **client program** runs on your PC and works in conjunction with a companion **server program** that runs on the Internet host computer. The client program contacts the server program, and they work together to give you access to the resources on the Internet server. Client programs are designed to work with one or more specific kinds of server programs (for example, the Internet Explorer client software works with the companion Internet Explorer server software). A single server computer might have several different server programs running on it, enabling it to accommodate a variety of clients.

A *browser* is one kind of client. Browsers are application software that provide you with a graphical interactive interface for searching, finding, viewing, and managing information over any network. Microsoft Internet Explorer and Netscape Communicator are the two most popular browsers. Both are used in the examples throughout this book. Most information on the Internet is accessed and viewed in the workspace of browser client programs. You give the browser an Internet address, called the *URL*, and it goes out over your Internet connection, finds the server site identified in the URL, then downloads the requested file for viewing on your browser. The operation of browsers is discussed in Chapter 9.

Uniform Resource Locator: The Internet Address

The **URL** or **uniform resource locator** (pronounced "*U-R-L*" or "*earl*") is the Internet equivalent of an address. Just as postal addresses progress from general to specific (country, state, city, to street address), URLs do the same. The URL gives those who make information available over the Internet a standard way to designate where Internet elements, such as server sites, documents, files, bulletin boards (newsgroups), and so on, can be found. Let's break down one of the following URLs from the Long and Long INTERNET BRIDGE, the companion Internet site for this book.

http://www.prenhall.com/long/computers6e/main.html

- *http://www.prenhall.com/long/computers6e/main.html.* That portion of the URL before the first colon (http in the example) specifies the access method. This indicator tells your local software how to access that particular file. The http tells the software to expect an **http (HyperText Transport Protocol)** file. Http is the primary access method for interacting with the Internet. Other common access methods include *ftp* (File Transfer Protocol) for transferring files, *news* for bulletin board–like newsgroups, *gopher* for accessing information via a Gopher menu tree, and *telnet* for logging into a remote computer. When on the Internet, you will encounter URLs like these.

handwritten: e-mail jportello@sunyopt.edu

handwritten: gets things

ftp://ftp.prenhall.com/ (Prentice Hall ftp site)

http://www.hotbot.com/ (Internet search engine)

news://alt.tennis (tennis newsgroup)

telnet://bbs.nightowl.net (Internet-based bulletin board)

gopher://wiretap.spies.com/00/Library/Classic/twocity.txt (African National Congress Information)

- *http://www.prenhall.com/ long/computers6e/main.html.* That portion following the double forward slashes (//), *www.prenhall.com,* is the server address, or the domain name. The **domain name,** which is a unique name that identifies an Internet host site, will always have at least two parts, separated by dots (periods). This host/network identifier adheres to rules for the domain hierarchy. The part to the right of the domain name is the most general and that part on the left is the most specific. At the top of the domain hierarchy (the part on the right) is the country code for all countries except the United States. For example, the address for the Canadian Tourism Commission is *info.ic.gc.ca.* Other common country codes are *au* (Australia), *dk* (Denmark), *fr* (France), and *jp* (Japan). Within the United States, the country code is replaced with a code denoting affiliation categories. Colleges are in the *edu* category. Other categories are shown in Figure 7–4. The next level of the domain hierarchy identifies the host network or host provider, which might be the name of a business or college *(prenhall or stateuniv).* Large organizations might have networks within a network and need subordinate identifiers. The example Internet address *cis.stateuniv.edu* identifies the *cis* local area network at *stateuniv.* The Physics Department LAN at State University might be identified as *physics.stateuniv.edu.*

- *http://www.prenhall.com/long/computers6e/main.html.* What follows the domain name is a *directory* containing the resources for a particular topic. The resource directory *long/* in this example refers to the Long and Long INTERNET BRIDGE (the companion Internet site for all Prentice Hall books by Larry and Nancy Long). Several

U.S. Top-level Domain Affiliation ID	Affiliation
com	Commercial
edu	Education
firm	Businesses
gov	Government
info	Purveyors of information
int	International
mil	Military
net	Network resources
nom	Users desiring personal nomenclature
org	Usually nonprofit organizations
rec	Entities dealing in recreational activities
store	Retailers
web	Businesses related to the web

FIGURE 7–4 United States Top-level Domains

books are covered within this INTERNET BRIDGE resource, so subordinate directories are needed to reference a specific book (*computers6e,* meaning *Computers,* sixth edition).

- *http://www.prenhall.com/long/computers6e/main.html.* At the end of the URL is the specific file that is retrieved from the server (www.prenhall.com in this example) and sent to your PC over the Internet. The html extension (after the dot) in the filename *main.html* indicates that this is an html file. **HTML (HyperText Markup Language)** is the language used to compose and format most of the content you see when cruising the Net.

Going Online

Internet Resources and Applications

The Internet offers a broad spectrum of resources, applications, and capabilities. First we'll discuss those that let you access information and services. Then we'll discuss those capabilities that let you communicate with people.

ACCESSING INFORMATION AND SERVICES: THE WEB, FTP, TELNET, AND MORE

World Wide Web servers have emerged as the choice for cruising the Internet; however, other not-so-user-friendly types of servers contain useful information not available from World Wide Web sources. These systems, which pre-date the World Wide Web, include *FTP, Gopher, WAIS,* and *Telnet.* Critical resources on these servers are being re-formatted and modernized for distribution via World Wide Web servers, but this may take a while. In the meantime these resources remain available from these effective but old-fashioned servers. This section describes modern and traditional servers on the Internet.

WWW: World Wide Web. The **World Wide Web** is affectionately called **the Web.** The World Wide Web is an Internet system that permits linking of multimedia documents among servers on the Internet. By establishing a linked relationship between World Wide Web documents, related information becomes easily accessible. These linked relationships are completely independent of physical location. These attributes set Web servers apart from other Internet servers.

- *User-friendly.* World Wide Web resources are designed to be accessed with Internet browsers. These easy-to-use browsers, with their graphical user interfaces, let users point-and-click their way around the Internet.

- *Multimedia documents.* Information on the Web, which may be graphics, audio, video, animation, and text, is viewed in **pages.** A Web page can contain text plus any or all of these multimedia elements. It might help to think of a Web page as a page in an alternative type of book, one with non-sequential linked documents at a Web site. Each Web page is actually a file with its own URL. When you navigate to a particular Web site (perhaps that of your college), the first page you will normally view is the site's **home page.** The home page is the starting point for accessing information at a site or in a particular area. A college's home page might be at URL http://stateuniv.edu, but each college or department might have a home page as well (for example, http://stateuniv.edu/cis for the Computer Information Systems Department's home page). A page is a scrollable file; that is, when it is too large for the viewing area, you can scroll up or down to view other parts of the page.

- *Hypertext and hypermedia links.* Web documents are created using HTML (HyperText Markup Language), a "tag" language that is used to format and transmit Web pages. Multimedia resources on the Web are linked via **hypertext** links. Words or phrases within HTML files can be marked (tagged) and highlighted (see Figure 7–5) to create interactive links to related text or multimedia information. Hypertext links on the Web are displayed differently from accompanying text, usually as colored (often blue) and underlined text. Links need not be

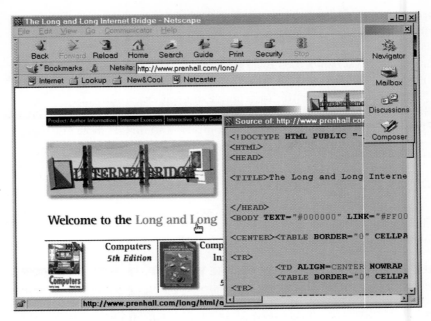

FIGURE 7–5 A Web Page and Its HTML Source Document

limited to text, though. Web pages can also have **hypermedia** links. Hypermedia links encompass hypertext links and any multimedia object on the page (images, animated objects, and so on) that is associated with a link. When the cursor is positioned over a hypertext or hypermedia link, it changes to a hand with a pointing finger. When you click on the link (the highlighted word[s] or image), you are electronically whisked away to the URL (uniform resource locator) address specified in the HTML document for the selected hypertext link. The link could take you to another location in the same document or to another document on the same Web server or to a Web server on another continent. The transition between hypertext links and hypemedia links, collectively called **hyperlinks,** appears seamless to the Web user.

- *Interactive.* The World Wide Web system, with its pages, enables interactivity between users and servers. There are many ways to interact with the World Wide Web. The most common form of interactivity is clicking on hyperlinks to navigate around the Internet. Some pages have input boxes into which you can enter textual information. You can click on radio buttons to select desired options. **Radio buttons** are circle bullets in front of user options that when selected include a dot in the middle of the circle. Each time you enter information in a text box or make selections, you will normally have to click on a *submit* button to transmit the information to the server computer.

- *Frames.* Some Web sites present some or all of their information in frames. **Frames** is the display of more than one independently controllable section on a single Web page (see Figure 7–6). When you link to a Web page that uses frames, the URL of that page is that of a *master HTML file* that defines the size, position, and content of the frames. Ultimately your request for a frames page results in multiple HTML files being returned from the Web server. The frames capability may be used to display the main site options in one small frame and primary information page in another larger frame. Sometimes a third frame displays context-sensitive instructions.

FTP: *Downloads for the asking* The **File Transfer Protocol (FTP)** allows you to download and upload files on the Internet. FTP has been around for a long time, so thou-

Prescreening of Online Communications

MILLIONS OF PEOPLE HAVE ACCESS TO AND PARTICIPATE IN the bulletin boards and online forums. Some information services feel obligated to give their subscribers an environment that is free of offensive language. These information services use an electronic scanner to "read" each message before it is posted to a bulletin board or a forum. In a split second the scanner flags those words and phrases that do not comply with the information service's guidelines. The scanner even catches words or phrases that may be disguised with asterisks and so on. Generally the guidelines are compatible with accepted norms in a moral society. These include the use of grossly repugnant material, obscene material, solicitations, and threats. The scanner also scans for text that may be inappropriate for a public discussion, such as the use of pseudonyms, attempts at trading, presentation of illegal material, and even speaking in foreign languages. Messages that do not pass the prescreening process are returned automatically to the sender.

Some might cry that their rights to freedom of expression are violated. This, of course, is a matter that may ultimately be decided in a court of law. In the meantime, those who wish a more open discussion have plenty of opportunities. On some national bulletin boards and information services, anything goes.

Discussion: Is prescreening of electronic communications a violation of freedom of expression?

sands of FTP sites offer millions of useful files—most are free for the asking. *FTPing* is a popular activity on the Net. You can download exciting games, colorful art, music from up-and-coming artists, statistics, published and unpublished books, maps, photos, utility and applications programs—basically anything that can be stored digitally. Many FTP sites invite users to contribute (upload) files of their own.

FIGURE 7–6 A Web Page with Frames

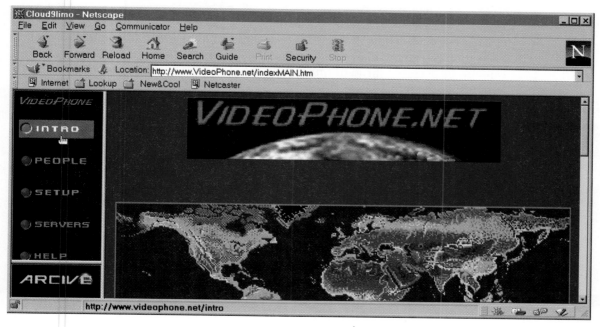

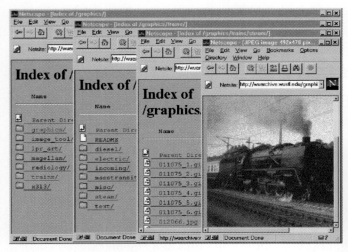

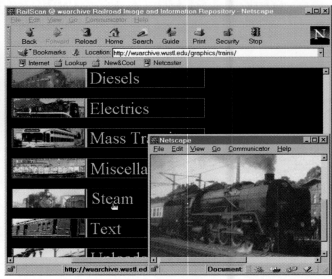

FIGURE 7–7 FTPing on the Internet

The browser image on the left illustrates how you might navigate through the directories at an anonymous FTP site. The user proceeded from the /graphics/ directly to the /graphics/train/ directory to the /graphics/train/steam/ directory to the 012066.jpg file (the locomotive image). The FTP site shown here, however, has been converted to a more user-friendly world-wide-web format (right). Other major FTP sites have or are undergoing a similar transformation.

You must be an authorized user (know the password) to access many FTP sites. Most, however, are **anonymous FTP** sites that maintain public archives. Anonymous FTP allows anyone on the Net to transfer files without prior permission. Once you navigate to the FTP site, you will be asked to enter a username and a password. Don't panic. Just enter "anonymous" or "ftp" at the username prompt and enter your e-mail address (or just tap the enter key) at the password prompt.

The trick to successful FTPing is knowing where to look. Fortunately, you can connect to ftp sites using a Web browser. Figure 7–7 demonstrates the hierarchical organization of FTP files.

Gopherspace and WAIS: Go-for information. The **Gopher** system, which pre-dates the World Wide Web, was developed at the University of Minnesota, the home of the Golden Gophers. Think of the Gopher system as a huge menu tree that allows you to keep choosing menu items until you find the information you want. Gopher resources can also be accessed through Internet browsers. Figure 7–8 illustrates the results of a gopherspace search.

WAIS (pronounced "*ways*") offers another approach to information retrieval. WAIS servers allow you to search by content, rather than poking around a hierarchy of menus to find the information you need.

Telnet: Remote login. Telnet refers to a class of Internet application programs that let you log into a remote computer using the Telnet communication protocol. **Telnet** is a *terminal emulation* protocol that allows you to work from a PC as if it were a terminal linked directly to a host computer. Thousands of Internet sites around the world have Telnet interfaces. Once online to one of these sites, you can run a normal interactive session as if you were sitting at an on-site terminal. You can run programs, search databases, execute commands, and take advantage of many special services. For example, you can search through the county library's electronic card catalog, play chess with students from other campuses, scan the pages of *USA Today*, or run programs to analyze data from an experiment.

MEMORY BITS

On the Internet

Accessing Information and Services
- World Wide Web
- FTP
- Gopher
- WAIS
- Telnet

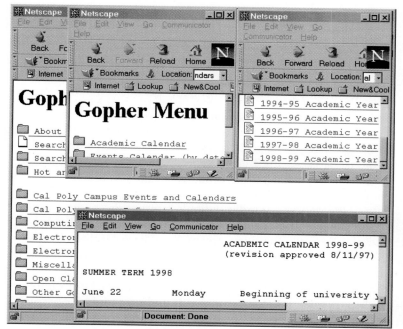

FIGURE 7–8 The Results of a Gopher Search
This gopher site (the California Institute of Technology's Gopher server) contains file folders full of documents. The user navigated through the folders to view the current school year's academic calander (see document on bottom right).

GETTING INFORMATION ON THE INTERNET The information on the Internet is out there, but getting to it can be challenging and fun. We can search for it or just wander around the Internet until we find it. Or, we can be passive about it and let the information come to us.

Searching and browsing the Internet. The Internet has thousands of databases, such as the *Congressional Record,* NIH clinical information, a list of job openings for the entire United States, the lyrics to "Yesterday" by the Beatles—you name it and it's probably on the Net. There is no organization that monitors or tracks information on the Internet. Consequently, there is no single comprehensive source or index that tells you what information is on the Net or how to find it. To get the information you want, you must look for it. There are three ways to search the Internet: *search, browse,* or *ask someone.*

- *Searching the Net.* The Net helps those who help themselves. It offers a variety of resource discovery tools, called **search engines,** to help you find the information or service you need. Generally, these search engines, such as Infoseek, AltaVista, HotBot, and WebCrawler are business ventures. Most of them let you find information by *key word(s)* searches. You can search the Net by keying in one or more key words, or perhaps a phrase, that best describes what you want (perhaps, information on "Julia Roberts" or who might offer a "masters degree biomedical engineering"). The results of the search are seldom exhaustive; so you may need to go to one of the listed sites; then follow the hyperlinks to find the information you need.

  The companies sponsoring these widely used search engines make money by selling advertising. Some sell priority rights to a particular word or phrase. For example, if you enter the key words "long-distance telephone," the company that purchased the rights to these words or this phrase would be listed in a priority position (first or possibly alone).

- *Browsing the Net.* **Web guides** let you browse through menu trees of *categories.* Web guides, such as Yahoo, Excite, Infoseek, Lycos, and SEARCH.COM, group resources on the Net into general categories, such as government, employment, news, and so on. Upon selecting a category, you are presented with another list of subcategories from which to choose. You may browse through three to ten levels of sub-categories before finding what you want. You can search Web guides by key words.

- *Asking someone.* People on the Net are a family, ready to help those in need. Don't hesitate to post an inquiry to the Net when you need help. Also, the Net is full of **FAQ** (frequently asked questions) pages and files that you can view or download. Your question has probably been asked and answered before.

Webcasting: Internet broadcasting.   Until recently, all Internet sites were more or less passive, waiting for Net surfers to find them. It's now apparent that the Internet can be a broadcast medium as well. For example, thousands of radio stations now **webcast** their audio signals over the Internet (see Figure 7–9). If you have an Internet connection and a multimedia PC, there is no reason for you to miss the radio broadcast of any of your favorite team's games. To tune in to the game, simply use your browser to navigate to the webcasting radio station's Internet site, then request a *real-time audio stream* of the game. You may need a program, such as Real Networks' RealPlayer, to receive and play the audio or video stream. RealPlayer lets listeners preset "stations" and scan them, much as you would in a car radio. Can TV broadcasting be far behind?

Several companies, including PointCast, broadcast news and other information that can be customized to your information needs. For example, you can request news on a particular topic (personal computing, politics) or from a particular country, weather for a particular region, stock quotes for selected companies, business news for selected industries, sports news relating to a sport (even to your teams), and so on. The company periodically scans available net sources; then downloads the information to you for viewing (see Figure 7–10).

COMMUNICATING WITH PEOPLE: E-MAIL, NEWSGROUPS, MAILING LISTS, AND MORE   The Internet is not just a resource for information and services; it is also an aid to better communication. There are several ways for people to communicate over the Internet, including e-mail, newsgroups, mailing lists, and videophone.

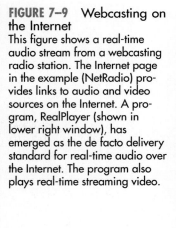

FIGURE 7–9   Webcasting on the Internet
This figure shows a real-time audio stream from a webcasting radio station. The Internet page in the example (NetRadio) provides links to audio and video sources on the Internet. A program, RealPlayer (shown in lower right window), has emerged as the de facto delivery standard for real-time audio over the Internet. The program also plays real-time streaming video.

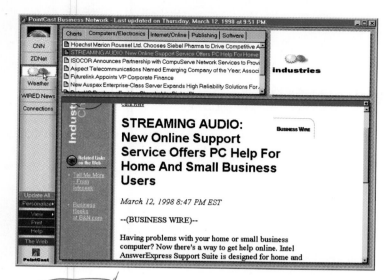

FIGURE 7–10 PointCast: A Customizable Information Service
PointCast gathers news according to preset user specifications, then delivers it periodically via the Internet.

Jporiello@suny/opt.edu

E-mail on the Net. You can send e-mail to and receive it from anyone with an Internet e-mail address, which is just about everyone who uses the Internet. Each Internet user has an electronic mailbox to which e-mail is sent. E-mail sent to a particular person can be "opened" and read only by that person. To send an e-mail message, the user simply enters the address of the recipient (for example, *TroyBoy@mindspring.com*), keys in a message, adds a subject in the subject line, and clicks the send icon to place the message in the recipient's electronic mailbox.

Internet e-mail is like company e-mail, but with a great many more electronic mailboxes. You can send an e-mail message to anyone on the Net, even the President of the United States *(president@whitehouse.gov)*. You can even use Internet e-mail to give your congressperson a few political hints. Figure 7–11 illustrates the use of Internet e-mail.

MEMORY BITS

Communicating with People
- E-mail
- Newsgroups
- Mailing list (listserv)
- IRC (chat)
- Audio mail
- Internet telephone
- Videophone

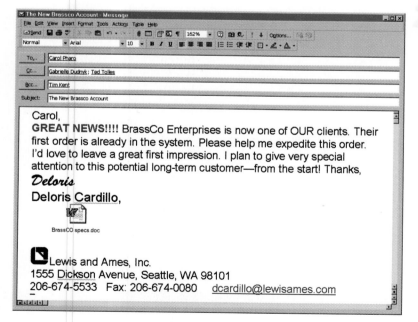

FIGURE 7–11 E-mail on the Internet
The e-mail format for Microsoft Outlook 98 (shown here) is representative of other Internet e-mail formats: To, cc (copy to), bcc (blind copy to), Subject, text of message, and attached file. The attached file is sent with the message. This e-mail client software (the software you use to receive and send e-mail) permits messages to be sent and viewed in rich text format, that is with variations in font attributes and embedded graphics. The option "personal information" placed automatically at the end of each message is called a *signature*. People usually include name, address, and communications information in the signature.

EMERGING TECHNOLOGY

Cybertalk: A New Way to Communicate

When online, we key in, rather than speak, our words and emotions. People who frequent bulletin boards and on-line forums have invented keyboard shortcuts and "emoticons" (emotion icons), called smileys, to speed up the written interaction and convey emotions. These are among the most frequently used keyboard shortcuts.

AFJ	April fool's joke	LOL	Laughing out loud
< –AFK	Away from keyboard	ROFL	Rolling on the floor laughing
BRB	Be right back	TPTB	The powers that be
BTW	By the way . . .	TTYL	Talk to you later
F2F	Face-to-face	< VBG>	Very big grin
FAQ	Frequently asked questions	WAG	A guess
< GG >	Grin	Wizard	A gifted or experienced user
IMHO	In my humble opinion. . .	YKYBHTLW	You know you've been hacking too long when. . .
IRL	In real life		

To shout online, key in entries in all capital letters. Do this only when you really wish to make a point.

In cyberspace there is no eye contact or voice inflection, so cybernauts use smileys to express emotions. They must be effective because many couples who meet on the information highway are eventually married. Their courtship may have involved some of these smileys.

@—>—>—	A rose	[[[***]]]	Hugs and kisses

Creating smileys has emerged as a pop art. These smileys were created by online users with a sense of humor. Turn the page sideways and see if you recognize any familiar faces.

:-)X	Sen. Paul Simon	< :(	Dunce
+-(:-)	The Pope	:-/	Skeptical
==:-D	Don King	:-o	Amazed
[8-]	Frankenstein	O :-)	Angel
==)-)=	Abe Lincoln	:-|	Bored
@@@@@@@@:)	Marge Simpson	;-)	Wink
/:-)	Gumby	:-I	Indifferent
*	Kiss	:c)	Pigheaded
:~~)	User with a cold	8-)	Wearing sunglasses
:-)	Smiling	@—>—>—	A rose
:-@	Screaming	7:-)	Ronald Reagan
:'-(	Crying (sad)	/	FDR
:-&	Tongue tied	8-]	FDR
:'-)	Crying (happy)	*<(:')	Frosty the Snowman
:-Q	Smoker	(8-o	Mr. Bill
:-(	Sad	~ 8-)	Alfalfa
:-D	Laughing	@;^:[)	Elvis

Your Internet e-mail address is your online identification. Once you get on the Internet, you will need to let other users and other computers know how to get a hold of you. All of your interaction will be done using your Internet address. Think of an Internet address as you would your mailing address. Each has several parts with the most encompassing part at the end. When you send mail outside the country, you note the country at the end of the address. The Internet address has two parts and is separated by an @ symbol. Consider this Internet address:

kay_spencer@cis.stateuniv.edu

- *Username.* On the left side of the @ separator is the username (usually all or part of the user's name). Organizations often standardize the format of the username so users don't have to memorize so many usernames. One of the most popular formats is simply the first and last name separated by an underscore (kay_spencer). Some organizations prefer an abbreviated format to help minimize strokes. For example, some have adopted a username format in which the first five letters of the last name are prefaced by the first letter of the first name (kspenc).

- *Domain name for the host/network.* That portion to the right of the @ identifies the host or network that services your e-mail, sometimes called the **e-mail server.** This is normally the Internet address for your Internet service provider (for example, worldnet.com), information service (for example, aol.com), your college (for example, stateuniv.edu), or your company (for example, prenhall.com).

The e-mail client software is the software that interacts with the e-mail server to enable sending and receiving of e-mail. Early e-mail client software packages limited messages to simple ASCII text. However, most modern e-mail client software lets you embed graphics and do fancy formatting as you might in a word processing document. Also, you can attach a file to an e-mail message. For example, you might wish to send a program or a digitized image along with your message. The **attached file** is routed to the recipient's e-mail server computer where it can be downloaded by the recipient.

The typical e-mail client software has some very handy features. For example, you can send copies of your e-mail to interested persons. Or, you can forward to another person(s) e-mail messages that you received. You can even send your e-mail to a fax machine. E-mail features and services continue to grow. One of the information services translates e-mail messages posted in French and German into English, and vice versa.

POP stands for both point-of-presence on the Internet (discussed earlier in this chapter) and **Post Office Protocol.** Post Office Protocol refers to the way your e-mail client software gets your e-mail from the server. When you get a SLIP or PPP access from an Internet service provider, you also get a POP account. When you set up your e-mail client software, you will need to specify this POP account name to get your mail. The POP is usually your username.

The combined volume of mail handled by the United States Postal Service is about the same as the volume of electronic communications sent each day. As more people send birthday invitations and greetings cards via e-mail and business communications continues its trend away from "snail mail" to e-mail, look for substantial increases in e-mail volume and commensurate decreases in traditional mail. E-mail has resulted in tremendous changes in the business world, as did the invention of the telephone. The telephone, however, is essentially one-to-one communication, but e-mail can be one-to-one, one-to-many, or many-to-many—and it's written.

Newsgroups: Electronic bulletin boards. A **newsgroup** is the cyberspace version of a bulletin board. A newsgroup can be hosted on Internet servers and on USENET servers. **USENET** is a worldwide network of servers that can be accessed over the Internet. Newsgroups is a misnomer in that you seldom find any real news. They are mostly electronic discussion groups. Tens of thousands of newsgroups entertain global discussions on thousands of topics, including your favorite celebrities. If you're unable to reach celebrities via e-mail, you can talk about them on an Internet newsgroup. For example, *alt.fan.letterman* (the newsgroup's name) is a David Letterman newsgroup. Sometimes Dave joins the fun. If Letterman is not your cup of tea, you can join another newsgroup and talk about Rush Limbaugh (*alt.fan.rush-limbaugh.tv-show*), Madonna (*alt.fan.madonna*), or Elvis (*alt.fan.elvis-presley*). Real Elvis fans can learn about recent Elvis sightings on the *alt.elvis.sighting* newsgroup.

Newsgroups are organized by topic. The topic, and sometimes subtopics, is embedded in the newsgroup name. Several major topic areas include: news, *rec* (recreation), *soc* (society), *sci* (science), and *comp* (computers). For example, *rec.music.folk* is the name of a music-oriented newsgroup in the recreation topic area whose focus is folk music. Another example is *rec.sport.tennis*.

You need *newsreader client software* or similar software that is built into most Internet browser clients. Generally newsgroups are public, but if you wish to keep up with the latest posting in a particular newsgroup, you will want to subscribe to it (at no charge). The newsreader software lets you read previous postings (messages), add your own messages to the newsgroup, respond to previous postings, and even create new newsgroups. Figure 7–12 illustrates interaction with a newsgroup.

People who frequent newsgroups refer to the original message and any posted replies to that message as a **thread.** The newsreader sorts and groups threads according to the original title. For example, a thread that begins with a message titled "Pete Sampras's forehand" includes all of the replies titled "RE: Pete Sampras's forehand." If you post a message with an original title or reply to a message and change the title, you start a new thread. For example, posting a reply titled "Pete Sampras's backhand" begins a new thread.

Mailing lists: Listserv's. The Internet **mailing list** is a cross between a newsgroup and e-mail. Mailing lists, which are also called **listserv's,** are like newsgroups in that they allow people to discuss issues of common interest. There are mailing lists for most, if not all, of your personal interest areas. To find one of interest, you scan or search available mailing lists from any of a number of sources. Web guides, like Yahoo, summarize and describe thousands of listserv's by description, name, and subject. When you find one you like, you simply send an e-mail message containing the word *sub* or *subscribe* plus your name to the mailing list sponsor, and the sponsor puts you on the list. Most mailing lists are handled automatically by computerized administrators with the username *listserv.* For example, you can subscribe to the Women's History mailing list at *listserv@h-net.msu.edu.*

Generally there is no subscription fee. Once on the list, you receive every e-mail message sent to that list by other subscribers. Sending mail to the list is as easy as sending an e-mail message to its mailing list address. Subscribing to a mailing list can

FIGURE 7–12 Newsgroups on the Internet
People frequenting this newsgroup (rec.music.folk) post messages related to folk music. In the example, a response to a "Do you know this song?" message is displayed in the small window.

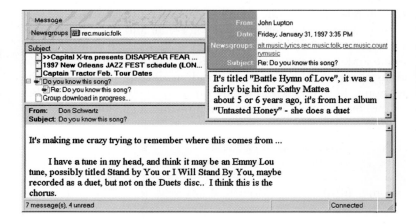

be stimulating and, possibly, overwhelming—remember each message posted is broadcast to all on the list. If you subscribe to a couple of active mailing lists, your Internet mailbox could be filled with dozens if not hundreds of messages—each day! So, if you can't get enough of David Letterman through a newsgroup, you can subscribe to a mailing list whose theme is Letterman.

Internet Relay Chat: Chit-Chat The **Internet Relay Chat (IRC)** protocol allows users to join and participate in group chat sessions. A chat session is when two or more Internet users carry on a typed, real-time, online conversation. Chatting is a favorite pastime of millions of cybernauts. They do this by establishing a link with a chat server; that is, an Internet server that runs the IRC protocol.

Chat servers let users join chat sessions called *channels*. A single chat server can have dozens, even thousands, of chat channels open at the same time. The name of the channel will usually reflect the general nature of the discussion. Usually, channel names are unchanged, but topics on the channels are continuously changing. For example, in a channel called "Personal Computing" the topic might be "Macintosh tips" one day and "Windows 97 trouble-shooting" the next day.

The channel operator creates or moderates the channel and sets the topic. This way, chat participants can exchange ideas about common interests. Chats are ideal for group discussions. For example, many organizations schedule chat sessions as a way to exchange information between employees and customers. Universities schedule chat sessions to exchange technical information and advice. When you log into a chat session, you can "talk" by keying in messages that are immediately displayed on the screens of other chat participants (see Figure 7–13). Any number of people can join a channel discussion. The rate at which you communicate is, of course, limited by your keyboarding skills.

Audio mail: Just say it. E-mail is just text, but new software, such as MidiSoft's Sound bar software, lets you speak your message instead of typing it. Users send sound files over the Internet (rather than e-mail), thus producing a form of worldwide audio messaging. Proponents of **audio mail** tout it as a faster and more effective way to communicate over the Internet. It eliminates the need to key in, edit, and spell-check text before sending a message, a time-consuming task for many of us. Also, audio mail conveys humor and other emotions that may be lost in e-mail messages. Audio mail is just evolving, but it's inevitable that this system of worldwide audio messaging will continue to grow and mature.

The Internet telephone: The best long-distance plan. To make a phone call we simply pick up a telephone, which is linked to a worldwide communications network, and speak into its microphone and listen through its speaker. Guess what? Millions of Internet users with multimedia PCs have these same capabilities: access to a worldwide network (the Internet), a mike, and a speaker. The only other thing needed to make

FIGURE 7–13 An IRC Chat Session

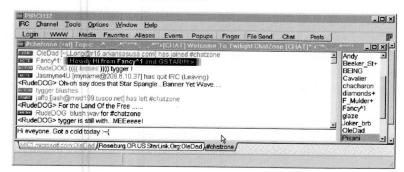

telephone calls via the Internet is Internet telephone software. The Internet phone capability lets you call people at other computers on the Internet. These computers must have the same capabilities (multimedia PC, phone software, and Internet access). By now, you are probably wondering about cost. There is no added cost over the cost of your PC and your Internet connection. People routinely use this capability to talk for hours on international calls!

Here is how the Internet telephones work. First you establish a connection with the Internet, then open your Internet telephone software. The software automatically notifies the host server supporting the **User Location Service (ULS)** that you selected when you installed the software. The ULS is simply an Internet-based listing of Internet users who are currently online and ready to receive Internet telephone calls. If you and your brother, who lives in Germany, wanted to talk via Internet telephone, you would both have to be online with Internet telephone software running and be registered with the same ULS. A number of Internet servers maintain multiple User Location Services. When you make an Internet call you speak just as you would on a regular speakerphone. Whether your Internet phone conversation is *half-duplex* or *full-duplex* depends primarily on the capabilities of your sound card and the speed of your PC. Half-duplex conversations require that one party stop speaking before the other can speak.

The Internet telephone conversation can be a much richer experience than a regular telephone call. This is because both parties have the capabilities of the Internet and their PCs at their fingertips. These capabilities can take place during the conversation.

- *Conferencing.* A two-way voice telephone conversation can be expanded to a conference that lets others listen in and add to the conversation via a chat box (an area on the screen that allows text entry). Those participants in chat mode provide input to the conversation by entering text in the chat box. All people in the conference hear the spoken words and see all textual entries simultaneously.

- *Whiteboarding.* Most Internet phone software packages support whiteboarding. **Whiteboarding** enables participants to sketch and illustrate ideas. When one person runs the whiteboard option, it automatically appears on everyone's screen. Everything that is drawn on the whiteboard is displayed for all to see.

- *Application sharing.* Another very helpful feature of Internet phone software enables you to share an application with others participating in the conversation. When you share an application (for example, a spreadsheet), you can work alone while others in the conference watch you wor3k, or you can allow them to take turns working in the application.

The videophone: Videoconferencing. The next dimension in Internet communications is the videophone, and it's here now. People who have a multimedia PC with a camera and video compression hardware, access to the Internet over an ordinary telephone line, and videophone software can see each other while talking. While they are talking they can continue to browse the Web, exchange electronic photos, or even play games. Relatively few people have PCs configured with cameras and related hardware, but they can add these peripherals for around $100.

Commercial videoconferencing has been available for many years, but it can cost hundreds of dollars an hour. Now you can see and hear your family members, friends, and colleagues during conversations for pennies (see Figure 7–14). It's quite possible that video-based Internet communications will be as mainstream as e-mail by the turn of the century!

The videophone is far from the last word in personal communications over the Internet. In the mid-1990s relatively few people even used the Internet and those that did communicated with one another by text-based e-mail and newsgroups. These remain the most popular means of personal communications over the Internet, but now

Telecommuting

FIGURE 7-14 Internet Videophone Capability
When this schoolgirl talks with her grandparents about her class project, she can see them and show them her project.

we have other choices: audio mail, chat, Internet phone, and Internet videophone. If recent history is an indication, we will have even more and better options next year.

The Intranet: A Closed Internet

An **intranet** is essentially a closed or private version of the Internet. An intranet employs the same technology as the Internet, but its scope is restricted to the networks within a particular organization. The main objective of most intranets is to share information and computing resources among employees. Some intranets are extended to customer locations as well. The interface is the same for both the Internet and intranets—user-friendly browsers. All of the capabilities discussed in this chapter from interactive Web pages to videophones to webcasting are possible.

Intranets within an enterprise are set up to permit access to the Internet through a firewall. A **firewall** is software that is designed to restrict access to an organization's network or its intranet. The firewall screens electronic traffic in both directions so that organizational security is maintained. The screening process can be adjusted to various levels of security.

Internet Issues

The Internet is a digital Wild West, without law and order. Nevertheless, the lure of this new frontier has an endless stream of wagon trains "heading west." Like the Wild West, anyone can come along. The Internet is public land; therefore, accessibility is one of the inherent problems on the Internet. With unlimited accessibility come mischievous hackers, the plague of computer networks. Such hackers are continually doing what they can to disrupt the flow of information. These electronic assaults are on the routers and other communications devices that route data from node to node on the Net. Such actions are like changing the road signs along the interstate highway system. Hackers don't stop at changing the road signs. They also plant computer viruses on the Internet, disguised as enticing downloadable files. Once downloaded, the virus infects the PC and creates havoc, often destroying files and sometimes even entire hard disks. Hackers have stolen valuable software, traded secrets, hijacked telephone credit-card numbers, distributed copyrighted photos and songs, and run online securities scams.

People on the Internet reflect real life—most are good and a few are bad. The bad elements deal in garbage. Some Internet newsgroups are dominated by bigots and cranks who push everything from neo-Nazi propaganda to pornographic images. Women on the

Internet are sometimes hounded by electronic lechers, and the language spoken in the heat of a passionate electronic debate can range from rude to libelous. Fortunately, responsible people are fighting back. When somebody posts something outlandish, inappropriate, or out of phase with the societal norms to a newsgroup or mailing list, he or she gets **flamed**. Flaming results in a barrage of scathing messages from irate Interneters.

And then there's spam—what we used to think of as junk mail, except that now it's in the cyberworld as well. **Spam** is unsolicited junk e-mail, mostly advertising for commercial products or services. Occasionally **spammers**, or those who send spam, spam unsuspecting people with political messages. Though most of us would prefer not to be spammed, it's as difficult to rid the public Internet of spam as it is to rid our mail boxes of junk mail. Just like at home, we must sort through the spam to find our legitimate e-mail. Also, people are concerned that spam is taking up valuable bandwidth on the Internet, stressing the information capacity of the Net. As you might have guessed, the origin of the term *spam* is the popular lunchmeat of the same name.

The Internet rivals the towering majesty of Mount Everest, but there is a dark side of every mountain. At the foot of this great mountain of information is a rocky pasture. Watch your step as you cross this pasture, then enjoy the climb up Mount Internet.

Cruising the Net

Vast, enormous, huge, immense, massive—none of these words is adequate to describe the scope of the Internet. Perhaps *the Internet* may someday emerge as a euphemism for anything that is almost unlimited in size and potential. There are at least as many applications on the Internet as there are streets in Moscow. To truly appreciate Moscow, you would need to learn a little of the Russian language and the layout of the city. Navigating the Internet also requires a little bit of knowledge. Gaining this knowledge takes time and a lot of practice. In this brief space, we can hope to expose you only to some of the thoroughfares. As you gain experience and confidence, you can veer off onto the Internet's side streets.

What follows is an attempt to give you a feel for the seemingly endless variety of things to see and do on the Internet.

- *Electronic Newsstand.* The Electronic Newsstand opened for business in 1993 with eight magazines: *The Economist,* the *New Yorker, National Review, The Source, The New Republic, New Age Journal, Journal of NIH Research,* and *Outside Magazine.* Today the Newsstand has several hundred extremely diverse magazines and is growing. The Electronic Newsstand doesn't include everything in the current issue of each magazine it carries, but it does include a table of contents and one or two selected articles from the current issue. Also, excerpts from past issues are included in archival files.

- *MUDers on the Internet.* One of the exits on the Internet highway leads to MUD (Multi-User Domain), online role-playing adventure games. MUDs are challenging games that provide text descriptions of circumstances and situations rather than the graphic images of video games. Think of them as the online version of *Dungeons and Dragons.* This scenario description is typical for a MUD: "You have fallen down a secret passageway into a chamber that is lit only by the full moon shining through a small opening in the ceiling. On the east wall there is a Latin inscription and a wooden door that is bolted on the outside. Distant voices are barely audible through the door." A player explores his or her realm by entering simple commands such as "go," "east," "west," and so on. As you might expect, not-so-nice creatures occupy the same realm and are out to get you. Each day tens of thousands of players spend hours, even days, online slaying evil creatures and joining other adventurers on their quest.

- *Love and war.* The Internet is a romance connection. Many married couples met and courted over the Net. Talk show host Rush Limbaugh had an electronic

Serendipitous Surfing:
Magazines

courtship that led to matrimony. Of course, where there is marriage there is divorce. Some couples prefer to negotiate their divorce settlement over Internet e-mail. This written approach to arbitration allows parties to choose their words more carefully and to keep records of exactly what has been said.

- *The electronic confessional.* Confess your sins over the Internet. To do so, choose a sin from a menu, enter the date of your last confession, then receive your penance.

- *Be an informed traveler.* Savvy travelers often shop around for the best deal on a hotel room, make their own reservations, and get information on local attractions and nearby restaurants—all over the Net.

- *Subscription services.* The Net offers subscription services for just about every interest area. Subscription services are available for the international intelligence community, podiatrists, CD-ROM manufacturers, tennis players, high school football coaches, and hundreds of other groups. The services supply e-mail, newsletters, reports, scores, images, or whatever the service is designed to provide.

- *E-mail and geography.* A Wisconsin teacher encourages her fifth graders to correspond with e-mail pen pals in all 50 states. The teacher conceived the idea to help students learn geography and practice communication skills. Kids ask their "pen pals" about everything from pizza prices to politics.

As you can see, the Internet offers a vast treasure trove of information and services. The number of users continues to explode as more and more newbies begin to cruise the Net. By the turn of the century, about 200,000,000 people will pass through the newbie stage on their way to becoming seasoned travelers on the Internet.

Emotions of newbies run high when they enter the Net for the first time. They simultaneously are shocked, amazed, overwhelmed, appalled, and enlightened. The Internet is so vast that these same emotions are experienced by seasoned users as well. Figure 7–15 includes examples of a few of the millions of stops along the Internet.

FIGURE 7–15 Surfing the World Wide Web

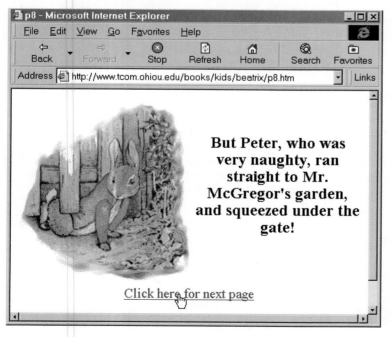

Story Hour There is something for children of all ages on the Net. The Internet Public Library offers a story hour section that contains many wonderful illustrated stories, including "The Tale of Peter Rabbit" (shown here).

(**Figure 7–15** *continues on next page*)

FIGURE 7–15 (continued)

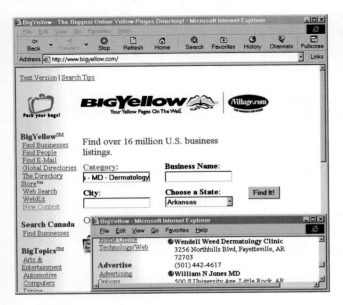

The Yellow Pages   Use the Big Yellow pages on the Net to quickly find any business in the United States. A search "Physicians & Surgeons–MD—Dermatology" and "Arkansas" listed Dr. Wendell Weed (shown here) and 58 other Arkansas dermatologists.

Special Interest Pages   No matter what your interests or hobbies, whether basket weaving or skydiving, there is a wealth of information about it (or them) on the Internet. This skydiving site has an image gallery (background window) filled with exciting mid-air photos, each of which can be expanded or downloaded for better viewing. The user simply double-clicks on one of the many thumbnail images to expand it (see foreground window).

The Titanic   The *Titanic* movie has its own official Web page (shown here), along with many other unofficial sites, where fans can learn more about the Titanic, the filmmakers, the actors, and other elements of the famous movie. The foreground window shows one of several available video clips of the movie. This clip shows the Titanic departing for its maiden voyage. Movie studios usually create Web sites for their high-profile films prior to their release and later to promote ticket sales, Academy Awards consideration, and video rentals and sales.

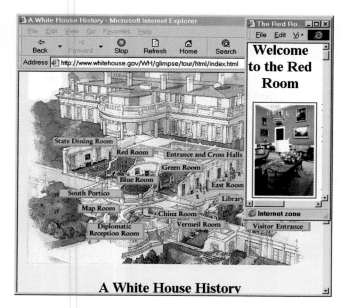

A White House History

White House Tour When you take your cybertour of the White House, be sure to sign the guest book. During the tour you can listen to the comments of the President and the Vice President, meet the first family, and see the White House. In the breakout of the White House, you just click on a room to learn more about it.

The Ultimate Travel Brochure The Internet has emerged as "the" source for travel information. It's easy to get information about any destination, including Sri Lanka (shown here), or any other popular vacation haven.

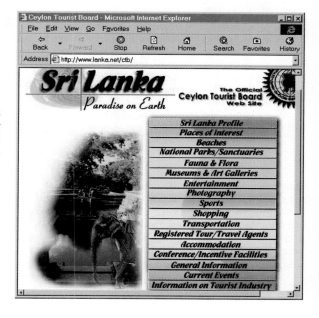

Peeping In on the CIA See your taxpayer dollars at work on the CIA Web server. The site contains some very interesting information on the CIA mission, current maps, and several online books, including the most recent *The World Fact Book*. *The World Fact Book* has comprehensive information on every country in the world.

(**Figure 7–15** *continues on next page*)

FIGURE 7–15   (continued)

Online Newspapers   The *Los Angeles Times,* The *Washington Post* and many other newspapers, even weekly newspapers in small towns, sponsor Internet Web sites. The comprehensive *Los Angeles Times* site provides up-to-the-minute news by category (news, entertainment, sports, business, classifieds, and Southern California), as well as a variety of other information-based services.

Shopper's Paradise   The Internet is becoming a shopper's paradise. Hundreds of businesses that now run stores in the traditional storefront manner are opening virtual stores so their customers have the option of walking in or logging on. At L. L. Bean (shown here) customers can view products in an online catalog, then place their orders online.

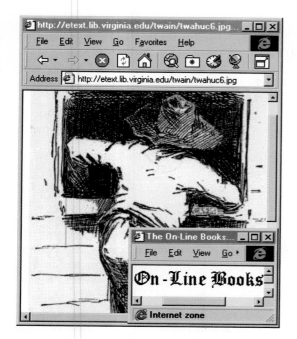

Online Books Mark Twain's *Huckleberry Finn*, with full text, original illustrations (shown in background window), and early reviews can be found at a number of Internet sites, including the Online Books site at the University of Virginia. Thousands of public domain works of literature, from *Beowulf* to the complete works of Shakespeare, can be found on the Net.

Commercial Web Presence Most businesses, including the publisher of this book, Prentice Hall, have a presence on the Internet. Prentice Hall has a comprehensive Web site over which students and professors can communicate with one another and download important class materials. Users can thumb through the Prentice Hall College Division's catalog to obtain information about any book it offers. Many Prentice Hall books, including this one, have a companion Web site. These are accessed from the Web Gallery.

Interactive Study Guide
Chapter 7

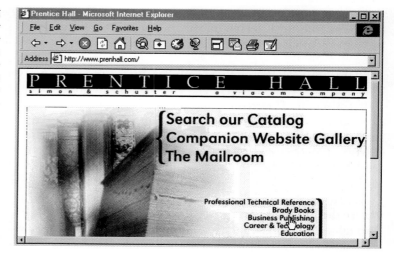

IMPORTANT TERMS AND SUMMARY OUTLINE

anonymous FTP 206
attached file 211
audio mail 213
browser 191
client program 201
dialup connection 200
domain name 202
e-mail server 211
FAQ 208
File Transfer Protocol (FTP) 204
firewall 215

flamed 216
frames 204
Gopher 206
home page 203
HTML (HyperText Markup Language) 203
http (HyperText Transport Protocol) 202
hyperlink 204
hypermedia 204
hypertext 203

Internet Relay Chat (IRC) 213
Internet service provider (ISP) 200
intranet 215
listserv 212
mailing list 212
newbie 201
newsgroup 211
packets 200
page 203
POP (point-of-presence) 200
POP (Post Office Protocol) 211

7-1 THE ONLINE WORLD The online world offers a vast network of resources, services, and capabilities. Most of us enter it by simply plugging the phone line into our PC's modem and running our communications software. More and more knowledge workers opt to **telecommute** to work over the digital highways.

7-2 INFORMATION SERVICES: AMERICA ONLINE, COMPUSERVE, AND MANY MORE When you subscribe to a commercial information service such as America Online or CompuServe, you get communications software, a username and password, and a user's guide. The communications software may be designed specifically to work with an information service network or it may be an Internet **browser.** Information services are continually updating and adding new services.

7-3 THE INTERNET: A WORLDWIDE WEB OF COMPUTERS AND INFORMATION The Internet (a worldwide collection of *inter*connected *net*works) is comprised of thousands of independent networks in virtually every type of organization. The Department of Defense's ARPANET project was the genesis of the Internet. Volunteers from many nations coordinate the Internet. InterNIC provides registration services for the Internet community.

There are three levels at which you can connect your PC to the Internet. The easiest way to gain access is through a commercial information service's gateway. Or you can make the connection via a **dialup connection** through an **Internet service provider (ISP).** To use this kind of connection, you must have software that enables a direct link via **Transmission Control Protocol/Internet Protocol (TCP/IP).** The *Transmission Control Protocol* sets the rules for the packaging of information into the **packets.** The *Internet Protocol* handles the address, such that each packet is routed to its proper destination. When you dialup an ISP's local **POP (point-of-presence),** your dialup connection is made through a SLIP or PPP connection to an Internet host. At the third level, there is direct connection to the Internet where your PC is wired directly into the Internet. Such connections often use an ISDN (128 K bps), an ADSL (up to 9 M bps), a **T-1 line** (1.544 M bps), or a **T-3 line** (44.736 M bps) line.

A **client program** runs on your PC and works in conjunction with a companion **server program** that runs on the Internet host computer. The client program contacts the server program, and they work together to give you access to the resources on the Internet server. A *browser* is one kind of client.

The **URL (uniform resource locator),** which is the Internet equivalent of an address, progresses from general to specific. That portion of the URL before the first colon (usually http) specifies the access method. The http tells the software to expect an **http (HyperText Transport Protocol)** file. That portion following the double forward slashes (//) is the server address, or the **domain name.** It has at least two parts, separated by dots (periods). What follows the domain name is a directory containing the resources for a particular topic. At the end of the URL is the specific file that is retrieved from the server. **HTML (HyperText Markup Language)** is the language used to compose and format most files on the Net.

The **World Wide Web (the Web)** is an Internet system that permits linking of multimedia documents among servers on the Internet. By establishing a linked relationship between World Wide Web documents, related information becomes easily accessible. World Wide Web resources are designed to be accessed with easy-to-use browsers. Information on the Web, which may be graphics, audio, video, animation, and text, is viewed in **pages.** The first page you will normally view at a site is its **home page.** Web documents are created using HTML (HyperText Markup Language), a "tag" language. Multimedia resources on Web are linked via **hypertext** links. Web pages can also have **hypermedia** links. The transition between hypertext links and hypermedia links, collectively called **hyperlinks,** appears seamless to the Web user. The Web enables interactivity between users and servers. For example, you can click on **radio buttons** to select desired options. Some Web sites present some or all of their information in **frames.**

The **File Transfer Protocol (FTP)** allows you to download and upload files on the Internet. Most are **anonymous FTP** sites. The **Gopher** system is a huge menu tree that allows you to keep choosing menu items until you find the information you want. **WAIS** servers allow you to search by content. **Telnet** is a *terminal emulation* protocol that allows you to work from a PC as if it were a terminal linked directly to a host computer.

There are three ways to search the Internet: *search, browse,* or *ask someone.* You can search using a variety of resource discovery tools, including **search engines** and **Web guides.** Web guides also let you browse through menu trees of *categories.*

People on the Net are ready to help those in need. There are also **FAQ** pages and files.

Webcasting (Internet broadcasting) has emerged as a popular Internet application.

The Internet is an aid to better communication. You can send e-mail to and receive it from anyone with an Internet e-mail address. The Internet e-mail address has two parts and is separated by an @ symbol, the username and the domain name. The latter identifies the **e-mail server**. An **attached file** can be sent with an e-mail message. **Post Office Protocol (POP)** refers to the way your e-mail client software gets your e-mail from the server.

A **newsgroup**, which is like a bulletin board, can be hosted on Internet servers and on **USENET** servers. People who frequent newsgroups refer to the original message and any posted replies to that message as a **thread**. The Internet **mailing list (listserv)** is a cross between a newsgroup and e-mail.

The **Internet Relay Chat (IRC)** protocol allows users to participate in group chat sessions. A chat session is when two or more Internet users carry on a typed, real-time, online conversation.

Audio mail lets you speak your Internet message instead of typing it.

The Internet phone capability lets you call people at other computers on the Internet. The telephone software automatically notifies the host server supporting the **User Location Service (ULS)** when you are ready to talk. Other Internet telephone capabilities include *conferencing*, **whiteboarding**, and *application sharing*. The next dimension in Internet communications, the videophone, permits videoconferencing.

An **intranet** is a closed or private version of the Internet. An intranet employs the same technology as the Internet, but its scope is restricted to the networks within a particular organization. **Firewalls** restrict access to an organization's network or its intranet.

People who send discourteous communications over the Net are frequently **flamed**. **Spam**, the electronic equivalent of junk mail, is sent by **spammers**.

The Internet offers a vast treasure trove of information and services. The number of users continues to explode as more and more **newbies** begin to cruise the Net.

REVIEW EXERCISES

Concepts

1. Name at least three things that you do now without the aid of online communications that may be done in the online environment in the near future.
2. Name three commercial online information services.
3. Briefly describe the function of an Internet browser.
4. Briefly describe four America Online channels.
5. What is a newbie?
6. What is the organizational affiliation of these Internet addresses: smith_jo@mkt.bigco.com; politics@washington.senate.gov; and hugh_roman@cis.stuniv.edu.
7. In an Internet address, how are levels separated in the host/network identifier?
8. Expand the following acronyms: TCP/IP, ISP, and URL.
9. List these communications channels by capacity (from least to most): T-1, ADSL, ISDN, and T-3.
10. In the URL, http://www.abccorp.com/pr/main.htm, what is the http component?
11. In the URL, http://www.abccorp.com/pr/main.htm, what is the www.abccorp.com component?
12. Briefly describe one of the three levels at which you can connect your PC to the Internet.
13. In what ways is the World Wide Web different from other servers on the Internet?
14. Which action would result in more Internet e-mail, posting a message to a newsgroup or subscribing to a popular mailing list?
15. What services are provided by Infoseek, AltaVista, and WebCrawler?
16. Name and briefly describe two types of hyperlinks.

Discussion and Problem Solving

17. Describe five things you would like to do on the Internet.
18. Discuss the pros and cons of FTPing on the Internet.
19. What kind of work would you like to be doing in five years? Explain how you might telecommute to accomplish part or all of your work.
20. The Internet is a digital Wild West. Should access be more tightly controlled to help bring law and order to the Internet?
21. Discuss how you would justify spending $15 to $25 a month to subscribe to an online information service.
22. Gambling could be one of the most profitable computer applications ever. Americans spent 70 times as much on gambling last year as they spent on movies. Gambling is being proposed as a possible application on the information superhighway. Argue for or against this proposal.
23. The federal government is calling for "universal

service" such that everyone has access to the "information superhighway." Is this an achievable goal?

24. Videophones are available on the Internet now. In all probability they will be available to the mass market in the near future. Is this new innovation in personal communications something you are looking forward to or dreading? Explain.

25. Discuss the advantages and disadvantages of using the Internet phone (relative to the traditional method of telephoning people).

SELF-TEST (BY SECTION)

7–1 Some knowledge workers _____ to work over the digital highways.

7–2 a. The monthly service charge for most commercial information services is set by law at $5 per month for unlimited usage. (T/F)

b. Which of the following does not come with a subscription to an information service: (a) communications software; (b) a username; or (c) a PC?

c. Which of the following is not an online commercial information service: (a) Microsoft Network; (b) the Web; or (c) AOL?

d. America Online has a private worldwide network that it uses to distribute online services to its subscribers. (T/F)

e. You would look for a forum on your favorite hobby in which AOL channel: (a) Shopping; (b) Personal Finance; or (c) Interests?

7–3 a. The Internet is not a commercial information service like Prodigy. (T/F)

b. ARPANET was the first commercially available communications software package. (T/F)

c. TCP/IP is the communications protocol for: (a) the Net; (b) sending faxes; or (c) all internal e-mail?

d. An _____ is a company that provides people with access to the Internet.

e. The first page you will normally view at a Web site is its: (a) home page, (b) banner page, or (c) master page?

f. To eliminate the spread of viruses, only downloading of files is permitted on the Internet. (T/F)

g. In the e-mail address, mickey_mouse@disney.com, the username is (a) mickey_mouse; (b) mouse; or (c) disney.com?

h. Which server on the Internet offers hypertext links: (a) WAIS; (b) the Web; or (c) Gopher?

i. The IRC protocol allows users to join and participate in group chat sessions. (T/F)

j. Yahoo is a site on the Internet that can be used to browse the Net by content category. (T/F)

k. Which of the following labels is associated with an Internet address: (a) bps; (b) pbs; or (c) http?

l. The Internet is short for (a) International Network; (b) interconnected networks; or (c) internal net e-mail terminal?

Self-test Answers.   **7–1** telecommute. **7–2 (a)** F; **(b)** c; **(c)** b; **(d)** T; **(e)** c. **7–3 (a)** T; **(b)** F; **(c)** a; **(d)** information service provider (ISP); **(e)** a; **(f)** F; **(g)** a; **(h)** b; **(i)** T; **(j)** T; **(k)** c; **(l)** b.

Appendix to Core
The Windows Environment

A-1 Concepts and Terminology

What Is Windows?

Windows 95, Windows 98, and *Windows NT,* all operating systems from Microsoft Corporation, dominate the PC-compatible environment. Windows 98 is the successor to Windows 95. The Microsoft master plan has all Windows users eventually migrating to Windows NT. The users of *Windows 3.1,* an earlier Microsoft operating system, are upgrading to either Windows 98 or Windows NT. Today's new PCs come with Windows 98 or the business-oriented Windows NT operating system installed on the hard disk. Windows 98 works well in the home or the office, but Windows NT with its security and networking capabilities is better suited for networking on a local area network (LAN).

The terms, concepts, and features discussed in this appendix generally apply to Windows 95, Windows 98, and Windows NT; however, the examples show the most recent home/office version—Windows 98. The name *Windows* describes basically how the software functions. The GUI-based Windows series runs one or more applications in *windows*—rectangular areas displayed on the screen. The Windows operating system series has introduced a number of new concepts and terms, all of which apply to the thousands of software packages that have been and are being developed to run on the Windows 98 and NT platforms. These two platforms run applications designed for Windows 3.1 and Windows 95 as well as legacy software from the MS-DOS operating system era (most of the 1980s).

Understanding Windows 98: <u>H</u>elp

Books, like this one, and tutorial software are *complementary* learning tools. Hands-on activity with Windows 98, Windows 95, or any other software package is essential to learning. The explanations in the following sections will make more sense once you begin interacting with Windows 98 or Windows 95 (collectively referred to as Windows 9x). We recommend that you visit your college's PC lab and run *Help* to learn more about your Windows 9x operating system (see Figure A-1). That is, click on the *Start* button in the *Taskbar* (usually positioned at the bottom of the screen), then click <u>H</u>elp. In addition, if you have Windows 98, you can take advantage of its excellent Web-based feature, called Web Help. This feature provides online access to compre-

FIGURE A-1 The Windows 98 Help Feature
The Help feature lets you find help by scanning a hierarchical table of *Contents.* Click on the *Index* tab to search an index similar to one you would find in a book (but without page references). Click on the *Search* tab to search the Help files by key word. Click on the *Web Help* button for Internet-based Windows 98 help and technical support.

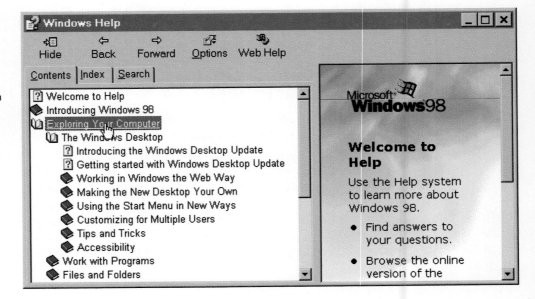

hensive, continually updated Help information. The Windows 9x Help capabilities include step-by-step tutorials that lead you through numerous common Windows 9x procedures. Also, the Windows 98 CD-ROM has several excellent multimedia tutorials that provide general computer competency instruction as well as specifics on how to use Windows 98, the mouse, and the keyboard.

Non-Windows versus Windows Applications

NON-WINDOWS APPLICATIONS   Any software application that does not adhere to the Microsoft Windows standard is a **non-Windows application**. Non-Windows applications will run under Windows 9x or Windows NT, but these software packages do not take advantage of many helpful Windows 9x features. Generally, non-windows programs are legacy software that was created for the earlier MS-DOS and Windows 3.1 platforms.

WINDOWS APPLICATIONS   Programs that adhere to Windows conventions are **Windows applications.** These conventions describe:

- Type and style of window
- Arrangement and style of menus
- Use of the keyboard and mouse
- Format for screen image display

Virtually all new software for the PC environment is designed to run on the Windows 9x or Windows NT platform. The GUI for Windows versions of Word, Quicken, Adobe Illustrator, and all other Windows applications have the same look and feel. *When you learn the GUI for Windows 9x, you also learn the GUI for all Windows 9x-based software packages.*

The Windows 9x graphical user interfaces use both a keyboard and a point-and-draw device for input. The point-and-draw device is often a mouse, but is increasingly a touchpad or some other such device. Such devices are also called **cursor control devices (CCDs)**. Interaction with Windows 9x or a Windows 9x application is most efficient when options are chosen with a mouse and characters are entered via the keyboard.

When working with the keyboard:

- Enter text as needed (for example, a path for a file: "C:\Program Files\Microsoft Office\Office\winword.exe").
- Activate the current menu bar by tapping the ALT key.
- Enter the underlined letter of the menu option in the active menu to choose that option.
- Use the arrow keys to highlight menu options in an active menu.
- Use the **shortcut key,** which can be a key or a key combination (for example, ALT+F4 to *Exit* and CTRL+C to *Copy*) to issue commands within a particular application without activating a menu.
- Use the **hotkey,** also a key or key combination, to cause some function to happen in the computer, no matter what the active application.

Input via a CCD, such as a mouse, is slightly different in Windows 9x and in Windows 98. When performing operating system functions in Windows 98 you can opt for the single-click mode or the traditional double-click mode of Windows 95. Single click mode is primarily for general Windows operations and may not be available in many applications. Figure A-2 summarizes the differences between the two modes of clicking. *Right clicking* (tapping the right button on a mouse set up for right-handed use) causes a context sensitive menu to be displayed. The resulting menu relates to the window, object, or whatever the cursor is on at the time of the right click.

Windows 9x Task	Double-Click Mode Windows 9x	Single-Click Mode Windows 98 only
Select an item	Point and click on item (and icon, a filename, a task bar program, and so on)	Point to item
Open (or choose) an item	Double-click on the item.	Click on the item.
Select a range of items	Press and hold the SHIFT key, then **click** the first and last items in a group of items (for example, files or words in a paragraph).	Press and hold the SHIFT key, and **point to** the first and last items in the group.
Select multiple individual items	Press and hold the CTRL key, and **click** individual items in a group	Press and hold down the CTRL key, and **point to** individual items in the group.
Drag and drop item	Point to an item, press and hold the mouse button, and drag the item to new location.	Same as double-click mode.

Differences between Windows 95 and Windows 98

Just as Windows 3.1 was used well into the Windows 9x era, Windows 95 will be used for several years after the 1998 release of Windows 98. Since Windows 95 will continue to be widely used, this section summarizes the major differences between Windows 95 and its successor Windows 98.

The Windows 95 GUI looks very much like that of Windows 98. What you see, however, tells only part of the story. The underlying software for Windows 98 reflects three years of improved and changing technology. The following summary Windows 98 features highlights of the differences between the two operating systems.

- *Easier to Use.* With Windows 98, users can manage their files and move between applications in the same intuitive way they browse the Internet. This new *Web page–oriented interface* may be the most significant visual different between Windows 95 and Windows 98. Windows 95 users can enjoy this feature by downloading and installing the most recent version of Internet Explorer, the Microsoft Internet browser, from the Microsoft Web site <http://www.microsoft.com>. The browser look is embedded in the functionality of the Windows 98 operating system. In most Windows 98 user activities, an Internet or Intranet connection is just a click away. It doesn't matter whether your files or applications are local (on the PC's hard disk), on a LAN server, or on the Internet, the user interface is the same.

  Several enhancements to the user interface make navigation easier. For example, being able to click the *forward/backward* buttons on the Web-page interface provides rapid navigation between applications and application views. The cumbersome double-clicking to open (choose) files in Windows 95 is replaced with a single-clicking option (see Figure A-2). With Windows 98, we simply point to an icon to select it.

- *Improved Performance.* Windows 98 is a newer, faster, and more feature-rich operating system. It boots, loads applications, and shuts down more quickly. It includes many new user-friendly tools that assist users in preparing their computer to run faster (for example, optimizing the location of frequently used files on the hard disk). A Tune-up **Wizard** (see Figure A-3) monitors your system, then suggests ways you can improve your system's performance. Wizards lead you step by step through many common user procedures such as installing new software or hardware.

- *Fully Integrated with the Internet.* With the Internet Explorer interface now a part of Windows 98, Internet access and viewing is integrated within any common office application (word processing, spreadsheet, e-mail, and so on). An Internet Connection Wizard even helps you get connected to an ISP (Internet service provider) so you can log on to the Internet. Plus, it has expanded support for other Internet connection options (for example, ISDN). Besides Internet Explorer, two other major Internet-based applications are distributed with Windows 98 including Outlook Express (for e-mail and newsgroups) and NetMeeting (for chat, Internet telephony, video conferencing, and application sharing over the Internet).

- *Enhanced Reliability.* Windows 98 is more reliable than Windows 95. Windows 98 actually looks for system concerns and either alerts you or fixes the problem automatically. Windows Update (see Figure A-4), a new Internet-based Microsoft resource site, will help you keep your system up to date and running smoothly with the latest **drivers** (the software that enables interaction between the operating system and peripheral devices) and operating system files.

- *Operational features.* Windows 98 provides support for recent hardware standards like Universal Serial Bus (USB), DVD, and the Accelerated Graphics Port (AGP) video accelerator cards. The USB is an advance over Plug and Play technology. With USB, you no longer need to reboot your PC to use new hardware. For gamers, Windows 98 surely enhances the entertainment experience with new digital audio capabilities, support for forced-feedback joysticks, and support for multiple monitors. The multiple monitor feature lets you connect up to eight monitors to a single PC, enabling a substantial increase in the size of your desktop (the viewing area). The Broadcast Architecture feature enables PCs to receive **enhanced television.** An enhanced TV presentation combines video, HTML (the language of the World Wide Web on the Internet), and general programming from broadcast, satellite, and cable networks.

The Desktop

The screen upon which icons, windows, and so on are displayed is known as the **desktop.** The Windows 9x desktop may contain a *background, one active window, one or more inactive windows, icons,* and *various bars showing processing options* (see Figure A-5). The background can be anything from a single-color screen to an elaborate artistic image as shown in Figure A-5. All windows and icons are superimposed over the background, be it plain or an artistic image. The Windows desktop reflects the user's personality as well as processing and information needs, so no two are the same.

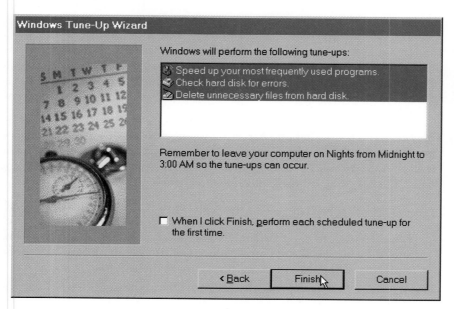

FIGURE A-3 The Windows 98 Tune-up Wizard
The Windows Tune-Up Wizard is one of many wizards that can guide you through common procedures. The Tune-Up Wizard can help you make your programs run faster, check your hard disk for problems, and free up hard disk space.

FIGURE A–4 Keeping Windows 98 Up-to-date
Windows Update feature helps you keep your Windows 98 system tuned and up-to-date by automating driver and system updates via the Internet. The registered user simply navigates to the Windows Update page, then downloads appropriate files.

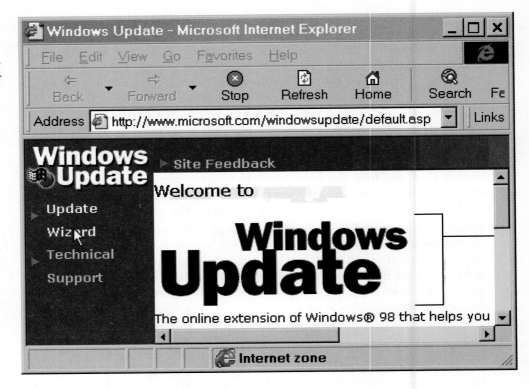

THE TASKBAR Typically, a Windows session begins with the **Start button** in the Taskbar. The **Taskbar**, which can be displayed all the time or hidden as desired, shows what programs are running and available for use. Click the *Start* button in the taskbar to display the Start menu and open the door to the resources on your PC. An application window can be opened in several ways, but usually people point and click on the desired application icon in the *Programs* option on the Start menu (see Figure A-6). Highlighting the Programs option presents a pop-out menu with either application options or folders containing other options (see Figure A-6). A Windows **folder** is a logical grouping of related files and subordinated folders.

THE WINDOW Figure A-7 shows a typical rectangular Windows **application window.** An application window contains an **open application** (a running application), such as Paint or Word. Several applications can be open or running simultaneously, but there is only one **active window** at any given time. Application commands issued via the keyboard or mouse apply to the active window. The active window's title bar (at the top of each application) is highlighted. There is no active window in Figure A-5 because the user has clicked on the Start button to open another program. The elements of an application window are: the title bar, the menu bar, the workspace, the scroll bars, and the corners and borders. Each is described in the following sections and illustrated in Figure A-7.

Title bar. The horizontal **title bar** at the top of each window runs the width of the window from left to right (see Figure A-7). The elements of the title bar include the *application icon, window title, minimize button, maximize/restore button, exit button,* and the *area.* Point and click/drag on these elements to change the presentation of the window.

- *Application icon in title bar.* The application icon is a miniature visual representation of the application and is displayed on the left end of the title bar. Double click on it to close the application. Click on it to display a pull-down control menu for the associated application. Control menu options vary, depending on the type of application being displayed in the window.

- *Window title.* The title bar displays the title of the application ("Microsoft Photo Editor" in Figure A-7).

If your PC is on a LAN, the *Network Neighborhood* icon provides ready access to its resources.

Windows 98 provides support for plug-and-play and USB peripherals. This means that your system can grow with your computing needs with considerably less effort on your part. All you have to do to add a new device, such as a video camera, is "plug" and "play" it.

A *Channel Bar* provides users with an opportunity to go directly to some of the more popular sites on the Internet.

Program icons, files, and folders (groups of related files) can be displayed directly on the desktop. The *My Computer* icon provides access to all files and folders.

The *Shortcut Bar* gives you single-click access to programs on the desktop, in a software suite such as Microsoft Office, or the "Favorites" folder.

A handy Start button provides easy access to most of the Windows tools and applications.

The Windows 98 *Explorer* (the file management program) redefines user friendliness, especially in the Web page format shown here, where files and folders are shown hierarchically and pictorially. Descriptive names for files and folders are now a reality with Windows 9x. Earlier operating systems limited names to eight characters.

The *Taskbar* keeps you abreast of active applications. Just click on the application button to switch to that application.

Windows 98 eliminates the need for MS-DOS (the original PC-compatible operating system) but offers complete backward compatibility for all MS-DOS and Windows 3.x software.

FIGURE A–5 The Windows 98 Desktop
The appearance of the Windows 98 desktop depends on the user's application mix and visual needs at a particular time. Windows 98 enables sophisticated multitasking, that is, running several programs at one time. This feature allows you to work on a word processing document while backing up files and checking e-mail on the Internet. This user has five open programs that are visible on the desktop. Several more are minimized (reduced to a button) in the task bar at the bottom of the desktop. The task bar lists all open applications.

- *Maximize/minimize/restore buttons.* Point and click on the minimize buttons (_), maximize or restore button (□ or ⊟), or the close button (✕) at the right end of the title bar in Figure A-7.

    Minimize (_) The *Minimize* option shrinks the active window to a button in the Taskbar (see Figure A-7). That is, the application in the window is deactivated and the window disappears from the screen, but the application remains open in the form of a button.

    Maximize (□) The *Maximize* option enlarges the active window to fill the entire screen. The Maximize button is dimmed if not available to the user.

    Restore (⊟) When maximized, the *Restore* button (⊟) replaces the maximize button in the title bar. Click it to restore an enlarged window to its previous size.

    Close (✕) Choosing *Close* deactivates and removes the active window (and its application) from the desktop.

- *Title area.* To *move* a window, the user simply points to the window title area (the band between the application icon and the minimize button) and drags the window to the desired location.

FIGURE A-6 The Start Menu
with Pop-out Menus
The *Start* menu *Program* option
is selected prompting a display
of available programs. Then, the
Norton Utilities folder is highlighted causing its contents (17
applications and two subordinate folders) to be displayed.
Highlighting one of these folders
shows two more application options.

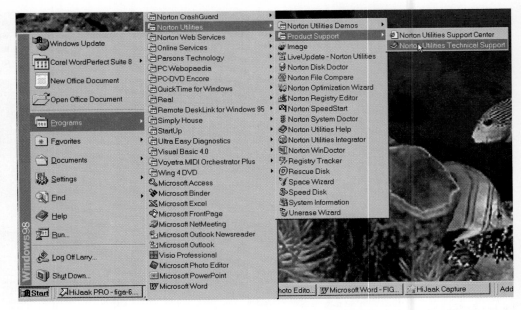

Menu bar. The menu bar for an application window runs the width of the window just below the title bar (see Figure A-7). The menu bar lists the menus available for that application. Choosing an option from the menu bar results in a pull-down menu. The *File, Edit, View,* and *Help* menus are available for most applications. Other menu options depend on the application.

Certain conventions apply to user interactions with any menu, whether a menu bar, a pull-down menu (see View menu in Figure A-7), or a pop-out menu (see *Measurements Units* menu in Figure A-7).

- *Only the boldface options can be chosen.* Dimmed options are not available for the current circumstances. For example, the *Copy* option would not be available in an Edit menu if nothing had been selected to be copied.

- *Choosing a menu option followed by an ellipsis (. . .) results in a dialog box.* The pop-up dialog box that would result from an action in a Figure A-7 menu would ask the user to choose parameters or enter additional information.

- *Corresponding shortcut keys are presented adjacent to many options in Windows menus.* For example, the *Open* option on the File menu in Figure A-7 can be executed by the Ctrl+O shortcut key combination.

- *Choosing a menu option followed by an arrow (▶) results in a pop-out menu.* The *Measurements Units* menu on Figure A-7 demonstrates the resulting pop-out menu.

- *A user-recorded check mark (✓) to the left of the menu option indicates that the option is active and applies to any related commands.* For example, many programs have a tool bar, ruler, and a status bar that can be hidden or displayed depending on whether or not there is a check mark next to the entry in the View pull-down menu. In Figure A-6, the *Toolbar* and *Status Bar* are checked. Simply click on the menu option to add/remove a check mark.

- *There are three ways to choose a menu option.*

  1. Point and click the mouse on the option.

  2. Enter the underlined letter key of the menu option in combination with the Alt key on a keyboard to (Alt+v for the *View* menu in Figure A-7). Tap the underlined letter of a pull-down menu option to choose that option (u for *Measurement Units* in Figure A-7).

3. Once the menu is activated (by mouse click or keyboard), you can use the keyboard cursor-control keys to select (highlight) the desired option and tap the Enter key to choose it.

On most application windows, the last option on the menu bar is *Help*. Choose the online Help menu whenever you need context-sensitive information regarding basic skills, shortcut keys, procedures, features, or commands.

Workspace. The **workspace** is the area in a window below the title bar or menu bar (see Figure A-7). Everything that relates to the application noted in the title bar is displayed in the workspace. For example, in Figure A-7, two photo images are displayed in the workspace of the Microsoft Photo Editor program. The workspace of a word processing program contains one or more word processing documents. If only one file/document is displayed in the workspace, then its filename appears in the title bar. If multiple files/documents are displayed, then filenames appear in the title bars of their windows (trees.jpg and mountaintop.jpg in Figure A-7 work area).

Scroll bars. Depending on the size of a window, the entire document may not be visible. When this happens, the window is outfitted with **vertical** and/or **horizontal scroll bars** (see Figure A-7). Each bar contains a **scroll box** and two **scroll arrows**. Use the CCD (usually a mouse) or keyboard to move a box up/down or left/right on a scroll bar to display other parts of the application. To move the scroll box with the mouse, simply drag it to another location on the scroll bar or click the scroll arrows.

Corners and borders. To resize a window, use CCD and point to a window's border or corner. The graphics cursor changes to a double arrow when positioned over a border or corner. Drag the border or corner in the directions indicated by the double arrow to the desired shape.

FIGURE A-7 Elements of an Application Window
In this example display, the work-space in this Microsoft Photo Editor application has two open document windows. The window with the highlighted title bar, trees.jpg, is the active document window.

TYPES OF WINDOWS: APPLICATION, DOCUMENT, AND DIALOG BOX   The three types of windows in the Windows 9x GUI are the *application window* (see Figure A-5), the *document window*, and the *dialog box*.

Document windows, which are windows within an application window, are displayed in the parent application window's workspace. For example, the Microsoft Photo Editor application in Figure A-7 has two open documents (trees.jpg and mountaintop.jpg), each of which is shown in a document window.

Typically, you, the user, must okay or revise entries in the dialog box before a command can be executed. The dialog box may contain any of these elements.

- *Tabs.*   The tabs enable similar properties to be grouped within a dialog box (for example, *Appearance* and *Background* in Figure A-8).

- *Text box.*   Enter text information in the text box or accept the default entry that is displayed (see Figure A-8).

- *Command buttons.*   Point and click on the *OK* command button to carry out the command with the information provided in the dialog box. Choose *Cancel* to retain the original information (see Figure A-8).

- *List boxes.*   A list box displays a list of available choices for a particular option (see Figure A-8). Long lists will have a vertical scroll bar.

- *Drop-down list boxes.*   The drop-down list box is an alternative to the list box (see Figure A-8) when the dialog box is too small for a list box to be displayed.

- *Drop-down color palette.*   The drop-down color palette displays a matrix of available font, line, and fill colors (see Figure A-8).

- *Radio buttons.*   Circular option buttons, called radio buttons, preface each item in a list of mutually exclusive items (only one can be activated). Point and click a button to insert a black dot in the button and activate the option.

- *Scroll bar adjustment.*   The scroll bar adjustment enables users to change parameters, such as the speed at which the cursor blinks or speaker volume.

ICONS   Icons, the graphical representation of a Windows element, play a major role in the Windows 9x GUI. Commonly used icons include *application icons, shortcut icons,*

FIGURE A–8   Elements of a Dialog Box
Many common dialog box elements are shown in the Display Properties dialog box. Not shown are the radio button and scroll bar adjustment elements.

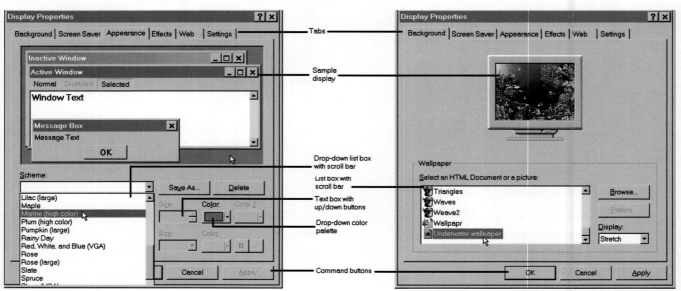

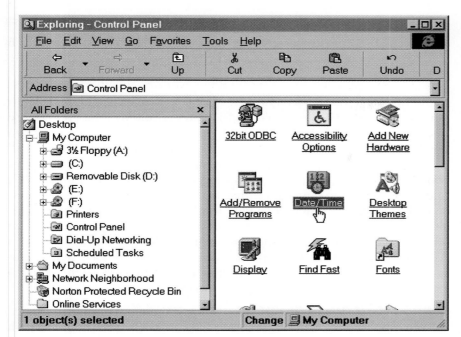

The Windows 98 Explorer makes resources on the computer readily accessible to the user. Click on a disk or folder icon to show its contents. The plus sign to the left of the icon indicates that the item has subordinate folders. Click the disk or folder icon to show its content, or click on an application icon to open the application.

document icons, and *disk drive icons.* The **Windows Explorer** in Figure A-9 shows the use of these icons. Use the Windows Explorer to perform file management tasks such as creating folders, copying files, moving files, deleting files, and other folder/file-related tasks. In Windows 9x, named **folders** are created to hold document and program files.

Application icons. An active application window can be minimized to a button on the Taskbar (see Figure A-5), thereby making it inactive. The **application icon,** usually a graphic rendering of the software package's logo, is positioned on the button. Point and click (or double-click in Windows 95) on the button or icon to restore the window and the application to active status. Typically, you would minimize application windows that may not be needed for a while to make room on the desktop for other windows.

Shortcut icons. A **shortcut icon** to any application, document, or printer can be positioned on the desktop, in a folder (see the Font icon in Figure A-9) or on a shortcut bar (see icons on the right edge of Figure A-5). The shortcut icon has an arrow in its lower left corner. Shortcuts are clicked (or double-clicked in Windows 95) to begin an application. They have other uses as well. For example, you can drag a file to a printer shortcut to print the file.

Document icons. The active document window, which is a window within an application window, can be minimized to a **document icon** within an application's workspace. Point and double-click on the document icon to restore the document window.

Disk-drive icons. The disk-drive icons graphically represent several disk-drive options: floppy, hard, network (hard), removable disk (for example, Zip disk drive), and CD-ROM (including DVD and CD-RW). The floppy (A), hard-disk (C), Zip disk (D), and CD-ROMs (E and F) icons shown in Figure A-9 resemble the faceplates of the disk drives or show the type of storage media. Typically, PCs have only one or two floppy drives, assigned to A and B.

TAKING IN THE SCENERY: VIEWING WINDOWS The Windows environment lets you view multiple applications in windows on the desktop display. Once open, a window can be resized, minimized (and restored), maximized (and restored), and, finally, closed.

Essentially, any applications software for the Windows 9x environment can be:

- Viewed and run in a window, the shape and size of which is determined by the user.
- Run full-screen (maximized); that is, filling the entire screen, with no other application windows or icons showing.

Some non-Windows applications run only as full-screen applications and cannot be run in a window. When multiple applications are running, the user can use the *Move* and *Resize* capabilities to arrange and size the windows to meet viewing needs. Of course, open windows can be minimized to free viewing space on the desktop.

Within a given application window, such as Microsoft Word, multiple document windows can be sized, shrunk, and arranged by the user within the workspace. As an alternative, the user can request that the document windows be automatically presented as **cascading windows** or **tiled windows** (see Figure A-10). Choose these options from the *Windows* menu option in the menu bar of any Windows application. The *Cascade* option overlaps open document windows so that all title bars are visible. The *Tile* option fills the workspace in such a way that no document window overlaps another. Scroll bars are provided on those document windows for which the space is not adequate to display the window's content.

SWITCHING BETWEEN WINDOWS   In the Windows environment, users can open as many applications as available RAM will permit. The active window is always highlighted in the **foreground.** When located in the foreground all parts of the window are visible. Other open windows are in the **background,** or behind the foreground (see Figure A-5). Do the following to switch between open applications.

- Point and click anywhere on the desired inactive window
- Point and click (double-click in Windows 95) the desired application button in the Taskbar or an application icon.

MOVING ON: TERMINATING AN APPLICATION AND A WINDOWS SESSION   Perform three operations before ending a Windows session.

FIGURE A-10 Arrangement of Windows
Here, four open applications are tiled on the Windows 98 desktop (clockwise from top left: Hijaak Pro, Internet Explorer, Word, and Outlook 98). The applications, as well as documents within an application's workspace, can be presented as cascading (top left HiJaak Pro documents overlap such that all title bars are visible) or they can be tiled vertically (bottom right Word documents) or horizontally.

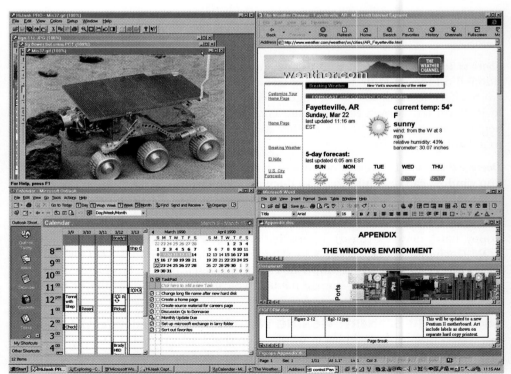

1. *Save your work.* The *Save* option in the *File* menu updates the existing file to reflect the changes made during the session. The *Save as* option allows users to save the current file under another filename.
2. *Close all open windows.* After saving your work, exit each window by pointing and clicking the close button in the title bar. You may also exit a Windows application through its menu bar (*File* then *Exit*).
3. *Shut down Windows 9x.* Click *Start* in the Taskbar, then click on the *Shut Down* radio button in the Windows Shut–down dialog box.

A-2   Sharing Information Among Applications

One of the most inviting aspects of the Windows environment is the ability to copy and move information (text, graphics, sound clips, video clips, or a combination) from one application to another. Windows offers several methods for sharing information.

The Clipboard: The Information Way Station

The most common method of sharing information among applications is to use the Windows **clipboard** and the *Edit* option in the menu bar. Think of the clipboard as an intermediate holding area for information. The information in the clipboard can be en route to another application or it can be copied anywhere in the current document. *Edit* is an option in the menu bar of most Windows applications and an option in the control menu of most non-Windows applications. Choosing Edit results in a pull-down menu from the menu bar. Options common to most Edit menus are *Cut, Copy, Paste,* and *Delete.* The **source application** and **destination application** can be one and the same or they can be entirely different applications.

The procedure for transferring information via the clipboard is demonstrated in Figure A-11. This example illustrates the *Copy* procedure. Choosing the *Cut* option causes the specified information to be removed from the source application and placed on the Windows clipboard. Whether *Copy* or *Cut* is chosen, the clipboard contents remain unchanged and can be pasted as many times as needed.

Object Linking and Embedding: OLE

Another way to link applications is through **object linking and embedding** or **OLE.** Loosely, an **object** is the result of any Windows application. The object can be a block of text, all or part of a graphic image, or even a sound clip. OLE gives us the capability to create a **compound document** that contains one or more objects from other applications. A document can be a word processing newsletter, a Corel Photo House drawing, a spreadsheet, and so on. The object originates in a **server application** and is linked to a destination document of a **client application.** For example, when a Corel Photo House (server application) drawing (object) is linked to a Word (client) newsletter (destination document), the result is a compound document (see Figure A-12).

OBJECT LINKING: DYNAMIC CONNECTION   OLE lets you *link* or *embed* information. When you link information, the link between source and destination documents is dynamic; that is, any change you make in the source document is reflected in the destination document. Object linking is demonstrated in Figure A-12. Linking doesn't actually place the object into the destination document: It places a pointer to the source document (a disk-based file). In linking, the object is saved as a separate file from the source document. The source document must accompany the destination to maintain the integrity of the destination document (a compound document); that is, if you give a friend a copy of the destination document, you must also give the friend the source as well. Your friend's PC must have both the server and client ap-

FIGURE A-11 Copy and Paste via the Clipboard
This walkthrough demonstrates the procedure for transferring information among multiple Windows applications: Paint (a paint program), Word (a word processing program), and a CD-ROM-based encyclopedia. In the example, the face of the Sphinx image in a Paint document is marked and copied (to the clipboard), then pasted to a Word document. Supporting text in the *1998 Grolier Multimedia Encyclopedia* is marked and copied to the same Word document via the clipboard.

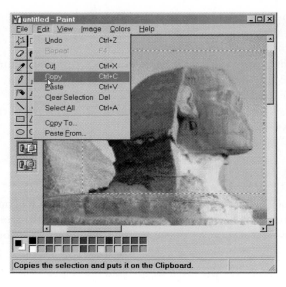

1. *Mark the information.* Drag the select cursor (the Pick tool in Paint) from one corner of the information to be copied to the opposite corner of the area and release the mouse button. The information to be transferred is highlighted.

2. *Copy the marked information to the clipboard.* Choose Edit in the source application's (Paint) menu bar to display the options. Choose Copy to place the specified information in the Windows clipboard, leaving the source application unchanged.

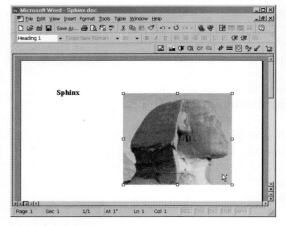

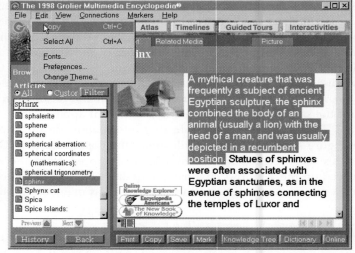

3. *Switch to the destination application and place the graphics cursor at the desired insertion point.*

4. *Paste the marked information.* Choose Edit in the destination application's (Word) menu bar to display the applicable options. Choose the Paste option to copy the contents of the clipboard to the cursor position in the destination application.

5. *Mark the information.* Use the cursor to highlight the information to be copied in the source application (*1998 Grolier Multimedia Encyclopedia*).

6. *Copy the marked information to the clipboard.*

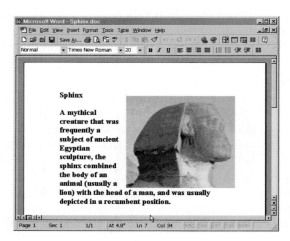

7. *Switch to the destination application and place the graphics cursor at the desired insertion point.*

8. *Paste the marked information.*

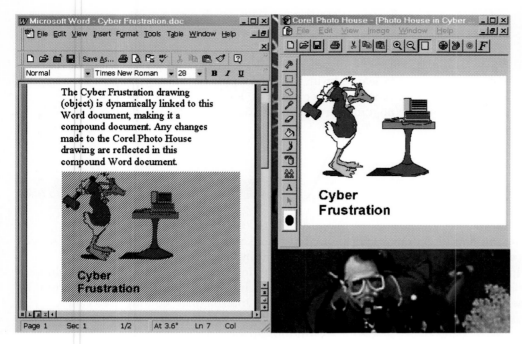

FIGURE A-12 Object Linking
An image is linked to a Word
document (left) to create a compound document. The original
object did not include the phrase
"Cyber Frustration." The image
was modified in Corel Photo
House (right) and the linked object was updated automatically
in Word.

plication to display the compound document. Linking is helpful when the object is used in several destination documents because when you change the source, it is updated in all documents to which it is linked.

Object Embedding: Implant Operation

When you embed information, you insert the actual object, not just a pointer. Where linking is dynamic, embedding is not. You can change the source within the destination document, but the original (if there is one) is unchanged. A source document is not required in object embedding.

A Thousand Look-Alikes

The discussion in Sections A-1 and A-2 is intended to introduce you to fundamental concepts and terminology associated with the Windows environment. Thousands of software packages written specifically for the Windows environment have adopted these same concepts and terminology and are designed to take advantage of Windows capabilities. Once you understand the Windows environment, you will feel comfortable with the user interfaces of all software written for this environment.

A-3 Migrating to Windows 98

More than seven years transpired before the original Microsoft Windows passed the 50% installed plateau for the PC compatibles. After seven years on the market, 50% of the users still preferred the original PC operating system, MS-DOS. If history repeats itself, acceptance of Windows 98 may be slow in coming for Windows 3.1 (users who never upgraded to Windows 95) and Windows 95 users. Millions of PC users who feel comfortable with the earlier Windows platforms may be reluctant to migrate to Windows 98. Some users must either upgrade their PC's, RAM, and/or hard disk before Windows 95 becomes an option. Many will opt to get a new PC with Windows 98 or Windows NT installed. Forecasters are predicting that a large group of Windows

95 users will bypass Windows 98 and go directly to Windows NT, the final destination for all Window users according to the Microsoft plan.

Windows 98 has full backward compatibility with MS-DOS and Windows programs. Those who plan to upgrade to Windows 98 will find that most of the concepts and terminology they learned with Windows apply to Windows 98 as well. They will also find a number of very enticing features. Earlier versions of Windows may linger for a while, but the migration has begun to Windows 98 or Windows NT, its business-oriented cousin.

REVIEW EXERCISES

1. In the Windows 98 environment, how is an item, such as an application program or a menu option, selected with a mouse? How is the item opened? How does selection and opening differ in Windows 95?
2. In the Windows environment, what is the screen area called upon which icons, windows, and so on are displayed?
3. List four elements of the Windows application window.
4. What area is just below the Windows title bar or menu bar?
5. Name three types of windows in the Windows graphical environment.
6. What results when a Windows menu option, which is followed by an ellipsis (. . .), is chosen?
7. In the Windows environment, is the active window highlighted in the foreground or the background?
8. What is the intermediate holding area called through which information is transferred between Windows applications?
9. In what type of presentation are open windows overlapped such that all title bars are visible?
10. What is displayed in a Windows 98 taskbar?
11. What does OLE stand for?

GLOSSARY

Absolute cell address A cell address in a spreadsheet that always refers to the same cell.

Access arm The disk drive mechanism used to position the read/write heads over the appropriate track.

Access time The time interval between the instant a computer makes a request for a transfer of data from a secondary storage device and the instant this operation is completed.

Accumulator The computer register in which the result of an arithmetic or logic operation is formed. (Related to *arithmetic and logic unit.*)

Active window The window in Microsoft Windows or Windows 95 with which the user may interact.

Address (1) A name, numeral, or label that designates a particular location in primary or secondary storage. (2) A location identifier for nodes in a computer network.

Address bus Pathway through which source and destination addresses are transmitted between RAM, cache memory, and the processor. (See also *data bus.*)

ADSL (Asymmetric Digital Subscriber Line) A technology that enables very high-speed downstream data transmission over POTS lines as well as high-speed upstream transmission.

AGP (Accelerated Graphics Port) board A graphics adapter that permits interfacing with video monitors.

Alpha (1) A reference to the letters of the alphabet. (Compare with *numeric* and *alphanumeric.*) (2) A RISC-based microprocessor from Digital Equipment Corporation.

Alphanumeric Pertaining to a character set that contains letters, digits, punctuation, and special symbols. (Related to *alpha* and *numeric.*)

America Online (AOL) An online information service.

Analog signal A continuous wave form signal that can be used to represent such things as sound, temperature, and velocity. (See also *digital signal.*)

Animation The rapid repositioning of objects on a display to create movement.

Anonymous FTP site An Internet site that permits FTP (file transfer protocol) file transfers without prior permission.

ANSI The American National Standards Institute is a non–government standards–setting organization which develops and publishes standards for "voluntary" use in the United States.

Applet A small program sent over the Internet or an intranet that is interpreted and executed by Internet browser software.

Application window A rectangular window containing an open, or running, application in Microsoft Windows.

Applications programmer A programmer who translates analyst-prepared system and input/output specifications into programs. Programmers design the logic, then code, debug, test, and document the programs.

Applications software Software designed and written to address a specific personal, business, or processing task.

Argument That portion of a function which identifies the data to be operated on.

Arithmetic and logic unit That portion of the computer that performs arithmetic and logic operations. (Related to *accumulator.*)

Arithmetic operators Mathematical operators (add [+], subtract [−], multiply [*], divide [/], and exponentiation [^]) used in programming and in spreadsheet and database software for computations.

Artificial intelligence (AI) The ability of a computer to reason, to learn, to strive for self-improvement, and to simulate human sensory capabilities.

ASCII [*American Standard Code for Information Interchange*] An encoding system.

ASCII file A generic text file that is stripped of program-specific control characters.

Assembler language A second generation programming language that uses easily recognized symbols, called mnemonics, to represent instructions.

Assistant system This knowledge-based system that helps users make relatively straightforward decisions. (See also *expert system.*)

Asynchronous transmission A protocol in which data are transmitted at irregular intervals on an as-needed basis. (See also *synchronous transmission.*)

Attached file A file that is attached and sent with an e-mail message.

Audio mail An electronic mail capability that lets you speak your message instead of typing it.

Audio file A file that contains digitized sound.

Authoring software Software that lets you create multimedia applications that integrate sound, motion, text, animation, and images.

Automatic teller machine (ATM) An automated deposit/withdrawal device used in banking.

Back-end applications software This software on the server computer performs processing tasks in support of its clients, such as tasks associated with storage and maintenance of a centralized corporate database. (See also *front-end applications software.*)

Backbone A system of routers and the associated transmission media that facilitates the interconnection of computer networks.

Background (1) That part of RAM that contains the lowest priority programs. (2) In Windows, the area of the display over which the foreground is superimposed. (Contrast with *foreground.*)

Backup file Duplicate of an existing file.

Backup Pertaining to equipment, procedures, or databases that can be used to restart the system in the event of system failure.

Badge reader An input device that reads data on badges and cards.

Bar code A graphic encoding technique in which printed vertical bars of varying widths are used to represent data.

Bar graph A graph that contains bars that represent specified numeric values.

Batch processing A technique in which transactions and/or jobs are collected into groups (batched) and processed together.

Baud (1) A measure of the maximum number of electronic signals that can be transmitted via a communications channel. (2) Bits per second (common-use definition).

Binary A base-2 numbering system.

Bit A *binary digit* (0 or 1).

Bit-mapped Referring to an image that has been projected, or mapped, to a screen based on binary bits. (See also *raster graphics*.)

Bits per second (bps) The number of bits that can be transmitted per second over a communications channel.

BMP A popular format for bit-mapped files.

Boilerplate Existing text in a word processing file that can in some way be customized to be used in a variety of word processing applications.

Boot The procedure for loading the operating system to primary storage and readying a computer system for use.

Bridge A protocol-independent hardware device that permits communication between devices on separate local area networks.

Browsers Programs that let you navigate to and view the various Internet resources.

Bug A logic or syntax error in a program, a logic error in the design of a computer system, or a hardware fault. (See also *debug*.)

Bulletin-board system (BBS) The electronic counterpart of a wall-mounted bulletin board that enables users in a computer network to exchange ideas and information via a centralized message database.

Bus An electrical pathway through which the processor sends data and commands to RAM and all peripheral devices.

Bus topology A computer network that permits the connection of terminals, peripheral devices, and microcomputers along an open-ended central cable.

Button bar A software option that contains a group of pictographs that represent a menu option or a command.

Byte A group of adjacent bits configured to represent a character or symbol.

C A transportable programming language that can be used to develop software.

C++ An object-oriented version of the C programming language.

Cache memory High-speed solid-state memory for program instructions and data.

CAD See *computer-aided design*.

Carrier Standard-sized pin connectors that permit chips to be attached to a circuit board.

Cascading menu A pop-up menu that is displayed when a command from the active menu is chosen.

Cascading windows Two or more windows that are displayed on a computer screen in an overlapping manner.

Cathode-ray tube See *CRT*.

CBT See *computer-based training*.

CD production station A device used to duplicate locally produced CD-ROMs.

CD writer A peripheral device that can write once to a CD-R disk to create an audio CD or a CD-ROM.

CD-R [*Compact Disk-Recordable*] The medium on which CD writers create CDs and CD-ROMs.

CD-ROM disk [*Compact-Disk Read-Only Memory disk*] A type of optical laser storage media.

CD-ROM drive A storage device into which an interchangeable CD-ROM is inserted for processing.

CD-ReWritable (CD-RW) This technology allows users to rewrite to the same CD media.

Cell address The location—column and row—of a cell in a spreadsheet.

Cell The intersection of a particular row and column in a spreadsheet.

Central processing unit (CPU) See *processor*.

Centronics connector A 36-pin connector that is used for the electronic interconnection of computers, modems, and other peripheral devices.

CGM A popular vector-graphics file format.

Channel capacity The number of bits that can be transmitted over a communications channel per second.

Channel The facility by which data are transmitted between locations in a computer network (e.g., terminal to host, host to printer).

Chief information officer (CIO) The individual responsible for all the information services activity in a company.

Chip See *integrated circuit*.

Choose To pick a menu item or icon in such a manner as to initiate processing activity.

CISC [*Complex Instruction Set Computer*] A computer design architecture that offers machine language programmers a wide variety of instructions. (Contrast with *RISC*.)

Click A single tap on a mouse's button.

Client application (1) An application running on a networked workstation or PC that works in tandem with a server application. (See also *server application*.) (2) In object linking and embedding, the application containing the destination document.

Client computer Typically a PC or a workstation which requests processing support or another type of service from one or more server computers. (See also *server computer*.)

Client/server computing A computing environment in which processing capabilities are distributed throughout a network such that a client computer requests processing or some other type of service from a server computer.

Clip art Prepackaged electronic images that are stored on disk to be used as needed in computer-based documents.

Clipboard An intermediate holding area in internal storage for information en route to another application.

Clone A hardware device or a software package that emulates a product with an established reputation and market acceptance.

Coaxial cable A shielded wire used as a medium to transmit data between computers and between computers and peripheral devices.

COBOL [*Common Business Oriented Language*] A third-generation programming language designed to handle business problems.

Code (1) The rules used to translate a bit configuration into alphanumeric characters and symbols. (2) The process of compiling computer instructions into the form of a computer program. (3) The actual computer program.

Command An instruction to a computer that invokes the execution of a preprogrammed sequence of instructions.

Common carrier A company that provides channels for data transmission.

Common User Access (CUA) The standard by which all software applications designed to be run under Microsoft's Windows must adhere.

Communications channel The facility by which data are transmitted between locations in a computer network.

Communications protocols Rules established to govern the way data in a computer network are transmitted.

Communications server The LAN component that provides external communications links.

Communications software (1) Software that enables a microcomputer to emulate a terminal and to transfer files between a micro and another computer. (2) Software that enables communication between remote devices in a computer network.

Compatibility Pertaining to the ability of computers and computer components (hardware and software) to work together.

Compile To translate a high-level programming language into machine language in preparation for execution.

Compiler A program that translates the instructions of a high-level language to machine-language instructions that the computer can interpret and execute.

Compound document A document, such as a word processing document, that contains one or more linked objects from other applications.

CompuServe An online information service.

Computer An electronic device capable of interpreting and executing programmed commands for input, output, computation, and logic operations.

Computer competency A fundamental understanding of the technology, operation, applications, and issues surrounding computers.

Computer matching The procedure whereby separate databases are examined and individuals common to both are identified.

Computer monitoring Observing and regulating employee activities and job performance through the use of computers.

Computer network An integration of computer systems, terminals, and communications links.

Computer operator One who performs those hardware-based activities needed to keep production information systems operational in the mainframe environment.

Computer system A collective reference to all interconnected computing hardware, including processors, storage devices, input/output devices, and communications equipment.

Computer virus See *virus*.

Computer-aided design (CAD) Use of computer graphics in design, drafting, and documentation in product and manufacturing engineering.

Computer-aided software engineering (CASE) An approach to software development that combines automation and the rigors of the engineering discipline.

Computer-based training (CBT) Using computer technologies for training and education.

Computerese A colloquial reference to the language of computers and information technology.

Configuration The computer and its peripheral devices.

Connectivity Pertains to the degree to which hardware devices, software, and databases can be functionally linked to one another.

Context-sensitive Referring to an on-screen explanation that relates to a user's current software activity.

Control clerk A person who accounts for all input to and output from a computer center.

Control unit The portion of the processor that interprets program instructions, directs internal operations, and directs the flow of input/output to or from RAM.

Cooperative processing An environment in which organizations cooperate internally and externally to take full advantage of available information and to obtain meaningful, accurate, and timely information. (See also *intracompany networking*.)

Coprocessor An auxiliary processor that handles a narrow range of tasks, usually those associated with arithmetic operations.

CPU See *processor*.

Cracker An overzealous hacker who "cracks" through network security to gain unauthorized access to the network. (Contrast with *hacker*.)

Cross-platform technologies Enabling technologies that allow communication and the sharing of resources between different platforms.

CRT [*Cathode-Ray Tube*] The video monitor component of a terminal.

Cryptography A communications crime-prevention technology that uses methods of data encryption and decryption to scramble codes sent over communications channels.

CSMA/CD access method [*Carrier Sense Multiple Access/Collision Detection*] A network access method in which nodes on the LAN must contend for the right to send a message.

Current window The window in a GUI in which the user can manipulate text, data, or graphics.

Cursor, graphics Typically an arrow or a cross hair which can be moved about a monitor's screen by a point-and-draw device to create a graphic image or select an item from a menu. (See also *cursor, text*.)

Cursor, text A blinking character that indicates the location of the next keyed-in character on the display screen. (See also *cursor, graphics*.)

Cursor-control keys The arrow keys on the keyboard that move the cursor vertically and horizontally.

Custom programming Program development to create software for situations unique to a particular processing environment.

Cyberphobia The irrational fear of, and aversion to, computers.

Cylinder A disk storage concept. A cylinder is that portion of the disk that can be read in any given position of the access arm. (Contrast with *sector.*)

Data Representations of facts. Raw material for information. (Plural of *datum.*)

Data bits A data communications parameter that refers to a timing unit.

Data bus A common pathway between RAM, cache memory, and the processor through which data and instructions are transferred. (See also *address bus.*)

Data cartridge Magnetic tape storage in cassette format.

Data communications The collection and distribution of the electronic representation of information between two locations.

Data communications specialist A person who designs and implements computer networks.

Data compression A method of reducing secondary storage requirements for computer files.

Data entry The transcription of source data into a machine-readable format.

Data entry operator A person who uses key entry devices to transcribe data into machine-readable format.

Data file This file contains data organized into records.

Data flow diagram A design technique that permits documentation of a system or program at several levels of generality.

Data item The value of a field. (Compare with *field.*)

Data mining An analytical technique that involves the analysis of large databases, such as data warehouses, to identify possible trends and problems.

Data path The electronic channel through which data flows within a computer system.

Data processing (DP) Using the computer to perform operations on data.

Data processing (DP) system Systems concerned with transaction handling and record-keeping, usually for a particular functional area.

Data transfer rate The rate at which data are read/written from/to secondary storage to RAM.

Data warehouse A relational database created from existing operational files and databases specifically to help managers get the information they need to make informed decisions.

Data warehousing An approach to database management that involves moving existing operational files and databases from multiple applications to a data warehouse.

Database The integrated data resource for a computer-based information system

Database administrator (DBA) The individual responsible for the physical and logical maintenance of the database.

Database record Related data that are read from, or written to, the database as a unit.

Database software Software that permits users to create and maintain a database and to extract information from the database.

Debug To eliminate bugs in a program or system. (See also *bug.*)

Decision support system (DSS) An interactive information system that relies on an integrated set of user-friendly hardware and software tools to produce and present information targeted to support management in the decision-making process. (Contrast with *MIS* and *EIS.*)

Decode To reverse the encoding process. (Contrast with *encode.*)

Decoder That portion of a processor's control unit that interprets instructions.

Dedicated keyboard port A port built into the system board specifically for the keyboard.

Dedicated mouse port A port built into the system board specifically for the cursor-control device.

Default options Preset software options that are assumed valid unless specified otherwise by the user.

Density The number of bytes per linear length or unit area of a recording medium.

Desktop The screen in Windows upon which icons, windows, a background, and so on are displayed.

Desktop film recorders An output device that permits the reproduction of high-resolution computer-generated graphic images on 35-mm film.

Desktop PC A non-portable personal computer that is designed to rest on the top of a desk. (Contrast with *laptop PC* and *tower PC.*)

Desktop publishing (DTP) Refers to the capability of producing typeset-quality camera-ready copy for publication from the confines of a desktop.

Desktop publishing software Software that allows users to produce near–typeset–quality copy for newsletters, advertisements, and many other printing needs, all from the confines of a desktop.

Destination application, clipboard The software application into which the clipboard contents are to be pasted. (Contrast with *source application.*)

Detailed system design That portion of the systems development process in which the target system is defined in detail.

Device controller Microprocessors that control the operation of peripheral devices.

Device driver software Software that contains instructions needed by the operating system to communicate with the peripheral device.

Dial-up line See *switched line.*

Dialog box A window that is displayed when the user must choose parameters or enter further information before the chosen menu option can be executed.

Digital camera A camera that records images digitally rather than on film.

Digital convergence The integration of computers, communications, and consumer electronics, with all having digital compatibility.

Digital signal Electronic signals that are transmitted as in strings of 1s and 0s. (See also *analog signal.*)

Digital videodisk (DVD) The successor technology to the CD-ROM that can store up to about 10 gigabytes.

Digitize To translate data or an image into a discrete format that can be interpreted by computers.

Dimmed A menu option, which is usually gray, that is disabled or unavailable.

Digitizer tablet and pen A pressure-sensitive tablet with the same *x-y* coordinates as a computer-generated screen. The outline of an image drawn on a tablet with a stylus (pen) or puck is reproduced on the display.

DIMM [*Dual In*-line *Memory Module*] A small circuit board, capable of holding several memory chips. It has a 64-bit data path and can be easily connected to a PC's system board. (Contrast with *SIMM*.)

Direct conversion An approach to system conversion whereby operational support by the new system is begun when the existing system is terminated.

Direct access See *random access*.

Direct-access file See *random file*.

Direct-access processing See *random processing*.

Direct-access storage device (DASD) A random-access secondary storage.

Disk, magnetic A secondary storage medium for random-access data storage available in permanently installed or interchangeable formats.

Disk address The physical location of a particular set of data or a program on a magnetic disk.

Disk caching A hardware/software technique in which frequently referenced disk-based data are placed in an area of RAM that simulates disk storage. (See also *RAM disk*.)

Disk cartridge An environmentally sealed interchangeable disk module that contains one or more hard disk platters.

Disk density The number of bits that can be stored per unit of area on the disk-face surface.

Disk drive, magnetic A magnetic storage device that records data on flat rotating disks. (Compare with *tape drive, magnetic*.)

Disk optimizer A program that reorganizes files on a hard disk to eliminate file fragmentation.

Diskette A thin interchangeable disk for secondary random-access data storage (same as *floppy disk*).

Docking station A device into which a notebook PC is inserted to give the notebook PC expanded capabilities, such as a high-capacity disk, interchangeable disk options, a tape backup unit, a large monitor, and so on.

Document file The result when work with an applications program, such as word processing, is saved to secondary storage.

Document icon A pictograph used by Windows within an application to represent a minimized document window.

Document window Window within an application window that is used to display a separate document created or used by that application.

Document-conversion program Software that converts files generated on one software package into a format consistent with another.

Domain expert An expert in a particular field who provides the factual knowledge and the heuristic rules for input to a knowledge base.

Domain name That portion of the Internet URL following the double forward slashes (//) that identifies an Internet host site.

DOS [*Disk Operating System*] See *MS-DOS*.

Dot pitch The distance between the centers of adjacent pixels on a display.

Dot-matrix printer A printer that arranges printed dots to form characters and images.

Double click Tapping a button on a point-and-draw device twice in rapid succession.

Download The transmission of data from a remote computer to a local computer.

Downsizing Used to describe the trend toward increased reliance on smaller computers for personal as well as enterprise-wide processing tasks.

Downtime The time during which a computer system is not operational.

DP See *data processing*.

Drag A point-and-draw device procedure by which an object is moved or a contiguous area on the display is marked for processing.

Drag-and-drop software Software that lets users drag ready-made shapes from application-specific stencils to the desired position on the drawing area to do drawings for flowcharting, landscaping, business graphics, and other applications.

Draw software Software that enables users to create electronic images. Resultant images are stored as vector graphics images.

Driver module The program module that calls other subordinate program modules to be executed as they are needed (also called a *main program*).

DTP See *desktop publishing*.

DVD See *digital videodisk*.

Dynamic RAM (DRAM) A type of RAM technology that requires stored data to be refreshed hundreds of times per second.

E-commerce (electronic commerce) Business conducted online, primarily over the Internet.

E-mail See *electronic mail*.

E-mail server A host or network that services e-mail.

E-time See *execution time*.

EBCDIC [*Extended Binary Coded Decimal Interchange Code*] An 8-bit encoding system.

Echo A host computer's retransmission of characters back to the sending device.

Enhanced Data Output (EDO) DRAM Dynamic RAM which is up to 50 percent faster than conventional DRAM.

Education coordinator The person within an organization who coordinates all computer-related educational activities.

Edutainment software Software that combines *edu*cation and enter*tainment*.

EFT [*Electronic Funds Transfer*] A computer-based system allowing electronic transfer of money from one account to another.

EGA [*Enhanced Graphics Adapter*] A circuit board that enables the interfacing of high-resolution monitors to microcomputers.

Electronic commerce See *e-commerce*.

Electronic data interchange (EDI) The use of computers and data communications to transmit data electronically between companies.

Electronic dictionary A disk-based dictionary used in conjunction with a spelling-checker program to verify the spelling of words in a word processing document.

Electronic document See *online document.*

Electronic funds transfer See *EFT.*

Electronic mail A computer application whereby messages are transmitted via data communications to "electronic mailboxes" (also called *E-mail*). (Contrast with *voice message switching.*)

Electronic messaging A workgroup computing application that enables electronic mail to be associated with other workgroup applications.

Electronic money (e-money) A payment system in which all monetary transactions are handled electronically.

Encode To apply the rules of a code. (Contrast with *decode.*)

Encoding system A system that permits alphanumeric characters and symbols to be coded in terms of bits.

Encryption/decryption The encoding of data for security purposes. Encoded data must be decoded or deciphered to be used.

Enterprise–wide information system Information systems which provide information and processing capabilities to workers throughout a given organization.

Ergonomics The study of the relationships between people and machines.

Exception report A report that has been filtered to highlight critical information.

Executable program file A file that contains programs that can be executed run.

Execution time The elapsed time it takes to execute a computer instruction and store the results (also called *E-time*).

Executive information system (EIS) A system designed specifically to support decision making at the executive levels of management, primarily the tactical and strategic levels.

Exit routine A software procedure that returns you to a GUI, an operating system prompt, or a higher-level applications program.

Expansion board These add-on circuit boards contain the electronic circuitry for many supplemental capabilities, such as a fax modem, and are made to fit a particular type of bus (also called *expansion cards*).

Expansion bus An extension of the common electrical bus which accepts the expansion boards that control the video display, disks, and other peripherals. (See also *bus.*)

Expansion card See *expansion board.*

Expansion slots Slots within the processing component of a microcomputer into which optional add-on circuit boards may be inserted.

Expert system An interactive knowledge-based system that responds to questions, asks for clarification, makes recommendations, and generally helps users make complex decisions. (See also *assistant system.*)

Expert system shell The software that enables the development of expert systems.

Export The process of converting a file in the format of the current program to a format that can be used by another program. (Contrast with *import.*)

Extended ASCII An 8-bit extension of the ASCII encoding system that includes 128 non–standard ASCII symbols.

Facsimile (fax) The transferring of images, usually of hardcopy documents, via telephone lines to another device that can receive and interpret the images.

FAQ A frequently asked question.

Fault tolerant Referring to a computer system or network that is resistant to software errors and hardware problems.

Fax modem A modem that enables a PC to emulate a facsimile machine. (See also *modem.*)

Fax See *facsimile.*

Feedback loop A closed loop in which a computer-controlled process generates data that become input to the computer.

Fetch instruction That part of the instruction cycle in which the control unit retrieves a program instruction from RAM and loads it to the processor.

Fiber optic cable A data transmission medium that carries data in the form of light in very thin transparent fibers.

Field The smallest logical unit of data. Examples are employee number, first name, and price. (Compare with *data item.*)

File (1) A collection of related records. (2) A named area on a secondary storage device that contains a program or digitized information (text, image, sound, and so on).

File allocation table (FAT) MS-DOS's method of storing and keeping track of files on a disk.

File compression A technique by which file size can be reduced. Compressed files are decompressed for use.

File format The manner in which a file is stored on secondary storage.

File server A dedicated computer system with high-capacity disk for storing the data and programs shared by the users on a local area network.

File Transfer Protocol (FTP) A communications protocol that is used to transmit files over the Internet.

Filtering The process of selecting and presenting only that information appropriate to support a particular decision.

Firewall Software that is designed to restrict access to an organization's network or its Intranet.

Fixed disk See *hard disk.*

Flaming A barrage of scathing messages from irate Internet users sent to somebody who posts messages out of phase with the societal norms.

Flash memory A type nonvolatile memory that can be altered easily by the user.

Flat files A file that does not point to or physically link with another file.

Flat-panel monitor A monitor, thin from front to back, that uses liquid crystal and gas plasma technology.

Floating menu A special-function menu that can be positioned anywhere on the work area until you no longer need it.

Floppy disk See *diskette.*

Floppy disk drive A disk drive that accepts either the 3.5-inch or 5.25-inch diskette.

FLOPS [Floating point operations per second] A measure of speed for supercomputers.

Flowchart A diagram that illustrates data, information, and work flow via specialized symbols which, when connected by flow lines, portray the logic of a system or program.

Flowcharting The act of creating a flowchart.

Font A typeface that is described by its letter style, its height in points, and its presentation attribute.

Footprint (1) The evidence of unlawful entry or use of a computer system. (2) The floor or desktop space required for a hardware component.

Foreground (1) That part of RAM that contains the highest priority program. (2) In Windows, the area of the display containing the active window. (Contrast with *background*.)

Formatted disk A disk that has been initialized with the recording format for a specific operating system.

FORTRAN [*FOR*mula *TRAN*slator] A high-level programming language designed primarily for scientific applications.

Fourth–generation language (FOURTH GENERATION LANGUAGE) A programming language that uses high-level English-like instructions to retrieve and format data for inquiries and reporting.

Frame A rectangular area in a desktop publishing-produced document into which elements, such as text and images, are placed.

Frames (web page) The display of more than one independently controllable section on a single Web page.

Front-end applications software Client software that performs processing associated with the user interface and applications processing that can be done locally.

Front-end processor A processor used to offload certain data communications tasks from the host processor.

Full-duplex line A communications channel that transmits data in both directions at the same time. (Contrast with *half-duplex line*.)

Full-screen editing This word processing feature permits the user to move the cursor to any position in the document to insert or replace text.

Function A predefined operation that performs mathematical, logical, statistical, financial, and character-string operations on data in a spreadsheet or a database.

Function key A special-function key on the keyboard that can be used to instruct the computer to perform a specific operation.

Function-based information system An information system designed for the exclusive support of a specific application area, such as inventory management or accounting.

Functional specifications Specifications that describe the logic of an information system from the user's perspective.

Gb See *gigabit*.

GB See *gigabyte*.

General system design That portion of the systems development process in which the target system is defined in general.

General-purpose computer Computer systems that are designed with the flexibility to do a variety of tasks, such as CAI, payroll processing, climate control, and so on.

Geosynchronous orbit An orbit that permits a communications satellite to maintain a fixed position relative to the surface of the earth.

GFLOPS A billion FLOPS. (See *FLOPS*).

GIF A popular format for bit-mapped files.

Gigabit (Gb) One billion bits.

Gigabyte (GB) One billion bytes.

Gopher A type of menu tree to "go for" items on the Internet, thus bypassing complicated addresses and commands.

Graceful exit Quitting a program according to normal procedures and returning to a higher-level program.

Grammar and style checker An add-on program to word processing software that highlights grammatical concerns and deviations from effective writing style in a word processing document.

Graphical user interface (GUI) A user-friendly interface that lets users interact with the system by pointing to processing options with a point-and-draw device.

Graphics adapter A device controller which provides the electronic link between the motherboard and the monitor.

Graphics-conversion program Software that enables files containing graphic images to be passed between programs.

Graphics file A file that contains digitized images.

Graphics mode One of two modes of operation for PC monitors. (Contrast with *text mode*.)

Graphics software Software that enables you to create line drawings, art, and presentation graphics.

Gray scales The number of shades of a color that can be presented on a monochrome monitor's screen or on a monochrome printer's output.

Green computing Environmentally sensible computing.

Group windows A window within the Windows Program Manager that contains groups of program-item icons.

Groupware Software whose application is designed to benefit a group of people. (Related to *workgroup computing*.)

Hacker A computer enthusiast who uses the computer as a source of recreation. (Contrast with *cracker*.)

Half-duplex line A communications channel that transmits data in one direction at the same time. (Contrast with *full-duplex line*.)

Half-size expansion board An expansion board that fits in half an expansion slot.

Handheld PC Any personal computer that can be held comfortably in a person's hand (usually weighs less than a pound). (See also *personal digital assistant*.)

Handshaking The process by which both sending and receiving devices in a computer network maintain and coordinate data communications.

Hard copy A readable printed copy of computer output. (Contrast with *soft copy*.)

Hard disk A permanently installed, continuously spinning magnetic storage medium made up of one or more rigid disk platters. (Same as *fixed disk*; contrast with *interchangeable disk*.).

Hard disk drive See *hard disk*.

Hardware The physical devices that comprise a computer system. (Contrast with *software*.)

Help command A software feature that provides an online explanation of or instruction on how to proceed.

Help desk A centralized location (either within an organization or outside of it) where computer-related questions about product usage, installation, problems, or services are answered.

High-level language A language with instructions that combine several machine-level instructions into one instruction. (Compare with *machine language* or *low-level language*.)

Home page The web page that is the starting point for accessing information at a site or in a particular area.

Horizontal scroll bar A narrow screen object located along the bottom edge of a window that is used to navigate side to side through a document.

Host computer The processor responsible for the overall control of a computer system.

Host mode A mode of PC operation in which remote users can call in and establish a communications link via terminal emulation. (Contrast with *terminal emulation*.)

Hot plug A universal serial bus (USB) feature that allows peripheral devices to be connected to or removed from the USB port while the PC is running.

Hotkey A seldom used key combination that, when activated, causes the computer to perform the function associated with the key combination.

HTML (HyperText Markup Language) The language used to compose and format most of the content found on the Internet.

Http (HyperText Transfer Protocol) The primary access method for interacting with the Internet.

Hub A common point of connection for computers and devices in a network.

Hyperlinks A collective reference to hypertext links and hypemedia links.

Hypermedia Software that enables the integration of data, text, graphics, sounds of all kinds, and full-motion video. (See also *hypertext*.)

Hypertext Data management software that provides links between key words in the unstructured text-based documents. (See also *hypermedia*.)

I/O [*Input/Output*] Input or output or both.

I-time See *instruction time*.

IBM Personal Computer (IBM PC) IBM's first personal computer (1981). This PC was the basis for PC-compatible computers.

Icons Pictographs used in place of words or phrases on screen displays.

Idea processor A program or word processing feature that allows the user to organize and document thoughts and ideas in outline form.

Image processing A reference to computer applications in which digitized images are retrieved, displayed, altered, merged with text, stored, and sent via data communications to one or several remote locations.

Image scanner A device which can scan and digitize an image so that it can be stored on a disk and manipulated by a computer.

Impact printer A printer that uses pins or hammers which hit a ribbon to transfer images to the paper.

Import The process of converting data in one format to a format that is compatible with the calling program. (Contrast with *export*.)

Inference engine The logic embodied in the software of an expert system.

Information Data that have been collected and processed into a meaningful form.

Information resource management (IRM) A concept advocating that information be treated as a corporate resource.

Information service A commercial network that provides remote users with access to a variety of information services.

Internet service provider (ISP) Any company that provides individuals and organizations with access to, or presence, on the Internet.

Information society A society in which the generation and dissemination of information becomes the central focus of commerce.

Information superhighway A metaphor for a network of high-speed data communication links that will eventually connect virtually every facet of our society.

Information system A computer-based system that provides both data processing capability and information for managerial decision making.

Information technology A collective reference to the integration of computing technology and information processing.

Information-based decision See *nonprogrammed decision*.

Infoseek An Internet search engine.

Infrared port See *IrDA port*.

Intelligent agent See *software agent*.

Ink-jet printer A nonimpact printer in which the print head contains independently controlled injection chambers that squirt ink droplets on the paper to form letters and images.

Input Data entered to a computer system for processing.

Input/output A generic reference to input and/or output to a computer.

Input/output-bound operation The amount of work that can be performed by the computer system is limited primarily by the speeds of the I/O devices.

Insert mode A data entry mode in which the character entered is inserted at the cursor position.

Instruction A programming language statement that specifies a particular computer operation to be performed.

Instruction register The register that contains the instruction being executed.

Instruction time The elapsed time it takes to fetch and decode a computer instruction (also called *I-time*).

Integrated circuit (IC) Thousands of electronic components that are etched into a tiny silicon chip in the form of a special-function electronic circuit.

Integrated information system An information system that services two or more functional areas, all of which share a common database.

Integrated Services Digital Network (ISDN) A digital telecommunications standard.

Interactive Pertaining to online and immediate communication between the user and the computer.

Interchangeable disk A magnetic disk that can be stored off-line and loaded to the computer system as needed. (Contrast with *hard disk*, or *fixed disk*.)

Internet, the (the Net) A global network that connects more than tens of thousands of networks, millions of large multiuser computers, and tens of millions of users in more than 100 countries.

Internet site specialist The person responsible for creating and maintaining one or more Internet sites.

Interoperability The ability to run software and exchange information in a multiplatform environment.

Intranet An Internet-like network whose scope is restricted in the networks within a particular organization.

Invoke Execute a command or a macro.

IrDA port Enables wireless transmission of data via infrared light waves between PCs, printers, and other devices (also called *infrared port*).

Jaz cartridge An interchangeable 3½-inch hard disk cartridge that can store up to 1 GB of information.

Jaz drive A disk drive that uses interchangeable Jaz cartridges.

Joystick A vertical stick that moves the cursor on a screen in the direction in which the stick is pushed.

Jukebox A storage device for multiple sets of CD–ROMs, tape cartridges, or disk modules enabling ready access to vast amounts of online data.

Kb See *kilobit*.

KB See *kilobyte*.

Kernel An operating system program that loads other operating system programs and applications programs to RAM as they are needed.

Key field The field in a record that is used as an identifier for accessing, sorting, and collating records.

Key pad That portion of a keyboard that permits rapid numeric data entry.

Keyboard A device used for key data entry.

Keyboard templates Typically, a plastic keyboard overlay that indicates which commands are assigned to particular function keys.

Kilobit (Kb) 1024, or about 1000, bits.

Kilobyte (KB) 1024, or about 1000, bytes.

Knowledge base The foundation of a knowledge-based system that contains facts, rules, inferences, and procedures.

Knowledge engineer Someone trained in the use of expert system shells and in the interview techniques needed to extract information from a domain expert.

Knowledge worker Someone whose job function revolves around the use, manipulation, and dissemination of information.

Knowledge-acquisition facility That component of the expert system shell that permits the construction of the knowledge base.

Knowledge-based system A computer-based system, often associated with artificial intelligence, that helps users make decisions by enabling them to interact with a knowledge base.

LAN operating system The operating system for a local area network.

LAN server A high-end PC on a local area network whose resources are shared by other users on the LAN.

Landscape Referring to the orientation of the print on the page. Printed lines run parallel to the longer side of the page. (Contrast with *portrait*.)

Laptop PC Portable PC that can operate without an external power source. (Contrast with *desktop PC* and *tower PC*.)

Laser printer A page printer that uses laser technology to produce the image.

Layout A reference to the positioning of the visual elements on a display or page.

Leased line See *private line*.

Librarian The person in a computer center who keeps track of interchangeable disks and tapes, and maintains a reference library of printed and computer-based material.

Line printer A printer that prints a line at a time.

Listserv An Internet mailing list.

Load To transfer programs or data from secondary to primary storage.

Local area network (LAN or local net) A system of hardware, software, and communications channels that connects devices on the local premises. (Contrast with *wide area network*.)

Local bus A bus that links expansion boards directly to the computer system's common bus.

Local net See *local area network*.

Log off The procedure by which a user terminates a communications link with a remote computer. (Contrast with *log on*.)

Log on The procedure by which a user establishes a communications link with a remote computer. (Contrast with *log off*.)

Logic error A programming error that causes an erroneous result when the program is executed.

Logical operators AND, OR, and NOT operators can be used to combine relational expressions logically in spreadsheet, database, and other programs. (See also *relational operators*.)

Logical security That aspect of computer-center security that deals with user access to systems and data.

Loop A sequence of program instructions executed repeatedly until a particular condition is met.

Low-level language A language comprising the fundamental instruction set of a particular computer. (Compare with *high-level programming language*.)

Mac OS The operating system for the Apple family of microcomputers.

Machine cycle The cycle of operations performed by the processor to process a single program instruction: fetch, decode, execute, and place result in memory.

Machine language The programming language that is interpreted and executed directly by the computer.

Macintosh Apple Computer's mainline personal computer.

Macintosh System The operating system for the Apple Macintosh line of personal computers.

Macro A sequence of frequently used operations or keystrokes that can be invoked to help speed user interaction with microcomputer productivity software.

Macro language Programming languages whose instructions relate specifically to the functionality of the parent software.

Magnetic stripe A magnetic storage medium for low-volume storage of data on badges and cards. (Related to *badge reader*.)

Magnetic tape cartridge Cartridge-based magnetic tape storage media.

Magnetic tape drive See *tape drive, magnetic.*

Magnetic tape See *tape, magnetic.*

Magnetic-ink character recognition (MICR)

Magneto-optical disk An optical laser disk with read and write capabilities.

Magneto-optical technology An erasable recording technology that incorporates attributes of both magnetic and optical storage technologies.

Mail merge A computer application in which text generated by word processing is merged with data from a database (e.g., a form letter with an address).

Mailing list An Internet-based capability that lets people discuss issues of common interest via common e-mail.

Main menu The highest-level menu in a menu tree.

Main program Same as *driver module.*

Mainframe computer A large computer that can service many users simultaneously in support of enterprise-wide applications.

Management information system (MIS) A computer-based system that optimizes the collection, transfer, and presentation of information throughout an organization, through an integrated structure of databases and information flow. (Contrast with *decision support system* and *executive support system.*)

Massively parallel processing (MPP) An approach to the design of computer systems that involves the integration of thousands of microprocessors within a single computer.

Master file The permanent source of data for a particular computer application area.

Mb See *megabit.*

MB See *megabyte.*

Megabit (Mb) 1,048,576, or about one million, bits.

Megabyte (MB) 1,048,576, or about one million, bytes.

Megahertz (MHZ) One million hertz (cycles per second).

Memory See *RAM.*

Menu A display with a list of processing choices from which a user may select.

Menu bar A menu in which the options are displayed across the screen.

Menu tree A hierarchy of menus.

Message A series of bits sent from a terminal to a computer, or vice versa.

Metafile A class of graphics that combines the components of raster and vector graphics formats.

MHZ See *megahertz.*

MICR See *magnetic-ink character recognition.*

MICR inscriber An output device that enables the printing of characters for magnetic ink character recognition on bank checks and deposit slips.

MICR reader-sorter An input device that reads the magnetic ink character recognition data on bank documents and sorts them.

Microcomputer (or micro) A small computer (See also *personal computer, PC*).

Microprocessor A computer on a single chip. The processing component of a microcomputer.

Microsecond One millionth of a second.

Microsoft Network (MSN) An online information service sponsored by Microsoft Corporation.

Microwave signal A high-frequency line-of-sight electromagnetic wave used in wireless communications.

MIDI [*M*usical *I*nstrument *D*igital *I*nterface] An interface between PCs and electronic musical instruments, like the synthesizer.

MIDI file A non-waveform file result for MIDI applications.

Millisecond One thousandth of a second.

Minicomputer (or mini) A midsized computer.

Minimize Reducing a window on the display screen to an icon.

MIPS Millions of instructions per second.

MIS planner The person in a company who has the responsibility for coordinating and preparing the MIS plans.

Mnemonics A memory aid often made up from the initials of the words in a term or process.

Modem [*MO*dulator-*DEM*odulator] A device used to convert computer-compatible signals to signals that can be transmitted over the telephone lines, then back again to computer signals at the other end of the line.

Monitor A televisionlike display for soft-copy output in a computer system.

Morphing Using graphics software to transform one image into an entirely different image. The term is derived from the word *metamorphosis.*

Motherboard See as *system board.*

Mouse A point-and-draw device that, when moved across a desktop a particular distance and direction, causes the same movement of the cursor on a screen.

Mouse pen A point-and-draw device that is rolled across the desktop like a mouse and held like a pen.

MS-DOS [*Micro*S*oft-*D*isk *O*perating *S*ystem] A microcomputer operating system.

Multifunction expansion board An add-on circuit board which contains the electronic circuitry for two or more supplemental capabilities (for example, a serial port and a fax modem).

Multifunction printer Multifunction machines that can handle several paper-related tasks such as computer-based printing, facsimile, scanning, and copying.

Multimedia upgrade kit A kit containing the necessary hardware and software to upgrade a PC to run multimedia applications (CD-ROM, sound card, and so on).

Multimedia application Computer applications that involve the integration of text, sound, graphics, motion video, and animation.

Multiplatform environment A computing environment which supports more than one platform.

Multiplexor A communications device that collects data from a number of low-speed devices, then transmits the combined data over a single communications channel. At the destination, it separates the signals for processing.

Multitasking   The concurrent execution of more than one program at a time.

Multiuser microcomputer   A microcomputer that can serve more than one user at any given time.

Nanosecond   One billionth of a second.

National Information Infrastructure (NII)   Refers to a futuristic network of high-speed data communications links that eventually will connect virtually every facet of our society. See also *information superhighway*.

Natural language   A programming language in which the programmer writes specifications without regard to the computer's instruction format or syntax—essentially, using everyday human language to program.

Navigation   Movement within and between a software application's work areas.

Net PC   Same as *network computer* (*NC*).

Network, computer   See *computer network*.

Network address   An electronic identifier assigned to each computer system and terminal/PC in a computer network.

Network administrator   A data communications specialist who designs and maintains local area networks (LANs) and wide area networks (WANs).

Network bus   A common cable in a bus topology which permits the connection of terminals, peripheral devices, and microcomputers to create and computer network.

Network computer (NC)   A single-user computer, usually diskless, that is designed to work with a server computer to obtain programs and data (also called *Net PC*).

Network interface card (NIC)   A PC expansion card or PCMCIA card that facilitates and controls the exchange of data between the PC and its network.

Network topology   The configuration of the interconnections between the nodes in a communications network.

Neural network   A field of artificial intelligence in which millions of chips (processing elements) are interconnected to enable computers to imitate the way the human brain works.

Newsgroup   Internet-based electronic discussion groups.

Node   An endpoint in a computer network.

Non–Windows application   A computer application that will run under Windows but does not conform to the Common User Access (CUA) standards.

Nondestructive read   A read operation in which the program and/or data that are loaded to RAM from secondary storage reside in both RAM (temporarily) and secondary storage (permanently).

Nonimpact printer   A printer that uses chemicals, lasers, or heat to form the images on the paper.

Nonprogrammed decision   A decision that involves an ill-defined and unstructured problem (also called *information-based decision*).

Nonvolatile memory   Solid-state RAM that retains its contents after an electrical interruption. (Contrast with *volatile memory*.)

Notebook PC   A notebook-size laptop PC.

NuBus   The architecture of high-end Apple Macintosh computers.

Numeric   A reference to any of the digits 0-9. (Compare with *alpha* and *alphanumeric*.)

Numeric key pad   An input device that permits rapid numeric data entry.

Object   A result of any Windows application, such as a block of text, all or part of a graphic image, or a sound clip.

Object linking and embedding   See *OLE*.

Object program   A machine-level program that results from the compilation of a source program. (Compare with *source program*.)

Object-oriented language   A programming language structured to enable the interaction between user-defined concepts that contain data and operations to be performed on the data.

Object-oriented programming (OOP)   A form of software development in which programs are built with entities called objects, which model any physical or conceptual item. Objects are linked together in a top-down hierarchy.

OCR   See *optical character recognition*.

OCR scanner   A light-sensitive input device that bounces a beam of light off an image to interpret printed characters or symbols.

Off-line   Pertaining to data that are not accessible by, or hardware devices that are not connected to, a computer system. (Contrast with *online*.)

OLE   [*object linking and embedding*] The software capability that enables the creation of a compound document that contains one or more objects from other applications. Objects can be linked or embedded.

Online   Pertaining to data and/or hardware devices accessible to and under the control of a computer system. (Contrast with *off-line*.)

Online document   Documents that are designed to be retrieved from secondary storage (locally or over a network) and viewed on a monitor. (Same as *electronic document*.)

Online service   A commercial information network that provides remote users with access to a variety of information services.

Online thesaurus   Software that enables a user to request synonyms interactively during a word processing session.

Open application   A running application.

Open architecture   Refers to micros that give users the flexibility to configure the system with a variety of peripheral devices.

Operating system   The software that controls the execution of all applications and system software programs.

Optical character recognition (OCR)   A data entry technique that permits original-source data entry. Coded symbols or characters are scanned to retrieve the data.

Optical laser disk   A secondary storage medium that uses laser technology to score the surface of a disk to represent a bit.

OS/2   A multitasking PC operating system.

Output   Data transferred from RAM to an output device for processing.

Packet   Strings of bits that contain information and a network address that are routed over different paths on the Internet according to a specific communications protocol.

Page   (Web) The area in which information is presented on the World Wide Web.

Page printer   A printer that prints a page at a time.

Paint software   Software that enables users to "paint" electronic images. Resultant images are stored as raster graphics images.

Palmtop PC   See *pocket PC.*

Parallel transmission   Pertaining to the transmission of data in groups of bits versus one bit at a time. (Contrast with *serial transmission.*)

Parallel conversion   An approach to system conversion whereby the existing system and the new system operate simultaneously prior to conversion.

Parallel port   A direct link with the microcomputer's bus that facilitates the parallel transmission of data, usually one byte at a time.

Parallel processing   A processing procedure in which one main processor examines the programming problem and determines what portions, if any, of the problem can be solved in pieces by other subordinate processors.

Parameter   A descriptor that can take on different values.

Parity checking   A built-in checking procedure in a computer system to help ensure that the transmission of data is complete and accurate. (Related to *parity error.*)

Parity error   Occurs when a bit is dropped in the transmission of data from one hardware device to another. (Related to *parity checking.*)

Password   A word or phrase known only to the user. When entered, it permits the user to gain access to the system.

Patch   A modification of a program or an information system.

PC card   Same as *PCMCIA card.*

PC   [*P*ersonal *C*omputer] A small computer design for use by an individual. See also *microcomputer.*

PC specialist   A person trained in the function and operation of PCs and related hardware and software.

PCI local bus   [*P*eripheral *C*omponent *I*nterconnect] Intel's local bus. (See *local bus.*)

PCMCIA card   A credit-card-sized module that is inserted into a PCMCIA-compliant interface to offer add-on capabilities such as expanded memory and fax modem (also called *PC card*).

PDF   See *Portable Document Format.*

Peer-to-peer LAN   A local area network in which all PCs on the network are functionally equal.

Pen-based computing   Computer applications that rely on the pen-based PCs for processing capability.

Pen-based PC   Same as *slate PC.*

Pentium   An Intel microprocessor.

Pentium II   An Intel microprocessor that is more advanced and faster than its predecessors, the Pentium and Pentium Pro microprocessors.

Pentium Pro   An Intel microprocessor that is more advanced than the Pentium microprocessor.

Peripheral device   Any hardware device other than the processor.

Personal computer (PC)   See *PC.*

Personal computing   A computing environment in which individuals use personal computers for domestic and/or business applications.

Personal digital assistant (PDA)   Handheld personal computers that support a variety of personal information systems.

Personal identification number (PIN)   A code or number that is used in conjunction with a password to permit the user to gain access to a computer system.

Phased conversion   An approach to system conversion whereby an information system is implemented one module at a time.

Photo illustration software   Software that enables the user to create original images and the modification of existing digitized images.

Physical security   That aspect of computer-center security that deals with access to computers and peripheral devices.

Picosecond   One trillionth of a second.

Picture element   See *pixel.*

Pie graph   A circular graph that illustrates each "piece" of datum in its proper relationship to the whole "pie."

Pilferage   A special case of software piracy whereby a company purchases a software product without a site-usage license agreement, then copies and distributes it throughout the company.

Pilot conversion   An approach to system conversion whereby the new system is implemented first in only one of the several areas for which it is targeted.

Pixel   [*p*icture *e*lement] An addressable point on a display screen to which light can be directed under program control.

Platform   A definition of the standards by which software is developed and hardware is designed.

Plotter   A device that produces high-precision hard-copy graphic output.

Plug-and-play   Refers to making a peripheral device or an expansion board immediately operational by simply plugging it into a port or an expansion slot.

Pocket PC   A handheld personal computer (also called *palmtop PC*).

POP (point-of-presence)   An access point to the Internet.

POP (Post Office Protocol)   Refers to the way an e-mail client software gets e-mail from its server.

Pointer   The highlighted area in a spreadsheet display that indicates the current cell.

Polling   A line-control procedure in which each terminal is "polled" in rotation to determine whether a message is ready to be sent.

Pop-out menu   A menu displayed next to the menu option selected in a higher-level pull-down or pop-up menu.

Pop-up menu   A menu that is superimposed in a window over whatever is currently being displayed on the monitor.

Port   An access point in a computer system that permits communication between the computer and a peripheral device.

Port replicator   A device to which a notebook PC can be readily connected to give the PC access to whatever external peripheral devices are connected to its common ports (keyboard, monitor, mouse, network, printer, and so on).

Portable document An electronic document that can be passed around the electronic world as you would a print document in the physical world.

Portable Document Format (PDF) A standard, created by Adobe Corporation, creating portable documents.

Portrait Referring to the orientation of the print on the page. Printed lines run parallel to the shorter side of the page. (Contrast with *landscape*.)

Post-implementation review A critical examination of a computer-based system after it has been put into production.

POTS Short for *p*lain *o*ld *t*elephone *s*ervices, the standard voice-grade telephone service common in homes and business.

Power up To turn on the electrical power to a computer system.

PowerPC processor A RISC-based processor used in Apple Macintosh and other computers.

Presentation graphics Business graphics that are used to present information in a graphic format in meetings, reports, and oral presentations.

Presentation graphics software User-friendly software that allows users to create a variety of visually appealing and informative presentation graphics.

Prespecification An approach to system development in which users relate their information processing needs to the project team during the early stages of the project.

Primary storage See *RAM*.

Print server A LAN-based PC that handles LAN user print jobs and controls at least one printer.

Printer A device used to prepare hard-copy output.

Private line A dedicated communications channel provided by a common carrier between any two points in a computer network (same as *leased line*.)

Procedure–oriented language A high-level language whose general-purpose instruction set can be used to produce a sequence of instructions to model scientific and business procedures.

Process and device control Using the computer to control an ongoing process or device in a continuous feedback loop.

Processor The logical component of a computer system that interprets and executes program instructions.

Processor-bound operation The amount of work that can be performed by the computer system is limited primarily by the speed of the computer.

Program–item icon A pictograph used in Windows to represent an application.

Program (1) Computer instructions structured and ordered in a manner that, when executed, causes a computer to perform a particular function. (2) The act of producing computer software. (Related to *software*.)

Program register The register that contains the address of the next instruction to be executed.

Programmed decision Decisions that address well-defined problems with easily identifiable solutions.

Programmer One who writes computer programs.

Programmer/analyst The title of one who performs both the programming and systems analysis function.

Programming The act of writing a computer program.

Programming language A language programmers use to communicate instructions to a computer.

PROM [*P*rogrammable *R*ead-*O*nly *M*emory] ROM in which the user can load read-only programs and data.

Prompt A program-generated message describing what should be entered.

Proprietary software package Vendor-developed software that is marketed to the public.

Protocols See *communications protocols*.

Prototype system A model of a full-scale system.

Prototyping An approach to systems development that results in a prototype system.

Pseudocode Nonexecutable program code used as an aid to develop and document structured programs.

Pull-down menu A menu that is "pulled down" from an option in a higher-level menu.

Quality assurance specialist A person assigned the task of monitoring the quality of every aspect of the design and operation of information systems.

Query by example A method of database inquiry in which the user sets conditions for the selection of records by composing one or more example relational expressions.

Radio signals Signals which enable data communication between radio transmitters and receivers.

Radio buttons Circle bullets in front of user options that when selected include a dot in the middle of the circle.

RAM disk That area of RAM that facilitates disk caching. (See also *disk caching*.)

Random-access memory See *RAM*

RAM [*R*andom-*A*ccess *M*emory] The memory area in which all programs and data must reside before programs can be executed or data manipulated. (Same as *primary storage*, compare with *secondary storage*.)

Random access Direct access to records, regardless of their physical location on the storage medium. (Contrast with *sequential access*.)

Random file A collection of records that can be processed randomly. (Same as *direct-access file*.)

Random processing Processing data and records randomly. (Same as *direct-access processing*, contrast with *sequential processing*.)

Range A cell or a rectangular group of adjacent cells in a spreadsheet.

Rapid prototyping Creating a nonfunctional prototype system.

Raster graphics A method for maintaining a screen image as patterns of dots. (See also *bit-mapped*.)

RDRAM (Rambus DRAM) A new RAM technology capable of very high-speed transfer of data (600 MHz) to/from the processor.

Read The process by which a record or a portion of a record is accessed from the secondary storage medium and transferred to primary storage for processing. (Contrast with *write*.)

Read/write head That component of a disk drive or tape drive that reads from and writes to its respective secondary storage medium.

Read-only memory (ROM) A memory chip with contents permanently loaded by the manufacturer for read-only applications.

Record A collection of related fields (such as an employee record) describing an event or an item.

Register A small high-speed storage area in which data pertaining to the execution of a particular instruction are stored.

Relational database A database, made up of logically linked tables, in which data are accessed by content rather than by address.

Relational operators Used in formulas to show the equality relationship between two expressions (= [equal to], < [less than], > [greater than], <= [less than or equal to], >= [greater than or equal to], <> [not equal to]). (See also *logical operators.*)

Relative cell address Refers to a cell's position in a spreadsheet in relation to the cell containing the formula in which the address is used.

Report generator Software that automatically produces reports based on user specifications.

Resident font A font that is accessed directly from the printer's built-in read-only memory.

Resolution Referring to the number of addressable points on a monitor's screen or the number of dots per unit area on printed output.

Responsibility matrix A matrix that graphically illustrates when and to what extent individuals and groups are involved in each activity of a systems development process.

Rewritable optical disk A secondary storage medium that integrates optical and magnetic disk technology to enable read-*and*-write storage.

RGB monitor Color monitors that mix red, green, and blue to achieve a spectrum of colors.

Ring topology A computer network that involves computer systems connected in a closed loop, with no one computer system the focal point of the network.

RISC [*Reduced Instruction Set Computer*] A computer design architecture based on a limited instruction set machine language. (Contrast with *CISC.*)

Robot A computer-controlled manipulator capable of locomotion and/or moving items through a variety of spatial motions.

Robotics The integration of computers and industrial robots.

ROM [*Read-Only Memory*] RAM that can be read only, not written to.

Root directory The directory at the highest level of a hierarchy of directories.

Routers Communications hardware that enables communications links between LANs and WANs by performing the necessary protocol conversions.

RS-232C connector A 9-pin or 25-pin plug that is used for the electronic interconnection of computers, modems, and other peripheral devices.

Run To open and execute a program.

Scalable system A system whose design permits expansion to handle any size database or any number of users.

Scalable typeface An outline-based typeface from which fonts of any point size can be created.

Scanner A device that scans hard copy and digitizes the text and/or images to a format that can be interpreted by a computer.

Scheduler Someone who schedules the use of hardware resources to optimize system efficiency.

Screen image projector An output device that can project a computer-generated image onto a large screen.

Screen-capture programs Memory-resident programs that enable users to transfer all or part of the current screen image to a disk file.

Screen saver A utility program used to change static screens on idle monitors to interesting dynamic displays.

Screen generator A systems design tool that enables a systems analyst to produce a mockup of a display while in direct consultation with the user.

Scroll arrow Small box containing an arrow at each end of a scroll bar that is used to navigate in small increments within a document or list.

Scroll box A square object that is dragged along a scroll bar to navigate within a document or list.

Scrolling Using the cursor keys to view parts of a document that extends past the bottom or top or sides of the screen.

SCSI bus [*Small Computer System Interface*] This hardware interface allows the connection of several peripheral devices to a single SCSI expansion board (or adapter).

SCSI port A device interface to which up to 15 peripheral devices can be daisy-chained to a single USB port. (Contrast with *USB port.*)

SDRAM (Synchronous dynamic RAM) RAM that is able to synchronize itself with the processor, enabling high-speed transfer of data (600 MHz) to/from the processor.

Search engine An Internet resource discovery tool that lets people find information by keyword(s) searches.

Secondary storage Permanent data storage on magnetic disk, CD-R, and/or magnetic tape. (Compare with *primary storage* and *RAM.*)

Sector A disk storage concept of a pie-shaped portion of a disk or diskette in which records are stored and subsequently retrieved. (Contrast with *cylinder.*)

Sector organization Magnetic disk organization in which the recording surface is divided into pie-shaped sectors.

Select Highlighting an object on a windows screen or a menu option.

Sequential access Accessing records in the order in which they are stored. (Contrast with *random access.*)

Sequential files Files containing records that are ordered according to a key field.

Sequential processing Processing of files that are ordered numerically or alphabetically by a key field. (Contrast with *direct-access processing* or *random processing.*)

Serial transmission Pertaining to processing data one bit at a time. (Contrast with *parallel transmission.*)

Serial port A direct link with the microcomputer's bus that facilitates the serial transmission of data.

Serial representation The storing of bits one after another on a secondary storage medium.

Serpentine A magnetic tape storage scheme in which data are recorded serially in tracks.

Server A LAN component that can be shared by users on a LAN.

Server application (1) An application running on a network server that works in tandem with a client workstation or PC application. (See also *client application*.) (2) In object linking and embedding, the application in which the linked object originates.

Server computer Any type of computer, from a PC to a supercomputer, which performs a variety of functions for its client computers, including the storage of data and applications software. See also *client computer*.

Shell Software that provides a graphical user interface alternative to command-driven software.

Shortcut key A key combination that chooses a menu option without the need to display a menu.

Shut down The processes of exiting all applications and shutting off the power to a computer system.

Simultaneous click Tapping both buttons on a point-and-draw device at the same time.

SIMM [*Single In-line Memory Module*] A small circuit board, capable of holding several memory chips. It has a 32-bit data path and can be easily connected to a PC's system board. (Contrast with *DIMM*.)

Slate PC A portable personal computer that enables input via an electronic pen in conjunction with a pressure-sensitive monitor/drawing surface.

Smalltalk An object-oriented language.

Smart card A card or badge with an embedded microprocessor.

Soft copy Temporary output that can be interpreted visually, as on a monitor. (Contrast with *hard copy*.)

Soft font An electronic description of a font that is retrieved from disk storage and downloaded to the printer's memory.

Soft keyboard A keyboard displayed on a touch sensitive screen such that when a displayed key is touched with a finger or stylus, the character or command is sent to memory for processing.

Software The programs used to direct the functions of a computer system. (Contrast with *hardware*, related to *program*.)

Software agent Artificial intelligence-based software that has the authority to act on a person or thing's behalf.

Software engineer A person who develops software products to bridge the gap between design and executable program code.

Software engineering A term coined to emphasize an approach to software development that embodies the rigors of the engineering discipline.

Software installation The process of copying the program and data files from a vendor-supplied master disk(s) to a PC's hard disk.

Software package One or more programs designed to perform a particular processing task.

Software piracy The unlawful duplication of proprietary software. (Related to *pilferage*.)

Software suite An integrated collection of software tools that may include a variety of business applications packages.

Sort The rearrangement of fields or records in an ordered sequence by a key field.

Source application, clipboard The software application from which the clipboard contents originated. (Contrast with *destination application*.)

Source data Original data that usually involve the recording of a transaction or the documenting of an event or an item.

Source data automation Entering data directly to a computer system at the source without the need for key entry transcription.

Source document The original hard copy from which data are entered.

Source program The code of the original program (also called *source code*). (Compare with *object program*.)

Source program file This file contains high-level instructions to the computer which must be compiled prior to program execution.

Spam Unsolicited junk e-mail.

Spammer A person who distributes spam.

Speech synthesis Converting raw data into electronically produced speech.

Speech synthesizers Devices that convert raw data into electronically produced speech.

Speech-recognition system A device that permits voice input to a computer system.

Spelling checker A software feature that checks the spelling of every word in a document against an electronic dictionary.

Spreadsheet file A file containing data and formulas in tabular format.

Spreadsheet software Refers to software that permits users to work with rows and columns of data.

Star topology A computer network that involves a centralized host computer connected to a number of smaller computer systems.

Static RAM (SRAM) A RAM technology whose chips do not require a refresh cycle. (Contrast with *DRAM*.)

Stop bits A data communications parameter that refers to the number of bits in the character or byte.

Structure chart A chart that graphically illustrates the conceptualization of an information system as a hierarchy of modules.

Structured system design A systems design technique that encourages top-down design.

Subroutine A group or sequence of instructions for a specific programming task that is called by another program.

Supercomputer The category that includes the largest and most powerful computers.

Switched line A telephone line used as a regular data communications channel (also called *dial-up line*).

Switching hub A type of hub that accepts packets of information sent within a network, then forwards them to the appropriate port for routing to their network destination based on the network address contained in the packet.

Synchronous transmission A communications protocol in which the source and destination points operate in timed alignment to enable high-speed data transfer.

Syntax The rules that govern the formulation of the instructions in a computer program.

Syntax error An invalid format for a program instruction.

Sysop [*system op*erator] The sponsor who provides the hardware and software support for an electronic bulletin-board system.

System Any group of components (functions, people, activities, events, and so on) that interface with and complement one another to achieve one or more predefined goals.

System board A microcomputer circuit board that contains the microprocessor, electronic circuitry for handling such tasks as input/output signals from peripheral devices, and memory chips (same as *motherboard*).

System check An internal verification of the operational capabilities of a computer's electronic components.

System life cycle A reference to the four stages of a computer-based information system—birth, development, production, and death.

System maintenance The process of modifying an information system to meet changing needs.

System operator See *sysop*.

System prompt A visual prompt to the user to enter a system command.

System software Software that is independent of any specific applications area.

System specifications (specs) Information system details that include everything from the functionality of the system to the format of the system's output screens and reports.

Systems analysis The examination of an existing system to determine input, processing, and output requirements for the target system.

Systems analyst A person who does systems analysis.

Systems development methodology Written standardized procedures that depict the activities in the systems development process and define individual and group responsibilities.

Systems programmer A programmer who develops and maintains system software.

Systems testing A phase of testing where all programs in a system are tested together.

T-1 line A high-speed digital link to the Internet (1.544 M bps)

T-3 line A high-speed digital link to the Internet (44.736 M bps)

Tape backup unit (TBU) A magnetic tape drive designed to provide backup for data and programs.

Tape drive, magnetic The hardware device that contains the read/write mechanism for the magnetic tape storage medium. (Compare with *disk drive, magnetic*.)

Tape, magnetic A secondary storage medium for sequential data storage and back up.

Target system A proposed information system that is the object of a systems development effort.

Task The basic unit of work for a processor.

TCP/IP [Transmission Control Protocol/Internet Protocol] A set of communications protocols developed by the Department of Defense to link dissimilar computers across many kinds of networks.

Telecommunications The collection and distribution of the electronic representation of information between two points.

Telecommuting "Commuting" via a communications link between home and office.

Telemedicine Describes any type of health care administered remotely over communication links.

Telephone Access Server (TAS) A system that permits users to access their electronic mailboxes remotely via a touchtone telephone.

Telephony The integration of computers and telephones.

Telnet A terminal emulation protocol that allows users to work from a PC as if it were a terminal linked directly to a host computer.

Template A model for a particular microcomputer software application.

Terabyte (TB) About one trillion bytes.

TFLOPS A trillion FLOPS. (See *FLOPS*).

Terminal Any device capable of sending and receiving data over a communications channel.

Terminal emulation mode The software transformation of a PC so that its keyboard, monitor, and data interface emulate that of a terminal.

Text mode One of two modes of operation for PC monitors. (Contrast with *graphics mode*.)

Thesaurus, online See *online thesaurus*.

Third-generation language (3GL) A procedure–oriented programming language that can be used to model almost any scientific or business procedure. (Related to *procedure–oriented language*.)

Thread (newsgroup) An original Internet newsgroup message and any posted replies to that message.

Throughput A measure of computer system efficiency; the rate at which work can be performed by a computer system.

Throwaway system An information system developed to support information for a one-time decision, then discarded.

Tiled windows Two or more windows displayed on the screen in a non-overlapping manner.

Tiny area network (TAN) A term coined to refer to very small local area networks, typically installed in the home or small office.

Title bar A narrow Windows screen object at the top of each window that runs the width of the window.

Toggle The action of pressing a single key on a keyboard to switch between two or more modes of operation, such as insert and replace.

Total connectivity The networking of all hardware, software, and databases in an organization.

Touch-screen monitors Monitors with touch-sensitive screens that enable users to choose from available options by simply touching the desired icon or menu item with their finger.

Tower PC A PC that includes a system unit that is designed to rest vertically. (Contrast with *laptop PC* and *desktop PC*.)

Track, disk That portion of a magnetic disk-face surface that can be accessed in any given setting of a single read/write head. Tracks are configured in concentric circles.

Track, tape That portion of a magnetic tape that can be accessed by any one of the tape drives read/write heads. A track runs the length of the tape.

Trackball A ball mounted in a box that, when moved, results in a similar movement of the cursor on a display screen.

Trackpad A point-and-draw device with no moving parts that includes a touch-sensitive pad to move the graphics cursor.

Tracks per inch (TPI) A measure of the recording density, or spacing, of tracks on a magnetic disk.

Transaction A procedural event in a system that prompts manual or computer-based activity.

Transaction file A file containing records of data activity (transactions); used to update the master file.

Transaction-oriented processing Transactions are recorded and entered as they occur.

Transmission medium The central cable along which terminals, peripheral devices, and microcomputers are connected in a bus topology.

Transparent A reference to a procedure or activity that occurs automatically and does not have to be considered by the user.

TSR [*terminate-and-stay-resident*] Programs that remain in memory so they can be instantly popped up over the current application by pressing a hotkey.

Turnaround document A computer-produced output that is ultimately returned to a computer system as a machine-readable input.

Twisted–pair wire A pair of insulated copper wires twisted around each other for use in transmission of telephone conversations and for cabling in local area networks.

Typeface A set of characters that are of the same type style.

Typeover mode A data entry mode in which the character entered overstrikes the character at the cursor position.

ULS (User Location Service) An Internet-based listing of Internet users who are currently online and ready to receive Internet telephone calls.

Unicode A 16-bit encoding system.

Uninterruptible power source (UPS) A buffer between an external power source and a computer system that supplies clean, continuous power.

Unit testing That phase of testing in which the programs that make up an information system are tested individually.

URL (uniform resource locator) An Internet address for locating Internet elements, such as server sites, documents, files, bulletin boards (newsgroups), and so on.

Universal product code (UPC) A 10-digit machine-readable bar code placed on consumer products.

Universal Serial Bus (USB) A bus standard that permits up to 127 peripheral devices to be connected to an external bus.

UNIX A multiuser operating system.

Upload The transmission of data from a local computer to a remote computer.

Uptime That time when the computer system is in operation.

USB port (Universal Serial Bus port) A high-speed device interface to which up to 127 peripheral devices can be daisy-chained to a single USB port. (Contrast with *SCSI port.*)

USENET A worldwide network of servers, often hosting newsgroups, that can be accessed over the Internet.

User The individual providing input to the computer or using computer output.

User-friendly Pertaining to an online system that permits a person with relatively little experience to interact successfully with the system.

User interface A reference to the software, method, or displays that enable interaction between the user and the software being used.

User liaison A person who serves as the technical interface between the information services department and the user group.

User sign-off A procedure whereby the user manager is asked to "sign off," or commit, to the specifications defined by the systems development project team.

Utility program An often-used service routine, such as a program to sort records.

Vaccine An antiviral program.

VDT [*Video Display Terminal*] A terminal on which printed and graphic information are displayed on a televisionlike monitor and into which data are entered on a typewriterlike keyboard.

Vector graphics A method for maintaining a screen image as patterns of lines, points, and other geometric shapes.

Vertical scroll bar A narrow screen object located along the right edge of a window that is used to navigate up and down through a document or list.

VGA [*Video Graphics Array*] A circuit board that enables the interfacing of very high-resolution monitors to microcomputers.

Video display terminal See *VDT.*

Video file This file contains digitized video frames that when played rapidly produce motion video.

Video RAM (VRAM) RAM on the graphics adapter.

Video display terminal See *VDT.*

Videophone An Internet-based capability that permits two parties to both see and hear one another during a conversation.

Virtual machine The processing capabilities of one computer system created through software (and sometimes hardware) in a different computer system.

Virus A program written with malicious intent and loaded to the computer system of an unsuspecting victim. Ultimately, the program destroys or introduces errors in programs and databases.

Vision-input systems A device that enables limited visual input to a computer system.

Visual programming An approach to program development that relies more on visual association with tools and menus than with syntax-based instructions.

Visual Basic A visual programming language.

Visual C++ A visual programming language.

VL-bus [*VESA Local–BUS*] A local bus based on the Video Electronics Standards Association's recommendations.

Voice message switching Using computers, the telephone system, and other electronic means to store and forward voice messages. (Contrast with *electronic mail.*)

Voice-response system A device that enables output from a computer system in the form of user-recorded words, phrases, music, alarms, and so on.

Volatile memory Solid-state semiconductor RAM in which the data are lost when the electrical current is turned off or interrupted. (Contrast with *nonvolatile memory.*)

WAIS [*wide area information server*] A database on the Internet that contains indexes to documents that reside on the Internet.

Wand scanner Handheld OCR scanner.

Wave file A windows sound file.

Web guide An Internet resource discovery tool that groups Internet resources in a hierarchical manner by category to assist people in navigating to a desired site.

Webcasting The broadcasting of real-time audio and/or video streams over the Internet.

Wide area network (**WAN**) A computer network that connects nodes in widely dispersed geographic areas. (Contrast with *local area network.*)

Window A rectangular section of a display screen that is dedicated to a specific document, activity, or application.

Window panes Simultaneous display of subareas of a particular window.

Windows A software product by Microsoft Corporation that provides a graphical user interface and multitasking capabilities for the MS-DOS environment.

Windows 95 An operating system by Microsoft Corporation.

Windows 9x A generic reference to any successor to the Windows 95 operating system.

Windows 98 An operating system by Microsoft Corporation (the successor to Windows 95).

Windows application An application that conforms to the Microsoft Common User Access (CUA) standards and operates under the Microsoft Windows platform.

Windows CE A Microsoft operating system, whose GUI is similar to Windows 9x operating systems, that is designed to run on handheld PCs, PDAs, and other small computers.

Windows NT A powerful client/server operating system.

Windows NT Server The server-side portion of the Windows NT operating system.

Windows NT Workstation The client-side portion of the Windows NT operating system.

Wintel PC A personal computer using a Microsoft *Windows* operating system in conjunction with an *Intel* Corporation or Intel-compatible processor.

WMF (**Windows metafile**) A popular format for metafiles.

Word For a given computer, an established number of bits that are handled as a unit.

Word processing Using the computer to enter, store, manipulate, and print text.

Word wrap A word processing feature that automatically moves, or "wraps," text to the next line when that text would otherwise exceed the right margin limit.

Work space The area in a window below the title bar or menu bar containing everything that relates to the application noted in the title bar.

Workgroup computing Computer applications that involve cooperation among people linked by a computer network. (Related to *groupware.*)

Workstation A high-performance single-user computer system with sophisticated input/output devices that can be easily networked with other workstations or computers.

World Wide Web (the Web, WWW, W3) An Internet server that offers multimedia and hypertext links.

Worm A program that erases data and/or programs from a computer system's memory, usually with malicious intent.

WORM disk [*Write-Once Read-Many disk*] An optical laser disk that can be read many times after the data are written to it, but the data cannot be changed or erased.

WORM disk cartridge The medium for WORM disk drives.

Write To record data on the output medium of a particular I/O device (tape, hard copy, PC display). (Contrast with *read.*)

WYSIWYG [*What You See Is What You Get*] A software package in which what is displayed on the screen is very similar in appearance to what you get when the document is printed.

X terminal A terminal that enables the user to interact via a graphical user interface (GUI).

Yahoo A Web guide site on the Internet.

Zip drive A storage device that uses optical technology together with magnetic technology to read and write to an interchangeable floppy-size 100-MB Zip disk.

Zip disk The storage medium for Zip drives.

Year 2000 problem An information systems problem brought on by the fact that many legacy information systems still treat the year field as two digits (98) rather than four (1998).

Zoom An integrated software command that expands a window to fill the entire screen.

INDEX

Crystal oscillator, C52
CSMA/CD access method, C179
Cursor, **C91-94**, C204, C223, C234, C238
    graphics, C91, **C93-94**, C132, C233,
        C238
    text, **C92**
Cursor control device (CCD), C227, C233
Cyberphobia, C2
Cylinder, C109

D

Data, **C5-6**
    demographic, C118
    entering, C12, C21, C91-94, C132-33,
        C134, C136-37, C140
Data cartridge, C113
Data communications, C39, C135, **C162**,
    C167, C170, C175-78, C198
Data file (*see* File, data)
Data path, C85
Data transfer rate, **C110**, C114
Database
    attribute, C83
    national, C118
    software (*see* Software, database)
Debug, **C38**
Decode, **C44**, C53
Decoder, C48
Default option, **C89**, C96
Desktop (Windows), C227
Desktop mainframe, C11
Desktop PC (*see* Personal computer,
    desktop)
Desktop publishing (DTP), **C25**, C27,
    C103, C142, C146, C230
Destination application, C237-38
Device controller, **C49**, C141
Dialog box, **C96**, C232-34
Dialup
    connection, C200
    line, C170
Dictionary (online), C121, **C138**, C166
Difference engine, C34
Digital, C42
Digital camera, C6, C13, C137, **C140**
Digital convergence, **C158-59**, C162
Digital Equipment Corporation, C38
Digital signals, **C42-43**, C141, C162-63,
    C165, C169
Digital videodisk (DVD), C117, **C120-22**,
    C148, C159, C229, C235
Digitize, C6, C8, **C43**, C102-4, C117,
    C122, C133, C135-40, C159, C162,
    C211
Digitizer tablet and pen, **C132-33**
DIMM (*see* Dual in-line memory module)
Dimmed, C37, **C95**, C231

Direct access, C105, C136
Direct-access storage device (DASD),
    C111
Directory, C232
Disk, C10
    access arm, C108-10, C117
    address, C108-9
    caching, C110
    cartridge, C122
    cylinder, C108-9
    density, C107-8
    drive, C44, C56, C79, **C103**, C105-6,
        C107, C109-11, C114, C148,
        C235
    fixed, C106-8
    floppy, **C15**, C107, C140
    floppy drive, C15
    hard, **C15**, C61, C76, C89, C104,
        C106-11, C113, C115-16, C123,
        C148, C181, C183, C192, C215,
        C226, C228, C239
    hard drive, **C15**, C107
    interchangeable, C106-8
    Jaz cartridge, C108
    Jaz drive, C108
    magnetic, C21, C43-44, C60, C87,
        C102-3, C105-6, C108, C110-11,
        C113-14, C117, C119-20, C122-23
    optical laser, C43, **C103**, C105, C117,
        C121-23, C135
    read/write head, **C108-10**, C114,
        C117, C120
    rewritable optical, C117, **C122-23**
    sector, C108
    WORM, C117, **C122**
    WORM cartridge, C122
    Zip, **C106-7**, C116, C235
    Zip drive, **C107**, C116, C235
Diskette, **C15**, C106-10, C116, C140
Docking station, **C12-14**
Document
    compound, **C237**, C239
    source, C237, C239
    window, C230
Domain name, **C202**
Dot pitch, C141
Dots per inch (dpi), C145
Download, **C8-9**, C60, C104, C158, C174,
    C191, C194, C204-5, C208, C221
Downsizing, C174
Downstream rate, C166
Downtime, **C23**
DRAM (*see* Dynamic RAM)
Dual in-line memory module (DIMM),
    C46
DVD (*see* Digital videodisk)
Dynamic RAM (DRAM), **C46**, C48

flat-panel, **C141-43**
monochrome, C141-42
non-interlaced, C142
pixels, **C141-42**
resolution, **C17**, C141
RGB, C142
touch screen, C142
Motherboard, **C56-60**, C141
Motorola Corporation, C56-57, C85
Motorola processors, C12, **C56-57**
Mouse, **C9**, C15, C17, C55, C58, C77,
C87, C93-94, C96, C132, C151,
C227, C230-32
click, C93, C227-28
double-click, C94, C227-28
drag, C94, C227-28
pen, C132
point, C227-28
simultaneous click, C94
MS-DOS (*see* Operating system, MS-DOS)
Multimedia, C15, C26-27, C57, C78, C82,
C107-8, C119-21, C143, C148-50,
C152, C203-4, C208, C213-14, C227
application, **C15**, C57, C82, C108,
C120-21
Multiplatform environment, C86
Multiplexor, **C162-65**, C168, C181
Multitasking, **C75-76**, C231

N

Nanosecond, C22
NASA, C28, C118
National Information Infrastructure
(NII), **C4**, C198
Natural language (*see* Programming lan-
guage, natural)
Navigation, C91, C228
Netscape Communicator, C201
NetWare, C183
Network, **C6**, C157-84
address, C164
bus, C172
portable, C184
topologies, **C171-72**, C178
Network computer (NC), C12, **C14-15**,
C152
Network interface card (NIC) (*see* Ex-
pansion board, network interface
card)
Network Neighborhood (Windows), C231
Networking
intercompany, C161
intracompany, C160
Newbie, **C201**, C216-17
Newsgroup, C202, **C211-13**, C216
Node, C171
Nondestructive read, C47
Nonvolatile memory, C46

Novell Corporation, C183
Numeric characters, C44
Numeric key pad, C91-92

O

Object, C235
Object linking and embedding (OLE),
C237
Object-oriented
Language (*see* Programming language,
object-oriented)
programming (OOP), C80-81
Offline operation, **C8**
Online
operation, **C8**
service, C60, **C191**
Open application, C227
Operating system, C12, C39, **C73-78**,
C83-90, C104, C109, C111, C165,
C182-83, C226
LAN, C182-83
Mac OS, C12, **C85**
MS-DOS, C39, **C77**, C84-85, C90,
C104, C226-27, C231, C239
multiuser, C75
platform, C12, **C57**, **C83-86**, C237-38
System 7, C104
UNIX, **C86**
Windows CE, C85
Windows 9x/NT, **C12**, C226-39
Windows 95, C57, C77, **C84-85**, C89-
90, C104-5, C119, C183, **C226-39**
cascading, C233-34
tiled, C233-34
Windows 3.1, C226-29
Windows 98, C12, C56, C75, C77,
C78, **C84-85**, C182, C213, **C226-39**
Windows NT, C57, C75, **C83-85**, C183,
C226-27
Windows NT Server, **C85**, C183
Windows NT Workstation, C85
Optical character recognition (OCR),
C133-36, C140
Optical laser disk (*see* Disk, optical laser)
Output, C3
Output device, C18, C21, C89, C131,
C141-47, C150

P

Packets, C200
Page, C203
Pages per minute (ppm), C145
Palmtop PC (*see* Personal computer,
palmtop)
Parallel port (*see* Port, parallel)
Parallel processing, C51
Parallel transmission, C58
Parameter, **C96**, C232, C234

procedure-oriented, **C79-80**, C82
Visual Basic, C50, C78, **C81**, C83
PROM (*see* Programmable read-only
   memory)
Prompt, C77, **C90**, C164, C183, C206
Protocols, C165, C175
Prototype system, C150
Punched cards, C35-36

Q

QIC-80 minicartridge, C114

R

Radio button, **C204**, C234
Radio signals, **C166-67**, C171
RAM (*see* Random-access memory)
Rambus dynamic RAM (RDRAM), C46
Random
   access, C107, C123
   processing, C105
Random-access memory (RAM), **C9-10**,
   C14, C43-53, C56, C58, C61, C75-
   76, C79, C89, C91, C102-3, C105,
   C107, C109, C110, C114, C117,
   C123, C141, C151, C181-83, C236,
   C239
RDRAM (*see* Rambus dynamic RAM)
Read/write head, C108
Record, **C6**, C76, C109, C111, C114, C136
Register, C48
   instruction, **C48**, C50
   program, C48
Resolution (*see* Monitor, resolution)
Ring topology, **C171-72**, C180
RISC, C51
Router, C162-63, **C165**, C177, C201
RS-232C connector, C58

S

Satellite, C88, C118, C167-68, C190, C229
Scanner, C55, C59, C60, **C133-35**, C140,
   C152, C177, C205
   image, C59, **C135**, C137, C140
   label, C134
   laser, C132, **C134**
   page, C135
   wand, C134
Screen image projector, C141, **C150**
Scroll bar, C230, **C233-34**
   arrow, C233
   box, C233
   horizontal, C233
   vertical, C233
Scrolling, C92
SCSI
   adapter, C59, C61
   bus, C59
   interface card, C60

port, C58-59
SDRAM (*see* Synchronous dynamic RAM)
Search engine, C202, **C207**
Secondary storage (*see* Storage, secondary)
Sector, C108
   organization, C108
Sequential
   access, **C105**, C107, C116
   processing, **C105**, C113
Serial
   representation, C44, C108, **C114**, C116
   transmission, C58
Serial port (*see* Port, serial)
Server, **C20-21**, C211, C213-14, C219,
   C237
   application, C237
   communications, C181
   computer, **C20**, C85, C152, C160,
      C164, C173-74, C197, C200, C201-4
   dedicated, C182-83
   e-mail, C211
   file, **C181**, C183
   LAN, **C182**, C228
   print, C181-82
   program, C201
Shareware, C194
Shell, C113
Shortcut Bar (Windows), C231
Shortcut key, **C227**, C232-33
Shrink, C229
Shut down procedure, C90
Silicon wafers, C66
Single in-line memory module (SIMM),
   C46, C48
SIMM (*see* Single in-line memory module)
Slate computer (*see* Personal computer,
   slate)
SLIP connection, **C201**, C211
Smalltalk, C80
Smart card, **C136**
Soft copy, **C9**, C141
Soft key, C91
Software, **C3**
   applications, C20, C40, **C74-75**, C82,
      C84, C89, C113, C164, C173-74,
      C182-83, C236
   back-end applications, C174
   command-driven, **C77**, C84
   communications, **C27**, C190-92
   database, **C27**
   desktop publishing, **C25**
   edutainment, C28
   front-end applications, C174
   general-purpose, C183
   graphics, **C26-27**, C94-96
   installing, C89
   piracy, C83
   portfolio, **P81**